John Locke's Theology

OXFORD STUDIES IN HISTORICAL THEOLOGY

Series Editor
Richard A. Muller, Calvin Theological Seminary

Founding Editor
David C. Steinmetz †

Editorial Board
Robert C. Gregg, Stanford University
George M. Marsden, University of Notre Dame
Wayne A. Meeks, Yale University
Gerhard Sauter, Rheinische Friedrich-Wilhelms-Universität Bonn
Susan E. Schreiner, University of Chicago
John Van Engen, University of Notre Dame
Robert L. Wilken, University of Virginia

THE UNACCOMMODATED CALVIN
Studies in the Foundation of a Theological Tradition
Richard A. Muller

THE CONFESSIONALIZATION OF HUMANISM IN REFORMATION GERMANY
Erika Rummell

THE PLEASURE OF DISCERNMENT
Marguerite de Navarre as Theologian
Carol Thysell

REFORMATION READINGS OF THE APOCALYPSE
Geneva, Zurich, and Wittenberg
Irena Backus

WRITING THE WRONGS
Women of the Old Testament among Biblical Commentators from Philo through the Reformation
John L. Thompson

THE HUNGRY ARE DYING
Beggars and Bishops in Roman Cappadocia
Susan R. Holman

RESCUE FOR THE DEAD
The Posthumous Salvation of Non-Christians in Early Christianity
Jeffrey A. Trumbower

AFTER CALVIN
Studies in the Development of a Theological Tradition
Richard A. Muller

THE POVERTY OF RICHES
St. Francis of Assisi Reconsidered
Kenneth Baxter Wolf

REFORMING MARY
Changing Images of the Virgin Mary in Lutheran Sermons of the Sixteenth Century
Beth Kreitzer

TEACHING THE REFORMATION
Ministers and Their Message in Basel, 1529–1629
Amy Nelson Burnett

THE PASSIONS OF CHRIST IN HIGH-MEDIEVAL THOUGHT
An Essay on Christological Development
Kevin Madigan

GOD'S IRISHMEN
Theological Debates in Cromwellian Ireland
Crawford Gribben

REFORMING SAINTS
Saint's Lives and Their Authors in Germany, 1470–1530
David J. Collins

GREGORY OF NAZIANZUS ON THE TRINITY AND THE KNOWLEDGE OF GOD
In Your Light We Shall See Light
Christopher A. Beeley

THE JUDAIZING CALVIN
Sixteenth-Century Debates over the Messianic Psalms
G. Sujin Pak

THE DEATH OF SCRIPTURE AND THE RISE OF BIBLICAL STUDIES
Michael C. Legaspi

THE FILIOQUE
History of a Doctrinal Controversy
A. Edward Siecienski

ARE YOU ALONE WISE?
Debates about Certainty in the Early Modern Church
Susan E. Schreiner

EMPIRE OF SOULS
Robert Bellarmine and the Christian Commonwealth
Stefania Tutino

MARTIN BUCER'S DOCTRINE OF JUSTIFICATION
Reformation Theology and Early Modern Irenicism
Brian Lugioyo

CHRISTIAN GRACE AND PAGAN VIRTUE
The Theological Foundation of Ambrose's Ethics
J. Warren Smith

KARLSTADT AND THE ORIGINS OF THE EUCHARISTIC CONTROVERSY
A Study in the Circulation of Ideas
Amy Nelson Burnett

READING AUGUSTINE IN THE REFORMATION
The Flexibility of Intellectual Authority in Europe, 1500–1620
Arnoud S. Q. Visser

SHAPERS OF ENGLISH CALVINISM, 1660–1714
Variety, Persistence, and Transformation
Dewey D. Wallace, Jr.

THE BIBLICAL INTERPRETATION OF WILLIAM OF ALTON
Timothy Bellamah, OP

MIRACLES AND THE PROTESTANT IMAGINATION
The Evangelical Wonder Book in Reformation Germany
Philip M. Soergel

THE REFORMATION OF SUFFERING
Pastoral Theology and Lay Piety in Late Medieval and Early Modern Germany
Ronald K. Rittgers

CHRIST MEETS ME EVERYWHERE
Augustine's Early Figurative Exegesis
Michael Cameron

MYSTERY UNVEILED
The Crisis of the Trinity in Early Modern England
Paul C. H. Lim

GOING DUTCH IN THE MODERN AGE
Abraham Kuyper's Struggle for a Free Church in the Netherlands
John Halsey Wood, Jr.

CALVIN'S COMPANY OF PASTORS
Pastoral Care and the Emerging Reformed Church, 1536–1609
Scott M. Manetsch

THE SOTERIOLOGY OF JAMES USSHER
The Act and Object of Saving Faith
Richard Snoddy

HARTFORD PURITANISM
Thomas Hooker, Samuel Stone, and Their Terrifying God
Baird Tipson

AUGUSTINE, THE TRINITY, AND THE CHURCH
A Reading of the Anti-Donatist Sermons
Adam Ployd

AUGUSTINE'S EARLY THEOLOGY OF IMAGE
A Study in the Development of Pro-Nicene Theology
Gerald Boersma

PATRON SAINT AND PROPHET
Jan Hus in the Bohemian and German Reformations
Phillip N. Haberkern

JOHN OWEN AND ENGLISH PURITANISM
Experiences of Defeat
Crawford Gribben

MORALITY AFTER CALVIN
Theodore Beza's Christian Censor and Reformed Ethics
Kirk M. Summers

THE PAPACY AND THE ORTHODOX
A History of Reception and Rejection
A. Edward Siecienski

DEBATING PERSEVERANCE
The Augustinian Heritage in Post-Reformation England
Jay T. Collier

THE REFORMATION OF PROPHECY
Early Modern Interpretations of the Prophet & Old Testament Prophecy
G. Sujin Pak

ANTOINE DE CHANDIEU
The Silver Horn of Geneva's Reformed Triumvirate
Theodore G. Van Raalte

ORTHODOX RADICALS
Baptist Identity in the English Revolution
Matthew C. Bingham

DIVINE PERFECTION AND HUMAN POTENTIALITY
The Trinitarian Anthropology of Hilary of Poitiers
Jarred A. Mercer

THE GERMAN AWAKENING
Protestant Renewal after the Enlightenment, 1815–1848
Andrew Kloes

THE REGENSBURG ARTICLE 5 ON JUSTIFICATION
Inconsistent Patchwork or Substance of True Doctrine?
Anthony N. S. Lane

AUGUSTINE ON THE WILL
A Theological Account
Han-luen Kantzer Komline

THE SYNOD OF PISTORIA AND VATICAN II
Jansenism and the Struggle for Catholic Reform
Shaun Blanchard

CATHOLICITY AND THE COVENANT OF WORKS
James Ussher and the Reformed Tradition
Harrison Perkins

THE COVENANT OF WORKS
The Origins, Development, and Reception of the Doctrine
J. V. Fesko

RINGLEADERS OF REDEMPTION
How Medieval Dance Became Sacred
Kathryn Dickason

REFUSING TO KISS THE SLIPPER
Opposition to Calvinism in the Francophone Reformation
Michael W. Bruening

FONT OF PARDON AND NEW LIFE
John Calvin and the Efficacy of Baptism
Lyle D. Bierma

THE FLESH OF THE WORD
The extra Calvinisticum *from Zwingli to Early Orthodoxy*
K.J. Drake

JOHN DAVENANT'S HYPOTHETICAL UNIVERSALISM
A Defense Of Catholic And Reformed Orthodoxy
Michael J. Lynch

RHETORICAL ECONOMY IN
AUGUSTINE'S THEOLOGY
Brian Gronewoller

GRACE AND CONFORMITY
The Reformed Conformist Tradition and the Early Stuart Church of England
Stephen Hampton

MAKING ITALY ANGLICAN
Why the Book of Common Prayer Was Translated Into Italian
Stefano Villani

AUGUSINE ON MEMORY
Kevin G. Grove

UNITY AND CATHOLICITY IN CHRIST
The Ecclesiology of Francisco Suarez, S.J.
Eric J. DeMeuse

RETAINING THE OLD EPISCOPAL DIVINITY
John Edwards of Cambridge and Reformed Orthodoxy in the Later Stuart Church
Jake Griesel

CALVINIST CONFORMITY IN POST-REFORMATION ENGLAND
The Theology and Career of Daniel Featley
Gregory A. Salazar

BEARDS, AZYMES, AND PURGATORY
The Other Issues that Divided East and West
A. Edward Siecienski

BISSCHOP'S BENCH
Contours of Arminian Conformity in the Church of England, c.1674–1742
Samuel David Fornecker

JOHN LOCKE'S THEOLOGY
An Ecumenical, Irenic, and Controversial Project
Jonathan S. Marko

John Locke's Theology

An Ecumenical, Irenic, and Controversial Project

JONATHAN S. MARKO

OXFORD
UNIVERSITY PRESS

Oxford University Press is a department of the University of Oxford. It furthers
the University's objective of excellence in research, scholarship, and education
by publishing worldwide. Oxford is a registered trade mark of Oxford University
Press in the UK and certain other countries.

Published in the United States of America by Oxford University Press
198 Madison Avenue, New York, NY 10016, United States of America.

© Oxford University Press 2023

All rights reserved. No part of this publication may be reproduced, stored in
a retrieval system, or transmitted, in any form or by any means, without the
prior permission in writing of Oxford University Press, or as expressly permitted
by law, by license, or under terms agreed with the appropriate reproduction
rights organization. Inquiries concerning reproduction outside the scope of the
above should be sent to the Rights Department, Oxford University Press, at the
address above.

You must not circulate this work in any other form
and you must impose this same condition on any acquirer.

Library of Congress Cataloging-in-Publication Data
Names: Marko, Jonathan S., author.
Title: John Locke's theology : an ecumenical, irenic, and
controversial project / Jonathan S. Marko.
Description: New York, NY, United States of America :
Oxford University Press, [2023] |
Series: Oxford STU in historical theology series |
Includes bibliographical references and index.
Identifiers: LCCN 2022053518 (print) | LCCN 2022053519 (ebook) |
ISBN 9780197650042 (hardback) | ISBN 9780197650066 (epub)
Subjects: LCSH: Locke, John, 1632–1704. | Theology, Doctrinal.
Classification: LCC B1298.R4 M37 2023 (print) | LCC B1298.R4 (ebook) |
DDC 192—dc23/eng/20230302
LC record available at https://lccn.loc.gov/2022053518
LC ebook record available at https://lccn.loc.gov/2022053519

DOI: 10.1093/oso/9780197650042.001.0001

Printed by Integrated Books International, United States of America

For
Craig Stevens Marko and Pamela Susann Marko, née Beahn
Proverbs 1:8–9

Contents

Preface   xvii

1. Introduction: The Problems of Understanding John Locke   1
    Inconsistent Labeling   1
    Overall Argument   3
    Scholarship   4
        Problematic Tendencies   4
        On the Ecumenical Intent of *ROC*   4
        Focusing on the Narratives and Singular Issues   6
    Figures and Doctrines that Could Have Been Given Their Own Essays   7
    Approach of the Book   8

PART I: THE REASONABLENESS OF REDEMPTION

2. John Locke's Preoccupation with Theology and Eternal Salvation in His "Non-Theological" Works   15
    Locke's Major Works: An Overview   19
        The Reasonableness of Christianity   19
        Locke's Major Non-Theological Works   23
    Theology in the *Two Treatises on Civil Government*   26
    Theology in *A Letter Concerning Toleration*   30
    Theology in *An Essay Concerning Human Understanding*   36
    Theology in *Some Thoughts Concerning Education*   41
    Conclusions   44

3. John Locke on Justification and Some Concomitant Doctrines   46
    Historical Context: Debating Christology, Pneumatology, and Soteriology Before and During the Enlightenment   50
        Christology and Pneumatology   50
        Soteriology   51
    Preliminary Evidence of Ecumenical and Irenic Intent in *The Reasonableness of Christianity*   53
    ROC's Fundamental Articles and Christology   57
    ROC's Soteriology, Pneumatology, and Targets   59
    Heretical Red Herrings in *ROC*   69

4. Why John Locke Thought that the Fundamental Articles Must Be Minimal … 73
   Historical Context: Fundamental Articles Debate … 76
     Historical Overview … 76
     Locke's Fundamentals … 79
     The Fundamentals of Other Doctrinal Minimalists … 82
   Fundamental Epistemological Principle: Unreasoned Faith Is Implicit Faith … 85
   Theology Is Not to Be Done in Isolation … 90
   The Necessity of the Number of Articles Being Minimal and Clear: God's Concern for the Vulgar or Commoner … 92
     Locke … 92
     Others … 95
   The Reasonableness of the Fundamental Articles Given Expressly from the Messiah: Continuity of the Church and the Definition of a Christian … 97
     ROC and Its *Vindications* … 97
     Locke's *Letter* and Express "Fundamentals" … 100
     Lim's Study on Baxter: "Antient Simplicity" and "Scripture Sufficiency" … 102
   Corollary: Toleration … 103
     Context … 103
     Locke and Toleration … 106

PART II: THE REASONABLENESS OF REVELATION

5. John Locke on the Necessity of Scripture Amidst the Innate Idea Controversy and the Rise of Deism … 111
   Historical Context: Two Theological Debates … 115
     The Innate Ideas Controversy … 115
     The Rise of Deism or Natural Religion … 119
   Locke's Assault on Innate Principles … 123
     Lord Herbert's Innate Principles … 123
     Locke's Assault … 125
   Mutual Reinforcement between Locke's Assault on Innate Ideas and His Argument for the Need of Divine Revelation … 128
   The Church and the Christian as the Salvation of Society … 134

6. John Locke on the Necessity of Miracles for Divine Revelation … 138
   Historical Context: The Use of Historical Testimonies of Miracles as an Evidentiary Basis for the Divinity of Scripture in Locke's Era … 143
     Marks of Divinity in the Protestants … 143
     The Rise of the Use of Miracles in the Moderate Empiricists and Probability Arguments in Theology … 146
     Lockean-Era Theologians on Miracles … 148

Locke's Writings on Miracles 155
Miracles, Testimonies, and Their Reasonable Evidentiary
 Use in *An Essay Concerning Human Understanding* 155
Miracles, Testimonies, and Their Reasonable Evidentiary Use
 in *The Reasonableness of Christianity* 160
Miracles, Testimonies, and Their Reasonable Evidentiary Use
 in "A Discourse on Miracles" 164
Ease of Assent for the Poor and Uneducated 167
The Unnatural Advancement of Morality 170
Conclusions 174

PART III: PARALLELS IN LOCKE'S LARGER CORPUS

7. John Locke and the "Free Will" Controversies: Why "Of
 Power" Is Not a Metaphysical Pronouncement 179
    Historical Context: The Multivalent Free Will Controversies
     and Issues of the 1600s 183
        Introduction 183
        Traditional Theological Elements Pertinent or Central to
         Free Will Discussions 184
        The Hobbes–Bramhall Debate's Foci 186
        Faculties and Free Will 190
        Malebranche's Liberty and Suspension 191
        Final Comments on Locke's Context 194
    Locke's Admission of Avoidance of Metaphysical Pronouncement 195
        James Harris's Argument from *Of Liberty and Necessity* 195
        Evidence from the Locke–Molyneux Correspondence that
         Supports the Theory that He Is Attempting to Avoid Metaphysical
         Pronouncements 197
    The Theological Message of "Of Power" that Eludes Sectarian
     Categorization 201
        Covering Some Familiar Ground before Culling the Theological
         Message 201
        The Theological Message of "Of Power" 206
        Eluding Theological Categorization Points to Avoiding Metaphysical
         Categorization 212
    Conclusions 214

8. John Locke and the Above Reason Controversy 215
    Historical Context: The Debate over Things Above Reason 218
        Introduction 218
        Precursors to the 1690s Debate Concerning Things Above Reason 219
            Cambridge Platonists 219
            Francis Turretin's Protestant Scholasticism 224

xiv CONTENTS

The Formal Above Reason Debate	231
Robert Boyle's *Reflections upon a Theological Distinction*	231
John Norris's Response to Boyle	235
Locke's Treatment of Reason, Faith, and Categorization of Propositions	239
Locke's Treatment of Reason and Assent	239
Locke's Categorization of Propositions from IV.XVII.23	244
Further Comments on Locke and the Incomprehensible	249
Toland's Treatment of Reason, Faith, and Categorization of Propositions	250
Toland's Treatment of Reason and Assent	250
Toland's Categorization of Propositions	253
Conclusions	256
9. Can One Assent to The Doctrine of the Trinity According to Lockean Epistemological Principles?	**257**
Historical Context: Two Intertwined Controversies	263
English Trinitarian Debates in the Time of Locke	263
The Mature Doctrine	263
Incomprehensibility of the Doctrine of the Holy Trinity	264
British Trinitarian Debates of the 1690s	265
Brief Remarks upon the Locke–Stillingfleet Debate	268
Ideas and Incomprehensibility	269
Introduction to the So-Called Way of Ideas	269
The Way of Ideas and Incomprehensibility	271
Epistemological Limitations and Ideas	274
Important Qualification to Incomprehensibility and Ideas	277
Knowledge of and Assent to the Incomprehensible in Locke?	279
Knowledge and Ideas	279
Propositions and Doctrines	282
Must We Have Knowledge for Assent?	284
Contexual Support for Denominating Locke's Epistemology as Antitrinitarian	288
Richard Burthogge	288
John Toland	291
William Stephens, Anthony Collins, and Other Deists and Free-Thinkers	295
Implications	297
Way-Of-Ideas-Trinitarians and Contexual Support for Arguing that Locke's Epistemology Was Not Antitrinitarian	298
John Norris and Potential Implications	298
Peter Browne and Potential Implications	301
Problems with Rejecting the Incomprehensible	306
Summary	306

    Human Free Choice and God's Attributes   306
    Problems of Ideas and Images   310
  Conclusions   311

Epilogue: The Coherence of John Locke and his Theological Project   313
  Overall Argument Briefly Stated   313
  The Pervasive Theme of Salvation and Its Impact on His Corpus   313
    Some Restatements   313
    Freedom of Religion   314
  Review of His Personal and Programmatic Doctrine   315
    Personally Held Doctrine, Namely the Fall   315
    Programmatic Doctrine   315
    Locke's Prescribed Approach to Scripture: Personal and Programmatic   316
  Pastoral Issues Not (Sufficiently) Addressed by Locke   317
  Who Locke Is: Narratives and Labels   318

Bibliography   319
Index   337

Preface

My fascination with John Locke and the thinkers of his era sprouted through two concurrent doctoral seminars at Calvin Theological Seminary in 2009, one led by Ronald J. Feenstra ("Prolegomena") and the other led by Richard A. Muller ("17th-century Metaphysics"). These two loved doctors opened new vistas for us and trained us to be clear, careful, and charitable. My main fruits from the seminars were a paper on the categories of propositions promulgated by John Locke and John Toland and another on the Anthony Collins–Samuel Clarke debate on liberty and necessity. By the end of the term, I was hooked on this era, especially philosophical and theological thinkers coming from the British Isles. I went on to write my dissertation (later published), building upon the work I had already done on Locke and Toland. It proved to be a fine beachhead for further exploration of the Enlightenment.

This book is mostly the culmination of my research to date in Locke while joyfully teaching at Cornerstone University and through conference papers mostly delivered at the Evangelical Theological Society's regional and national conferences. These two institutions have been crucial to the writing of my book. One provided me with a "due date" for drafts of chapters and venues in which to receive feedback, among many other benefits. The other gave me supportive colleagues, financial resources, insightful and fun students, and time. Cornerstone awarded me a full-semester sabbatical for this book in the fall of 2019. And its librarians, particularly Gina Bolger, consistently and quickly delivered works to me that were not part of our library's holdings.

There are so many other people for whom I am grateful. I am thankful for the individuals in whose company I happily find myself on occasion who have given me theologically rich conversations and friendship: John Duff, Matthew Everhard, Benjamin Marko (brother), Drew McGinness, and Michael Wittmer, just to name a few. They all love the Lord and truth. The person to whom I owe the most gratitude in this group is Richard A. Muller. His best scholarly accomplishments might not be the great number of brilliant articles, chapters, books, and series he has penned and edited, but rather the great number of scholars he has mentored and the camaraderie he has helped cultivate amongst his students. We are not only better scholars, but better people because of him.

I would also like to express gratitude for my families. There is of course my church family. They have been a constant source of friendship, support, and theological dialogue. Also, without the support of my wife, this book would never have been written. While I have cheered on or come alongside of her for the last seventeen years, she has done likewise for me but much better. I am thankful to my three daughters. They have brought me unforeseen joy. I dedicate this book to my parents, Craig Stevens Marko and Pamela Susann Marko, née Beahn, residing in my hometown, Cuyahoga Falls, Ohio. They taught me and my beloved siblings much. Two mindsets they instilled in us often come to mind when I think about our upbringing: the importance of valuing good company and how to persist.

I also need to thank the unknown reviewers, editors, and the many people who have had a hand in the completion of this book. The insights of the initial reviewers and Muller were invaluable. I count them as collaborators on this work. I learned so much from them along the way.

Gratitude is due to a few others as well. Without the work of the collaborators and collectors of the Post-Reformation Digital Library (PRDL), my work would have been greatly slowed. I visit it and recommend it often. I also want to thank the editors of the *Journal of Markets and Morality* (Acton Institute) (*JMM*) and *Philosophy and Theology* (Marquette University) (*PT*) for publishing some of my work on Locke and allowing me to publish greatly expanded and re-worked journal articles as chapters in this book: Chapter 3 (*PT*), Chapter 5 (*JMM*), and Chapter 7 (*PT*).

Finally, I have a few comments on the structure of this book. Each chapter can stand on its own. I give a full bibliographical first reference of works used in each chapter, partly for this reason. But each chapter also has a complementary chapter. The final arrangement of the book has separated two companion chapters into different ends of the book. Chapters 3 (justification in *The Reasonableness of Christianity* [*ROC*]) and 4 (fundamental articles in *ROC*) are mutually supportive, as are Chapters 5 (special revelation in *ROC*) and 6 (miracles in *ROC*). Chapters 8 (the question of Locke's use of "above reason") and 9 (the question of Locke's position on the Trinity) are also mutually reinforcing. But Chapters 2 (soteriology and theology in

Locke's "non-theological" works) and 7 (free will in the *Essay*) nicely complement each other. But the foci of Chapter 2, its introduction of Locke's body of writing, and its comparative simplicity make it the most fitting chapter with which to start Part I.

Jonathan S. Marko
Cascade Township, MI

1
Introduction

The Problems of Understanding John Locke

Inconsistent Labeling

John Locke published *The Reasonableness of Christianity* (*ROC*) in 1695. It is a somewhat lengthy theological treatise that starts with explication of certain points of doctrine that was deemed heterodox by traditional Protestants. The bulk of the book contains a painstaking proof of what the fundamental articles of the Christian faith are and why. He does discuss miracles, morality, and other theological and philosophical topics. But, interestingly, it perhaps received more attention for what was not in it. Locke avoided making explicit references to standard Christian doctrines such as the doctrine of the Holy Trinity and the atonement. Theologian John Edwards lambasted Locke's writings for being Socinian and this resulted in a protracted debate that pulled in others. Edwards attacked Locke in a number of works and the latter responded in kind. From this debate came two vindications of Locke's theological treatise: the first, *A Vindication of The Reasonableness of Christianity*, was a shorter work; and *A Second Vindication* was a comparatively massive work that contains many cutting responses, clarifications of *ROC*, and reveals much of Locke's theological programmatic intent of *ROC*.[1]

---

[1] John Locke, *The Reasonableness of Christianity, as Delivered in the Scriptures*, 2nd ed. (London: Printed for Awnsham and John Churchil, 1696); John Locke, *A Vindication of the Reasonableness of Christianity, etc., From Mr. Edwards's Reflections* (London: Awnsham and John Churchil, 1695). This was published along with the 1696 second edition of *ROC*. John Locke, *A Second Vindication of the Reasonableness of Christianity, etc.* (London: A. and J. Churchil, 1697); John Locke, *An Essay Concerning Human Understanding*, ed. Peter H. Nidditch (Oxford: Clarendon Press, 1979). Pertinent works from Edwards and Bold are as follows: John Edwards, *Some Thoughts Concerning the Several Causes and Occasions of Atheism, Especially in the Present Age. With Some Brief Reflections on Socinianism: And on a Late Book Entituled The Reasonableness of Christianity as Deliver'd in the Scriptures* (London: Printed for J. Robinson, 1695); John Edwards, *Socinianism Unmask'd. A Discourse Shewing the Unreasonableness of a Late Writer's Opinion Concerning the Necessity of Only One Article of Faith; and of His Other Assertions in His Late Book, Entituled, The Reasonableness of Christianity as Deliver'd in the Scriptures, and in His Vindication of It. With a Brief Reply to Another (Professed) Socinian Writer* (London: Printed for J. Robinson, 1696); John Edwards, *The Socinian Creed: or, A Brief Account of the Professed Tenents and Doctrines of the Foreign and*

Locke would soon have other issues. Bishop Edward Stillingfleet soon accused Locke not of heresy, but for unwittingly paving the way for the heterodox opinions promulgated in the infamous book, *Christianity Not Mysterious*, by John Toland. Locke's works were again associated with Socinian thought. Even though Locke defended himself well in both controversies, getting the best of both of his interlocutors in the minds of many, he would never be rid of a dogged association with Socinianism. There is wisdom, then, in Locke's comment to Stillingfleet amidst their debate: "It is an Observation, I have somewhere met with, That whoever is once got into the Inquisition, Guilty or not Guilty, seldom ever gets clear out again."[2] Yet, in the minds of some he did escape. Instead of being portrayed as heterodox, he is consistently portrayed as being "orthodox" (or at least relatively so) by scholars who focus upon the rise of natural religion or deism narrative. There he is routinely juxtaposed against John Toland who is portrayed as appropriating his epistemological fundamentals not into Socinianism, as was the original charge, but deism.

There are a few observations I would like to make about the above account that has pertinence to this present work. First, the application of labels like heterodox and orthodox (and even Socinian) all depend upon against whom Locke is being compared. This is perhaps not so surprising. Second, the context in which Locke wrote and thought was very contentious and complicated. It is convenient and somewhat efficient to discuss him in the context of the advancement of Socinianism or in the rise of deism or natural religion, but there is so much more going on during that period. England was rife with theological and philosophical controversy, not to mention similar trends in other spheres of life and thought. So, in this present book we will

---

English Socinians. Wherein Is Shew'd the Tendency of Them to Irreligion and Atheism. With Proper Antidotes Against Them (London: Printed for J. Robinson, 1697). Samuel Bold's *A Collection of Tracts, Publish'd in Vindication of Mr. Lock's Reaosnableness of Christianity, as Deliver'd in the Scriptures, etc.* (London: Printed for A. and J. Churchil, 1706) has the following relevant tracts: *A Short Discourse of the True Knowledge of Christ Jesus* (London: Printed for A. and J. Churchil, 1697); *Some Passages in* The Reasonableness of Christianity, etc. *and Its Vindication. With Some Animadversions on Mr. Edwards's Reflections on the Reasonableness of Christianity, and on His Book, Entituled, Socinianism Unmask'd* (London: Printed for A. and J. Churchil, 1697); and *A Reply to Mr. Edwards's Brief Reflections on A Short Discourse of the True Knowledge of Christ Jesus, etc. To Which is Prefixed a Preface, Wherein Something Is Said Concerning Reason and Antiquity, in the Chief Controversies with the Socinians* (London: Printed for A. and J. Churchil, 1697). For a nice collection of excerpts of contemporary works related to ROC: *John Locke and Christianity: Contemporary Responses to The Reasonableness of Christianity*, ed. and intro. Victor Nuovo (Bristol: Thoemmes Press, 1997).

[2] John Locke, *Mr. Locke's Reply to the Right Reverend the Lord Bishop of Worcester's Answer to His Letter, Concerning Some Passages Relating to Mr. Locke's Essay of Humane Understanding: In Late Discourse of His Lordships, In Vindication of the Trinity* (London: Printed by H. Clark, for A. and J. Churchill, 1697), 107.

not only explore the theological and philosophical works of Locke, but also the controversies in which they were forged.

Overall Argument

The primary argument of this book is that John Locke's intent for *ROC* was to describe and defend his version of the foundational or fundamental doctrines of Christianity during a very theologically and philosophically controversial time and not his own personal views. Locke desired to describe what makes one a Christian in the simplest and most irenic terms and to argue for the necessity of Scripture and the reasonableness of God's means of conveying his messages. Both revelation and the promulgated redemption are eminently reasonable.

Locke's theological writings, namely *ROC* and its two vindications, are an intentionally ecumenical and irenic project written amidst numerous complex theological and philosophical controversies. He argued for the simplicity of the Christian faith, to which the uneducated and the laborers could assent. The writings themselves were inadvertently controversial and regarded as suspect due in part to Locke's refusal to assert more than he thought warranted or desired, his lack of accommodation to the theological terminology and paradigms of his day, a studious avoidance of metaphysical pronouncement, and his failure to realize that most readers will not make a distinction between his personal and programmatic positions. His lack of doctrinal specificity often incensed self-professed orthodox thinkers and nettled metaphysicians, who did not recognize or accept the aims of his program. And the project was personal or individually focused in the sense that through it he foisted the burden of understanding the Bible and arriving at theological convictions on the autonomous individual, including the uneducated, and dismissed basing one's doctrinal opinions on so-called authorities as epistemologically illegitimate. This advancement of an individualized or personal orthodoxy and his accompanying theological framework for Christians to build upon was intended to refine the Reformation and counter certain Post-Reformation trends: adherence to his project would yield more and better Christians, less negative priestly influence and thus fewer unhelpful controversies and less sectarianism, and a thriving society. What is more, the claim of his intentional ecumenicity is bolstered by the ease of appropriation of his thoughts by orthodox and heterodox thinkers alike, a particular point not dealt with here, but demonstrated elsewhere by others. All of this helps explain the difficulty scholarship has had in labeling Locke along the lines of more traditional Christian sects. Of course, there were certain theological positions and worldviews that he vigorously opposed, such as deism, enthusiasm, and antinomianism.

Scholarship

Problematic Tendencies

There are a few trends that are present in many works on Locke that have been counterproductive to understanding his writings. First, there are far too many compartmentalized approaches. Locke was not simply an epistemologist, or political scientist, or a theologian, etc. He was a polymath, and a rather systematic one. As I will note in the next chapter, even his major "non-theological" works have strands of theological thought in them. As a case in point, his *A Letter Concerning Toleration* is arguably just as much a theological work as it is a political one. Thus, approaching one of his works attempting to isolate one of Locke's mental spheres makes one's reading of him liable to distortion. Second, the theological context of Locke's works is far more complex than most realize. For instance, Calvinism and Arminianism, terms frequently used in recent Locke scholarship, do not describe two monoliths at odds. Not only do these terms reference varied theological movements, but there are also other traditions engaged in Locke's conversation, notably the Lutherans and Anabaptists. Third, there has been a lack of appreciation that Locke's theology in *ROC* is more programmatic than it was personal. He says as much in *ROC*, but there are some reasons many conflate the two. As I will argue, there are important differences between understanding Locke's *ROC* as programmatic as opposed to being personal. In what follows, I am less interested in trying to decipher Locke's personal views than in understanding his theological program, its implications, and to some degree how it ties in to or is adumbrated in other Lockean works.

On the Ecumenical Intent of *ROC*

In the main, I will be interacting with scholarship that focuses on *ROC*, what Locke intended to do with it, and why it is notably different in certain respects from his *Essay*, etc. There is no perfect way in which to divide them, but there are certain patterns of argument into which scholars have frequently fallen pertaining to Locke's professed ecumenical and irenic intent for *ROC* and the authority of Scripture advanced therein. First, there is what I will call the surreptitious group. This is a significant group of scholars, like Leo Strauss, Michael S. Rabieh, and Steven Forde, who read Locke as religiously surreptitious (because corrosive). They think that such characteristics such as inconsistencies between the *Essay* and *ROC* or a seeming meager defense of miracles is evidence that Locke appeals to the Bible (exoterically) while simultaneously trying to undercut its authority (esoterically). His claims of irenicism and ecumenism are, thus, wholly feigned. There is a small and related group, consisting at least of Nicholas Jolley and Michael Ayers—who focus on the *Essay*—who think Locke is undercutting Christianity but do not emphasize an attempt on Locke's part to hide it.[3] The next group, the sectarian group, find his ecumenical claims insincere or Locke to be rather obtuse in making them and read *ROC* as being religiously sectarian. While earlier this group tended to frame him and *ROC* as Socinian (as John Edwards did) some more recent thinkers have described both as Arminian.[4] There are some well-noted scholars in this group, such as Victor Nuovo, John Marshall, and Stephen D. Snobelen, to name a few.

The other group of scholars that stand in contrast to those named immediately above, I will call the sincere group. They tend to read Locke's claims

---

[3] The following are notable examples of those who read Locke as being religiously surreptitious: Steven Forde, "Natural Law, Theology, and Morality in Locke," *American Journal of Political Science* 45, no. 2 (April 2001): 396–409 [ref. pp. 407–8]; Leo Strauss, *Natural Right and History* (Chicago: The University of Chicago Press, 1953); Leo Strauss, *Persecution and the Art of Writing* (Chicago: The University of Chicago Press, 1952; Reprint, 1988); Michael S. Rabieh, "The Reasonableness of Locke, or the Questionableness of Christianity," *Journal of Politics* 53, no. 4 (November 1991): 933–57; Jonathan Donald Conrad, "Locke's Use of the Bible in: *The Two Treatises, The Reasonableness of Christianity*, and *A Letter Concerning Toleration*" (Ph.D. diss., Northern Illinois University, 2004); David Foster, "The Bible and Natural Freedom in John Locke's Political Thought," in *Piety and Humanity*, ed. Douglas Kries (Lanham: Rowman and Littlefield, 1997), 181–212. Foster's earlier claims are in the same vein as Conrad's. He concludes his essay with the suggestion that Locke rejects "crucial elements of the biblical teaching on God, property, and the family." See also: Nicholas Jolley, "Locke on Faith and Reason," in *The Cambridge Companion to Locke's "Essay Concerning Human Understanding"*, ed. Lex Newman (Cambridge: Cambridge University Press, 2007), 436–55; Michael Ayers, *Locke Volume 1: Epistemology* (New York: Routledge, 1991), 122.

[4] Maurice Cranston, *John Locke: A Biography* (New York: The MacMillan Company); John Marshall, "Locke, Socinianism, 'Socinianism', and Unitarianism," in *English Philosophy in the Age of Locke*, ed. M. A. Stewart (Oxford: Clarendon Press, 2000), 111–82; Victor Nuovo, "Locke's Theology, 1694-1704," in *English Philosophy in the Age of Locke*, ed. M. A. Stewart (Oxford: Clarendon Press, 2000), 183–216; Victor Nuovo, *Christianity, Antiquity, and Enlightenment: Interpretations of Locke* (New York: Springer, 2011); Stephen D. Snobelen, "Socinianism, Heresy and John Locke's *Reasonableness of Christianity*," *Enlightenment and Dissent* 20 (2001), 88–125; Dewey Wallace, "Socinianism, Justification by Faith, and the Sources of John Locke's *The Reasonableness*

of ecumenical and irenic intent for *ROC* and his claims of the authority of Scripture as being sincere, although they will often admit perplexity how to understand or reconcile various places in Locke's works that pertain to religion, or they claim that he has made honest errors. This is perhaps the largest of the three groups and carries with it some very prominent names in Locke scholarship across the various fields: Nicholas Wolterstorff, John Dunn, Alan P. F. Sell, and Richard Ashcraft, to name a few.[5] In following this line of argument, I will offer a richer and broader theologically oriented context for *ROC*. I will also be more attentive to the distinction between Locke's personal and programmatic theologies. In so doing, I believe I have reconciled some of the major concerns over cohesiveness among Locke's major works.

Focusing on the Narratives and Singular Issues

There are several scholarly narratives of which Locke is often a part that will be engaged in this book. As already mentioned above, Locke is sometimes found in works covering or commenting on the advance of Socinianism or Unitarianism in England like those of McLachlan or John Marshall.[6] Locke

---

of Christianity," *Journal of the History of Ideas* 45, no. 1 (January–March 1984): 49–66. Cf. Hans Boersma, *A Hot Pepper Corn: Richard Baxter's Doctrine of Justification in Its Seventeenth-Century Context of Controversy* (Vancouver: Regent College Publishing, 2004); Joanne Tetlow, "John Locke's Covenant Theology," *Lock Studies* 9 (2009): 167–99; Donald Thomas Smith, "John Locke's Concept of Reasonable Christianity" (Ph.D. diss., Southern Methodist Seminary, 1997); Diego Lucci, *John Locke's Christianity* (Cambridge: Cambridge University Press, 2020). Lucci believes that Locke's "moralist soteriology" in *ROC* has Socinian and Arminian roots (7, 52–53, 211). He asserts Locke did intend *ROC* to be irenic while simultaneously contending that Locke's religion is unique (8).

[5] Alan P. F. Sell, *John Locke and the Eighteenth-Century Divines* (Cardif: University of Wales Press, 1997), 186–88 [quotation, p. 188]; John C. Higgins-Biddle, Introduction to *The Reasonableness of Christianity: As Delivered in the Scriptures*, ed. John C. Higgins-Biddle (Oxford: Clarendon Press, 1999), xv–cxv [reference, pp. lxxiv, cviii–cxv]; John Dunn, *The Political Thought of John Locke: An Historical Account of the Argument of the 'Two Treatises of Government'* (Cambridge: Cambridge University Press, 1969); Nicholas Wolterstorff, "John Locke's Epistemological Piety: Reason is the Candle of the Lord," *Faith and Philosophy* 11, no. 4 (October 1994): 572–91; Richard Ashcraft, "Faith and Knowledge in Locke's Philosophy," in *John Locke: Problems and Perspectives*, ed. John W. Yolton (Cambridge: Cambridge University Press, 1969), 194–223; Stuart Brown, "Locke as Secret 'Spinozist': The Perspective of William Carroll," in *Disguised and Overt Spinozism Around 1700: Papers Presented at the International Colloquium held at Rotterdam, 5-8 October 1994*, ed. Wiep Van Bunge and Wim Klever (New York: E. J. Brill, 1996), 213–34; Steven M. Dworetz, *The Unvarnished Doctrine: Locke, Liberalism, and the American Revolution* (Durham: Duke University Press, 1990); Greg Forster, *John Locke's Politics of Moral Consensus* (Cambridge: Cambridge University Press, 2005), 141–42; J. T. Moore, "Locke on the Moral Need for Christianity," *The Southwestern Journal of Philosophy* 11 (1980): 61–68.

[6] H. McLachlan, *The Religious Opinions of Milton, Locke and Newton* (Manchester: University of Manchester Press, 1941); Marshall, "Locke, Socinianism, 'Socinianism.'"

is perhaps most often mentioned in the account of the rise of deism or natural religion in England. These works tend to mention Locke and John Toland and give little or no analysis other than mentioning their differences in their respective categorizations of propositions. Works mainly focusing on Toland will routinely juxtapose him with Locke in the same way, but those comparisons are also typically shallow.[7] Locke's relationships to the Latitudinarians (during his years of publishing) and their intellectual forbearers in a sense, the Cambridge Platonists, are also the foci of some good Lockean scholarship coming from those like Griffin Martin, John Marshall, G. A. J. Rogers, and Patrick Müller.[8]

There are also particular issues in religion for which Locke receives attention. Some of them overlap with some of the above categories. For instance, it is commonplace for narratives covering the rise of deism to at least broach the topic of the relationship of revelation and reason or the categorization of propositions by pointing out that Toland rejects doctrines and propositions that are above reason while Locke accepts them. Locke's treatment of miracles and of the doctrine of the Holy Trinity are other topics that have been explored.

Figures and Doctrines that Could Have Been Given Their Own Essays

There are a few figures and doctrines about which so much is said in the book that it would not have been too much of a stretch for one or more of them to have been the primary foci of their own chapter. In terms of figures,

---

[7] For example, James Livingston, *Modern Christian Thought*, 2 vols., 2nd ed. (Minneapolis: Fortress Press, 2006), namely 1:18-21; Robert E. Sullivan, *John Toland and the Deist Controversy: A Study in Adaptations* (Cambridge: Harvard University Press, 1982), 79; William Uzgalis, "Anthony Collins" in Stanford Encyclopedia of Philosophy (first published on August 25, 2002 with substantive revisions February 23, 2009; accessed on March 13, 2009) http://plato.stanford.edu/entries/collins, 13-14; Gerald R. Cragg, *Reason and Authority in the Eighteenth Century* (Cambridge: Cambridge University Press, 1964), 67, 78, 83; Lucci, *John Locke's Christianity*, 24.

[8] Martin I. J. Griffin, Jr., *Latitudinarianism in the Seventeenth-Century Church of England*, ann. Richard H. Popkin and ed. Lila Freedman (New York: E. J. Brill, 1992). John Marshall, "John Locke and Latitudinarianism," in *Philosophy, Science, and Religion in England 1640-1700*, ed. Richard Kroll, Richard Ashcraft, and Perez Zagorin (New York: Cambridge University Press, 1992), 253-82; G. A. J. Rogers, "Locke and the Latitude-Men: Ignorance as a Ground of Toleration," in *Philosophy, Science, and Religion in England 1640-1700*, ed. Richard Kroll, Richard Ashcraft, and Perez Zagorin (New York: Cambridge University Press, 1992), 230-52; Patrick Müller, *Latitudinarianism and Didacticism in Eighteenth-Century Literature: Moral Theology in Fielding, Sterne, and Goldsmith* (New York: Peter Lang, 2009).

an essay on Samuel Bold would arguably fit well. He seemed to understand Locke's *ROC* better than any other commentator, past or present. They are very similar in many respects, which will be pointed out during the course of the book. Bold was very much an irenic and ecumenically minded thinker in a very similar vein to Locke (Something similar could be said about John Toland regarding the *Essay*, although Locke might not approve of where he actually deviated from him or that Toland's personal–programmatic balance weighed too heavily toward the personal). In terms of doctrines that could have been given a more direct or singular chapter are the traditional attributes of Scripture—authority, necessity, perspicuity, and sufficiency—and interpretation principles. The former topic would be easily culled from Locke's express words, while the latter would mostly need to be inferred.

Approach of the Book

While this book sets out to describe and show the coherence of Locke's theological and philosophical responses to certain theological controversies, it is not a full systematizing of Locke's published theology. If one were to develop a full "theology of Locke," it would be rather general and biblical. What is more, Locke did not set forth this irenic and ecumenical approach in all his works, even though one can observes glimpses of it elsewhere. In many of his works, he simply held back from making hasty conclusions or pronouncing upon issues for which there was no urgency to do so. His avoidance of taking sides in the Trinitarian and free will debates was intentional.

Taken together, the following chapters answer major questions that could not have been feasibly answered and defended through just one essay. Chapter 2 offers an overview of Locke's major works. I hold that Locke's major "non-theological" works demonstrate a sincere preoccupation with biblical Christianity, especially eternal salvation, the primary focus of *ROC*. I am not yet claiming that the Bible or theology or his concern over the salvation of souls is the singular key to observing the coherence of these works or that they were his main motivating factor for them. But theology in general and soteriology in particular are leitmotifs that cannot be ignored in studying Locke's corpus. Moreover, this argument can be viewed as evidence of Locke being a rather systematic and meticulous polymath. I am not aware of any study that has traced the theme of eternal salvation in Locke's major works.

The rest of Part I, Chapters 3 and 4, focus on Locke's soteriology within *ROC*. Both chapters have the overarching theme of how reasonable Locke finds the Christian religion's soteriology to be. And this is where the book starts to focus on Locke's program of basic Christianity. In Chapter 3, I situate *ROC* in the context of the justification debates of Locke's era and controversies focusing on the doctrines of Christ and the Holy Spirit. I argue that Locke's presentation of justification, the primary topic in *ROC*, and the soteriological framework in which it is placed are intended to be broad enough to encompass all "Christian" views on the topics except antinomian ones. Much the same can be said of his Christology and Pneumatology. The focus of *ROC* is not Locke's *personal* views of justification, the broader doctrine of salvation, or any other theological topic. Locke intended for the work to be ecumenical and irenic in its core.

In Chapter 4, I look at *ROC* and its vindications from the standpoint of the fundamental articles debate taking place in the years of Locke's writing. I maintain that Locke argues that the fundamental articles are reasonably minimal and explicitly from the Messiah. This position supports religious toleration and is not wholly novel. Locke thought that because people must be able to cull for themselves (although not wholly in isolation) any articles from Scripture to claim that they believe them—lest they be guilty of a brand of illegitimate, implicit faith—it is perfectly reasonable that the fundamental articles in Scripture are few in number and clear—otherwise the vulgar or commoners are practically ruled out from being saved—and expressly from the Messiah Himself—lest, among other things, the continuity of the church be disrupted and the definition of a Christian be subject to change. A corollary to this is the need for a relatively high degree of religious toleration. Moreover, while Locke tied these elements systematically together, there were others in the era who advanced one or more of these elements. Finally, in so arguing for the above, I will direct the reader's attention to Locke's keen concern for and interest in the eternal salvation of humans.

In Part II, namely Chapters 5 and 6, I continue to cull Locke's understanding of basic Christianity, but this time pointing out how reasonable he finds God's means of conveyance of the message of salvation (among other doctrines) to be. Chapter 5 focuses on Locke's understanding of the necessity of Scripture, set within the historical context of the controversy over innate ideas and the closely related rise of natural religion or deism. There, I argue that John Locke's belief that Christianity is epistemologically vital to the spread and maintenance of right morals in society is demonstrated by the mutual reinforcement between his argument against innate ideas and principles, which is most prominent in the *Essay*, and his conclusion in *ROC* that a great shift in moral thinking started with Christ's advent. Right moral principles, although demonstrable, are neither easily wrought nor innate but can seem to be so to the many who have taken for granted their Christian (or Christianized) milieu in which they have been raised, such as the deists. As a result, the removal of Scripture's position of authority from the public square will result in an inevitable decline in the quality and safety of it as it starts toward a morality of convenience. The conclusions of this chapter run counter to the frequent claims that Locke's advancement of the Christian faith is feigned or in some way intentionally divisive and establish an important logical link between two of Locke's greatest works. They further index why Locke did not alter the *Essay* based on what he wrote in *ROC* regarding the epistemology of moral principles.

Chapter 6 turns to an issue for which Locke is frequently criticized: miracles. Due to the great importance miracles play in his identification of revelation as such, those who think that his professed faith is sincere often critique him for offering a lackluster defense of miracles. Others point out that Locke intentionally set Christianity up for a fall by placing so much emphasis on miracles. This chapter looks at *ROC* in the context of the late seventeenth-century debate on the use of miracles as an evidentiary basis for the divinity of Scripture. I argue that Locke is one of many Christian theologians in the era with a strong emphasis on the evidentiary utility of the historical testimonies of miracles for proving the divinity of Scripture. But, for those who reject miracles as such an evidentiary basis and the need for special revelation, such as the deists, Locke asks them to consider: (1) the reasonableness of revealing Scripture as Locke thinks God did; and (2) the extraordinary advancement in right morality between Christ and the best thinkers preceding Him. The former consideration, the reasonableness of God using miracles, involves the ease of legitimate assent to the Christian faith that miracles provide for the poor and uneducated, a heretofore untreated element in the Locke-miracles discussion, and also a factor that I contend solidified the importance he continued to give to miracles in his works, notwithstanding any problems with incorporating them.

Part III is dedicated to showing other areas of Locke's works where he apparently took an irenic and ecumenical approach due to the controversies surrounding those issues. Chapter 7 anchors Locke's famed chapter "Of Power" in the *Essay* into the multivalent free will controversies in Locke's era.

It also builds upon James Harris's understanding of Locke's free will chapter in Harris's excellent work, *Of Liberty and Necessity*. It is my contention here that "Of Power" is not a metaphysical pronouncement but a description of our experience of freedom of the will.

Chapter 8 sets Locke within the debate over the categorization of propositions and disputes the perceived opposition of Locke and John Toland. There, I will argue that, for Locke, propositions "above reason" simply refer to that which Scripture tells the individual that is beyond the discovery of the application of his or her faculty of reason; but he is unclear to what extent this encompasses incomprehensible doctrines. This position is closer, than traditionally thought, to that of John Toland who does not deny biblical revelation that surpasses our natural abilities of discovery, but only incomprehensible doctrines of a particular sort derived from revelation. In short, John Locke's orthodoxy is more open to question than it is often claimed, and John Toland's heterodoxy is less drastic than it is consistently presented.

Chapter 9 picks up where the previous chapter left off. In the chapter, however, Locke will be approached from two different historical phenomena: the loose tradition or philosophical approach known as the "way of ideas" and the 1690s debates over the doctrine of the Holy Trinity. Here I will argue that while there are comments Locke makes, positions he takes, and qualifications made by critics that could be added to his published thought to make his epistemology accepting of incomprehensible doctrines, including the Trinity, there are other positions Locke takes and appropriators' interpretations and adaptations of his thought that are incompatible with incomprehensible doctrines. He could have given clarity to his position if he were reading his appropriators and their critics, but he offered none. Thus, I affirm the hesitancy of those Locke scholars who are wary of making a definitive pronouncement on Locke's orthodoxy on the Trinity; but I will argue the point by a different path than has previously been taken.

PART I
THE REASONABLENESS OF REDEMPTION

2

John Locke's Preoccupation with Theology and Eternal Salvation in His "Non-Theological" Works

John Locke's profession of the Christian faith and the recurrent biblical and theological themes and arguments he employs in his non-theological works have been the subjects of notable conversations among scholars in the last few decades. Due to the variety of his output, these scholarly, integrative explorations have proved to be difficult undertakings because they draw on multiple areas of expertise. Two interrelated questions are often in the background of these studies: (1) how do Locke's major works intellectually cohere—more specifically, how do one or more of his major non-theological works and *The Reasonableness of Christianity* (*ROC*) cohere or what part do Christian or "religious" themes play in them?—and (2) how crucial is the biblical faith to Locke's corpus—in other words, are his biblical and theological incorporations superficial, surreptitious (or secretly corrosive to the faith), or are they in some way truly vital? All do not address both questions and the range of his works investigated varies significantly from study to study. What is more, some implicitly cast doubt on the pursuit of the two questions by portraying Locke as a brilliant, but somewhat hasty thinker, liable to inconsistencies.[1]

---

[1] Nicholas Wolterstorff, *John Locke and the Ethics of Belief* (Cambridge: Cambridge University Press, 1996), xv. In the preface, Wolterstorff explains what he thinks is the root of Locke's inconsistencies: "A typical strategy of Locke, when discussing a topic, is first to present his thought in eloquent visionary unqualified language, then to elaborate and articulate his thought with great philosophical craftsmanship, and then to close by returning to the visionary. Unfortunately, he never brings these two sides of his genius into harmony with each other. For what he says in the detailed working out of his thought regularly undercuts the visionary statement; the qualifications and elaborations not only amplify but deconstruct the official formulations." Timothy Stanton, "Locke and His Influence," in *The Oxford Handbook of British Philosophy in the Eighteenth Century*, ed. James A. Harris (Oxford: Oxford University Press, 2013), 21-40. Stanton has a more straightforward take on Locke's perceived inconsistencies: "Apparent confusions, contradictions, and omissions were a part of Locke's thinking and writing as anybody else's" (22). Richard Ashcraft, "Faith and Knowledge in Locke's Philosophy," in *John Locke: Problems and Perspectives*, ed. John W. Yolton (Cambridge: Cambridge University Press, 1969), 194-222. He finds Locke's *Essay* and *ROC* as being

There has been a relative dearth of exploration and commentary on Locke's *Some Thoughts Concerning Education* (*STCE*), let alone rigorous discussion over the part and importance the Christian faith plays in that work. Works by John Yolton and by Ruth Grant and Benjamin Hertzberg set forth how a number of Locke's works relate to *STCE* and they comment upon a few of the Christian themes in his pedagogical book. For instance, Yolton thinks that when seriously considering Locke's *Two Treatises on Civil Government* (*Treatises*), *An Essay Concerning Human Understanding* (*Essay*), *STCE*, and their Christian themes, Locke's overarching programmatic goal is to produce "a socialized and Christianized individual."[2]

Most scholarly treatments, however, that explore the ramifications of Christian thought in Locke's non-theological works focus on the *Essay*, *Treatises*, or *A Letter Concerning Toleration*.[3] (I have treated the works of

---

inconsistent on the issues of faith and reason. All of this said, Locke does admit a degree of haste or carelessness in the preface to *An Essay Concerning Human Understanding*, but it is probably better to assume he was more careful than his humble comments might lead one to believe. Many of his works went through multiple editions and he would frequently change minor details, as the critical editions will attest. Furthermore, he would frequently seek feedback on his thinking and writing as a perusal through his correspondence will reveal.

[2] John Locke, *Some Thoughts Concerning Education* (London: Printed for A. and J. Churchill, 1693); John W. Yolton, "Locke: Education for Virtue," in *Philosophers on Education: New Historical Perspectives*, ed. Amélie Oksenberg Rorty (New York: Routledge, 1998), 173-89 [quotation, p. 173]; Ruth W. Grant and Benjamin R. Hertzberg, "Locke on Education," in *A Companion to Locke*, ed. Matthew Stuart (Oxford: Blackwell, 2016), 448-65. In this essay, Grant and Hertzberg argue that Locke's *STCE* and his posthumously published "The Conduct of the Understanding" work in concert and that the writing of *STCE* likely helped Locke think through some of his issues on his chapter "Of Power" in the *Essay*. Cf. Jonathan S. Marko, "Why Locke's 'Of Power' Is Not a Metaphysical Pronouncement: Locke's Response to Molyneux's Critique," *Philosophy and Theology* 29, no. 1 (2017): 41-68. Clarence W. Joldersma has a very intriguing and novel take on *STCE* and its Christian themes, but he does not seriously treat Locke in his historical context: "Providential Deism, Divine Reason, and Locke's Educational Theory," *Journal of Educational Thought* 45, no. 2 (Autumn 2011): 113-25.

[3] John Locke, *The Reasonableness of Christianity, as Delivered in the Scriptures*, 2nd ed. (London: Awnsham and John Churchil, 1696); John Locke, *The Reasonableness of Christianity: As Delivered in the Scriptures*, ed. John C. Higgins-Biddle (Oxford: Clarendon Press, 1999). Higgins-Biddle's critical edition of *ROC* is based, in part, upon the "Harvard copy" of *ROC*. The Harvard copy is a first edition *ROC* that contains Locke's notes, emendations, and corrections (cxxxiv). I have consulted both but reference only the pagination of the second edition John Locke, *A Vindication of the Reasonableness of Christianity, etc, from Mr. Edwards's Reflections* (London: Awnsham and John Churchil, 1695). This was published along with the 1696 second edition of *ROC*. John Locke, *A Second Vindication of the Reasonableness of Christianity, etc.* (London: A. and J. Churchill, 1697); John Locke, *An Essay Concerning Human Understanding*, ed. Peter H. Nidditch (Oxford: Clarendon Press, 1979); John Locke, *A Letter to Edward Ld Bishop of Worcester, Concerning Some Passages Relating to Mr. Locke's Essay of Humane Understanding: In a Late Discourse of His Lordships, In Vindication of the Trinity* (London: Printed for A. and J. Churchill, 1697); John Locke, *Mr. Locke's Reply to the Right Reverend the Lord Bishop of Worcester's Answer to His Letter, Concerning Some Passages Relating to Mr. Locke's Essay of Humane Understanding: In a Late Discourse of His Lordships, In Vindication of the Trinity* (London: Printed by H. Clark for A. and J. Churchill, and E. Castle, 1697); John Locke, *Mr.*

those who solely focus on the religious epistemology of the *Essay* elsewhere.[4]) There are scholars who frame Locke's incorporation of biblical themes as being, in some way, disingenuous. One could claim that such an incorporation was unimportant and superficial and was merely added to lend credibility to his writings or, alternatively, that they were part of a surreptitious ploy of actually leading people to what were in fact unbiblical conclusions. Examples of those who hold this latter view to one degree or another are Leo Strauss, Michael S. Rabieh, and David Foster, to name a few. There are also those who do not expressly charge Locke with insincerity, but view his writings as corrosive to Christianity, like Michael Ayers and Nicholas Jolley.[5]

The larger grouping of integrative scholars, those who accept Locke's profession of Christianity as sincere and who think that his Christian faith is in some way vital to his larger corpus, is also complex. There are those like Greg

---

Locke's Reply to the Right Reverend the Lord Bishop of Worcester's Answer to His Second Letter (Printed by H. C. for A. and J. Churchill and E. Castle, 1699).

John Locke, *A Letter Concerning Toleration*, 2nd ed., corrected (London: Printed for Awnsham Churchill, 1690); John Locke, *A Second Letter Concerning Toleration* (London: Printed for Awnsham and John Churchill, 1690); John Locke, *A Third Letter for Toleration, to the Author of the Third Letter Concerning Toleration* (London: Printed for Awhsham and John Churchill, 1692); John Locke, "Part of a Fourth Letter for Toleration," in *Posthumous Works of Mr. John Locke* (London: Printed by W. B. for A. and J. Churchill, 1706), 235-77; John Locke, *Two Treatises on Government: In the Former, The False Principles and Foundation of Robert Filmer, and His Followers Are Detected and Overthrown. The Latter Is an Essay Concerning the True Original, Extent, and End of Civil Government* (London: Printed for Awnsham and John Churchill, 1698).

[4] Jonathan S. Marko, *Measuring the Distance between Locke and Toland: Reason, Revelation, and Rejection during the Locke-Stillingfleet Debate* (Eugene, OR: Pickwick Publications, 2017).

[5] Leo Strauss, *Natural Right and History* (Chicago: The University of Chicago Press, 1953), 202-32; cf. Leo Strauss, *Persecution and the Art of Writing* (Free Press, 1952; Reprint: The University of Chicago Press, 1988), 7-36; Michael S. Rabieh, "The Reasonableness of Locke, or the Questionableness of Christianity," *Journal of Politics* 53, no. 4 (Nov. 1991): 933-57; David Foster, "The Bible and Natural Freedom in John Locke's Political Thought," in *Piety and Humanity*, ed. Douglas Kries (Lanham: Rowman and Littlefield Publishers, Inc., 1997), 181-212. His earlier claims are in the same vein as Conrad's (see next reference). He concludes his essay with the suggestion that Locke rejects "crucial elements of the biblical teaching on God, property, and the family." Jonathan Donald Conrad, "Locke's Use of the Bible in: *The Two Treatises, The Reasonableness of Christianity,* and *A Letter Concerning Toleration*" (Ph.D. diss., Northern Illinois University, 2004). Conrad arrives at a tentative conclusion that would not be welcomed in the majority of Locke scholarship: that Locke "is an esoteric writer who may have been attempting to undermine the authority of the Bible while simultaneously appealing to it" (abstract). Michael Ayers and Nicholas Jolley, while not asserting to my knowledge that Locke intentionally inserted logical inconsistencies, do think that Locke's *An Essay Concerning Human Understanding*, properly understood, is highly corrosive to Christianity. Nicholas Jolley "Locke on Faith and Reason," in *The Cambridge Companion to Locke's "Essay Concerning Human Understanding,"* ed. Lex Newman (Cambridge: Cambridge University Press, 2007), 436-55; Michael Ayers, *Locke Volume 1: Epistemology* (New York: Routledge, 1991), 122. There is a host of scholars that think that Locke's expressed ecumenicity is feigned and that he is instead advancing a biblical but sectarian agenda. This line of scholarship will not be addressed here but in coming chapters. Cf. Jonathan S. Marko, "Justification, Ecumenism, and Heretical Red Herrings in John Locke's *The Reasonableness of Christianity*," *Philosophy and Theology* 26, no. 2 (2014): 245-66.

Forster and İsmail Kurun, who adamantly argue for the foundational importance his faith plays in his political works, but functionally see Christianity as a placeholder for a more indefinite "religion."[6] Others conclude that Locke's biblical faith, in particular, and not religion, in general, is key to understanding some of Locke's non-theological works. Relying on other anti-Straussians like Yolton, Dunn, and Pocock, Steven M. Dworetz argues that Strauss has put Locke on the procrustean bed of the twentieth-century mindset and that Lockean liberalism emerges from Locke's overriding concern of the individual's relationship to God and salvation. John Dunn argues that all of Locke's works are more theologically driven than anything else; and Joshua Mitchell argues the following regarding the *Letter*: "The meaning of Christ's fulfillment is absolutely central for understanding Locke's position [of toleration]. Contemporary attempts to resurrect Locke's doctrine of toleration which all the while disregard the significance of Christ are, I think, quite misguided." I have recently argued how the innate ideas that figure most prominently in the *Essay*, the necessity of Scripture that does so in *ROC*, and the nature of faith often associated with the *Letter* are mutually reinforcing. Peter Myers has a somewhat similar conclusion regarding Locke's thinking on faith, reason, toleration, and political thought. He thinks that these notions must not be set in opposition to one another.[7] Finally, there

---

[6] Greg Forster, *John Locke's Politics of Moral Consensus* (Cambridge: Cambridge University Press, 2005). Forster plays loose with the term "religion." He does have a commendable explanation of the incorporation of Christianity in Locke's works in his Chapter 4. Furthermore, through a series of misreadings that will be addressed later in this book, he argues in his fourth and fifth chapters that Locke's real point is that the moral laws of the community must have *divine* backing to be effective and create a moral consensus. But this need not be a biblical faith or even a monotheistic one according to Forster. İsmail Kurun, *The Theological Origins of Liberalism* (New York: Lexington Books, 2016). The thrust of Kurun's book is actually to help us navigate our increasingly religiously pluralistic societies better than we are today and he thinks Locke, among others, can help us with this. He does think, however, that Locke saw not (general) religion as being of paramount importance to his program but theism (although, still, not more specifically Christianity or a biblical faith).

[7] Steven M. Dworetz, *The Unvarnished Doctrine: Locke, Liberalism, and the American Revolution* (Durham: Duke University Press, 1990), 117-32. Building upon comments from John Dunn, Dworetz writes, "Lockean individualism, for example, emerges from the individual's relationship with God; its basis is the individual's responsibility—Locke calls it his 'duty and interest'—to judge for himself in matters pertaining to his own salvation." He thinks that when one removes Locke's concern for the relationship between the individual and God, one no longer has a basis for reading John Locke and understanding his theological liberalism as the great thinker intended (132). John Dunn, *The Political Thought of John Locke: An Historical Account of the Argument of the 'Two Treatises of Government,'* (Cambridge: Cambridge University Press, 1969), 262-67; Joshua Mitchell, "John Locke and the Theological Foundation of Liberal Toleration: A Christian Dialectic of History," *The Review of Politics* 52, no. 1 (Winter 1990): 64-83 [quotation, p. 65]. This work was re-published in 1993: Joshua Mitchell, "Locke: The Dialectic of Clarification and the Politics of Reason," in *Not by Reason Alone: Religion, History, and Identity in Early Modern Political Thought* (Chicago: The University of Chicago Press, 1993), 73-97; cf. Jonathan S. Marko, "The Promulgation of Right Morals: John Locke on the Church and the Christian as the Salvation of Society," *Journal of Markets and Morality* 19, no.

are those like Timothy Stanton and Alex Tuckness who seem more interested in directing attention to certain aspects of the religiosity of Locke's texts and away from others. Stanton tries to help some refocus on themes in Locke like the church and the fall and away from the often discussed Lockean claim that persecution could not lead to legitimate belief. Tuckness generally has the same latter aim as does Stanton. Tuckness directs the conversation to other Lockean writings on toleration but notes that, despite what other scholars might say, "Locke sees nothing intrinsically good about religious diversity. His theory of toleration is thus not a celebration of pluralism. Nor does it defend toleration on the basis of a general skepticism about our ability to make moral judgments."[8]

This chapter will argue that Locke's major "non-theological" works demonstrate a sincere preoccupation with biblical Christianity, especially eternal salvation, the primary focus of *ROC*. I do not claim that the Bible or theology or his concern over the salvation of souls is the singular key to observing the coherence of these works or that they were his main motivating factor for them. But theology in general and soteriology in particular are leitmotifs that cannot be ignored in studying Locke's corpus. Moreover, this argument can be viewed as evidence of Locke being a rather systematic and meticulous polymath. I am not aware of any study that has traced the theme of eternal salvation in Locke's major works.

Locke's Major Works: An Overview

The Reasonableness of Christianity

The Reasonableness of Christianity is Locke's major theological treatise, first published in 1695, with a second edition in 1696. It drew the ire of some, like John Edwards, who labeled it "Socinian," a not uncommon charge bandied about in those days. But others, like Samuel Bold, came to Locke's defense, extolling the work's irenic and reasonable character. Locke's response to

---

1 (2016): 41–59; Peter C. Myers, "Locke on Reasonable Christianity and Reasonable Politics," in *Piety and Humanity*, ed. Douglas Kries (New York: Rowman and Littlefield Publishers, Inc., 1997), 145–80.

[8] Timothy Stanton, "Locke and the Politics and Theology of Toleration," *Political Studies* 54 (2006): 84–102; Cf. Timothy Stanton, "Locke and His Influence"; Alex Tuckness, "Locke on Toleration," in *A Companion to Locke*, ed. Matthew Stuart (Oxford: Blackwell, 2016), 433–47 [quotation, p. 446].

these attacks and his gratitude toward Bold were the impetus behind two *Vindications* of *ROC*, the first being a very brief work, and the second a bit longer than *ROC* itself. It is worth mentioning that Edwards was a Calvinist whereas many of Locke's notable supporters, like Limborch, were not.[9] This surely affects scholars who maintain that *ROC* is sectarian despite express Lockean protestations to that supposition or conclusion within the treatise.

In this tumultuous era, where numerous doctrines were being debated in Britain, it is not surprising that *ROC* created discomfort in some of its readers. By the first several pages he denies that all humans are guilty and corrupt by virtue of Adam's transgression. In the first paragraph he dismisses those who "would have all *Adam's* Posterity doomed to Eternal Infinite Punishment for the Transgression of *Adam*, whom Millions had never heard of, and no one had authorized to transact for him, or be his Representative." What he says that humanity lost was immortality and bliss. This is no injury, however, in Locke's mind, to the progeny of Adam: "Nay, if God afford them a Temporary Mortal Life, 'tis his Gift, they owe it to his Bounty, they could not claim it is as their Right, nor does he injure them when he takes it from them. Had he taken from Mankind any thing, that was their Right ... this indeed would be hard to reconcile with the notion we have of Justice." So, among other things, he dismisses the very idea of eternal conscious punishment of the unrighteous.[10]

---

[9] John Edwards, *Some Thoughts Concerning the Several Causes and Occasions of Atheism, Especially in the Present Age. With Some Brief Reflections on Socinianism: And on a Late Book Entituled The Reasonableness of Christianity as Deliver'd in the Scriptures* (London: Printed for J. Robinson, 1695); John Edwards, *Socinianism Unmask'd. A Discourse Shewing the Unreasonableness of a Late Writer's Opinion Concerning the Necessity of Only One Article of Faith; and of His Other Assertions in His Late Book, Entituled, The Reasonableness of Christianity as Deliver'd in the Scriptures, and in His Vindication of It. With a Brief Reply to Another (Professed) Socinian Writer* (London: Printed for J. Robinson, 1696); John Edwards, *The Socinian Creed: or, A Brief Account of the Professed Tenents and Doctrines of the Foreign and English Socinians. Wherein Is Shew'd the Tendency of Them to Irreligion and Atheism. With Proper Antidotes Against Them* (London: Printed for J. Robinson, 1697). Samuel Bold's *A Collection of Tracts, Publish'd in Vindication of Mr. Lock's Reasonableness of Christianity, as Deliver'd in the Scriptures, etc.* (London: Printed for A. and J. Churchil, 1706) has the following relevant tracts: *A Short Discourse of the True Knowledge of Christ Jesus* (London: Printed for A. and J. Churchil, 1697); *Some Passages in The Reasonableness of Christianity, etc. and Its Vindication. With Some Animadversions on Mr. Edwards's Reflections on The Reasonableness of Christianity, and on His Book, Entituled, Socinianism Unmask'd* (London: Printed for A. and J. Churchil, 1697); and *A Reply to Mr. Edwards's Brief Reflections on A Short Discourse of the True Knowledge of Christ Jesus, etc. To Which is Prefixed a Preface, Wherein Something Is Said Concerning Reason and Antiquity, in the Chief Controversies with the Socinians* (London: Printed for A. and J. Churchil, 1697). For a nice collection of excerpts of contemporary works related to *ROC*: *John Locke and Christianity: Contemporary Responses to The Reasonableness of Christianity*, edited and introduced by Victor Nuovo (Bristol: Thoemmes Press, 1997). William Stephens, *An Account of the Growth of Deism in England* (London: 1696). Stephens extols *ROC* in his pamphlet.

[10] Locke, *ROC*, 1-13 [quotations, pp. 1-2 and 8, respectively].

This was an inauspicious beginning to an otherwise well-thought-out treatise. These early heterodox points distracted many readers from the ecumenical and irenic thrust of the work. What reads like a heretical treatise at the beginning will often be read as one throughout. The following comment by mathematician Johannes Hudde on Locke's *ROC* was conveyed to him by his good friend Philip Van Limborch: "as it is, many in whose minds that opinion [the common opinion regarding original sin] is deeply rooted are offended on reading the beginning of the book before they come to its main argument, and accordingly conceive a prejudice against the author, so that they do not read what follows with the requisite serenity of mind."[11] As additional proof of his heretical design for some, he never expressly affirms or defends certain cherished points of orthodoxy like the divinity of Christ, the doctrine of the Holy Trinity, or the atonement in *ROC*.[12] Nonetheless, Limborch, Samuel Bold, and many others were able to see past the indiscretions of the first pages and extol the work because of Locke's designs for it and its overall execution.

Locke's main point in *ROC* was not to discuss his heterodox stance on theological doctrines, but rather to answer the question, "How is somebody saved unto eternal life?" The bulk of the book is spent proving from the Gospels and Acts that there were two propositions one must believe to be justified: there is one almighty, creator God and that Jesus is the Messiah foretold of in the Old Testament. The first does not recur in the Gospels nearly as frequently as the second, but that is because, Locke explains, Christ's audience was typically Jewish and already monotheistic.[13] Any other propositions that Christ or the apostles proclaimed with the gospel were in truth in support of these two fundamental propositions.[14] He writes, "For whatsoever is brought as an Argument to prove another Truth, cannot be thought to be the principal thing aimed at in that argumentation; though it may have so strong and immediate a connexion with the Conclusion, that you cannot deny it without denying even what is inferr'd from it, and is therefore the fitter to be an Argument to prove it."[15]

---

[11] Philip Van Limborch, "L2318. Philippus Van Limborch to John Locke, 28 September 1697," in *The Correspondence of John Locke*, vol. 6, ed. E. S. de Beer (Oxford: Clarendon Press, 1976) 206–10 [Hudde quotation/paraphrase, p. 207].

[12] For a fuller argument on the thrust of this paragraph: Marko, "Justification, Ecumenism, and Heretical Red Herrings."

[13] Locke, *ROC*, 25, 43.

[14] Locke, *ROC*, 30–31, 33, 34–35, 188, 293–94.

[15] Locke, *A Second Vindication*, 269.

Eternal life was not obtained, however, only through these two propositions. "For if they believed him to be the *Messiah* their King, but would not obey his Laws, and would not have him to Reign over them, they were but greater Rebels; and God would not Justifie them for a Faith that did but increase their Guilt, and oppose Diametrically the Kingdom and Design of the Messiah."[16] The truly justified person will evidently take Christ as their King or, from a different angle, a monotheist who actively takes Christ as King should be considered justified. This is not simply an intellectual faith.[17] It is active. Moreover, a true believer in Christ should obey Scripture as best he or she understands it: "And as for the rest of Divine Truths, there is nothing more required of him, but that he receive all the parts of Divine Revelation, with a docility and disposition prepared to imbrace, and assent to all Truths coming from God; And submit his mind to whatsoever shall appear to him to bear that Character." If one finds some text too difficult to understand or multiple texts too difficult to reconcile after fair endeavors one should "suspend his Opinion."[18] And to those who find his version of Christianity too easy, Locke writes, "And the all-merciful God seems herein to have consulted the poor of this World, and the bulk of Mankind. These are Articles that the labouring and illiterate Man may comprehend. This is a Religion suited to vulgar Capacities."[19]

Moreover, while the main message of *ROC* was simple, the theological backdrop of it was not. Locke identifies deists and those finding themselves engaged in debates over justification as some of the targets of his book. He mentions his desire to disabuse the former of their position that "Jesus Christ [is] nothing but the Restorer and Preacher of pure Natural Religion."[20] On a related point, he argues that the Bible is necessary for more assuredly delivering moral principles because our reasoning is weak.[21] In the final pages, where he notes that justification is the primary topic of the treatise, he chastises those from Dissenting and Conformist churches involved in the justification debate for adversely affecting others in their bodies who do not have the wherewithal to follow the complexities of it.[22] But justification and deism are not the only topics of concern. For instance, there was also

---

[16] Locke, *ROC*, 213; cf. 47; cf. Locke, *A Second Vindication*, 194–95.
[17] Locke, *ROC*, 194–97; Locke, *A Second Vindication*, 194–96.
[18] Locke, *ROC*, 303–4.
[19] Locke, *ROC*, 305.
[20] Locke, *ROC*, 2.
[21] Cf. Marko, "The Promulgation of Right Morals."
[22] Locke, *ROC*, 306–7.

widespread disagreement over what were the fundamental—fundamental in a variety of senses—articles of the faith among the traditions, to which Locke directly responds. There are still more that will be discussed as the book proceeds, and as I show his attempted navigation through and around certain controversies.

Locke's Major Non-Theological Works

One—or two, if you count the following as separate works—of Locke's major political works is the *Two Treatises on Civil Government*. There were many people, writings, and events that influenced and compelled Locke to write the *Treatises* such as his own exile, Charles II, James VII, The Glorious Revolution, Richard Hooker's *Ecclesiastical Polity*, etc.[23] But the controversy that appears to be the catalyst of the *Treatises* is that over the so-called divine right of kings. Some held that the monarchy is the only legitimate, God-sanctioned government and that a king had absolute power over his people. Locke turned his sights on Robert Filmer's work, *Patriarcha; or The Natural Power of Kings*.[24] Filmer had been long dead, but Locke confides that he would not have given the book any notice had it not been referenced or used in so many sermons in then-recent times. Locke decries that the book has one point, "*That all Government is absolute Monarchy*," built upon the ground "*That no Man is Born free.*"[25] Argumentation against these two assertions is the aim of the *Treatises*, the first treatise assailing the former and the second treatise the latter. But it is the first treatise that is the most concerted and direct assault against *Patriarcha*. In it, Locke is unceasing in his attacks on Filmer's reasoning and exegesis. The second of the *Treatises* is *An Essay Concerning the True Original, Extent, and End of Civil Government*. In it, contrary to Filmer, Locke contends that all men are naturally in a "State of perfect Freedom to order their Actions, and dispose of their Possessions, and Persons as they think fit, within the bounds of the Law of Nature, without asking leave, or depending upon the Will of any other Man" and in a state of equality, "wherein all the Power and Jurisdiction is reciprocal, no one having

---

[23] Cf. Jacqueline Rose, "The Contexts of Locke's Political Thought," in *A Companion to Locke*, ed. Matthew Stuart (Oxford: Blackwell, 2016), 45–63.
[24] Robert Filmer, *Patriarcha; or The Natural Power of Kings* (London: Printed for Ric. Chiswell, 1680).
[25] Locke, *Treatises*, I.1.2.

more than another, there being nothing more evident, than that Creatures of the same species and rank promiscuously born to all the same advantages of Nature, and the use of the same faculties, should also be equal one amongst another without Subordination or Subjection."[26] In the latter treatise, he offers biblical argumentation, among other reasoning, as to why government must be by consent of the people.

Locke's other major political work, *A Letter Concerning Toleration*, could be categorized as also a theological one. In it he outlines, among other things, the boundaries between the church and the state: "I esteem it above all things necessary to distinguish exactly the Business of Civil Government from that of Religion, and to settle the just bounds that lie between the one and the other;" and he offers his purpose for doing so: "If this be not done, there can be no end put to the Controversies that will be always arising, between those that have, or at least pretend to have, on the one side, a Concernment for the Interest of Mens Souls, and on the other side, a Care of the Commonwealth."[27] One of the theological or ecclesiastical differences between Locke and his rather like-minded Latitudinarian brethren that serves as a backdrop of this letter is that Locke pushed for toleration outside of the bounds of the Church of England, while the latter pushed for toleration within the bounds of the Church or "comprehension."[28] In the preface, Locke writes that we neither need "Declarations of Indulgence, *nor* Acts of Comprehension" but "*Equal and Impartial Liberty*" in our society with respect to the sects. What is more, Locke wrote a *Second* and *Third Letter Concerning Toleration* in debate with clergyman Jonas Proast.[29] A *Fourth Letter* was posthumously published.

An Essay Concerning Humane Understanding is his magnum opus. It is widely known for attacking the position that we are born with innate moral principles:

---

[26] Locke, *Treatises*, II.2.4
[27] Locke, *Letter*, 7-8.
[28] Cf. Diana Stanciu, "Arminian Toleration, Irenicism and Latitudinarianism in Cudworth's Letters to Van Limborch: Text and Context," *Lias* 40, no. 2 (2013): 177-209; G. A. J. Rogers, "Locke and the Latitude-Men: Ignorance as a Ground of Toleration," in *Philosophy, Science, and Religion in England 1640-1700*, ed. Richard Kroll, Richard Ashcraft, and Perez Zagorin (New York: Cambridge University Press, 1992), 230–52; John Marshall, "John Locke and Latitudinarianism," in *Philosophy, Science, and Religion in England 1640-1700*, ed. Richard Kroll, Richard Ashcraft, and Perez Zagorin (New York: Cambridge University Press, 1992), 253–82.
[29] Jonas Proast, *The Argument of the Letter Concerning Toleration Briefly Consider'd and Answer'd* (Oxford: Printed for H. West and A. Clements, 1690); Jonas Proast, *A Third Letter Concerning Toleration: In Defence of the Argument of the Letter Concerning Toleration Briefly Consider'd and Answer'd* (Oxford: Printed by H. Lichfield for G. West and H. Clements, 1691).

> It is an established Opinion amongst some Men, That there are in the Understanding certain *innate Principles*; some primary Notions... stamped upon the Mind of Man, which the Soul receives in its very first Being; and brings into the World with it. It would be sufficient to convince unprejudiced Readers of the falseness of this Supposition, if I should only shew... how Men, barely by the Use of their natural Faculties, may attain to all the Knowledge they have, without the help of any innate Impressions; and may arrive at Certainty, without any such Original Notions or Principles.[30]

This theological debate in which Locke entered the lists was hardly a new one. Lord Herbert of Cherbury, one of Locke's principal targets of attack, had said decades earlier, "Let us have done with the theory that asserts that our mind is a clean sheet, as though we obtained our capacity for dealing with objects from objects themselves. For while we can think of the mind as a closed book in so far as it is not open to objects, it cannot be justly called a clean sheet, as an appeal to consciousness, the final test concerning objects, shows."[31] Moreover, with all the attention that the work received, there were only two respondents that evoked defenses from Locke: Thomas Burnet and Bishop Edward Stillingfleet. Over thirteen hundred pages were put in print between the three in the course of the debate, the vast majority of which came from Locke and Stillingfleet.[32]

---

[30] Locke, *Essay*, I.ii.1.

[31] Edward, Lord Herbert of Cherbury, *De Veritate*, trans. Merick H. Carré (Bristol: J. W. Arrowsmith, Ltd., 1937), 132.

[32] Concerning the Edward Stillingfleet and John Locke debate: Edward Stillingfleet, *A Discourse in Vindication of the Trinity with an Answer to the Late Socinian Objections Against It from Scripture, Antiquity and Reason*, 2nd ed. (London: Printed by J. H. for Henry Mortlock, 1697); John Locke, *A Letter to Edward Ld Bishop of Worcester*; Edward Stillingfleet, *The Bishop of Worcester's Answer to Mr. Locke's Letter, Concerning Some Passages Relating to His Essay of Humane Understanding, Mention'd in the Late Discourse in Vindication of the Trinity* (London: Printed by J. H. for Henry Mortlock, 1697); John Locke, *Mr. Locke's Reply ... Answer to His Letter*; Edward Stillingfleet, *The Bishop of Worcester's Answer to Mr. Locke's Second Letter; Wherein His Notion of Ideas Is Prov'd to Be Inconsistent with It Self, and with the Articles of the Christian Faith* (London: Printed by J. H. for Henry Mortlock, 1698); John Locke, *Mr. Locke's Reply ... Answer to His Second Letter*.

Concerning the Thomas Burnet and John Locke debate: Thomas Burnet, *Remarks upon An Essay Concerning Humane Understanding: In a Letter Address'd to the Author* (London: Printed for M. Wotton, 1697); Thomas Burnet, *Second Remarks upon An Essay Concerning Humane Understanding in a Letter Address'd to the Author. Being a Vindication of the First Remarks, against the Answer of Mr. Lock, at the End of His Reply to the Lord Bishop of Worcester* (London: Printed for M. Wotton, 1697); Thomas Burnet, *Third Remarks upon An Essay Concerning Humane Understanding: In a Letter Address'd to the Author* (London: Printed for M. Wotton, 1699). Locke's lone and brief reply to Burnet comes appended to *Mr. Locke's Reply to the Right Reverend the Lord Bishop of Worcester's Answer, etc.* and is entitled *An Answer to Remarks Upon an Essay Concerning Humane Understanding*.

The final major work of John Locke is *Some Thoughts Concerning Education*. It is one of the least treated and explored works of his that was not a defense or vindication of another work from his corpus. The book was addressed to Edward Clarke and was the fruits of his advice in letters to him over a period of years. His goal was to give suggestions to the English gentry about raising virtuous young men. This book not only conveys his thoughts on pedagogy but also on physical health.

Theology in the *Two Treatises on Civil Government*

The first of the *Treatises* is entirely theological and biblical. It is Locke's exegetical and biblical-theological riposte to Filmer's *Patriarcha*. Locke engages the relevant biblical texts in deconstructing Filmer's arguments, attempting to show that Filmer's assertions are not in fact supported by the Bible. He contends, in many instances, that Filmer's claims, the Bible aside, are contradictory or inconsistent. Much of the second of the *Treatises* also relies on arguments from the Bible. One might suggest that this is merely to keep with the heavy biblical incorporation of the first or that he is simply making accommodations for his mostly Christian audience. But there are biblical or theological themes woven throughout the second treatise that are introduced in the first, namely the state of humans at birth, specifically their equality and freedom, and God's sovereignty. The former is the main pillar of the second treatise, and it is founded upon the latter.

The theme of the state of natural humankind that he initially discusses in the first treatise is, thus, re-initiated at the start of the second.[33] Naturally, humans are born in the aforementioned states of "perfect Freedom" and "Equality." The only reason that we should disregard these notions, at least in particular cases, is if "the Lord and Master of them all, should by any manifest Declaration of his Will set one above another, and confer on him by an evident and clear appointment an undoubted Right to Dominion and Sovereignty."[34] He qualifies this natural state, however. He notes that this "State of Liberty" is not a "State of License." Individual humans have no right to destroy themselves or do injury to the life, health, liberty, or possessions of another. The reason that he gives is: "for Men being all the Workmanship

---

[33] Locke, *Treatises*, I.VI.50–54, 67.
[34] Locke, *Treatises*, II.II.4.

of one Omnipotent, and infinitely wise Maker; All the Servants of one Sovereign Master, sent into the World by his order and about his business, they are his Property, whose Workmanship they are, made to last during his, not one anothers Pleasure."[35] Thus, the position that we are all naturally equal and free is undergirded by the notion of God. He is the sovereign and the one to whom we owe our work and allegiance.

Even allowable violence or retribution done to another or punishment is based upon these two premises, our natural state and God's sovereignty. The person who deserves punishment is "the Offender [who] declares himself to live by another Rule, than that of reason and common Equity, which is that measure God has set to the actions of Men, for their mutual security, and so he becomes dangerous to Mankind."[36] And, as it is unwise for humans to be judges in their own cases, in part, due to an inclination we have to execute a disproportionately high punishment for offenses done against us, "God hath certainly appointed Government to restrain the partiality and violence of Men."[37] In fact, Locke argues in the next chapter that although "Men living together according to reason, without a common Superior on Earth, with Authority to judge between them, is properly the State of Nature," people tended to enter into society and quit this state of nature.[38] But when one enters society, the governors are not permitted to quit the notions of equality and freedom and do violence to the people whom they serve. To act unjustly toward one's people is to make war upon them. And, in that case, the only appeal that the sufferers have is "an appeal to Heaven," i.e., to rebel.[39] Locke closes his chapter on "The State of War" with this warning, regarding our so-called appeals to heaven, which alludes to God's sovereignty: "Of that I my self can only be Judge in my own Conscience, as I will answer it at the great Day, to the Supream Judge of all Men."[40] In other words, citizens must never be hasty when it comes to rebelling, as God will judge the legitimacy of their actions.

As intimated earlier, Locke expounds upon the states of equality and freedom into which all are born throughout the second treatise, typically tying it directly to God's sovereignty, or indirectly to it by indexing support for the notions in Scripture. In his chapter, "Of Slavery," he argues that we

---

[35] Locke, *Treatises*, II.II.6.
[36] Locke, *Treatises*, II.II.8; cf. 9-12.
[37] Locke, *Treatises*, II.II.13.
[38] Locke, *Treatises*, II.III.19-21 [quotation, p. 19].
[39] Locke, *Treatises*, II.III.20.
[40] Locke, *Treatises*, II.III.21.

have no superior power on earth but the law of nature. Slavery, in reality, Locke argues (in most situations), is an extended state of war. And he denies that the Jews ever sold themselves into slavery, although they did feel it necessary to put themselves to "drudgery," but only for a time; and even during those times, the so-called master could not do with the servant what he or she wished.[41] Furthermore, Locke, later, in a different chapter, argues that children are not under the absolute power of their parents (contra Filmer). He claims that while Adam and Eve were created with fully functioning and mature faculties, they, and all parents after them, were under the obligation of the law of nature to "preserve, nourish, and educate" their children, although, "not as their own Workmanship, but the Workmanship of their own maker, the Almighty, to whom they were to be accountable for them." In other words, parents are not kings or sovereigns over their children, but only stewards, who are to prepare them to serve God.[42] Later, where Locke discusses the birth of political societies, arguing that they were all based on the consent of free individuals, he draws on the historical narratives in the Old Testament as support for some of his ideas.[43] Even later, when he examines the legislative power of governments, he explains that this power is limited to the public good and so cannot enslave or impoverish. He asserts:

> Thus the Law of Nature stands as an Eternal Rule to all Men, Legislators as well as others. The Rules that they make for other Mens Actions, must as well as their own and other Mens Actions, be conformable to the Law of Nature, *i.e.* to the Will of God, of which that is a Declaration, and the fundamental Law of Nature being the preservation of Mankind, no Humane Sanction can be good, or valid against it.[44]

In short, God's law is put in place for our benefit and cannot be abrogated by agreement of humans; He is always sovereign. Furthermore, because people do not consent to their harm, if their government is harming them and there is no one to appeal to on earth, they, as mentioned earlier, can appeal to heaven, to their absolute Sovereign.[45] In the same vein and toward the end of the second treatise, Locke argues that when the king or legislature

---

[41] Locke, *Treatises*, II.IV.24.
[42] Locke, *Treatises*, II.VI.56; cf. 55. Later, he indicates that education of the child is the most power or influence the parents have over their children: II.VI.68.
[43] Locke, *Treatises*, II.VIII.95-109.
[44] Locke, *Treatises*, II.XI.135.
[45] Locke, *Treatises*, II.XIV.168; cf. II.XVI.176.

acts contrary to trust and there are no earthly judges, one can appeal to the true judge and sovereign, God. Humans are to judge for themselves whether someone has put themselves in a state of war against them and whether they should, like Jephtha of the Old Testament, appeal to the supreme judge.[46]

A few observations regarding the natural state of humans and divine sovereignty are worth mentioning. First, while the reader might assume metaphysical free choice or will is a crucial notion advanced in Locke's numerous comments on human agents and the divine sovereign, it is not expressly discussed. The focus is on the obligations of humans to one another and to God. Second, Locke's heterodox view of the fall of Adam, namely his dismissal of the idea that corruption and guilt were passed to all humans, is promulgated in the *Treatises* just as it was in *ROC*. In the former, when writing of the history of the world, he writes:

> But though the Golden Age (before vain Ambition, and *amor sceleratus habendi*, evil Concupiscence had corrupted Mens minds into a Mistake of true Power and Honour) had more Virtue, and consequently better Governours, as well as less vicious Subjects; and there was then no stretching Prerogative on the one side to oppress the People; nor consequently on the other any Dispute about Priviledge, to lessen or restrain the Power of the Magistrate; and so no consent betwixt Rulers and People about Governours or Government. Yet, when Ambition and Luxury, in future Ages would retain and increase the Power, without doing the Business for which it was given, and aided by Flattery, taught Princes to have distinct and separate Interests from their People, Men found it necessary to examine more carefully the Original and Rights of Government.[47]

Thus, humans, according to Locke, did not have a sinful corruption passed down to them. And it stands to reason that he would hold the same idea that they were not counted guilty either, in the *Treatises* just as in *ROC*. Third, while he portrays God as sovereign, He is, concomitantly, judge and the one to whom we must ultimately give account. It would be perhaps assumed by his readership, but he does make it express. Thus, he does demonstrate a concern for salvation, although not nearly as blatantly done elsewhere. Finally, the idea that God's sovereignty is the basis of our natural state is perhaps

---

[46] Locke, *Treatises*, II.XIX.240-41.
[47] Locke, *Treatises*, II.VIII.111.

where Kurun and Forster find support for their notions that one of Locke's key programmatic concerns is that people are monotheistic or more generally religious (not necessarily monotheistic) as opposed to particularly Christian. That Locke is largely intent on defending the necessity of monotheism or a broader idea of divinity are plausible but unlikely interpretations of the *Treatises*. ROC clearly demonstrates a strong preference for Christianity or a biblical sect, as was and will be shown.

Theology in *A Letter Concerning Toleration*

While there are a number of theological themes such as the church, fundamental articles, and the like treated in the *Letter*, the theme of eternal salvation is, perhaps, the most prominent. Even when it is not the doctrine or notion focused upon, it is not uncommon for Locke to show how salvation is related to the topic at hand. In the opening of his letter, he writes, "I esteem that Toleration to be the chief Characteristical Mark of the True Church."[48] One who is "destitute of Charity, Meekness, and Good-will in general towards all mankind, even to those that are not Christians" is not a true Christian.[49] He continues on to describe some deplorable practices done in the name of Christ: persecuting those who are not of the same sect, quarrelling over that which the common person does not have the capacity to understand, and being more concerned with external forms of worship than morality.[50] "If, like the Captain of our Salvation, they sincerely desired the Good of Souls, they would tread in the Steps, and follow the perfect Example of that Prince of Peace; who sent out his Soldiers to the subduing of Nations, and gathering them into his Church, not armed with the Sword, or other Instruments of Force, but prepared with the Gospel of Peace, and with the Exemplary Holiness of their Conversation."[51]

He claims that he desires "to settle the just Bounds that lie between" the business of religion and civil government in the *Letter* in order to end this non-mandated style of adversarial evangelism.[52] With this goal in mind, he offers three reasons that the civil magistrates' jurisdictions should reach only

---

[48] Locke, *Letter*, 1.
[49] Locke, *Letter*, 2.
[50] Locke, *Letter*, 2-6.
[51] Locke, *Letter*, 6.
[52] Locke, *Letter*, 8.

to civil concerns "and that it neither can nor ought in any manner to be extended to the Salvation of Souls."[53] First, Locke argues, God has not committed the care of the soul to any person other than the individual: "For no Man can, if he would, conform his Faith to the Dictates, of another. All the Life and Power of true Religion consists in the inward and full perswasion of the mind: And Faith is not Faith without believing."[54] In other words, implicit faith or the appropriation of a set of beliefs on account of some authority is not true belief or faith. And one cannot offer up worship to God with which one thinks God will be displeased.[55] Locke's second reason is very much like his first: while the power of the magistrate consists in outward force, "true and saving Religion consists in the inward perswasion of the Mind; without which nothing can be acceptable to God. And such is that nature of the Understanding, that it cannot be compell'd to the belief of any thing by outward Force."[56] In short, fear of penalties are not legitimate reasons of assent. And, thirdly, even if government machinations somehow had the ability to convince people, that means that conceivably "one Conntry [sic] alone would be in the right, and all the rest of the World would be put under an Obligation of following their Princes in the ways that lead to Destruction." He finds the idea that "Men would owe their eternal Happiness or Misery to the places of their Nativity" as highly absurd and unfitting of the notion of a deity.[57]

Thereafter, Locke considers the church. He offers the following definition emphasizing autonomy and salvation: "A Church then I take to be a voluntary Society of Men, joining themselves together of their own accord, in order to the publick worshipping of God, in such a manner as they judge acceptable to him, and effectual to the Salvation of their Souls."[58] He briefly considers various church governments, but argues that he must "have liberty . . . to join my self to that Society, in which I am perswaded those things are to be found which are necessary to the Salvation of my Soul."[59] And while he acknowledges differences among different communions, he does challenge Christians with the following:

---

[53] Locke, *Letter*, 9.
[54] Locke, *Letter*, 9.
[55] Locke, *Letter*, 10.
[56] Locke, *Letter*, 10.
[57] Locke, *Letter*, 12.
[58] Locke, *Letter*, 13; cf. 17. On p. 17, he writes, "The end of a Religious Society (as has already been said) is the Publick Worship of God, and by means thereof the acquisition of Eternal Life."
[59] Locke, *Letter*, 16.

> if it be more agreeable to the Church of Christ, to make the Conditions of her Communion consist in such things, and such things only, as the Holy Spirit has in the Holy Scriptures declared, in express Words, to be necessary to Salvation; I ask, I say, whether this be not more agreeable to the Church of Christ, than for men to impose their own Inventions and Interpretations upon others, as if they were of Divine Authority; and to establish by Ecclesiastical Laws, as absolutely necessary to the Profession of Christianity, such things as the Holy Scriptures do either not mention, or at least not expressly command. Whosoever requires those things in order to Ecclesiastical Communion, which Christ does not require in order to life Eternal; he may perhaps indeed constitute a Society accommodated to his own Opinion, and his own Advantage; but how that can be called the Church of Christ, which is established upon Laws that are not his, and which excludes such Persons from its Communion as he will one day receive into the Kingdom of Heaven, I understand not.[60]

So, if we were to rely on what is expressly clear in Scripture, we would have more unity and be more like Christ wanted us to be.

Locke then turns to the question of what religious toleration should look like. First, no church must retain a person that offends against the laws of the society. There is no civil injury done in excommunication. Second, "No private Person has any Right, in any manner, to prejudice another Person in his Civil Enjoyments, because he is of another Church or Religion."[61] Third, the ecclesiastical leader's authority is within the bounds of his particular church and it does not extend to the civil arena. Lastly, "That the Care of Souls does not belong to the Magistrate." By this he proscribes compulsion through punishments and laws but allows individuals, even magistrates in an unofficial capacity, to express "a charitable Care, which consists in teaching, admonishing, and persuading, [which] cannot be denied unto any man." Locke explains, "The Care therefore of every man's Soul belongs unto himself, and is to be left unto himself." It is not the government's role to keep a man from bringing financial ruin or illness upon himself and it is the same with salvation.[62] Even "God himself will not save men against their wills."[63] He sums up his argument for the last point with the following:

---

[60] Locke, *Letter*, 16-17.
[61] Locke, *Letter*, 20.
[62] Locke, *Letter*, 29.
[63] Locke, *Letter*, 30.

> But after all, The *Principal Consideration*, and which absolutely determines this Controversie, is this. Although the Magistrates Opinion in Religion be sound, and the way that he appoints be truly Evangelical, yet if I be not thoroughly perswaded thereof in my own mind, there will be no safety for me in following it. No way whatsoever that I shall walk in, against the Dictates of my Conscience, will ever bring me to the Mansions of the Blessed ... I cannot be saved by a Religion that I distrust, and by a Worship I abhor ... Faith only, and inward Sincerity, are the things that procure acceptance with God.[64]

Again, as he stated earlier in the letter, implicit faith is no saving faith at all. One must be persuaded for oneself.

Locke then shifts to outlining what tolerating churches might look like. In Locke's mind, there should be no distinction made here between "the National Church, and other separated Congregations" with respect to the application of toleration principles. He asserts, "For the business of these Assemblies of the People is nothing but what is lawful for every Man in particular to take care of: I mean the Salvation of their Souls."[65] He offers his thoughts on toleration in two specific areas: outward worship and doctrines. Regarding the former, he notes that people should not have forms of outward worship imposed upon them. Again, if they are not personally convicted of a particular form of worship and corresponding rites, compelling them to perform them "is in effect to command them to offend God; Which, considering that the end of all Religion is to please him, and that Liberty is essentially necessary to that End, appears to be absurd beyond expression."[66]

His thoughts on the toleration of doctrines are similar to those regarding outward worship and the theme of salvation therein is even more pronounced. Locke acknowledges that doctrines are practical and speculative, and because those of the latter category terminate in the understanding, "it is absurd that things should be enjoyned by Laws, which are not in mens power to perform. And to believe this or that to be true, does not depend upon our Will."[67] Furthermore, no preaching of speculative doctrines should be hindered as they have nothing to do with the civil rights of the subjects of the commonwealth.[68] What is more, "if Truth makes not her way into the

---

[64] Locke, *Letter*, 36-37.
[65] Locke, *Letter*, 38.
[66] Locke, *Letter*, 39.
[67] Locke, *Letter*, 55.
[68] Locke, *Letter*, 55-56.

Understanding by her own Light, she will be but the weaker for any borrowed force Violence can add to her."[69] In discussing practical doctrines, he says the following:

> Every man has an Immortal Soul, capable of Eternal Happiness or Misery; whose Happiness depending upon his believing and doing those things in this Life, which are necessary to the obtaining of Gods Favour, and are prescribed by God to that end; it follows from thence, 1*st*, That the observance of these things is the highest Obligation that lies upon Mankind, and that our utmost Care, Application, and Diligence, ought to be exercised in the Search and Performance of them; Because there is nothing in this World that is of any consideration in comparison with Eternity. 2*dly*, That seeing one Man does not violate the Right of another, by his Erroneous Opinions, and undue manner of Worship, nor is his Perdition any prejudice to another Mans Affairs; therefore the care of each Mans Salvation belongs only to himself.[70]

Thus, our greatest concern is eternal life. Everything pales in comparison. And because what we believe is so important to this end, and because belief cannot be compelled, each human must not be impeded from doing whatever he or she can to determine the path to God he or she thinks best. One still ought to preach, discuss, and charitably admonish regarding religious matters, but only as long as force and compulsion are not used.[71] Even so, "The principal and chief care of every one ought to be of his own Soul first, and in the next place of the publick Peace."[72] The peaceful public does give humans more opportunity to explore the questions of religion and salvation. Locke's prescribed second concern actually undergirds and bolsters his primary concern.

In the "Postscript" Locke sets out to define what makes different traditions count as different religions and what a heretic and schismatic are. Regarding the first issue, he asserts, "those who have one and the same Rule of Faith and Worship, are of the same Religion; and those who have not the same Rule of Faith and Worship, are of different Religions."[73] Muslims and Christians

---

[69] Locke, *Letter*, 56-57.
[70] Locke, *Letter*, 57-58.
[71] Locke, *Letter*, 58.
[72] Locke, *Letter*, 63.
[73] Locke, *Letter*, 81.

are different because they have different holy books as their rule. Lutherans and Roman Catholics, although both nominally "Christian," are different religions: while Scripture is a rule for both, Roman Catholics add to it papal decrees and tradition.[74]

Locke then fixes the reader's attention on those within the same religion that separate because of disagreements: heretics. He notes two kinds of heresies: (1) "a Separation made in Ecclesiastical Communion between men of the same Religion, for some Opinions no way contained in the Rule itself"; and (2) a separation of a communion of believers, who take Scripture as their lone rule, due to doctrines not found in the express words of Scripture.[75] Regarding the latter kind, there are two more specific types of heretics: (1) those who expel others from their communion "because they will not profess their Belief of certain Opinions which are not to be found in the express words of Scripture"; and (2) when an individual separates from a communion "because that Church does not publickly profess some certain Opinions which the Holy Scriptures do not expressly teach." Thus, heretics "lay down certain Propositions as fundamental, which are not in the Scripture."[76] Locke thinks that the fundamentals are only express words of Scripture and not deductions from the express words:[77] "For if they be conceived in the express words of Scripture, there can be no question about them; because those are acknowledged by all Christians to be of Divine Inspiration, and therefore fundamental."[78] He ends his treatment on heresy chiding various sects for their numerous and different fundamentals stating, "I cannot but wonder at the extravagant arrogance of those Men who think that they themselves can explain things necessary to Salvation more clearly than the Holy Ghost, the Eternal and Infinite Wisdom of God."[79]

In the last pages of the *Letter*, he briefly covers the topic of schism, a notion closely related to heresy, both signifying "an ill-grounded Separation in Ecclesiastical Communion, made about things not necessary." But whereas heresy is a separation over doctrinal concerns, namely doctrines not expressly stated in Scripture, schism is separation over worship or discipline forms not

---

[74] Locke, *Letter*, 81-82.
[75] Locke, *Letter*, 82.
[76] Locke, *Letter*, 83.
[77] This limitation applied to the fundamental articles is in opposition to chapter 1 of the Westminster Confession of Faith and Article VI of the Thirty-Nine Articles.
[78] Locke, *Letter*, 84. This is prior to his writing *ROC* where he argues for two so-called fundamental articles.
[79] Locke, *Letter*, 85.

expressly stated in Scripture: "Now nothing in Worship or Discipline can be necessary to Christian Communion, but what Christ our Legislator, or the Apostles, by Inspiration of the Holy Spirit, have commanded in express words." A heretic or schismatic separates over issues not expressly addressed by Scripture. Locke ends the *Letter* asserting the contrapositive: a professed follower of Christ who does not so split, cannot be a heretic or schismatic.[80] It is worth mentioning that the backdrop of Locke's comments on schism correspond to the theological concept of adiaphora: things not commanded or forbidden in Scripture. This was an important concern discussed in Locke's lifetime.[81]

A few concluding observations about the *Letter* are worth noting. First, most of the *Letter* is taken up with theological and ecclesiastical discussions. The distinction between the jurisdictions of the church and civil government is, nonetheless, the main purpose of the *Letter*. Second, his notions that factor prominently in *ROC*—that the fundamental articles are expressly stated in Scripture, that implicit faith is illegitimate and a concomitant concern for the uneducated, and that salvation is our utmost concern—are also used powerfully in the *Letter*. In fact, *ROC* and the *Letter* reinforce each other nicely regarding these themes. Third, the *Letter* and the *Treatises* complement one another on the issue of civil or political liberty.

Theology in *An Essay Concerning Human Understanding*

Locke's critique of innate principles is hardly the only theological theme in the *Essay*. There is brief mention of theological topics throughout the book, such as the incarnation of Christ and the infallibility of the Bible. Scholars from Locke's day to the present have also pondered the theological implications of some of the philosophical topics thoroughly covered in the *Essay*. His treatment of substance drew the scrutiny of Bishop Edward Stillingfleet and others. Stillingfleet thought that Locke's *Essay* had antitrinitarian implications, although initially, he assumed that Locke did not realize the

---

[80] Locke, *Letter*, 86.
[81] Cf. Sungho Lee, "All Subjects of the Kingdom of Christ: John Owen's Conceptions of Christian Unity and Schism" (Ph.D. diss., Calvin Theological Seminary, 2007); Henry M. Knapp, "John Owen, on Schism and the Nature of the Church," *Westminster Theological Journal* 72, no. 2 (2010): 333–58.

heretical implications.[82] Locke's discussion on identity in Book II has also been considered for its the potential implications for the incarnation and the doctrine of the holy Trinity.[83]

There are places in the *Essay* where Locke offers a sustained theological discussion. The most obvious place where he does this, Book IV, has drawn the attention of innumerable scholars. In chapter 10 of that book, Locke argues for the existence of God. The rest of Book IV is devoted to defining taxonomies of reason, faith, and divine revelation and explaining their relationships. He discusses, for instance, the differences between so-called original and traditional revelation and by what marks they can be reasonably assessed to be divine; but a positive reasonable assessment entails the assessor approaching the revelation (Scripture, in Locke's personal assessment) being prepared to have it overturn any previously held notion that is not "certain" (a precise technical term in the *Essay*), including moral precepts.[84] In his chapters on the degrees of assent and enthusiasm, he discusses the reasonableness of using miracles as evidence of the divine agency of a particular, alleged conveyer of revelation, a discussion he picks up later in *ROC*. In his chapter on reason, he briefly addresses the traditional categorization of propositions: above reason, according to reason, and contrary to reason. In his chapter on enthusiasm, he gives guidance to the reader how to approach modern-day claims of immediate revelation from God. The theological content of these chapters is infrequently overlooked by scholars.[85]

Analyses of Locke have largely ignored the relation between his concern for eternal salvation and his treatment of freedom and the will. Locke examines this topic in his chapter, "Of Power."[86] This chapter went through a major revision after the first edition and other smaller revisions after the second. That the theme of eternal salvation plays prominently in the first version can be observed by glancing through sections 29, 30, 35, 38, and 45 of that chapter. Even so, William Molyneux's letter to Locke, critiquing the first

---

[82] Cf. E. D. Kort, "Stillingfleet and Locke on Substance, Essence, and Articles of Faith," *Locke Studies* 5 (2005): 149–78; Edwin McCann, "Locke's Theory of Substance Under Attack!" *Philosophical Studies* 106 (2001): 87–105.

[83] See Udo Thiel, "The Trinity and Human Personal Identity," in *English Philosophy in the Age of Locke*, ed. M. A. Stewart (Oxford: Clarendon Press, 2000), 217–43.

[84] Cf. Marko, *Measuring the Distance*; Marko, "Promulgation of Right Morals."

[85] Much of the scholarship on the aforementioned issues in Book IV have been categorized and treated in Marko, *Measuring the Distance*, especially, chapters 2 and 3.

[86] Much of the scholarship has been categorized and treated in: Marko, "Why Locke's 'Of Power'" and in Chapter 7 of this text. In both, I acknowledge that not all have missed the theological aspects of the work.

edition of the chapter, reveals Molyneux's grasp that eternal salvation is one of the most prominent and important themes in it:

> The Next place I take Notice off as requiring some Farther Explication is Your Discourse about Mans Liberty and Necessity. [T]his Thread seems so wonderfully fine spun in your Book, that at last the Great Question of Liberty and Necessity seems to Vanish. and herein you seem to make all Sins to proceed from our Understandings, or to be against Conscience; and not at all from the Depravity of our Wills. Now it seems harsh to say, that a Man shall be Damn'd, because he understands no better than he does.[87]

Thus, Molyneux thinks that one might infer from the first edition of "Of Power," that people are damned for not understanding or reasoning well.

In Locke's second edition of "Of Power," he worked hard at explaining how humans are not damned by a mere lack of understanding or intelligence. At one point he admits that he made an error in the first edition. He notes that he thought that the greatest good apprehended by the human agent is what determined the will, "But yet upon a stricter enquiry, I am forced to conclude, that *good*, the *greater good*, though apprehended and acknowledged to be so, does not determine the *will*, until our desire, raised proportionably to it, makes us *uneasy* in the want of it." In short, we need to cultivate our desires. He asserts that any person who wants to do great things in this world or "hopes in the next," "his *will* will not be determin'd to any action in pursuit of this confessed greater good" until he trains himself to be uneasy in the want of the perceived greater goods.[88] Later, he again critiques his former position in the first edition:

> Were the *will* determin'd by the views of good, as it appears in Contemplation greater or less to the understanding, which is the State of all absent good, and that, which in the received Opinion the *will* is supposed to move to, and to be moved by, I do not see how it could ever get loose from the infinite eternal Joys of Heaven, once propos'd and consider'd as possible.[89]

---

[87] William Molyneux, "L1579. William Molyneux to Locke, 22 December 1692," in *The Correspondence of John Locke*, vol. 4, ed. E. S. de Beer (Oxford: Clarendon Press, 1979), 599–602 [quotation, pp. 600-1].
[88] Locke, *Essay*, II.xxi.35.
[89] Locke, *Essay*, II.xxi.38.

In short, the prospect of eternal and blissful life ought to compel our will if the greatest good determined our wills. We are clearly not so moved. Locke explains how other desires take the place of what should be our focus on eternal life and he writes of the seeming precariousness of the human condition:

> Though they cannot deny, but that it is possible, there may be a state of eternal durable Joys after this life, far surpassing all the good is to be found here. Nay they cannot but see, that it is more possible, than the attainment, and continuation of that pittance of Honour, Riches, or Pleasure, which they pursue; and for which they neglect that eternal State: But yet in full view of this difference, satisfied of the possibility of a perfect, secure, and lasting happiness in a future State, and under a clear conviction, that it is not to be had here, whilst they bound their happiness within some little enjoyment, or aim of this life, and exclude the joys of Heaven from making any necessary part of it, their desires are not moved by this greater apparent good, nor their *wills* determin'd to any action, or endeavour for its attainment.[90]

So, even if some were not completely convinced of the afterlife, all ought to acknowledge that it is a much better choice to focus their life on the pursuit of endless joys as opposed to earthly ephemeral ones; but, again, people are rarely so moved.

Locke's answer to Molyneux's critique is an addition of about thirty sections that are built upon his discussion of our "power to *suspend* the execution and satisfaction of any of its [the mind's] desires." This ability to rationally consider the best choice is important. In fact, for Locke, "This seems to me the source of all liberty; in this seems to consist that, which is (as I think improperly) call'd *Free will.*"[91] As the rest of the chapter continues, it is clear that this state of freedom is important because it offers us an opportunity to train ourselves to cultivate good desires and to disempower our

---

[90] Locke, *Essay*, II.xxi.44.
[91] Locke, *Essay*, II.xxi.47. In section 71, he writes: "But every *Good*, nay every *greater Good* does not constantly move *Desire*, because it may not make, or may not be taken to make any necessary part of our Happiness. For all that we desire is only to be Happy. But though this general *Desire* of Happiness operates constantly and invariably, yet the satisfaction of any particular *desire* can be suspended from determining the will to any subservient action, till we have maturely examin'd, whether the particular apparent good, which we then desire, makes a part of our real Happiness, or be consistent or inconsistent with it. The result of our judgment upon that Examination is what ultimately determines the Man, who could not be *free* if his *will* were determin'd by any thing, but his own *desire* guided by his own *Judgment*."

bad habits and desires and ultimately avoid damnation or loss of rewards. He mentions or discusses heaven or its joys throughout the rest of the chapter, using terms like "true happiness," "true felicity," "real Bliss," "Joys of a future State," "the future State of Bliss," and "infinite Happiness," etc.[92] In one of the final sections he writes the following:

> The Rewards and Punishments of another Life, which the Almighty has established, as the Enforcements of his Law, are of weight enough to determine the Choice, against whatever Pleasure or Pain this Life can shew, when the eternal State is considered but in its bare possibility, which no Body can make any doubt of. He that will allow exquisite and endless Happiness to be but the possible consequence of a good Life here, and the contrary state the possible Reward of a bad one, must own himself to judge very much amiss, if he does not conclude, That a vertuous Life, with the certain expectation of everlasting Bliss, which may come, is to be preferred to a vicious one, with the fear of that dreadful state of Misery, which 'tis very possible may overtake the guilty; or at best the terrible uncertain hope of Annihilation.[93]

In short, if one admitted the possibility of an afterlife, it is most reasonable for that person to apply his or her own faculties in pursuit and determination of the truest and most reasonable religion and to discover what he or she is obligated to believe and/or do. If there is no God and afterlife, a person who spent their time pursuing it will not have any regrets. But, if a person does not pursue the good, assuming only annihilation accompanies death and he or she is wrong, there will be infinite, enduring misery.

Thus, our true freedom lies in our ability to apply our faculty of reason to our choices and desires by suspending the immediate pursuit of any desire. Doing that well, in Locke's mind, is the difference between various rewards and punishment. Molyneux's letter to Locke commenting on the second edition of "Of Power" captures the former's appreciation for the latter's response to his earlier critique: "I was mightily pleased to find therein a Rational Account of what I have often wonderd at, viz., Why Men should content

---

[92] Locke, *Essay*, II.xxi.51, 52, 60, 64, 69, 70. He does also have corresponding comments on eternal misery.
[93] Locke, *Essay*, II.xxi.70.

themselves to stay in this Life for ever, tho at the same time they will grant, that in the next Life they expect to be infinitely Happy"[94]

Locke's very rational take on religion, even after responding to Molyneux's critique may not be as heterodox as one might claim. He seems to shy away from any metaphysical discussions. In fact, James Harris has recently suggested that Locke is trying to describe the experience of freedom and not engage in any sort of metaphysical or sectarian discussion.[95] This comports with the presentation of human liberty he incorporates in the *Treatises* and the *Letter*. It is also interesting that what he takes to be the hope of an atheist or skeptic—annihilation—if there is a God, is actually what he thinks will likely happen to the unrighteous. One need not see a development or change in his thinking between the two books, the *Essay* and *ROC*. It could simply be that although he finds annihilation a probable conclusion from the theologizing of the relevant passages of Scripture explored in *ROC*, nothing uncertain is worth the gamble on eternity. Finally, and on a related note, one might see *ROC* as a response, in part, to Locke's recurrent claim in the *Essay* that the height of irrationality is not giving due consideration to one's eternal state, even if one is not convinced there is an afterlife. *ROC* puts forth many reasonable arguments compelling one truly to believe that Christianity is the true faith.

Theology in *Some Thoughts Concerning Education*

Locke directly mentions eternal salvation in *STCE*, although not often. When he does, eternal salvation is connected with virtue, the general quality Locke is trying to help parents instill in their children throughout the book.[96] At one point in *STCE*, Locke discusses how reputation can be an indication of one's virtue. He notes, however, that it is not the true principle and measure, but rather the true metric is "the Knowledge of a Man's Duty, and the Satisfaction it is, to obey his Maker, in following the Dictates of that Light God has given him, with the Hopes of Acceptance and Reward."[97] In a later place, he writes of the importance of virtue: "I place *Vertue* as the first and

---

[94] William Molyneux, "L1763. William Molyneux to Locke, 28 July 1694, July 1693," in *The Correspondence of John Locke*, vol. 5, ed. E. S. de Beer (Oxford: Clarendon Press, 1979), 92-93 [quotation, p. 92].
[95] Marko, "Why Locke's 'Of Power,'" 41-45; cf. Harris, *Of Liberty and Necessity*, 19-31.
[96] Locke, *STCE*, dedication.
[97] Locke, *STCE*, 61 [§60].

most necessary of those Endowments, that belong to a Man or Gentleman, as absolutely requisite to make him valued and beloved by others, acceptable or tolerable to himself; without that, I think, he will neither be happy in this, nor the other World."[98] Immediately after, he offers his thoughts on educating children about God. Although he stresses caution in telling them too much and confusing their little minds, he does think it is important to imprint on their minds "a true Notion of *God*, as of the independent Supreme Being, Author and Maker of all Things, from whom we receive all our Good, that loves us, and gives us all Things; and consequent to it a Love and Reverence of him."[99] A few lines later he reiterates the final mandate, imploring parents to teach their children to "love and obey him."[100] Thus, eternal salvation is addressed in *STCE* in different places, but not always in a direct way.

There are several subsequent sections that focus heavily on biblical and theological education, among other pedagogical ideas and suggestions. Locke asserts that children should commit the Lord's Prayer and Ten Commandments to memory.[101] He believes that children should read from the Bible but not from a "promiscuous reading of it through, by Chapters, as they lie in order." Such reading will neither help advance principles of religion nor encourage nor pleasure them. To read all the parts indifferently without a grasp on genres and their functions will create an "odd jumble of Thoughts" in the child's head ("I am apt to think, that this in some Men has been the very Reason, why they never had clear and distinct Thoughts of it [the Bible] all their Life-time"). Locke doubts that children will get much from the laws of Moses, Song of Solomon, Prophecies, Epistles, and Revelation. Locke even maintains that some aspects of the Gospels and Acts are beyond children. That said, he thinks that the principles of religion are to be drawn from Scripture in its express words and not out of human-wrought systems and analogies.[102] He does think that children should be aware of stories like Joseph and his brothers, David and Goliath, David and Jonathan, and so on. He recommends Dr. Worthington's catechism for children, which is straight from the words of Scripture.[103] Thereafter, he suggests the reader make sure that children know and memorize the moral rules scattered

---

[98] Locke, *STCE*, 157 [§128].
[99] Locke, *STCE*, 157 [§129].
[100] Locke, *STCE*, 158 [§129].
[101] Locke, *STCE*, 185 [§149].
[102] Locke, *STCE*, 186–87 [§150].
[103] Locke, *STCE*, 187–88 [§151]. This catechism referenced represents a broadly latitudinarian approach. Many catechisms of the day were dogmatic and would broach doctrines like the Trinity.

throughout Scripture.[104] The importance of Scripture's moral principles is brought up later in the book. There he remarks, "I know not whether he should read any other Discourses of Morality, but what he finds in the Bible; or have any System of *Ethicks* put into his Hand, till he can read *Tully's Offices*, not as a School-Boy to learn *Latin*, but as one that would be informed in the Principles and Precepts of Vertue, for the Conduct of his Life."[105]

He continues his thoughts on theological and biblical education toward the end of the book, specifically regarding its utility for proper thinking in natural philosophy. Natural philosophy concerns spirits—or metaphysics—and other bodies.[106] Locke thinks that the study of the spirits "ought to go before the study of Matter, and Body, not as a Science that can be methodized into a System, and treated of upon Principles of Knowledge; but as an enlargement of our Minds towards a truer and fuller comprehension of the intellectual World to which are led both by Reason and Revelation."[107] In fact, revelation is from where most of what we know of other spirits and God comes. Locke even goes so far to make a suggestion that someone should craft a historical narrative derived from the Bible suitable for young people to read. This would help with instilling the notion and belief of spirits. This is crucial for natural philosophy, in Locke's mind, because "our Philosophy will be lame and defective in one main Part of it, when it leaves out the Contemplation of the most Excellent and Powerful Part of the Creation."[108] Locke gives further reasoning that the study of the history of the Bible that discusses spirits and doctrine of Scripture ought to precede the study of physical concerns:

> The Reason why I would have this premised to *the study of Bodies*; and the Doctrine of Scripture well imbibed, before young Men be entered in *Natural Philosophy*, is, because Matter being a thing, that all our Senses are constantly conversant with, it is so apt to possess the Mind, and exclude all other Beings, but Matter, that prejudice grounded on such Principles often leaves no room for the admittance of Spirits, or the allowing any such things as *immaterial Beings, in rerum natura*, when yet it is evident that by

---

[104] Locke, *STCE*, 189 [§151].
[105] Locke, *STCE*, 220 [§174].
[106] This is a shift away from the traditional limitation of natural philosophy to physics. Metaphysics was typically considered its own discipline.
[107] Locke, *STCE*, 225-26. [§178; this section is not labeled but his section on natural philosophy is evidently supposed to be 178].
[108] Locke, *STCE*, 226-27 [§178].

mere Matter and Motion, none of the great Phoenomena of Nature can be resolved...[109]

Because all our ideas of things come from our empirical senses, we have a natural proclivity to favor materialistic explanations or less supernatural explanations. Locke thinks this sort of bias will lead us astray in our philosophy.

The work does, however, have theological underpinnings. First, while STCE has the least relative amount of direct theological or biblical material of Locke's non-theological works, God's sovereignty is the motivating factor of virtue, the main concern of the book, and biblical morality delivers virtue's principles. Thus, God, eternal life, and the high importance of the Bible for morality, all elements that factor prominently in other works of Locke, are in the background here. Second, it is interesting that there is no discussion on so-called fundamental articles, a topic that importantly factors into ROC and the *Letter*. Perhaps children are to be left to discover these through their own religious investigations. Locke does make it a point, however, to emphasize learning doctrines from the express words of Scripture, as he has been shown to do elsewhere.

Conclusions

Locke's major "non-theological" works contain numerous theological and biblical themes that are very difficult to miss. What is more, Locke's concern for eternal salvation is prominent in the *Letter*, ROC, and the chapter on liberty and the will in the *Essay*. Although not prominent, the concern is also present in SCTE and the *Treatises*. This ever-abiding concern makes sense, as Locke held that the height of human irrationality is being unconcerned with the prospects of eternal life and eternal death. Not unrelated, obedience and morality, justly labeled theological themes, are highly prominent in all his works treated above.

There are other themes that are shared between two or more works. God is presented as our King in the *Treatises* and Jesus Christ is presented as King in ROC, although it is not clear he is intending to identify Christ as God. The theme of liberty is incorporated at least implicitly in all of Locke's

---

[109] Locke, STCE, 228 [§180].

works. Liberty is vital to the prospects for eternal salvation. Also, *ROC*, the *Essay*, *SCTE*, and the *Letter* treat the Bible as the surest deliverer of morality. There are also a few themes expressed in multiple works that Locke typically associates with eternal salvation: fundamental articles, doctrines presented in the express words of Scripture, and the illegitimacy of implicit faith. Taken together, these themes render the characterization of John Locke as a religiously or theologically concerned thinker convincing.

3
John Locke on Justification and Some Concomitant Doctrines

Written in a time of significant theological controversy, perhaps John Locke should not have been surprised that his irenic and ecumenical intentions with *The Reasonableness of Christianity* (*ROC*) would be misunderstood.[1] In this work he argues that there is only one article of faith necessary to be believed for justification for philosophical monotheists: Jesus is the Messiah. He acknowledges that one with true faith will not be content with or sanctified by staying at such a fundamental level. Nonetheless, John Edwards (1637–1716) vehemently attacked it as being a Socinian work prompting two subsequent *Vindications* (*First* and *Second*) of *ROC* from Locke, further assaults from others, and more responses from Edwards. Some noted thinkers, like Samuel Bold, came to Locke's defense.[2] Locke claims more than

---

[1] John Locke, *The Reasonableness of Christianity, as Delivered in the Scriptures*, 2nd ed. (London: Awnsham and John Churchil, 1696); John Locke, *The Reasonableness of Christianity: As Delivered in the Scriptures*, ed. John C. Higgins-Biddle (Oxford: Clarendon Press, 1999). Higgins-Biddle's critical edition of *ROC* is based off of, but not slavishly, the "Harvard copy" of *ROC*. The Harvard copy is a first edition *ROC* that contains Locke's notes, emendations, and corrections (cxxxiv). I have researched both and note the page numbers of the 1696.

[2] John Locke, *A Vindication of the Reasonableness of Christianity, etc, From Mr. Edwards's Reflections* (London: Awnsham and John Churchil, 1695). This was published along with the 1696 second edition of *ROC*. John Locke, *A Second Vindication of the Reasonableness of Christianity, etc.* (London: A. and J. Churchil, 1697); John Locke, *An Essay Concerning Humane Understanding*, 3rd ed. (London: Awnsham and John Churchill, 1695); John Locke, *An Essay Concerning Human Understanding*, ed. Peter H. Nidditch (Oxford: Clarendon Press, 1979). The 1695 third edition that existed at the writing of Locke's *ROC* and its two vindications has been consulted along with Nidditch's critical edition. Pertinent works from others are as follows: John Edwards, *Some Thoughts Concerning the Several Causes and Occasions of Atheism, Especially in the Present Age. With Some Brief Reflections on Socinianism: And on a Late Book Entituled The Reasonableness of Christianity as Deliver'd in the Scriptures* (London: Printed for J. Robinson, 1695); John Edwards, *Socinianism Unmask'd. A Discourse Shewing the Unreasonableness of a Late Writer's Opinion Concerning the Necessity of Only One Article of Faith; and of His Other Assertions in His Late Book, Entituled, The Reasonableness of Christianity as Deliver'd in the Scriptures, and in His Vindication of It. With a Brief Reply to Another (Professed) Socinian Writer* (London: Printed for J. Robinson, 1696); John Edwards, *The Socinian Creed: or, A Brief Account of the Professed Tenents and Doctrines of the Foreign and English Socinians. Wherein Is Shew'd the Tendency of Them to Irreligion and Atheism. With Proper Antidotes Against Them* (London: Printed for J. Robinson, 1697). Samuel Bold's *A Collection of Tracts, Publish'd in Vindication of Mr. Lock's Reasonableness of Christianity, as Deliver'd in the Scriptures, etc.* (London: Printed for A. and J. Churchil, 1706) has the following relevant tracts: *A Short Discourse*

once that his project is evangelistic—by his calling the deists to the biblical faith and Christ—and ecumenical—with his charge for religious toleration and his biblically based teaching on eternal salvation, among other things. Nevertheless, in his own day, he could not completely shake the perception that he had ulterior sectarian aims.

While modern-day scholarly adjudications of Locke's motives and intentions for *ROC* say little explicitly about his evangelistic efforts with the deists, they more often concentrate upon the professed ecumenicity of the work. Some imagine Locke to be sincerely attempting to create a "common doctrinal platform with a view to unity and peace in the Church" and, thus, in society.[3] In this respect, John C. Higgins-Biddle says *ROC* is the "cornerstone" of that Lockean, programmatic effort.[4] But, this is indeed a hard pill to swallow for many in light of scholars' acknowledgments that Locke's views on salvation place him at odds with the justification by faith alone of the Reformation.[5] Locke's proclaimed ecumenical thrust is feigned according to some, like Stephen D. Snobelen, given that *ROC* promulgates certain

---

of the True Knowledge of Christ Jesus (London: Printed for A. and J. Churchil, 1697); *Some Passages in The Reasonableness of Christianity, etc. and Its Vindication. With Some Animadversions on Mr. Edwards's Reflections on the Reasonableness of Christianity, and on his Book, Entituled, Socinianism Unmask'd* (London: Printed for A. and J. Churchil, 1697); and *A Reply to Mr. Edwards's Brief Reflections on A Short Discourse of the True Knowledge of Christ Jesus, etc. To Which is Prefixed a Preface, Wherein Something is Said Concerning Reason and Antiquity, in the Chief Controversies with the Socinians* (London: Printed for A. and J. Churchil, 1697). For a nice collection of excerpts of contemporary works related to *ROC*: *John Locke and Christianity: Contemporary Responses to The Reasonableness of Christianity*, edited and introduced by Victor Nuovo (Bristol: Thoemmes Press, 1997). William Stephens, *An Account of the Growth of Deism in England* (London: 1696). Francis Turretin, *Institutes of Elenctic Theology*, 3 vols., trans. George Musgrave Giger and ed. James T. Dennison, Jr. (Phillipsburg: P&R Publishing, 1997).

[3] Alan P. F. Sell, *John Locke and the Eighteenth-Century Divines* (Cardif: University of Wales Press, 1997), 186–88 [quotation, p. 188]; John C. Higgins-Biddle, Introduction to *The Reasonableness of Christianity*, ed. John C. Higgins-Biddle (Oxford: Clarendon Press, 1999), xv–cxv [reference, pp. lxxiv, cviii–cxv]; John Dunn, *The Political Thought of John Locke: An Historical Account of the Argument of the 'Two Treatises of Government,'* (Cambridge: Cambridge University Press, 1969); Nicholas Wolterstorff, "John Locke's Epistemological Piety: Reason is the Candle of the Lord," *Faith and Philosophy* 11, no. 4 (Oct 1994): 572–91; Richard Ashcraft, "Faith and Knowledge in Locke's Philosophy," in *John Locke: Problems and Perspectives*, ed. John W. Yolton (Cambridge: Cambridge University Press, 1969), 194–223; Stuart Brown, "Locke as Secret 'Spinozist': The Perspective of William Carroll," in *Disguised and Overt Spinozism Around 1700: Papers Presented at the International Colloquium Held at Rotterdam, 5–8 October 1994*, ed. Wiep Van Bunge and Wim Klever (New York: E. J. Brill, 1996), 213–34; Steven M. Dworetz, *The Unvarnished Doctrine: Locke, Liberalism, and the American Revolution* (Durham: Duke University Press, 1990); Greg Forster, *John Locke's Politics of Moral Consensus* (Cambridge: Cambridge University Press, 2005), 141–42; J. T. Moore, "Locke on the Moral Need for Christianity," *Southwestern Journal of Philosophy* 11 (1980): 61–68.

[4] Higgins-Biddle, Introduction, cxiv.

[5] Sell, *John Locke*, 189; Higgins-Biddle, Introduction, xvii–xviii. Sell does not explicitly say this but instead refers the reader to Dewey Wallace's views on the matter (cited below).

theological positions that the vast majority of erudite Christians at the time would call heresy.[6] Even so, the various discernibly sectarian positions that other scholars index in *ROC* prevent them from taking Locke's stated ecumenical intentions seriously.[7] Assessments of the treatise in the interpretive tradition of John Edwards have ranged from identification of it as being blatantly Socinian to noting curious doctrinal commonalities with that sect.[8]

---

[6] Stephen D. Snobelen, "Socinianism, Heresy and John Locke's *Reasonableness of Christianity*," *Enlightenment and Dissent* 20 (2001): 88–125 [reference, pp. 117, 122].

[7] James. C. Livingston, *Modern Christian Thought*, 2nd ed. (Minneapolis: Fortress Press, 2006), 19. Livingston flatly remarks that Locke "rejects much of traditional Christian belief that he finds contrary to reason" in *ROC*. Manfred Svensson, "John Owen and John Locke: Confessionalism, Minimalism, and Toleration," *History of European Ideas* 43, no. 4 (2017): 302–16. Svensson juxtaposes two different types of toleration projects via an exploration of John Owen—who merges his confessionalism and toleration—and John Locke—who unites toleration with a doctrinal minimalism. It would be surprising if Locke were to think that he could dissuade the theologians away from their varied and rigorous confessional standards. Successfully arguing for giving one another room and seeing important commonality, though difficult, is more plausible. Besides, Locke explicitly says toward the end of *ROC* that if one were convinced that a particular doctrine was in Scripture and one did not believe it, that person would not be taking Christ as King and should not be considered justified. Confessionalism does not bother Locke. It is denying the status of "Kingdom-brother" or "-sister" to someone with a different confession but who takes the historical Christ as King that bothers Locke. By contrast, Victor Nuovo argues against the idea that Locke's so-called fundamentalism is to be understood as promulgation of a doctrinal minimalism: Victor Nuovo, Introduction to *John Locke and Christianity: Contemporary Responses to The Reasonableness of Christianity*, ed. and intro. Victor Nuovo (Bristol: Thoemmes Press, 1997), ix–xli [reference, pp. xxiii–xxiv].

There are also scholars that believe Locke's promotion of the Bible as *an* or *the* authority is feigned and merely exoteric, while the real Locke will be found with an esoteric reading. See Chapter 1.

[8] Maurice Cranston, *John Locke: A Biography* (New York: The MacMillan Company); John Marshall, "Locke, Socinianism, 'Socinianism', and Unitarianism," in *English Philosophy in the Age of Locke*, ed. M. A. Stewart (Oxford: Clarendon Press, 2000), 111–82; Lucci, *John Locke's Christianity*; Victor Nuovo, "Locke's Theology, 1694–1704," in *English Philosophy in the Age of Locke*, ed. M. A. Stewart (Oxford: Clarendon Press, 2000), 183–216; Victor Nuovo, *Christianity, Antiquity, and Enlightenment: Interpretations of Locke* (New York: Springer, 2011); Stephen D. Snobelen, "Socinianism, Heresy"; Victor Nuovo, *John Locke: The Philosopher as Christian Virtuoso* (Oxford: Oxford University Press, 2017). On the one end of the spectrum Maurice Cranston notes, "The general character and tone of Locke's argument was plainly Unitarian or Socinian" (390). Moving down the continuum, John Marshall has recently done an extensive study of Locke's affinities to Socinianism, concluding that Locke's theological positions are the product of a cross pollination of Arminianism and Socinianism (117). Nevertheless, he does rightly acknowledge that Locke is attempting to avoid disputes regarding the Trinity and the atonement by his careful wording in *ROC* (167–70). Lucci's description of Locke's theology is very similar to Marshall's (7, 52–53, 211, 214). Victor Nuovo, in his earliest work, maintains that while Locke holds some positions in common with the Socinians—as indicated, among other places, in *ROC*—Locke's agenda is not Socinian (211). He later qualifies this, however, in his book, *Christianity, Antiquity, and Enlightenment*, by indicating that that there are at least three senses in which the label, "Socinian," was applied; and that Locke would be Socinian according to the last sense used: "The tradition [Socinianism in the third sense] is identifiable by its political conservatism, an aversion to radicalism and enthusiasm, an advocacy of toleration, scepticism with respect to abstruse metaphysical and theological issues, acceptance of the freedom of the will and of the possibility of universal salvation, and a view of Christianity as a moral religion" (48). Stephen D. Snobelen's arguments are largely an expanded version of Nuovo's 2000 article, but with more enthusiasm regarding Locke's theology being "homomorphic" with respect to Socinianism (115). Nuovo's most recent description of Locke's soteriology is more indicative of early, traditional Protestant thought. He writes, "Justification by faith, the imputation of righteousness to an individual by virtue of faith, remained a central theme of his discourse," (217) and "Jesus, although

And some, concentrating on different doctrinal positions advanced in *ROC*, have concluded that it is decidedly "anti-Calvinist" and "Arminian," as well as promulgating justification by faith and works.[9]

Recent scholarship commenting on *ROC* has suffered from two problems. First and foremost, it is simply taken as a matter of fact that Locke teaches justification by faith and works. Historically, indiscriminate quotations out of context have sufficed to silence any potential objectors. But a quick perusal of Samuel Bold's commentary on *ROC* alone should make a theologically perceptive reader realize that either Bold, Locke's contemporary who defended and earned the praise of Locke for his right interpretation of *ROC*, is gravely mistaken or that the received historical narrative is. Second, none have seemed to consider that perhaps Locke expected the reader to be able to demarcate his ecumenical treatment of soteriology in *ROC* from his own personal opinions on particular theological points that are obviously sectarian. Edwards did not, but Bold and others close to Locke did.[10]

Arguably, Locke's presentation of justification, the primary topic in *ROC*, and the soteriological framework in which it is placed is intended to be broad enough to encompass all "Christian" views on the topics except antinomian ones. Much the same can be said of Locke's Christology and Pneumatology. In other words, the focus of *ROC* is not Locke's *personal* views of justification, the broader doctrine of salvation, or any other theological topic. Locke

---

he perfected the law and its rigor, nevertheless allowed faith to be surrogate for works, and so offered a more attainable and therefore reasonable road to righteousness" (232).

[9] The terms "Calvinism" and "Arminianism" found in Locke scholarship tend to be used a bit indiscriminately or often with too little qualification. Nuovo, "Locke's Theology," 196; Nuovo, *Christianity, Antiquity, and Enlightenment*, 31–33; Lucci, *John Locke's Christianity*, 7, 52–53, 211, 214; Dewey Wallace, "Socinianism, Justification by Faith, and the Sources of John Locke's *The Reasonableness of Christianity*," *Journal of the History of Ideas* 45, no. 1 (January–March 1984): 49–66. Cf. Hans Boersma, *A Hot Pepper Corn: Richard Baxter's Doctrine of Justification in Its Seventeenth-Century Context of Controversy* (Vancouver: Regent College Publishing, 2004); Joanne Tetlow, "John Locke's Covenant Theology," *Lock Studies* 9 (2009): 167–99; Donald Thomas Smith, "John Locke's Concept of Reasonable Christianity" (Ph.D. diss., Southern Methodist Seminary, 1997), vi, 211. Other than being noteworthy for reading *ROC* as Arminian, when Smith comes to the discussion of justification in *ROC* he possibly errs with an inadvertent shift in thought, making his conclusions on the more general doctrine of salvation.

[10] Cf. Philippus Van Limborch, "L2318. Philippus Van Limborch to John Locke, 28 September 1697," in *The Correspondence of John Locke*, vol. 6, ed. E. S. de Beer (Oxford: Clarendon Press, 1981), 206–10. Interestingly Justin Champion seems to think that scholarship has allowed Locke's conclusions on various doctrinal points to have obscured the true intent of *ROC* as well. Champion suggests that it was primarily intended to demonstrate to the readers how to study Scripture; thus, to view it as firstly promoting definitive doctrinal claims is to miss the point. Justin Champion, "'A law of continuity in the progress of theology': Assessing the Legacy of John Locke's *Reasonableness of Christianity*, 1695-2004," *Eighteenth-Century Thought* 3 (2007): 111–42.

intended for the work to be ecumenical and irenic in its core. This has three significant implications. First, the irenic positing of one article of faith for monotheists, upon which all Christians are agreed, is not the only place for them to find common ground. The treatise builds a case for and presents an ecumenical statement of justification and places it in an ecumenical soteriological framework. And, while not his primary focus, the Christological and Pneumatological elements that are discussed in the context of soteriology are biblical but also very broad. Second, his attempt to correct antinomian leanings in addition to his explicitly attempted correction of deists, who reject the need for revelation and redemption, produce a message with balance: the deists undercut their own concerns of a moral religion by not taking revelation, Scripture, seriously, and the antinomians undercut their truth claims for the Bible by not taking morality and obedience seriously. Third, we must distinguish Locke's personal views from the bulk of *ROC* that focuses on an ecumenical statement of justification and salvation.[11]

Historical Context: Debating Christology, Pneumatology, and Soteriology Before and During the Enlightenment

Christology and Pneumatology

There were various overlapping debates and controversies raging or smoldering during Locke's day. This is certainly the case in controversies over the persons of Christ and the Holy Spirit brought to the fore by Socinians and Arians in the late 1600s. The present chapter focuses on soteriology and justification, reserving the Trinitarian debates for later chapters.

Questions have surrounded Christ and the Holy Spirit since early in the history of the church. Socinianism, the major form of Reformation-era antitrinitarianism, became a focus of debate in England after the mid-seventeenth century.[12] Socinians denied the full divinity of Christ and the

---

[11] The doctrine of justification is an aspect of the doctrine of salvation for Locke and orthodox Christian theologians. In theological works the terms can have a synecdochical relationship.

[12] On the Socinian-Unitarian movement in England, note: Stephen Nye, *A Brief History of the Unitarians, Called also Socinians. In Four Letters, Written to a Friend*, 2nd ed. (1691); Samuel Przypkowski, *The Life of that Incomparable Man, Faustus Socinus Senensis* (London: Printed for Richard Moone, 1653); *The Racovian Catechism, with Notes and Illustrations*, trans. Thomas Rees (London: Printed for Longman et al., 1818); Fausti Socini Senensis, *De Jesu Christo Servatore, Hoc Est, Cur & qua ratione Jesus Christus noster Servator sit* in *Fausti Socini Senensis Operum Tomus Alter Continens ejusdem Scripta Polemica* (Irenopoli, 1656); Joshua Toulmin, *Memoirs of the Life, Character,*

penal substitution theory of atonement, and tended to focus on the example set by Christ's faithful obedience in life and death. They also denied the personhood of the Holy Spirit.[13]

Arian Christology also arose during this period and was often associated with Socinianism. The Arians, however, unlike the Socinians, acknowledged that Christ was not merely a man, but was pre-existent. Stephen Nye identified both Socinians and Arians as "Unitarians," while recognizing their differences concerning Christ and the Holy Spirit. Nye pointed out that John Biddle acknowledged that the Spirit is a person and the "chief of the Heavenly Spirits." Although differing on their understandings on the personhood and divinity of the Son and Spirit, the Socinian sentiment toward the Arians appears to have been positive. As Nye argued: "This difference notwithstanding [regarding the Holy Spirit], because they agree in the principal Article, that there is *but one God*, or *but one who is God*; both Parties (*Socinians* and *Arians*) are called *Unitarians*, and esteem of one another as Christians and true Believers, as may be seen on the parts of the *Arians* in their Historian *Chr. Sandius* and for the *Socinians* in the Disputation of *Alba*."[14]

Soteriology

The Church of England, of which Locke was a part, was no stranger to the Reformation and post-Reformation controversies concerning justification. The question of what role the place of works had, if any, in the process of justification came to the fore in the Anglican Church in the latter half of the 1600s. Stephen Hampton's recent work, *Anti-Arminians*, outlines some of the debates that took place among the Anglicans over this issue. His focus on those involving George Bull and his interpretation of Pauline epistles in light of James 2:24 are particularly illuminating. Contrary to C. Fitzsimons

---

Sentiments, and Writings of Faustus Socinus (London: Printed for the author by J. Brown, 1777). *Votes of Parliament Touching the Book Commonly Called The Racovian Catechism* (London: Printed by John Field, Printer to the Parliament of England, 1652). In modern scholarship, see Earl Morse Wilbur, *History of Unitarianism in Transylvania England and America* (Boston: Beacon Press, 1945); Herbert Mclachlan, *Socinianism in Seventeenth Century England* (Oxford: Oxford University Press, 1951); Sarah Mortimer, *Reason and Religion in the English Revolution: The Challenge of Socinianism* (Cambridge University Press, 2010).

[13] *Racovian Catechism*, IV.1 and Nye, *A Brief History*, 6, 12.
[14] Nye, *A Brief History*, 12.

Allison, who argues that, according to Bull, Christ's righteousness is why our imperfect faith, repentance, and works are accepted as righteous and whereby we are justified, Hampton effectively argues that, for Bull, human obedience is not the *cause* of justification but the *condition*. And, for Bull, while Christ's merits are not mystically transferred or imputed to us, because of them our imperfect works of faith and obedience are acceptable as the *condition*. Bull denies, however, that works are the cause of justification but rather God's gracious decision is the (formal) cause of justification. Reformed Anglican Thomas Barlow fired back at Bull, arguing that Bull is mistaken and that in his contrived economy obedience is truly a cause of justification and no mere condition. Barlow readily admits that works are, nonetheless, necessary for salvation, not in the sense that they are part of the process of justification but in that they are instrumental to sanctification. Thus, Barlow contends, Pauline justification, as understood in Reformation-era Protestantism, does not lead to libertinism or antinomianism.[15]

The debate between Bull and Barlow was only one of the soteriological controversies in the Anglican Church in Locke's lifetime. Distinctions of high-church and low-church (as they came to be known) and the related discussions over comprehension and toleration aside, there existed multiple groups within the Anglican church: the "Arminians" or synergists; the Reformed; and the Latitudinarians, who, despite their generous orthodoxy, tended to be privately Arminian.[16] The Latitudinarian Gilbert Burnet, in an irenic move that was not widely appreciated, attempted to show that Arminian and Calvinist readings of the Anglican Church's 39 Articles are both legitimate.[17] There was also debate over the eternal fate of the noble pagans, whose philosophy seemed almost inspired.[18]

The Reformed Nonconformists definitely had their part to play in the debates of the era over soteriology and justification. In their argumentation against synergism, John Owen (1616–1683) and Richard Baxter (1615–1691) found themselves at odds. Owen thought Baxter's positions leaned

---

[15] Stephen Hampton, *Anti-Arminians: The Anglican Reformed Tradition from Charles II to George I* (Oxford: Oxford University Press, 2008), 36–98.

[16] Nicholas Tyacke, "From Laudians to Latitudinarians: A Shifting Balance of Theological Forces," in *The Later Stuart Church, 1660–1714*, ed. Grant Tapsell (New York: Manchester University Press), 46–67; cf. Hampton, *Anti-Arminians*, 2–38.

[17] Hampton, *Anti-Arminians*, 27–31.

[18] D. W. Dockrill, "'No Other Name': The Problem of Salvation of the Pagans in Mid-Seventeenth Century Cambridge," in *The Idea of Salvation: Papers from the Conference on the Idea of Salvation, Sacred and Secular, Held at St. Paul's College, University of Sydney, 22–25 August, 1986*, ed. D. W. Dockrill and R. G. Tanner (Auckland: the University of Auckland, 1988), 117–51.

toward Socinianism, while Baxter feared Owen's teachings involving justification were crypto-Antinomian.[19] Some in the era drew a line from the Calvinist conception of election to antinomianism. In the minds of some, election appeared to negate any sort of impetus for obedience. Other points were the subject of argument, such as the imputation of Christ's active and passive obedience and the relationship between justification, sanctification, and assurance.[20] The variations of theological opinion had become so fine that Locke, in *ROC*, when discussing the debates over justification, notes that even the teachers of the opposing factions do not realize the differences that divide them![21]

Preliminary Evidence of Ecumenical and Irenic Intent in *The Reasonableness of Christianity*

Locke indicates theological conversations and occasions that prompted or influenced the writing of *ROC*. The first such is that pertaining to the specter of deism. He names deism as the main target of *ROC*,[22] attributing to its adherents the positions, of which they need to be rectified, that there is no need of divine revelation and redemption.[23] Locke also explicitly desired to reach those who wondered which articles were necessary for salvation.[24] He expresses grave concern over the persecution, bloodshed, and division that have occurred amongst Christians over fundamentals.[25] (The issue of the fundamental articles as a point of dispute and the associated concerns regarding the necessity of toleration among seventeenth century theologians and in Locke's writings will be treated at length in the next chapter). Similarly, in the closing pages of the work, where he awkwardly states that justification

---

[19] Paul Chang-Ha Lim, *In Pursuit of Purity, Unity, and Liberty: Richard Baxter's Puritan Ecclesiology in Its Seventeenth-Century Context* (Boston: Brill, 2004), 182–90.

[20] Hans Boersma, *A Hot Pepper Corn: Richard Baxter's Doctrine of Justification in Its Seventeenth-Century Context of Controversy* (Vancouver: Regent College Publishing, 2003). Cf. Daniel Waterland, *An End to Discord: Wherein Is Demonstrated, That No Doctrinal Controversy Remains between the Presbyterian and Congregational Ministers, Fit to Justify Long Divisions. With a True Account of Socinianism as to the Satisfaction of Christ* (London: 1699), iii–vi, 11–26, in Victor Nuovo, *John Locke and Christianity*, 139–48.

[21] Locke, *ROC*, 306.

[22] Locke explicitly states that *ROC* is written to deists. Locke, *ROC*, 1–2; Locke, *A Second Vindication*, xvi–xviii, 151–52, 376, 465–66. Cf. Locke, *Vindication*, 9; Locke, *A Second Vindication*, 77–78.

[23] Locke, *A Second Vindication*, xvii–xviii; Locke, *ROC*, 2.

[24] Locke, *A Second Vindication*, xvii.

[25] Locke, *Vindication*, 7; Locke, *A Second Vindication*, 342–43. The Thirty Years War was going on during Locke's lifetime.

is the subject of *ROC*, he draws attention to the disputes over the doctrine taking place amidst Dissenters and Conformists. He asserts that all this disputing and wrangling with fine distinctions is oppressive to the bulk of simple people, the exact type for whom the Gospel was clearly expressed![26] Thus, there are at least three general arguments undergirding his evangelical and ecumenical efforts: (1) the need of divine revelation, namely Scripture; (2) the need for redemption; and (3) what the Gospels and Acts plainly say about salvation. In sum, Locke intended to counter deism and to procure agreement between Christian sects and Christian persons on a broad level.

There is other evidence of irenic and ecumenical intent found in statements Locke and Samuel Bold, his sympathizer, make about *ROC* in their vindications. In *Second*, Locke's closing remarks, addressed to Bold, indicate his intent in publishing *ROC*: "What it [*ROC*] contains, and how much it tends to Peace and Union amongst Christians, if they would receive Christianity as it is, you have discovered."[27] At the end of the tract, to which Locke is alluding, Bold, in his final assessment of *ROC*, writes the following:

> If you believe Mr. *Edwards*'s account of the *Reasonableness, etc.* you will conclude it likely to do abundance of *hurt*...
>
> Were the *Reasonableness of Christianity, etc.* generally read with *deliberation*, and rightly understood, and (what I apprehend to be) its *main design* well followed, it would be of eminent use, amongst other *good purposes*, to these two.
>
> First, *To effect an happy alteration in particular Persons.* For if more time and pains were employ'd, in bringing *People* to a *sound Conviction*, and *full persuasion*, that *Jesus is the Christ*, and only Saviour of Sinners, and of their *own personal need of Him*, and less of each in *Squabling* about *Terms*... there would not be such great numbers every where, who *pretend* to be *Christians*...
>
> Secondly, *To overthrow and ruine Faction in Religion*, and promote that *Concord*, and good *Affection amongst Christians*, which would render them mightily serviceable to one another, put them into a condition, to reap singular advantage from all Publick ministrations, which would make the whole number of Christians appear to the World as one entire and well compacted Body, and effectually remove those pernicious Prejudices against

---

[26] Locke, *ROC*, 304–6.
[27] Locke, *A Second Vindication*, xix.

our most sacred Profession, which too many take occasion to entertain, from the humoursome Separations, and groundless Devisions which do most unmercifuly prevail amongst Christians.[28]

This excerpt is clear testimony from an erudite thinker other than Locke how misguided Edwards's critiques of *ROC* are and how ecumenical and irenic the design of *ROC* is. What is more, in Bold's A *Short Discourse of the True Knowledge of Jesus Christ*, he, like Locke, argues for one proposition that must be owned to be a Christian; yet, in the midst of the tract, he offers his own opinions of what he thinks Christians should know *after* they become Christians: rejection of works-righteousness, the doctrine of Christ's satisfaction, and the full divinity and personhood of the Son and Spirit.[29] If Bold were to have thought that *ROC*'s main aim was to advance some variety of justification through works or something else clearly sectarian (or heretical), he could not reasonably offer approbation for the author's ecumenical and irenic intent. Moreover, in *Second*, responding to Edwards's lambasting him for not including a particular theory of the atonement in his discussion on the advantages of Christ's advent, Locke adds the following to his assertion in *First* that a charitable read would have discovered it there:[30] "I thought it most reasonable to offer such Particulars only as were agreed on by all Christians, and were capable of no Dispute, but must be acknowledged by every body to be needful."[31] Finally, Locke is clear and adamant that he is not writing from any specific communion but solely from Scripture.[32]

This irenic and ecumenical tenor of *ROC* becomes more pronounced when juxtaposed with the occasionally polemical undertones of his *Essay*. Both clearly display consideration for the common human who has not much leisure to attend to the study of morals and religion, but the said differences in intentions are drawn out most prominently in *Second*. There Locke remarks that all sincere Christians should endeavor to understand Christ's institution of communion, namely "*This is my Body*, and *This is my Blood*." He writes:

> And if upon his serious Endeavour to do it, he does understand them in a literal sence, that Christ meant that that was his Body and Blood, and nothing

---

[28] Bold, *Some Passages*, 49–51.
[29] Bold, *A Short Discourse*, 4, 40–45.
[30] Locke, *Vindication*, 6–7.
[31] Locke, *A Second Vindication*, 466.
[32] Locke, *A Second Vindication*, xvii–xviii.

else; must he not necessarily believe that the Bread and Wine in the Lord's Supper, is changed really into his Body and Blood, though he doth not know how? Or, if having his Mind set otherwise, he understands the Bread and Wine to be really the Body and Blood of Christ; without ceasing to be true Bread and Wine; Or else, if he understands them, that the Body and Blood of Christ are verily and indeed given and received in the Sacrament, in a Spiritual manner; Or lastly, If he understands our Saviour to mean by those words, only the Bread and Wine to be a Representation of his Body and Blood; In which way soever of these Four, a Christian understands these words of the Saviour to be meant by him, is he not obliged in that sence to believe them to be true, and assent to them? Or can he be a Christian, and understand these words to be meant by our Saviour, in one sence, and deny his assent to them as true, in that sence?[33]

In and surrounding this passage he makes room for four prevailing convictions on communion based on the associated interpretations of that piece of Scripture: Roman Catholic transubstantiation, Lutheran impanation, Reformed spiritual presence, and the Anabaptist memorial understanding of Christ's words. This is significantly different from the *Essay* where he is notably antagonistic toward transubstantiation. There he uses it as an example of what he calls the "grossest Absurdities."[34] It need not be taken as dishonest of Locke to make accommodations, in *ROC*, for those who are not necessarily capable of following his reasoning and arguments in the *Essay* and those who do not care to follow them. To do so would be inconsistent with his professed posture and consideration of the day-laborers and uneducated. Furthermore, he seems concerned with making sure all Christian sects are equally chided for their lack of agreement on fundamentals: Anabaptists, Quakers, Arminians, Socinians, Lutherans, Roman Catholics, and Calvinists, all of whom are explicitly named.[35]

---

[33] Locke, *A Second Vindication*, 408–09.
[34] More specifically, transubstantiation transgresses Locke's principle that an interpretation cannot overturn certain knowledge, which he believes sensitive knowledge should be treated as, and it contradicts our knowledge that it is impossible for one body to be in two places at once. Locke, *Essay*, IV.xviii.5; IV.xx.10 [IV.xix.10 from the first through third editions]. Locke does not, to my knowledge, explicitly critique the Lutherans for their view of impanation or consubstantiation.
[35] Locke, *A Second Vindication*, 52; cf. 103.

ROC's Fundamental Articles and Christology

ROC is perhaps best known for its proclamation that there are only two articles one must believe to be justified, but these are not without qualifiers. The first article that must be believed is adhered to historically by the Jews: the existence of the one eternal and invisible God, maker of heaven and earth. It is not always promulgated explicitly with Christ's and the apostles' proclamations of the second fundamental article because it is most often assumed by their audiences.[36]

The second fundamental article necessary for justification, as already stated above, is: Jesus is Messiah. This encompasses a number of concomitant articles "required as necessary to Justification," such as the articles of his being the prophet foretold of in the Old Testament, sinlessness, crucifixion, resurrection, ascension, rule, and coming again to judge the world.[37] Some of these concomitant articles were not necessarily incorporated into the fundamental article until after they were revealed, namely the crucifixion, resurrection, and ascension. When the apostles preached these, they were not to be understood as new articles necessary to be believed, but rather arguments for the fundamental article. He writes, "For whatsoever is brought as an Argument to prove another Truth, cannot be thought to be the principal thing aimed at in that argumentation; though it may have so strong and immediate connexion with the Conclusion, that you cannot deny it without denying even what is inferr'd from it, and is therefore the fitter to be an Argument to prove it."[38] Thus, any such concomitant article taken in itself proclaims Jesus as Messiah.[39]

Locke argues adamantly that these are the only two articles necessary for justification. Had there been more, Jesus and his apostles would have clearly stated them in the Gospels and Acts. By the time of Christ's last discourse with his disciples in John, Locke argues that Jesus had given them everything the disciples needed to know to be saved. This is supported by significant evidence such as Christ telling his disciples that he has told them all things he has heard from the Father (John 15:15), subsequently, the thief on the cross is saved by the one doctrine, and Jesus shares no new doctrines with his

---

[36] Locke, *ROC*, 25, 43.
[37] Locke, *ROC*, 30–31, 33, 34–35, 188, 293–94. Notice that nothing is said of Christ's divinity in these places.
[38] Locke, *A Second Vindication*, 269.
[39] Locke, *A Second Vindication*, 308. Christ's sinlessness, for instance, can serve the same function as it can be inferred from the fundamental article: Locke, *ROC*, 33.

disciples after his resurrection.[40] If there were new articles of faith necessary for justification and, thus, eternal salvation, the apostles would have pressed something alongside of the two fundamental articles in their preaching.[41]

In addition to his extensive commentary on the Gospels and Acts, Locke explains the need of the Epistles. They cannot contain doctrines necessary for justification as those to whom they are being written are already Christians.[42] Otherwise, the recipients of the letters would be believers and non-believers at the same time.[43] Nonetheless, the Epistles and their doctrines must be observed and are edifying.[44] They are the declared mind and will of the Lord and Master Messiah.[45] "Every word of Divine Revelation, is absolutely and indispensibly necessary to be believed, by every Christian, as soon as he comes to know it to be taught by our Savior or his Apostles, or to be of Divine Revelation."[46] To disbelieve a proposition stated in Scripture is to undercut belief in the second fundamental article, Jesus is Messiah.[47]

The fundamental articles have another characteristic to a greater degree than the other doctrines in the Bible: clarity. They are so clear that no one could dispute them.[48] Locke says the following regarding Scriptural clarity and interpretations:

> Where it is spoken plainly we cannot miss it, and it is evident, he requires our assent: where there is obscurity either in the Expressions themselves, or by reason of the seeming contrariety of other Passages, there a fair endeavour, as much as our Circumstances will permit, secures us from a guilty Disobedience to his Will, or a sinful Error in Faith, which way soever our en[qui]ry resolves the doubt, or perhaps leaves it unresolved. If he had required more of us in those Points, he would have declared his Will plainer

---

[40] Locke, *ROC*, 184–88.
[41] Recall that when Jesus and the apostles preached to the Jews—monotheists—they concentrated on the second fundamental article.
[42] Locke, *ROC*, 293–95. Locke writes, "There remains something to be said to those who will be ready to Object, If the believe [sic] of Jesus of *Nazareth* to be the *Messiah*, together with those concomitant Articles of his Resurrection, Rule, and coming again to Judge the World, be all the Faith required as necessary to Justification, to what purpose were the Epistles written; I say, if the belief of those many Doctrines contained in them, be not also necessary to Salvation?... They were writ to those who were in Faith, and true Christians already: And so could not be designed to teach them the Fundamental Articles and Points necessary to Salvation..."
[43] Locke, *A Second Vindication*, 133.
[44] Locke, *ROC*, 294.
[45] Locke, *A Second Vindication*, 76–77.
[46] Locke, *A Second Vindication*, 443; cf. Locke, *ROC*, 295.
[47] Locke, *ROC*, 302–3; cf. Locke, *A Second Vindication*, 83–88.
[48] Locke, *A Second Vindication*, 39, 76–77, 93–94.

to us; and discover'd the truth contain'd in those obscure, or seemingly contradictory places, as clearly, and as uniformly as he did that Fundamental Article, that we were to believe him to be the *Messiah* our King.[49]

The second fundamental article is as clear as a doctrine can possibly be. The other doctrines are not as readily clear to us, but they are also not necessary for justification. Christians are required honestly to try to understand passages that contain something that is doctrinal. They do not have to arrive at an assured final interpretation, but obedience requires making a fair attempt.

All valid, biblical doctrines are necessary to be believed and obeyed, but only two are necessary for justification, and thus only two to be a Christian. The others, once one is convinced of their meaning and sense, become necessary. For instance, it is not necessary for justificatory purposes to believe that Jesus and the Holy Spirit are God; but once convinced that this is what the Bible is asserting, then one must believe it if one is truly a Christian.[50] Locke undoubtedly had his own opinions on some of the many questions that tend to separate and divide followers of Christ, but to promulgate them all would be contrary to his intent.

ROC's Soteriology, Pneumatology, and Targets

Locke's treatment of salvation borrows from the covenantal framework found in Reformed works such as the Westminster Confession and some of the "law" terminology used by some of a more Arminian bent.[51] His specific treatment of salvation incorporates a Covenant of Works and a Covenant of Grace, which, for Locke, are governed respectively by the Law of Works and the Law of Faith. "The difference between the *Law of Works* and the *Law of Faith* is only this; that the *Law of Works* makes no allowance for failing on any occasion." Locke notes that the positive commands attributed to the Law of Works are occasionally for peculiar ends and suited for particular dispensations. Such is the Law of Moses that is tripartite, divided into Ceremonial, Civil, and Moral laws. It is only the last aspect that is eternally

---

[49] Locke, *A Second Vindication*, 76–77.
[50] Locke, *A Second Vindication*, 416–17. Lucci wrongly describes Locke as advancing "two levels of authority within Scripture" in *ROC*: Lucci, *John Locke's Christianity*, 64.
[51] For example, Hampton, *Anti-Arminians*, 94.

obligatory.[52] Although believers find themselves under the Law of Faith—"which is that Law whereby God Justifies a Man for Believing, though by his Works he be not Just or Righteous"—the Moral Law "is to all Men the Standing Law of Works."[53]

Locke appropriates teaching on the covenant of grace insofar as that covenant is conditional upon faith and obedience. Locke writes, "These two, Faith and Repentance, *i.e.* believing Jesus to be the *Messiah*, and a good Life; are the indispensible Conditions of the New Covenant to be performed by all those who would obtain Eternal Life."[54] This is very similar in certain respects to the teaching of noted Reformed theologian Francis Turretin, with which Locke was familiar, in *Institutes of Elenctic Theology*:

> For as there are two special benefits of the covenant on God's part (the remission of sins and the writing of the law upon the heart), so on the part of man two duties ought to answer to them—faith, which applies the pardon of sins to itself; and repentance (or the desire of sanctification), which reduces the law written upon the heart to practice by walking in its statutes.[55]

Locke, like Turretin in the quotation above, uses repentance, at times, broadly for obedience. It is sorrow for sins past, but also "(what is a Natural consequence of such sorrow, if it be real) a turning from them, into a new and contrary Life." Repentance and turning to God can be rendered as being "converted." Naturally, then, baptism for Locke is a part of repentance or our obedience to the covenant. Expounding upon the close relationship between faith and repentance, Locke writes, "Believing Jesus to be the *Messiah*, and Repenting, were so Necessary and Fundamental parts of the Covenant of Grace, that one of them alone is often put for both."[56]

In what Locke has said so far about salvation, there is nothing that should give many sects too much discomfort, other than, perhaps, his terminology and lack of specificity. He does mention that we are in no way justified by the

---

[52] Locke, *ROC*, 18–20.
[53] Locke, *ROC*, 22.
[54] Locke, *ROC*, 202.
[55] Turretin, *Institutes of Elenctic Theology*, XII.ii.29. Turretin goes on in the next section to write, "Although these two duties are commanded by God as works due from man, still they are also promised by him as his gifts. Thus they are here to be considered at the same time both as the duties of man and as the blessings of God." Cf. John Locke, "L 1901. Locke to Philippus Van Limborch, 10 May 1695," in *The Correspondence of John Locke*, vol. 5, ed. E. S. de Beer (Oxford: Clarendon Press, 1979), 368–72. Cf. Higgins-Biddle, Introduction, xxvi. Cf. John Locke, *ROC*, crit. ed., 5 fn 2.
[56] Locke, *ROC*, 198–201.

standing Law of Works.⁵⁷ That is impossible for us. Most "Christian" sects would agree—with the exception of the antinomians—that the moral law is not entirely abrogated.⁵⁸

Within his discussions of covenant, Locke works out *ROC*'s teaching on justification. He notes that "God alone does, or can, Justifie or make Just those who by their Works are not so: Which he doth by counting their Faith for Righteousness."⁵⁹ He uses similar "counting" language elsewhere, for instance in *A Second Vindication*, where he writes that the faith by which one believes the two articles, "God will impute to him for Righteousness."⁶⁰ Dewey Wallace understands this to be testimony from Locke, following Richard Baxter, that "faith justifies as it is accepted by God in place of full righteousness," which is "a position strikingly different from the Reformation Protestant view that it is Christ's righteousness imputed by God to the believer which justifies, faith being the instrument by which advantage is taken of this 'alien' righteousness."⁶¹ There are a few problems with such a "Baxterian" interpretation of Locke. It is inconsistent with Locke's claims of excluding anything regarding the advantages of Christ's coming that would not be accepted by everyone, and it is also such with Locke's dislike of superfine theological distinctions in a text directed, if not at, then, toward the wellbeing of the masses.⁶² In fact, at no point does he allude to or employ terms like "immediate causality" or "instrumental causality," the traditional terms used to make such soteriological distinctions, and he surely doesn't deny any of these concepts. And, most importantly, Locke clearly starts using counts-imputes language regarding righteousness in the immediate context of his discussion of Romans 4:3–8 where the uses of *logizomai* can be translated as impute, count as, reckon as, etc. In brief, it appears that Locke is avoiding controversy by adopting imputes-counts language—biblical language—near the beginning of *ROC*, using it throughout, and never delving into anything like causality or conditionality of justification discussions to avoid advancing a specific stance being promoted at the time or his own personal one. This

---

⁵⁷ Locke, *ROC*, 15.
⁵⁸ Turretin, *Institutes of Elenctic Theology*, XI.xxiii. Turretin writes, "Whether the moral law is abrogated entirely under the New Testament. Or whether in a certain respect it still pertains to Christians. The former we deny; the latter we affirm against the Antinomians."
⁵⁹ Locke, *ROC*, 22.
⁶⁰ Locke, *A Second Vindication*, 89.
⁶¹ Wallace, "Socinianism, Justification by Faith," 56.
⁶² It would be strikingly incongruous for Locke to scruple over not offending Christians in his list of the five advantages of Christ's advent while giving a highly contentious doctrine of justification—justification being the primary advantage we have in the coming of Christ.

use of biblical language or the express words of Scripture (as discussed in the last chapter) for the intent of irenic and ecumenical purposes is something that Paul Chang-Ha Lim has documented that Baxter and others did. It even led to Baxter being likened to Socinians.[63] So, Wallace is correct in pointing out similarities between Baxter and Locke, but he is incorrect regarding the details of those similarities. And, more importantly, Locke is hardly the first person to attempt avoiding controversy that is rooted in specificity by appropriating Scriptural terms.

Confusion arising from Locke's use of certain theological terms or lack thereof can also be observed in the responses of *ROC*'s very first major critic, John Edwards. At one point in *ROC*, Locke distinguishes between the faith had by devils and Christians by merely noting that the devils cannot repent—repent taken as sorrow and turning as mentioned above.[64] Edwards attacks Locke for making faith out to be merely assent to a proposition. Locke responds in the *A Second Vindication* by pointing out numerous places in *ROC* that prove such accusations unfounded and to be the result of passages in *ROC* being read out of context. He writes, "To prevent this Calumny, I in more places than one distinguished between Faith in a strict sense, as it is a bare assent to any Proposition, and that which is called Evangelical Faith, in a larger sense of the word; which comprehends under it something more than a bare simple assent..."[65] Soon thereafter he adds:

> By these, and more the like Passages in my Book, my meaning is so evident, that no body, but an *Unmasker* [*Edwards*], would have said, that when I spoke of *believing* as a bare Speculative assent to any Proposition as true, I affirm'd that was all that was required of a Christian for Justification: Though that in the strict sense of the word is all that is done in *believing*. And therefore, I say, as far as *meer believing* could make them Members of *Christ's* Body; plainly signifying, as much as words can, that the *Faith*, for which they were justified, included something more than a bare assent. This appears not only from these words of mine, *p. 196*. St. Paul *often in his Epistles, puts* Faith *for the whole Duty of a Christian*; but from my so often, and almost everywhere interpreting *believing him to be the Messiah, by taking him to be our King*; whereby is meant not a bare idle Speculation, a bare notional perswasion of any truth whatsoever in our Brains; but an active Principle

---

[63] Lim, *In Pursuit of Purity*, 157–89.
[64] Locke, *ROC*, 194ff.
[65] Locke, *A Second Vindication*, 194.

of Life, a *Faith* working by Love and Obedience. *To take him to be our King*, carries with it a right disposition of the will to honour, and obey him, joyn'd to that assent wherewith Believers imbrace this Fundamental Truth, that Jesus was the Person, who was by God sent to be their King; he that was promis'd to be their Prince and Saviour.[66]

So, while faith or believing can have a strict sense of assent, this is not only what Locke means by faith. Justifying faith includes a change of the will, a taking Christ as King, or a new disposition. Mere intellectual assent is not justifying.

The works of Samuel Bold, Locke's sympathizer, also make a distinction between mere intellectual assent and evangelical faith regarding belief in the one article that makes one a Christian. His one article, similar to Locke's, is that Jesus is the person that God sent, appointed, and commissioned by God to be our Savior.[67] Bold notes that one must be affected and influenced by their belief.[68] And it is not simply a notional and speculative knowledge (belief):

> it is such a Knowledge as doth effectually determine the Person, and cause him to *resign* up himself *entirely* to *Christ Jesus* to be saved by him in *his own way*. Such a knowledge of him, as makes the Person to *take* him for *his Lord*; so that he will use his *serious, honest,* and *best endeavours* to understand what he hath taught and revealed, and will *assent* to, *believe* and *observe* whatever he shall attain to know He hath taught or revealed; and will *depend* wholly on *Him* to receive from *Him* in his *own way*, the *benefits* He is *intrusted* to *dispence*.[69]

In short, he agrees with Locke that faith that saves is not simply assent but includes a change of the will and a new disposition. True belief results in true action. Moreover, in another work, where he explicitly comes to Locke's defense against Edwards's attacks, Bold points out to the reader that Edwards was not reading *ROC* carefully enough as evinced by Edwards's charge that Locke made faith plain intellectual assent.[70]

---

[66] Locke, *A Second Vindication*, 195–96.
[67] Bold, *A Short Discourse*, 5, 15, 52.
[68] Bold, *A Short Discourse*, 8–11.
[69] Bold, *A Short Discourse*, 7–8.
[70] Bold, *Some Passages*, 30–32.

There is another crucial aspect of Locke's teaching on justification, related to the last point, that has been consistently misunderstood by commentators. It involves a statement used near the beginning of *ROC* whose message is repeated throughout the work: "All, I say, that was to be believed for Justification [*Jesus is Messiah*]: For that it was not all that was required to be done for Justification, we shall see hereafter."[71] It is this idea, that something other than faith is to be *done* for justification, that leads most Locke scholars to believe Locke has ruled out if not all soteriologies from "Reformation Protestantism," then at least "Calvinist" soteriology.[72] One scholar writes, "Faith in Christ justifies a man before God—the Protestant doctrine of justification; however, Locke's view differs from the Reformed belief in justification by faith alone. Locke's doctrine of justification requires both faith *and* obedience."[73] Similarly, John C. Higgins-Biddle writes, "While he insisted on the necessity of both faith and obedience for salvation, they were for him clearly separate acts. This equation of faith with belief and its separation from obedience is in strong contrast to the position of John Calvin . . . For Locke the contrast was conscious."[74] These scholars are again trying to take more from Locke than he is offering. What is to be *done*, at a minimum, is what he clarifies above against Edwards: a turning to God or acquiescing to God, which added to the bare intellectual assent, makes trusting or evangelical faith. He does not say anything about specifics of the turning, just that there must be one. In his discourses about faith and works, Locke shows a tight relationship between the two; but he never ventures to explore the questions that gravitate toward the use of terms like "instrumental," "forensic," "infusion," "meritorious," "condition," or any others that create the subtle distinctions that scholars seem to expect. There are none of the theological intricacies and subtleties that characterized the Barlow–Bull debate or that between Baxter and Owen. There is instead the generous attitude displayed at times by one of the Reformed and Arminian conciliators of the Anglican Church, Latitudinarian Gilbert Burnet, so-called "moderate Calvinist" and Noncomformist Richard Baxter, and Lockean sympathizer Samuel Bold.

It does appear, however, that Locke has been conscientious also to avoid an incorporation of works in the process of justification as do the Roman

---

[71] Locke, *ROC*, 47; cf. Locke, *A Second Vindication*, 194–95.

[72] For example, Wallace believes that Locke's teaching on justification cannot be considered Reformation Protestant or Tridentine Roman Catholic. Wallace, "Socinianism, Justification by Faith," 56. Sell appears to follow Wallace's views put forth in his article. Sell, *John Locke*, 344 en 26.

[73] Tetlow, "John Locke's Covenant Theology," 191.

[74] Higgins-Biddle, Introduction, xvii. He gives no evidence how they were "clearly" separate acts.

Catholics. As Hampton's work points out, George Bull and John Tillotson incorporated works into the process of justification, but, go to lengths to deny that works were the cause or a cause of justification as Roman Catholics do.[75] Of Bull, Hampton writes, "Human obedience is for him the condition of justification, the means to justification, even the instrument of justification—but it is not the [formal] cause of justification."[76] Put another way, Bull thought that faith and obedience were necessary conditions for justification but were not in themselves a cause of it.[77] Even those Protestants who pushed the traditional boundaries of Protestantism, or, arguably, broke them, denied merit due to our works. Locke appears, although not explicitly, to deny the merit of works done by believers, at least, in the following passage: "But Christian Believers have the Priviledge to be under the *Law of Faith* too; which is that Law whereby God Justifies a Man for Believing, though by his Works he be not Just or Righteous, *i.e.* though he came short of Perfect Obedience to the Law of Works."[78]

Perhaps the most important thesis regarding justification and salvation that Locke advances is: "For if they believed him to be the *Messiah* their King, but would not obey his Laws, and would not have him to Reign over them, they were but greater Rebels; and God would not Justifie them for Faith that did but increase their Guilt, and oppose Diametrically the Kingdom and Design of the *Messiah*."[79] His wording is very careful. It is not evident whether it is Lutheran or Calvinist, how the Holy Spirit is incorporated, whether he is referring to initial or continued justification, as Baxter might posit,[80] and so on. It is not unclear; it is surprisingly unspecific. The main soteriological message of *ROC* is simply that we should count someone who believes and

---

[75] Hampton, *Anti-Arminians*, 45–49, 60–62.

[76] Hampton, *Anti-Arminians*, 51. "In other words, for Bull, Christian obedience is not part of the formal cause of justification. The formal cause of justification, the essential definition of that process, is simply the gracious divine decision to justify the sinner and admit her to eternal life. Good works, or Christian obedience, bear, in Bull's presentation of the matter, no causal relationship to that decision, though they are a necessary precondition for that decision to be made" (49).

[77] Hampton, *Anti-Arminians*, 53; cf. 54–58.

[78] Locke, *ROC*, 22. This arguably opens the door for Socinians. *Racovian Catechism* II.ii, in answer to the question of what is the way of salvation, responds, "It consists in the knowledge of God and of Christ, as the Lord Jesus has himself declared (John xvii.3). 'This is life eternal, that they might know thee, the only true God, and Jesus Christ whom thou has sent.'" And to explain this knowledge, it, not unlike Bold and Locke, pronounces: "By this knowledge I do not understand any merely barren and speculative acquaintance with God and Christ, but accompanied by its proper effects; that is, with a lively or efficacious faith, and a suitable and exemplary conduct." Whether Bull's conception of justification could fit into Locke's extraordinarily generous boundaries of justification remains to be investigated.

[79] Locke, *ROC*, 213.

[80] Boersma, *A Hot Pepper Corn*, 312.

takes Jesus as King as justified. Evidence of Locke's ecumenical intent in this regard can be adduced from a letter to Locke from Philip Van Limborch. There the latter quips that as *ROC*'s soteriology is too easy, wrought from Scripture, and not dependent on sectarian confessions, it amounts to a crime so great that its author assuredly deserves to be labeled "Socinian" or "atheist" by the systematicians.[81] The idea that Locke is specifically rejecting faith as alone the instrumental cause of justification and is solely advocating works-righteousness or some other view of justification outside of the pale of Reformation Protestant orthodoxy and is instead promulgating a soteriology in *ROC* that is intentionally Socinian, Socinian-like, Baxterian, or Arminian is unfounded. That many different scholars can read a particular view back into the text, or find traces of then-contemporary views, perhaps displays Locke's shrewdness.

This soteriological message is also articulated by Bold. When Bold discusses justifying "knowledge," he states that it is such that it "makes the Person to *take* him [Christ] for *his Lord*."[82] Bold personally rejects works-righteousness. He makes a similar remark in another work: "That which constitutes and makes a Man a Christian, a Believer, a Disciple, or Subject of Christ, is his believing Jesus to be the Christ, so as to yield up himself unreservedly to believe and practice whatsoever he shall attain to know he hath taught and commanded him."[83] In other words, a Christian believes that Jesus is Messiah and takes Him as king![84]

The above explains Locke's incorporation of Galatians 5:6 and James 2:24 in in a paragraph that defines justifying faith. The paragraph begins, "Now, that this is the Faith for which God of his free Grace Justifies a sinful Man." Locke goes onto argue that God would not justify people for a faith that resulted in them being greater rebels: "For if they believed him to be the *Messiah* their King, but would not obey his Laws, and would not have him to Reign over them, there were but greater Rebels; and God would not

---

[81] Philippus Van Limborch, "L2222. Philippus Van Limborch to John Locke, 16 March 1697," in *The Correspondence of John Locke*, vol. 6, ed. E. S. de Beer (Oxford: Clarendon Press, 1981), 42–53 [quotation, pp. 42–43]. In this letter Limborch commends the author of *ROC* for his defense of the treatise's main aim. He writes, "Moreover there are many things among them by which he excellently confirms the principal matter discussed in his book, which is that the faith that Jesus is the Christ is that faith by which we are justified" (44). In the latter part of the letter, he, also without specificity, decries the teaching of those who would set justification apart from repentance (52–53).

[82] Bold, *A Short Discourse*, 8.

[83] Bold, *Some Passages*, 37.

[84] Williams, *An Account*, 25–27. Williams has the same reading of *ROC* as Bold. There is one article (for monotheists), faith is not merely intellectual assent, and that "a Man should shew forth his Faith by an agreeable course of Life, in doing Justice, loving Mercy, and an humble walking with God" (27).

Justifie them for a Faith that did but increase their Guilt . . ." It is after this that he writes: "And therefore *St. Paul* tells the *Galatians*, That that which availeth is *Faith*; But *Faith working by Love*. And that *Faith* without *Works*, *i.e.* the Works of sincere Obedience to the Law and Will of Christ, is not sufficient for our Justification, St. *James* shews at large, *Chap.* II."[85] He again is outlining the nature of faith and it is a faith that is not merely intellectual assent, but a faith inseparable from obedience. Is faith that justifies simply faith that results in works? Are both faith and works in some way justifying? Are works a condition for justification? Again, he does not attempt to answer these questions. Rather he appropriates Scripture's words and lets the reader take from it what he or she will.

There are two other comments to make to bring this message, articulated above, into clearer focus. A faithful Roman Catholic might look at this message as being highly problematic because, although it describes themselves in their own minds, it is too general to account for the justifying aspects that can be delivered only by the Roman Catholic Church, namely the sacraments. As noted above, Locke might have intentionally ruled out the notion of infused righteousness that allows works to be meritorious or causative. It would perhaps be a long shot to try to prove to a rather indoctrinated Roman Catholic of the helpfulness of Locke's program. But, Protestants, likely Locke's main audience, could look at certain Roman Catholics as being justified even if their Roman doctrine has misinformed them of that which justifies. A Roman Catholic will be considered justified because he or she believes that Christ is the Messiah and takes Him as king, despite their errant views on baptism and the other sacraments.[86] Moreover, the Pneumatology incorporated within Locke's soteriological framework, like his Christology, is vague. He mentions the following regarding the Holy Spirit: His falling on the Gentiles in Acts, Christ's sending of the Holy Spirit to the Apostles and the concomitant enlightening, assurance, and miraculous enablement given, His assistance and mysterious working on us, His infallible authorship of Scripture, and our expected illumination by the Holy Spirit in reading Scripture.[87] Although Locke appears to speak of the Holy Spirit as a person, he never explicitly says so or defends the point as Bold does (who himself, undoubtedly like many others, including Richard Baxter,[88] does not hold the

---

[85] Locke, *ROC*, 212–14.
[86] The thinking of some bolster this toleration of certain Roman Catholics: e.g., Lucci, *John Locke's Christianity*, 190–92.
[87] Locke, *ROC*, 38, 176–81, 293; Locke, *A Second Vindication*, 272–73, 340–45, 466.
[88] Lim, *In Pursuit of Purity*, 157–89.

personhood and divinity of the Holy Spirit as an article one must hold to become a Christian).

While Locke's primary message of *ROC* is not sectarian by nature, it seems as though he is building two interconnected rejoinders regarding justification, each aimed at a different group. First, the deists, the advancers of the religion of morality, must add belief in Christ.[89] Locke spent significant time building his case for this: a need for revelation and subsequently the need of redemption that it clearly teaches. Toward the end of *ROC* Locke discusses the disagreement on aspects of morality that are witnessed between times and places to show the need and reasonableness of God giving a moral authority in Jesus Christ, whose Scripture is authoritative. Following the moral principles set forth in Scripture is far easier and, in a sense, more reasonable, especially for the common person, than trying to figure all of them out with our natural reason.[90] The second rejoinder is leveled at the antinomians who—being Libertine and misguided—must incorporate obedience based on morality into their view of salvation. This is what revelation clearly teaches and it has to do with taking Christ as king. They are not named explicitly as the deists, but they need not be.[91]

Both groups undercut the foundation of society in their own ways. The deists lose the sure source and basis of a shared and perfect morality. The human mind wanders into much error as Locke notes: "That 'tis too hard a thing for unassisted Reason, to establish Morality in all its parts upon its true foundations; with a clear and convincing light."[92] On the other hand, the antinomians are a law unto themselves, which is hardly a fine workable basis for state and church. Antinomian leanings are poison to the soul of individuals, church, and state. The deists' position undercuts their own concerns of a moral religion by not taking the divinity of Scripture seriously, and the antinomians undercut their truth claims for the Bible by not taking morality and obedience seriously. Locke understands that revelation has been functionally necessary for our morality. Thus, those who deny the need

---

[89] Locke explicitly states that *ROC* is written to deists. Locke, *ROC*, 2; Locke, *Second*, xvi–xviii, 151–52, 376, 465–66. Cf. Locke, *Vindication*, 9; Locke, *A Second Vindication*, 77–78.

[90] Locke, *ROC*, 267–85. See Chapter 5 for more on Locke's epistemology of moral principles.

[91] Limborch applauds Locke for attacking antinomian sentiments in *ROC*. Limborch, "L2222," 52–53.

[92] Locke, *ROC*, 268. Locke's discussion on this point is rather lengthy and notable. He makes a fine case for the need of revelation. See Chapter 5 for more on Locke's teaching on the necessity of Scripture.

of faith in Christ and those who deny the need of obeying him stand in eternally precarious positions.

Heretical Red Herrings in *ROC*

A question that is yet to be answered is: If Locke desired to produce an irenic and ecumenical treatise why would he include elements that are sectarian or even considered damnable heresy by some? Snobelen believes that Locke should have clearly stated Christ's deity and the Trinity if he wanted to be irenic. Locke's response to Snobelen and others would be: What about many ante-Nicene Christians, whose views would not be supported by post-Nicene developments? Snobelen's similar queries regarding a positive affirmation of annhilationism and mortalism and what is to him an explicit rejection of the concept of original sin in *ROC* perhaps have more force.[93]

Locke also speculated that perhaps one who has heard nothing of the Messiah might, following his God-given reason, be saved. Snobelen might have excluded this as not all self-identified Christians would find this heresy or because the picture Locke paints of the human condition in the pages following shows the unlikelihood of one coming to know God well enough to be assured that, by virtue of His attributes, He would forgive them if they repented and took Him as their ruler.[94] Locke writes, "Though the Works of Nature, in every part of them, sufficiently Evidence a Deity; yet the World made so little use of their Reason, that they saw him not" due to sense and lust, carelessness, fearful apprehensions, priests, and so on.[95]

A few things can be said in response to those suspicious of Locke's ecumenical intent in light of sectarian teachings in *ROC*. Locke, in building up to the law in the opening pages of *ROC*, is concerned with expunging the idea that eternal death refers to torment and the seminal and federal views of original sin.[96] It is rather intriguing why the thinker displeased with

---

[93] Snobelen, "Socinianism, Heresy," 111–12.
[94] Locke, *ROC*, 256.
[95] Locke, *ROC*, 259–60.
[96] Regarding the positions on original sin, the so-called seminal and federal views are two of the most popular. The first is the stance that we are implicated in the original sin of Adam because we were somehow (ontologically) in Adam. We therefore have the guilt of that sin assigned to us. The corruption associated with it is passed on organically because both the material and immaterial aspects of the human are derived from her parents. The federal view holds that Adam was the federal head of humanity and therefore the guilt of the original sin is imputed to all and, as a result, all are corrupt.

systems and the pushing of one onto others would begin with his own seeds of systematizing.[97] Surely the irony would not be lost on one such as Locke. It is possible that Locke was constructing a framework beginning with a teaching on original sin that might accommodate all views. This seems extraordinarily unlikely and makes him out to be rather naïve. Besides, it is his stated intention in what follows the first several pages to explain the Gospel as it was plainly presented in Scripture. Taking into consideration his surprisingly nonspecific treatment of justification, it is more likely the case that he assumed that readers would catch the shift: an introduction of his own thoughts, followed by a lengthy discussion of the fundamental articles and actions that make one a Christian—annhilationism and mortalism and original sin, clearly excluded as not being fundamental; one could make a similar argument for his articulation of inclusivism. *ROC* would have probably had a warmer reception if Locke would have discussed the fundamental articles and in what sense they are necessary first or simply the unorthodox views not at all; similar sentiments can be found in the letters to Locke. For instance, in a letter to Locke, Limborch shares Johannes Hudde's thoughts on the book, including its opening pages:

> Another man [Hudde] said that he had twice read through that treatise [*ROC*]; he praised it exceedingly and declared that the author had very solidly demonstrated the object of the Christian faith, which is the principal subject of the whole book. But he found one thing amiss: namely that from the very beginning the author had rejected and refuted the common opinion regarding original sin; the author, leaving that opinion untouched, could nonetheless have established the principal argument of his treatise; as it is, many in whose minds that opinion is deeply rooted are offended on reading the beginning of the book before they come to its main argument, and accordingly conceive a prejudice against the author, so that they do not read what follows with the requisite serenity of mind and are thus rendered the more averse, when rather their goodwill should have been courted, so that they might ponder with impartial judgment an opinion that indeed is true but that agrees little with the common craving of theologians, who almost all want something of their own to be admixed with the Christian faith, as if that faith were peculiar to their own religious body and others were excluded from that faith.[98]

---

[97] Locke, *Vindication*, 6–8.
[98] Limborch, "L2318," 206–07.

Instead, these unorthodox doctrines at the head cast a shadow of suspicion on *ROC*'s irenic and ecumenical material for many readers for centuries to come by virtue of their presence and positioning. Most scholarship focusing on Locke's soteriology has tended towards Edwards's approach to and reading of *ROC* that amounts to this: What reads like a Socinian or Socinianesque document at the beginning will read the same through until the end.[99]

Recent scholarship has acknowledged that "Socinian" is a slippery term and one not capable of engulfing Locke's own personal theological views. So, some scholars' sights have turned, as has been made evident, to an exploration of the question: From whom else, then, might Locke have borrowed in writing *ROC*? This in itself is a formidable task when studying past scholars who extensively cite many of their sources; but such referencing is definitely not characteristic of Locke, save his correspondence. Again, what has added to the confusion of the pursuit of Locke's specific sources for soteriology in *ROC* is that it was constructed so that numerous traditions are affirmed as Christian. Intentional maneuvers that make room for perhaps Baxterian types or Socinians, for instance, have been taken as influence by Baxter or Socinians of Locke's own specific soteriological views, which many mistakenly think is the focus of *ROC*.

Thus, the form of the response to Snobelen and those who interpret Locke as Socinian can also be applied to those who suggest that the anti-Calvinist sentiments made in the early pages of *ROC* exclude ecumenism and are evidence of the treatise promulgating a type of "Arminianism" throughout.[100] The approach of *ROC* by those who label it Socinian is merely appropriated by those who paint it Arminian: what reads like a type of Arminianism to some in the beginning has appeared to them as an Arminian document to the end because of the ecumenical treatment of soteriology. For instance, some scholars find support for an undergirding Arminian soteriology throughout *ROC* in Locke's assertions that the Holy Spirit gives us "assistance,"[101] despite the fact that a mere assertion of His giving assistance is hardly specific or technical and that directly after mentioning the "promise of assistance" of the Holy Spirit he writes, "'Twill be idle for us, who know not how our own

---

[99] Cf. *Racovian Catechism*, V.x.

[100] For example, Tetlow, "John Locke's Covenant Theology," 168, 179, 183–84; Smith, "John Locke's Concept," vi, 211. Marshall clearly asserts that Locke can be considered Arminian in some regards and Socinian in others. Marshall, "Locke, Socinianism, 'Socinianism,'" 117. Cf. Lucci, *John Locke's Christianity*, 7, 52–53, 211.

[101] Tetlow, "John Locke's Covenant Theology," 168; Wallace, "Socinianism, Justification by Faith," 54–55; Lucci, *John Locke's Christianity*, 95.

Spirits move and act us, to ask in what manner the Spirit of God shall work upon us... Can we suspect, that the Spirit and Wisdom of God should fail in it; though we perceive or comprehend not the ways of his Operation?"[102]

In closing, the main message of *ROC* is not Socinian or Arminian, although Locke's personal theology might have many conclusions similar to one or both. In fact, when he shows his hand in *ROC*, one or an amalgamation of both is probably not far off the mark. Promoting a certain system or sect, however, is hardly his goal. *ROC*'s doctrine of justification and its associated soteriological framework are Socinian, Arminian, Calvinist, Quaker, Anabaptist, and so on. They are not deist; they are not antinomian. *ROC* is probably one of the finest attempted ecumenical efforts from the time period. It is its opening pages, however, that serve as a prime example of an unintentional red herring.

---

[102] Locke, *ROC*, 292. In fact, none of the comments on the Holy Spirit's assistance to the believer point to any particular sect. Cf. Locke, *A Second Vindication*, 83–84.

4
Why John Locke Thought that the Fundamental Articles Must Be Minimal

The commentators on Locke's doctrinal minimalism are legion. His suggestion, in *The Reasonableness of Christianity* (*ROC*), that there were only two fundamental articles of faith, in the midst of a rigorous debate over the fundamental articles of the Christian faith, was met with approbation from some, like pastor Samuel Bold, and with ire from others, like theologian John Edwards.[1] And Locke has not been short on commentators

---

[1] John Locke, *The Reasonableness of Christianity, as delivered in the Scriptures*, 2nd ed. (London: Awnsham and John Churchil, 1696); John Locke, *The Reasonableness of Christianity: As Delivered in the Scriptures*, ed. John C. Higgins-Biddle (Oxford: Clarendon Press, 1999). Higgins-Biddle's critical edition of *ROC* is based on, but not slavishly, the "Harvard copy" of *ROC*. The Harvard copy is a first edition *ROC* that contains Locke's notes, emendations, and corrections (cxxxiv). I will reference only the 1696 edition.
John Locke, *A Vindication of the Reasonableness of Christianity, etc, From Mr. Edwards's Reflections* (London: Awnsham and John Churchil, 1695). This was published along with the 1696 second edition of *ROC*. John Locke, *A Second Vindication of the Reasonableness of Christianity, etc.* (London: A. and J. Churchil, 1697); John Locke, *An Essay Concerning Humane Understanding*, 3rd ed. (London: Awnsham and John Churchil, 1695); John Locke, *An Essay Concerning Human Understanding*, ed. Peter H. Nidditch (Oxford: Clarendon Press, 1979). The 1695 third edition that existed at the writing of Locke's *ROC* and its two vindications has been consulted along with Nidditch's critical edition. Pertinent works from Edwards and Bold are as follows: John Edwards, *Some Thoughts Concerning the Several Causes and Occasions of Atheism, Especially in the Present Age. With Some Brief Reflections on Socinianism: And on a Late Book Entituled The Reasonableness of Christianity as Deliver'd in the Scriptures* (London: Printed for J. Robinson, 1695); John Edwards, *Socinianism Unmask'd. A Discourse Shewing the Unreasonableness of a Late Writer's Opinion Concerning the Necessity of Only One Article of Faith; and of His Other Assertions in His Late Book, Entituled, The Reasonableness of Christianity as Deliver'd in the Scriptures, and in His Vindication of It. With a Brief Reply to Another (Professed) Socinian Writer* (London: Printed for J. Robinson, 1696); John Edwards, *The Socinian Creed: or, A Brief Account of the Professed Tenents and Doctrines of the Foreign and English Socinians. Wherein Is Shew'd the Tendency of Them to Irreligion and Atheism. With Proper Antidotes Against Them* (London: Printed for J. Robinson, 1697). Samuel Bold's *A Collection of Tracts, Publish'd in Vindication of Mr. Lock's Reaosnableness of Christianity, as Deliver'd in the Scriptures, etc.* (London: Printed for A. and J. Churchil, 1706) has the following relevant tracts: *A Short Discourse of the True Knowledge of Christ Jesus* (London: Printed for A. and J. Churchil, 1697); *Some Passages in The Reasonableness of Christianity, etc. and Its Vindication. With Some Animadversions on Mr. Edwards's Reflections on the Reasonableness of Christianity, and on his Book, Entituled, Socinianism Unmask'd* (London: Printed for A. and J. Churchil, 1697); and *A Reply to Mr. Edwards's Brief Reflections on A Short Discourse of the True Knowledge of Christ Jesus, etc. To*

regarding his doctrinal minimalism up through the present day. Elsewhere I have categorized scholars' approaches to Locke's religious intent with *ROC* and other works. Some read *ROC* as being surreptitious. That is, although he points to the Bible as authoritative, one of his goals is to undercut it. Others have found him to have sectarian aims despite his professed intent to create peace among the churches. Another group takes Locke at his word and the work as being his best attempt to find common ground for the various Christian sects[2] (one of their number thinks, however, that Locke's intent is not really so much doctrinal, but that his design is to showcase how one appropriately reads Scripture).[3] These categories could be applied to the narrower topic of what Locke's intent was regarding the doctrinal minimalism rendered in *ROC*. What is more, there is a group of scholars, most of whom take Locke as sincere, who are interested in how his doctrinal minimalism might have been influenced by the Cambridge Platonists, in his earlier years, and the Latitudinarians and Arminians in his most active writing years. Many of these take an interdisciplinary approach and are interested in how his minimalism and thoughts on toleration mutually reinforce

---

Which Is Prefixed a Preface, Wherein Something Is Said Concerning Reason and Antiquity, in the Chief Controversies with the Socinians (London: Printed for A. and J. Churchil, 1697). For a nice collection of excerpts of contemporary works related to *ROC*: *John Locke and Christianity: Contemporary Responses to The Reasonableness of Christianity*, ed. and intro. Victor Nuovo (Bristol: Thoemmes Press, 1997). Other works that will assist in understanding Locke's historical context are as follows: Locke–Limborch correspondence from *The Correspondence of John Locke*, ed. E. S. de Beer (Oxford: Oxford University Press, 1977–1980) (referenced throughout the chapter); Philip Van Limborch, *A Compleat System, or Body of Divinity, Both Speculative and Practical, Founded on Scripture and Reason*, trans. William Jones (London: 1702); Gilbert Burnet, *Some Passages of the Life and Death of the Right Honourable John Earl of Rochester* (London: 1680); Gilbert Burnet, *A Treatise Concerning the Truth of the Christian Religion. To Which Is Added, A Discourse on Miracles, by John Locke Esq.* (Glasgow: Printed by Robert Foulis, 1743); Symon Patrick, *The Witnesses to Christianity; or, The Certainty of Our Faith and Hope: In a Discourse upon 1 S. John v. 7, 8* (London: Printed for R. Royston, 1675); Francis Turretin, *Institutes of Elenctic Theology*, 3 vols., trans. George Musgrave Giger and ed. James T. Dennison, Jr. (Phillipsburg: P & R Publishing, 1992); Richard A. Muller, *Post-Reformation Reformed Dogmatics: The Rise and Development of Reformed Orthodoxy, ca. 1520 to ca. 1725*, 2nd ed., vol. 1 (Grand Rapids: Baker Academic, 2003); Richard A. Muller, *Dictionary of Latin and Greek Theological Terms: Drawn Principally from Protestant Scholastic Theology*, 2nd ed. (Grand Rapids: Baker Academic, 2017); Leslie Stephen, *History of English Thought in the Eighteenth Century*, 2 vols., 3rd ed. (London: Harbinger, 1962).

[2] Jonathan S. Marko, "The Promulgation of Right Morals: John Locke on the Church and the Christian as the Salvation of Society," *Journal of Markets and Morality* 19, no. 1 (2016): 41–59.

[3] Justin Champion, "'A Law of Continuity in the Process of Theology': Assessing the Legacy of John Locke's Reasonableness of Christianity, 1695–2004," *Eighteenth-Century Thought* 3 (2007): 111–42; cf. Justin Champion, "'Directions for the Profitable Reading of the Holy Scriptures': Biblical Criticism, Clerical Learning and Lay Readers, c. 1650–1720," in *Scripture and Scholarship in Early Modern England*, ed. Ariel Hessayon and Nicholas Keene (Burlington: Ashgate Publishing Company, 2006), 208–30.

one another.⁴ It is these latter scholars' assertions and arguments to which I will be the most attentive in this chapter.

No scholar of whom I am aware has attempted to describe in detail the systematic coherence of Locke's defense of doctrinal minimalism from a variety of his writings along with its implications. It is not my intent to offer an explication of how Locke exegetically arrived at his fundamentals. Given the biblical conclusion, at least as arrived at by Locke, he thought that the paucity of fundamental articles and their origin, the mouth of the Messiah, was eminently reasonable.

Locke argues that the fundamental articles are reasonably minimal and explicitly from the Messiah. This position supports religious toleration and it is not wholly novel. As people must be able to cull for themselves (although not wholly in isolation) any articles from Scripture to claim that they believe them—lest they be guilty of a brand of illegitimate, implicit faith—it is perfectly

---

⁴ Martin I. J. Griffin, Jr., *Latitudinarianism in the Seventeenth-Century Church of England*, ann. Richard H. Popkin and ed. Lila Freedman (New York: E. J. Brill, 1992). Because of Locke's tolerance and doctrinal minimalism Griffin categorizes Locke as a Latitudinarian. But, Locke and others, "who held heterodox ideas on the Trinity, must be considered atypical seventeenth-century Latitudinarians, but were unexceptional ones of the eighteenth-century" (47). Griffin's book is also of interest for his attempts to define Latitudinarianism within its trajectory from the Cambridge Platonists. He thinks that the so-called Latitudinarians of the late seventeenth century were notably more orthodox than the eighteenth-century version. John Marshall, "John Locke and Latitudinarianism," in *Philosophy, Science, and Religion in England 1640-1700*, ed. Richard Kroll, Richard Ashcraft, and Perez Zagorin (New York: Cambridge University Press, 1992), 253–82. In this early work of Marshall on Locke, he compares Locke with those commonly known as Latitudinarians. Marshall writes the following: "There were, then, important personal and intellectual threads linking Locke to at least the most eirenic [sic] strands of latitudinarianism. Focus upon the parallels . . . however, obscures the many areas of disagreement . . . Generally . . . the latitudinarians emphasized comprehension, or toleration within the church, much more than toleration outside of its boundaries" (265). John Marshall, *John Locke, Toleration and Early Enlightenment Culture* (Cambridge: Cambridge University Press, 2006). This later work charts what he thinks might be Locke's development of his ideas on toleration. He notes that Locke roundly chastises all traditions for their insufficient tolerance (554). G. A. J. Rogers, "Locke and the Latitude-Men: Ignorance as a Ground of Toleration," in *Philosophy, Science, and Religion in England 1640-1700*, ed. Richard Kroll, Richard Ashcraft, and Perez Zagorin (New York: Cambridge University Press, 1992), 230–52. Rogers argues that Locke takes up the mantle of the Cambridge Platonists who recognized limits of our intellectual enquiry and thus the necessity of tolerance. Rogers notes that Locke's main difference from his intellectual forbearers is that he translated their thinking into a political theory of action. I will be attempting to go much further than Rogers and show some of these interconnections between Locke's *Essay*, *ROC*, and *Letter Concerning Toleration*. Diana Stanciu, "Arminian Toleration, Irenicism and Latitudinarianism in Cudworth's Letters to Van Limborch: Text and Contect," *Lias* 40, no. 2 (2013): 177-209. She asserts two points important for my purposes here. One, she echoes the comparative extremity of Locke's toleration in comparison to Limborch and Cudworth but, two, also notes that Locke's *Letter Concerning Toleration* was not all that novel. I will be repeating a similar point throughout this chapter. Patrick Müller, *Latitudinarianism and Didacticism in Eighteenth-Century Literature: Moral Theology in Fielding, Sterne, and Goldsmith* (New York: Peter Lang, 2009). Müller, following Victor Nuovo, thinks that Locke does not actually believe his minimalist creed and is simply trying to reduce fighting (26).

There is a trove of literature that helps give a better picture of Locke's immediate intellectual background concentrating on theological latitude. Paul Chang-Ha Lim, *In Pursuit of Purity, Unity, and Liberty: Richard Baxter's Puritan Ecclesiology in Its Seventeenth-Century Context* (Boston: Brill,

reasonable that the fundamental articles in Scripture are few in number and clear—otherwise the vulgar or commoners are practically ruled out from being saved—and expressly from the Messiah himself—lest, among other things, the continuity of the church be disrupted and the definition of a Christian be subject to change. A corollary of this is the need for a relatively high degree of religious toleration. While Locke tied these elements systematically together, there were others in the era who advanced one or more of these elements.

Historical Context: Fundamental Articles Debate

Historical Overview

The debate over fundamental articles of Christian faith hit full force in the late 1600s.[5] In the narrowest sense the fundamental articles were those one must

---

2004), 157–89. Lim's study on Richard Baxter is rather illuminating to the intellectual milieu in which Locke labored. Lim shows Baxter's hope that a return to "pre-Nicene [doctrinal] purity" and scriptural sufficiency would heal divisions within God's Church. His work is helpful as it shows a strong ecumenical fervor of an English thinker not typically associated or compared with Latitudinarians. What is more, Lim shows that Baxter (like Locke) likes to use Scriptural terms to avoid controversy. İsmail Kurun, *The Theological Origins of Liberalism* (New York: Lexington Books, 2016). Kurun has recently set Locke in a politico-theological trajectory that spans from the Reformation up to modern times. I agree with his narrative that Locke, the Enlightenment, political liberalism, and modernity were not the sharp break from medieval theological thinking that some have posited. He rightly stresses Locke's concern for the individual. My main quibble with Kurun is that he believes Locke is highly concerned with maintaining theism as it is the best foundation for moral and thus political liberalism (170). I have argued elsewhere (Marko, "The Promulgation of Right Morals"; see also Chapter 5) that Locke thought Christians who take Scripture as their authority is the best foundation for morality. Stephen Hampton, *Anti-Arminians: The Anglican Reformed Tradition from Charles II to George I* (Oxford: Oxford University Press, 2008). Hampton has, also recently, shown that the Anglican Church was much more soteriologically diverse, namely that Reformed thinking had a strong presence well into the 1700s despite common narratives to the contrary. He also showcases the amazingly subtle distinctions in the justification debates in the decades spanning the seventeenth and eighteenth centuries. Distinctions of so-called high-church and low-church aside, he shows how Reformed, Arminian, and Latitudinarians co-existed in the church. Nicholas Tyacke, "From Laudians to Latitudinarians: A Shifting Balance of Theological Forces," in *The Later Stuart Church, 1660–1714*, ed. Grant Tapsell (New York: Manchester University Press, 2012), 46–67. Although missing the degree to which the Reformed still influenced the Anglican Church as Hampton points out, Nicholas Tyacke provides a narrative how the High Church Laudians lost their influence to the Latitudinarians in the Restoration period. He helpfully brings out some of the characteristics and goals of both traditions. Isabel Rivers, *Reason, Grace, and Sentiment: A Study of the Language of Religion and Ethics in England, 1660–1780*, vol. 1 (New York: Cambridge University Press, 1991), 25–87. Isabel River's second chapter showcases the similarities and differences among the so-called Latitudinarians starting with the Cambridge Platonists and ending with some of the better known of the late 1600s like John Tillotson and Simon Patrick. She brings their anti-Hobbessian tendencies to the fore and also exposes the characteristics that led some to group them with the Socinians.

[5] Cf. Muller, PRRD, vol. 1, 406–430; Martin I. Klauber, "The Drive Toward Protestant Union in Early Eighteenth-Century Geneva: Jean-Alphonse Turrettini on the 'Fundamental Articles' of the

maintain to be saved. While the question was treated in the Reformation period, it received attention as the various traditions coming out of that era continued to draw clearer doctrinal lines. To get a better handle on the differences, I will briefly focus on Francis Turretin's *Institutes of Elenctic Theology*. He is not only paradigmatic of the period of high orthodoxy and a cataloguer of views on numerous theological issues, but Locke was also familiar with him. What is more, Turretin's work is rather removed from the Latitudinarian sentiment. As might be expected, the Reformed Turretin chastises those outside of his tradition for erring in either defect or excess. Of the Socinians he writes that they "err in defect who admit very few fundamentals (and those only practical, the theoretical being almost entirely set aside)." Arminians, in Turretin's learned opinion, also err in defect. He complains that they "reduce fundamentals to those heads which are placed beyond dispute among almost all Christians and are contained in these three: faith in the divine promises, obedience to the divine precepts and a due reverence for the Scriptures." Had Turretin been familiar with Locke, he would no doubt have complained of Locke's position on the fundamentals being close to that of the Arminians and/or Socinians. On the other side, the Roman Catholics and Lutherans are those guilty of excess. The former simply declare as fundamental "whatever the Romish church teaches" and "the more strict Lutherans who (to render union with us more difficult) extend fundamentals more widely than is just, turn almost every error into heresy and make necessary those things which are indifferent so as more easily to prove that we differ on fundamentals." Unsurprisingly, it is the Reformed in Turretin's estimation who get the balance right: "The orthodox [Reformed] hold the mean between both. As they necessarily build upon some fundamentals, so they neither restrict them too closely, nor extend them too far."[6]

What Turretin goes on to discuss, however, is riddled with distinctions. He notes that the personal and simple foundation of the faith is Christ but that the fundamental articles are that which one is "required to believe": "repentance from dead works, faith toward God, the doctrine of baptisms, the laying on of hands, the resurrection of the dead and eternal judgment." He

---

Faith," *Church History* 61, no. 3 (1992): 334–49; Martin I. Klauber, "Between Protestant Orthodoxy and Rationalism: Fundamental Articles in the Early Career of Jean LeClerc," *Journal of the History of Ideas* 54, no. 4 (1993): 611–36; Stephen Pickard, "The Purpose of Stating the Faith: An Historical and Systematic Inquiry into the Tradition of Fundamental Articles with Special Reference to Anglicanism" (PhD thesis, Durham University, 1990), 127–37.

[6] Turretin, *Institutes of Elenctic Theology*, I.xiv.1–3.

notes, however, that not all of these have the same degree of necessity: "These principles however have not an equal degree of necessity, some being necessary primarily and by themselves and others secondarily only and by reason of some other thing."[7] This is akin to the distinction between (primary) fundamental articles and secondary fundamental articles employed by the Lutheran orthodox.[8] It is also not a far leap from the distinction Locke makes in ROC between fundamental articles and those that are concomitant to them.[9] Turretin notes the complexity of the distinctions one ought to recognize when attempting to speak of certain articles of the faith as being fundamental:

> Hence some doctrines are necessary to be known simply for the existence of faith, others only relatively and for its well-being; some to the production of faith, others to its perfection (Heb. 6:1); some per se and absolutely to all whether babes or perfect, others accidentally only to these of full age and advanced (Heb. 5:13, 14). Some doctrines are relatively necessary to the instruction of others. This necessity again is to be taken in a certain degree of latitude according to the gifts, instruction, calling, sex and age, inasmuch as some belong to the flock, while others are pastors to whom are committed the oracles of God, whose duty it is to give instruction and to convince the gainsayers.[10]

In short, there are some things required for justifying faith and others for further sanctification; but one must consider a person's situation because there is a reasonable relativity in that regard.

Turretin recognizes that there will be a difference in articulation and enumeration of fundamental articles within his tradition. But, he thinks, the content would prove to be the same. The various articles cohere and mutually support one another and make it difficult to uniformly disentangle. And if someone rejects a particular fundamental article in the narrowest sense of the term, that person has in fact overthrown the rest. Moreover, his response to those from other traditions that push him and his Reformed brethren to enumerate fundamental articles is that such calls are "rash" and "also useless and unnecessary because there is no need of our knowing particularly the

---

[7] Turretin, *Institutes of Elenctic Theology*, I.xiv.4.
[8] Muller, s.v. "articuli fundamentales," "articuli fundamentales secundurii," "articuli non-fundamentales," *Dictionary*.
[9] See Chapter 3.
[10] Turretin, *Institutes of Elenctic Theology*, I.xiv.7.

number of such articles, if we can prove that they [their opponents] err fundamentally in one or more. And this can be done easily with regard to the papists, Socinians, Anabaptists and similar heretics."[11]

Muller highlights some of the characteristics that are emphasized above in Turretin's work. Different theologians of the era employed varied distinctions in their treatment of the issue of fundamental articles. Yet, Muller notes that, in the strictest sense, the fundamentals are "Only those doctrines absolutely necessary to faith and capable of being known by all—even the 'simple and illiterate'—either directly by reading or by obvious logical consequence of the text can be defined as fundamentals in the strictest sense."[12] He notes that it was not uncommon for the Reformed to avoid giving an explicit list of fundamental articles. But, in their defense, he asserts, "it is clear that the Reformed discussion of *articuli fundamentales* also maintained a precise and careful distinction between the status and function of Scripture, catechism, or confession, and theological system in the church, while demonstrating the theoretical and practical interrelation of these three forms of *doctrina*."[13] But it is the refusal by many theologians to articulate and enumerate the fundamental articles in the strictest sense of the term that resulted in a decline in confessionalism and polemics.[14] Even the Anglican church eventually permitted Arminian thinking into their ranks and even started to show signs of tolerating non-Nicene positions on the doctrine of the Holy Trinity.[15] This switch to Arminian thinking and non-Nicene positions is nicely outlined via explanation of a handful of debates and theologians in Hampton's *Anti-Arminians*.

Locke's Fundamentals

It is in the midst of this debate that Locke penned most of his works. But it is *ROC* that arguably faces the debate most directly. Locke spends the bulk of the book proving from the gospels and Acts that the only two articles that are consistently preached over and over are: (1) there is one God; and (2) Jesus Christ is the Messiah foretold of in the Old Testament. What he

---

[11] Turretin, *Institutes of Elenctic Theology*, I.xiv.24–25.
[12] Muller, *PRRD*, vol. 1, 406–30 [quotation, p. 417].
[13] Muller, *PRRD*, vol. 1, 427.
[14] Cf. Muller, *PRRD*, vol. 1, 430.
[15] Muller, *PRRD*, vol. 1, 429.

takes as requirements for salvation go beyond these, however. One must also take Christ as king of their life: "Only those who have believed *Jesus* to be the *Messiah*, and have taken him to be their King, with a sincere Endeavour after Righteousness, in obeying his Law, shall have their past sins not imputed to them."[16] Elsewhere in *ROC*, he notes that we "are Justified by God, for believing *Jesus* to be the *Messiah*, and so taking him for their King, whom they are resolved to obey, to the utmost of their Power."[17] All considered, it is not simply intellectual assent or historical faith that makes one a Christian.[18]

Locke does have some very helpful comments regarding all the other notions and doctrines that one might glean from Scripture. He does emphasize, however, that Christ did not preach any other articles as necessary for salvation. It is during the last supper where one would expect Christ to tell the disciples of anything else necessary to the faith beyond what he had already told them. But he does not tell them anything new.[19] In fact, as unequivocal support, Locke quotes Christ from John 15:15 "*Henceforth I call ye not Servants; for the Servant knoweth not what his Lord does: But I have called ye Friends; for ALL THINGS I have heard of my Father, I have made known unto you.*"[20] In response to those who think earlier believers could perhaps believe less to be saved, Locke asserts, if that were the case, John would have inserted such things because his gospel was written to people decades after the fact.[21] But Locke does note, similar to Turretin, that there are certain articles comprehended under "Jesus is the Messiah" that one cannot reject without rejecting the said fundamental article, such as his death, resurrection, and ascension. These are undeniable proofs of him being the Messiah.[22] "For whatsoever is brought as an Argument to prove another Truth, cannot be thought to be the principal thing aimed at in that argumentation; though it may have so strong and immediate connexion with the Conclusion, that you cannot deny it without denying even what is inferr'd from it, and is therefore the fitter to be an Argument to prove it."[23] This is why his resurrection was required to believe as a fundamental article and "sometimes solely insisted on."[24]

---

[16] Locke, *ROC*, 215.
[17] Locke, *ROC*, 246; cf. 212–18; 235.
[18] Locke, *ROC*, 194–202.
[19] Locke, *ROC*, 164–94.
[20] Locke, *ROC*, 185.
[21] Locke, *ROC*, 193–94.
[22] Locke, *ROC*, 30–31, 33, 34–35, 188, 293–94.
[23] Locke, *A Second Vindication*, 269.
[24] Locke, *ROC*, 30–31.

Locke has a similar position regarding all the doctrines promulgated or inferable from the epistles of the New Testament. They were written to those who were already Christians so there could not be any fundamental articles in the strictest sense promulgated therein.[25] That said, "They [doctrines promulgated in the epistles] are Truths whereof none that is once known to be such, may or ought to be disbelieved." Not believing would be a rejection of Christ as King: "For to acknowledge any Proposition to be of Divine Revelation and Authority, and yet to deny or disbelieve it, is to offend against the Fundamental Article and Ground of Faith, that God is true."[26]

John Edwards responded to Locke in his *Some Thoughts Concerning the Several Causes and Occasions of Atheism*. Locke responded with his (first) *Vindication*. Edwards volleyed back with *Socinianism Unmask'd*. Locke responded to that work with his lengthy *A Second Vindication*. Edwards accuses Locke of feigning good intentions, while he, in truth, is essentially wiping out centuries of theological work. In *Socinianism Unmask'd* he writes:

> Well, this cause must be carried on, and I can do it as well as any man by maintaining that there is but *One Article of Christian Faith necessarily to be believed to make a man a Christian,* necessarily to be believed in order to salvation. For if there be but One Point necessary to be believ'd, then the doctrines concerning the *Trinity,* concerning the *Incarnation* and *Divinity of Christ,* concerning his *Satisfaction,* etc. are rendred unnecessary as to making us Christians.[27]

It is the recurrent "etc." explicitly present, as in the excerpt above, or implicitly so throughout Edwards's works that becomes one of Locke's targets in their debate. Locke notes that the fundamental doctrines that he mentions in *Thoughts Concerning the Causes of Atheism* and *Socinianism Unmask'd* are different; thus, he calls on Edwards to clarify which of his "two Creeds" he prefers.[28] At another place he writes:

> 'Tis no wonder therefore, there has been such fierce Contests, and such cruel Havock made amongst Christians about Fundamentals: Whilst every

---

[25] Locke, *ROC*, 293–301.
[26] Locke, *ROC*, 302–3.
[27] Edward, *Socinianism Unmask'd*, 45–46.
[28] Locke, *A Second Vindication*, 69.

one would set up his System upon pain of Fire and Faggot in this, and Hell Fire in the other World; Though at the same time, whilst he is exercising the utmost Barbarities against others to prove himself a true Christian, he professes himself so ignorant that he cannot tell, or so uncharitable, that he will not tell, what Articles are absolutely necessary, and sufficient to make a man a Christian. If there be any such Fundamentals, as 'tis certain there are, 'tis as certain they must be very plain. Why then does every one urge and make a stir about Fundamentals, and no body give a List of them? But because, (as I have said) upon the usual Grounds, they cannot.[29]

Locke calls on Edwards and anyone who is willing to give an alternative list of fundamentals at a number of different places in his *A Second Vindication*.[30] As was observed in the case of Turretin, few, if any, were forthcoming with such a list.

The Fundamentals of Other Doctrinal Minimalists

Locke was hardly the only thinker in the era to promulgate the notion of two fundamental articles. For instance, Simon Patrick, in *The Witnesses of Christianity*, although likely assuming the first to be held by those to whom Christ preached, advanced that "Christ is the Messiah" is the basis of Christianity. He notes that Saint John tells us that "*whoever believeth that Jesus is the Christ, is born of God.*" He adds that elsewhere where Jesus is called the Son of God, that, too, should be understood as promulgating that Jesus is the Christ. "It is the very same Faith no doubt whereby we are *born of God*, and whereby we overcome the world; and therefore it is the very same thing to believe that *Jesus is the Christ* and believe that *Jesus is the Son of God.*"[31] Several pages later, he points out that in John 1:49 Nathaniel identifies "Son of God" and "King of Israel" in order to show that a true Christian will thus submit themselves "with the greatest devotion of spirit, and from whom we may expect Protection, Blessing, and the noblest Rewards." But right after he quotes Nathaniel's confession, Patrick writes: "This is the business upon which we are to examine these *Witnesses* [to Christianity]." In other words,

---

[29] Locke, *A Second Vindication*, 81–82.
[30] For example, Locke, *A Second Vindication*, 168–74, 460.
[31] Patrick, *Witnesses of Christianity*, 10; cf. Locke, *Vindication*, 39–40.

confessing Jesus as the Christ, or Messiah, or Son of God, or King, with a faith that takes him as such, is the starting point of Christianity.[32] Like Locke, he is not afraid to share his theological opinions in the midst of his argumentation for his main point of a book, although they would be likely a bit more acceptable, no doubt than those shared by Locke, who advances, for instance, unusual positions on the image of God, the resurrection, and original sin in the opening pages of *ROC*.[33]

Patrick was just one of a number of notable Latitudinarian theologians and churchmen in Locke's era. The Latitudinarians of the late 1600s were thought to be notably influenced by the preceding generation of Cambridge Platonists, who are also labeled by some as Latitudinarians. The Cambridge Platonists were less insistent on the acceptance of their theological opinions than many of the era and concerned about liberty of conscience. Similarly, the Latitudinarians of the latter decades of the seventeenth century were more accepting of theological diversity than many of the Anglicans of the time.[34] They required less specificity than what would have been expected of Anglican parishioners. They were still quite orthodox. In fact, according to Martin Griffin, Jr., the difference between the Latitudinarians of the eighteenth and the seventeenth century is that the latter were more traditional in their theology and conformed to the 39 Articles, whereas "Deists, Socinians, and Arians could be found under the protective wings of the eighteenth-century Latitudinarianism."[35] So, although less doctrinally rigid than some, they were not always as generous or express in the degree of tolerance that Locke advocated. One of the most noted differences between Locke and the Latitudinarians (and the earlier Cambridge Platonists) is that the latter desired to offer toleration without relinquishing their goals of comprehension or inclusion while Locke advocated toleration outside of the bounds of the Anglican Church.[36]

Other thinkers personally supported Locke's main argument in the *ROC*, although they offered more details regarding their personal theological opinions. One was Philip Van Limborch, the noted Dutch Arminian and author of *Theologia Christiana* (a systematic theology text) and numerous

---

[32] Patrick, *Witnesses to Christianity*, 21; cf. Locke, *Vindication*, 39–40.
[33] For example, Patrick, *Witnesses of Christianity*, 22.
[34] Hampton, *Anti-Arminians*, chs. 1–3; Rivers, *Reason, Grace, and Sentiment*, ch. 2; Tyacke, "From Laudians to Latitudinarians."
[35] Griffin, Jr., *Latitudinarianism*, 46–47 [quotation, p. 47].
[36] Stanciu, "Arminian Toleration"; Rogers, "John Locke and the Latitude-men"; Marshall, "John Locke and Latitudinarianism."

other works. In a letter to Locke, in response to *ROC*, Limborch writes: "I am reading it attentively with very great pleasure, and I assent especially to that argument which throughout the book discusses the object of the Christian faith." And, he adds, "I think that if this is rightly perceived the weightiest and bitterest disputes in the Christian Church can be happily settled; at least, notwithstanding diversity of opinions, peace can easily be restored to the Church." Limborch maintains that *ROC* makes it clear that "those things which are now insisted on by the majority as almost the sole foundation of Christianity are not included in the object of faith."[37] In another letter to Locke, Limborch admits that he has read *ROC* three times. Limborch notes that Locke "excellently confirms the principle matter discussed in his book, which is that the faith that Jesus is the Christ is that faith by which we are justified." He then adds: "I have taken notice of scarcely anything worth putting before you in so excellent a treatise; it commands my assent so thoroughly that those things which I have taken notice [as being disagreeable or questionable] are inconsiderable and not at all detrimental to it main object, and perhaps I have not fully understood them."[38]

Samuel Bold was a pastor-theologian and defender of Locke against the attacks of John Edwards who produced, similar to *ROC*, *A Short Discourse of the True Knowledge of Jesus Christ* (*Discourse*). To say that he approved of *ROC* would be an understatement:

> In short, if the *Reasonableness of Christianity as delivered in the Scripture*, doth merit no worse a *Character*, on any other account, than it doth justly deserve, because if advanceth and to fully proveth this Point, *That Christ and his Apostles did not propound any Articles as necessarily to be believed to make a man a Christian, but this, That Jesus is the Christ, or Messias*, I think it may with great Justice be reputed, one of the *best Books* that hath been published for at least *these Sixteen Hundred Years*.[39]

Bold similarly argues that the knowledge of Christ that brings justification, or, in other words, the gospel, "strictly and most properly considered," is: "That

---

[37] Phillippus Van Limborch, "L2110. Philipppus Van Limborch to Locke 14/24 July, 1696," in *The Correspondence of John Locke*, vol. 5, ed. E. S. de Beer (Oxford: Clarendon Press, 1979), 665–71 [quotations, p. 668].

[38] Phillipus Van Limborch, "L2222. Philippus Van Limborch to Locke, 16/26 March 1697," in *The Correspondence of John Locke*, vol. 6, ed. E. S. de Beer (Oxford: Clarendon Press, 1981), 42–53 [quotations, p. 44].

[39] Bold, *Some Passages*, 52.

Jesus is the Christ (the Person God hath commissioned to be the Saviour of Sinners)." That "is the *Proposition* I conceive the Apostle here speaks of, the object of that Knowledge here commended. And this is the *Gospel* strictly and most properly considered, *Luk.* 2. 10, 11. *Act.* 4.12."[40] But as Locke argues, this is not merely intellectual assent, but "it is such a Knowledge as doth effectually determine the Person, and cause him to *resign* up himself *entirely* to *Christ Jesus* to be saved by him in his *own way*. Such a knowledge of him, as makes the Person to *take* him for *his Lord*."[41] And, like Locke, although there is only one article of faith for monotheists, the Christian is to believe whatever they find in the Bible: "The true Christian is obliged to use his best endeavors to know what Christ hath revealed, and to assent unto, and make a right use of what he attains to know Christ hath revealed." If one does not endeavor to know more, that person had not taken Christ as Lord.[42] It would be hasty, however, to cast Bold as a mere epigone. He adds his own flavor and arguments to his works, not simply appropriating the reasoning of *ROC*. He, like Limborch, feels quite free to theologically opine and polemicize a bit all the while maintaining the same fundamentals as Locke held.

Fundamental Epistemological Principle: Unreasoned Faith Is Implicit Faith

Disambiguation is often required when one comes across the word "faith" in theology and philosophy. The sense in which Locke was most interested is the faith that defines one as a Christian. Traditional Protestants maintained that faith entailed knowledge of the actual content of the gospel, intellectual assent that acknowledges that truth, and trust, which is the volitional component. In short, true faith must be volitional and cannot be mere intellectual assent. The latter would often be called historical faith.[43] In the Reformation, however, the Reformers argued that the implicit faith of the Roman church was not legitimate faith. Implicit faith or blind faith was, in Griffin's words, "the resolution by the Roman Catholics of religious certainty into the authority and the infallibility of the Church" or in Muller's words, "faith that accepts as true 'what the church believes,' without knowing the objective

---

[40] Bold, *Discourse*, 6–7.
[41] Bold, *Discourse*, 7–8.
[42] Bold, *Discourse*, 32; cf. 44–45.
[43] Cf. Muller, s.v. "fides," *Dictionary*.

contents of the faith." Such implicit faith does not grasp the knowledge or content of the theological doctrine that the person is claiming to believe.[44]

Locke held that implicit faith was epistemologically illegitimate and was no faith at all. But to his understanding of what true faith is, he went beyond the Reformers. In Locke's reasoning, for faith to be legitimate, people had not only to understand what they are claiming to believe but they also had to cull those propositions, observing them from Scripture for themselves. Otherwise, they had implicit faith in the interpreter—pastor, theologian, or parent—that his or her interpretation and theological conclusion is correct. When discussing the grounds of probability, with which we regulate our assent, he notes that there is another ground people use, although it is no right ground of probability. He writes, "yet [it] is often made use of for one, by which Men most commonly regulate their Assent, and upon which they pin their Faith more than any thing else, and, that is, *the Opinion of others.*" This is serious matter as humans are teeming with errors.[45] In fact, he outlines how many so-called authorities abide with long-held errors in the penultimate chapter of the *Essay*.

In the *Essay*, Locke employs an argument in support of his assertions above but which also focuses on toleration, using the God-given gifts of humans, and the importance of religion:

> Are the current Opinions, and licensed Guides of every Country sufficient Evidence and Security to every Man, to venture his greatest Concernments on; nay, his everlasting Happiness, or Misery? Or can those be the certain and infallible Oracles and Standards of Truth, which teach one Thing in *Christendom*, and another in *Turkey*? Or shall a poor Counry-man be eternally happy, for having the Chance to be born in *Italy*; or a Day-Labourer be unavoidably lost, because he had the ill Luck to be born in *England*? How ready some Men may be to say some of these Things, I will not here examine: but this I am sure, that Men must allow one or other of these to be true, (let them chuse which they please;) or else grant, That GOD has furnished Men with Faculties sufficient to direct them in the Way they should take, if they will but seriously employ them that Way, when their ordinary Vocations allow them the Leisure. No Man is so wholly taken up with the

---

[44] Griffin, Jr., *Latitudinarianism*, 54; Muller, s.v. "fides implicita," *Dictionary*.
[45] Locke, *Essay*, IV.xv.6.

Attendance on the Means of Living, as to have no spare Time at all to think of his Soul, and inform himself in Matters of Religion.[46]

In short, Locke thinks that when it comes to the question of epistemological legitimacy in religion, either God allows us to base our eternal salvation on the opinions of another or he has given each individual the wherewithal and the responsibility to determine this on his or her own. There is no other viable third choice in his mind.

He is perhaps clearer and more emphatic on this point in *ROC* and its vindications. For instance, in *ROC*, toward the last pages of the book, he believes that it is incumbent upon believers in the fundamental articles of the faith, if they really take Christ as king, to accept all the divine truths that they read in Scripture. And if one cannot understand a text or make multiple texts cohere, that person should suspend their opinion after fair endeavors.[47] Locke believes if Scripture were to be put into the hands of people instead of the systems of others, there would be more Christians and they would be knowledgeable.[48] But he thinks that it is wrong for an authority to put Scripture into the hands of another only to make them understand it as a particular sect does. He then complains how mere humans assume for "themselves a Power of declaring Fundamentals, *i.e.* of setting up a Christianity of their own making . . . Thus Systems, the Inventions of Men, are turn'd into so many opposite Gospels."[49] "[E]very distinct Society of Christians Magisterially ascribes Orthodoxy to a select Set of Fundamentals distinct from those proposed in the Preaching of our Saviour and his Apostles." "[T]heir People are never sent to the Holy Scriptures, that true Fountain of Light, but hoodwink'd."[50] He explicitly blames Protestant sects for advocating implicit faith similar to the Roman Catholics:

> And thus we see how, amongst other good effects, Creed-making always has, and always will necessarily produce and propagate Ignorance in the World, however each Party blames others for it. And therefore, I have often wonder'd to hear Men of several Churches so heartily exclaim against the implicit Faith of the Church of *Rome*; when the same implicit Faith is as

---

[46] Locke, *Essay*, IV.xx.3 [IV.xix.3 in the third edition and earlier].
[47] Locke, *ROC*, 302–4; cf. Locke, *A Second Vindication*, 76–77.
[48] Locke, *A Second Vindication*, 211; cf. Locke, *Vindication*, 8.
[49] Locke, *A Second Vindication*, 212–13 [quotation, p. 213].
[50] Locke, *A Second Vindication*, 216–17.

much practised and required in their own, though not so openly professed, and ingenuously owned there.⁵¹

Although Roman Catholic implicit faith does not entail understanding, for all intents and purposes Locke thinks that the sects do what amounts to the same by advocating that one follow a certain list that the person did not cull for themselves and which is not clearly in Scripture in the way and for the purposes that the authority claims them to be.

Locke refuses to let up on this point in his final assault on Edwards. Locke thinks that we must acknowledge human fallibility in religion and assume errors in others. Calling one's own system orthodox, in comparison to another's, is presumptuous and foolhardy. Still, Locke comments, "'Tis not that I do not think every one should be perswaded of the Truth of those Opinions he professes. 'Tis what I contend for."⁵² Rather, the "Sticklers for Orthodoxy" have frequently not arrived at their system of ideas from their own detailed exploration of Scripture. Just as Locke is persuaded of the truths of Scripture, he allows that others can be likewise persuaded of the truths they find in Scripture without fear of reprisal.⁵³ Locke is not against Systems per se, but rather it is the ill use of them: "so far as they are set up by particular Men or Parties, as the just Measure of every Man's Faith, wherein every thing that is contained, is required and imposed to be believed to make a Man a Christian."⁵⁴

The same lines of thought can be found in the earlier *Letter Concerning Toleration*. There Locke is also concerned that people be persuaded by their own reasoned interaction with Scripture. He writes, "For no Man can, if he would, conform his faith to the Dictates, of another. All the Life and Power of true Religion consists in the inward and full perswasion of the mind."⁵⁵ Soon thereafter he asserts: "But true and saving Religion consist in the inward perswasion of the Mind; without which nothing can be acceptable to God. And such is the nature of the Understanding, that it cannot be compell'd to the belief of any thing by outward Force." Later, when arguing that the government should not force a particular sect on anyone, he offers more of his reasoning why this is so. He writes, "Every man has an Immortal Soul, capable of Eternal Happiness or Misery" and this depends upon following

---

[51] Locke, *A Second Vindication*, 217–18.
[52] Locke, *A Second Vindication*, 380.
[53] Locke, *A Second Vindication*, 380–81.
[54] Locke, *A Second Vindication*, 401.
[55] Locke, *A Second Vindication*, 10.

God's prescriptions to that end. Following God's prescriptions for the sake of our immortal soul is our highest obligation and thus should be attended to by the utmost care.[56] So, we should not be able to disrupt one another. Now Locke quickly qualifies this, noting that he "would not have this understood, as if I meant hereby to condemn all charitable Admonitions, and affectionate Endeavours to reduce Men from Errors; which are indeed the greatest Duty of a Christian" but rather "all Force and Compulsion are to be forborn." In short, no one should force someone to believe something that he or she did not determine on his or her own. In fact, that would not be true faith. "Every man, in that, has the supreme and absolute Authority of judging for himself. And the Reason is, because no body else is concerned in it [his immortal soul]."[57]

Some of what has been drawn out of Locke's works can be observed in Limborch. After asserting that all church councils are subject to error, he writes:

> From what has been said, 'tis plain that there is no visible standing Rule in the Church, whereby to determine with a definitive Sentence all the Controversies in Religion: Every one of the Faithful must be his own Judg to discern the genuine Sense of Scripture from what is False. Every one has his everlasting Salvation at stake, every one must give an account for himself to God both of his Belief and Practice, and therefore every one ought to be his own Judg of the true Sense of Scripture. However this Judgment ought to be Discretionary, for the direction of his own Conscience; not Authoritative, so as to impose his own private Opinions upon others as necessary: according to that of St. *Paul, Who are thou that judgest another Man's Servant? To his own Master he standeth or falleth.*[58]

He, like Locke, argues that we are all responsible for our own souls, and therefore, it is incumbent upon us to search these things out for ourselves and not rely on a fallible authority. And in a letter to Locke, while discussing the present-day Church of England and the ancient councils, he quips, "Popedom is a natural thing to all man, as Luther used to say in his time."[59]

---

[56] Locke, *Letter*, 57.
[57] Locke, *Letter*, 58.
[58] Limborch, *Compleat System*, 38–39.
[59] Philip Van Limborch, "L1112. Philippus Van Limborch to Locke, [2/12 April?] 1689," in *The Correspondence of John Locke*, vol. 3, ed. E. S. de Beer (Oxford: Oxford University Press, 1978), 586–89 [quotation, p. 588].

Simon Patrick also argues against this same sort of implicit faith against which Locke argues. He first complains about the seeming lack of concern about the Bible that many professed Christians have. They do not think upon the supposed ground of their beliefs and thus seem to believe like a Muslim.[60] They simply take claims of authorities at face value and examine no further. "Upon the very same account do many receive Jesus for the Son of God." This is a dishonor to Christ "to have no better subjects, nor a stronger hold, than this, of their hearts."[61] They, unfortunately, rely too heavily on Christ's ministers. All of this is quite like enthusiasm.[62] There are so many cheats in this world that we must exercise caution:[63]

> And we ought not to surrender our belief to any thing carelessly; nor, either out of idleness and sloth, or being over-awed by the confidence which any men assume to themselves, content our selves with an implicite faith: neglecting to search, and prove, and try all things, which demand to have no less than our Souls resigned up unto them. For that which commands our understanding, and hath got authority there, hath a right to govern our Will and command the whole man ... That wariness which was in an Heathen [believing upon authority] sure doth as much or more concern us Christians. Who ought to suspect those would have us believe them, without putting ourselves to the trouble of much search.[64]

Thus, Simon thinks that implicit faith is not believing without knowledge, but it is believing without having searched the doctrines out for oneself. In fact, he thinks it is the duty of the churches to encourage study and research among its people. Not to do so is an affront to Christ.

Theology Is Not to Be Done in Isolation

Locke's emphasis on the individuality of the Christian faith is quite explicit, although this does not mean that he eschewed dialogue and conversation. To

---

[60] Patrick, *Witnesses to Christianity*, 546.
[61] Patrick, *Witnesses to Christianity*, 547.
[62] Patrick, *Witnesses to Christianity*, 548.
[63] Patrick, *Witnesses to Christianity*, 550.
[64] Patrick, *Witnesses to Christianity*, 550–51.

this end, Champion notes, "Importantly for Locke the business of studying scripture was an inherently individual activity, although (as we have seen) he applauded the polishing of ideas by intellectual conversation."[65] There are thousands of pages in the eight volume set of *The Correspondence of John Locke* and in innumerable letters it is quite clear that he is regularly consulting other printed works and colleagues on a variety of theological matters. And the reader of the *Essay* learns that the impetus for the writing of the *Essay* came from a conversation that Locke had among friends. John Marshall notes that this practice was hardly unique to Locke and his circle. He praises a few scholars who have "refocused our attention from 'the Enlightenment' defined as a set of propositions or specific commitments to 'the Enlightenment' defined as a set of practices and processes of criticism and conversation, enquiry and curiosity."[66]

From his preface to *A Paraphrase and Notes on the Epistles of Paul* it is fairly plain why he seems to have emphasized the individuality of our faith and faith practices as opposed to focusing more on the corporate aspects in our research. He thinks that commentaries, for instance, do more harm than good in the hands of many. First, people often defer to the commentators' interpretations out of laziness or doubt in their own gifts, and then turn them into authorities. What is more, most commentators already have their systems in place that they are attempting to prove in the writing of their commentary. In a word, they have too much bias. Locke further notes that the nature of the epistles, for instance, requires reading them in one sitting and repeating that process until the general view and outline comes into focus. Locke found parceled reading with indiscriminate commentary use as being unhelpful.[67] Theology texts would also prove to be a snare to people in the same ways as outlined above. So, while printed materials and conversation with others is helpful, Locke would caution all not to allow such assists as doing too much of the heavy labor.

---

[65] Champion, "A Law of Continuity," 128.
[66] Marshall, *John Locke, Toleration*, 517.
[67] John Locke, *A Paraphrase and Notes on the Epistles of Paul to the Galatians, I and II Corinthians, Romans, and Ephesians. To Which Is Prefixed, An Essay for the Understanding of St. Paul's Epistles, by Consulting St. Paul Himself* (London: Printed for Thomas Tegg, W. Sharpe and Son, etc., 1823), x–xv.

The Necessity of the Number of Articles Being Minimal and Clear: God's Concern for the Vulgar or Commoner

Locke

For Locke, it was eminently reasonable, based on God's character and human frailty that He would make the fundamental articles abundantly clear and few in number. If this were not the case few people would be saved. This is a theme that can be found throughout a number of Locke's works. His most unequivocal statement to this effect is found in the closing pages of *ROC*:

> But considering the frailty of Man, apt to run into corruption and misery, he promised a Deliverer, whom in his good time he sent; And then declared to all Mankind, that whoever would believe him to be the Saviour promised, and take him now raised from the dead, and constituted the Lord and Judge of all Men, to be their King and Ruler, should be saved. This is a plain intelligible Proposition; And the all-merciful God seems herein to have consulted the poor of this World, and the bulk of Mankind. These are Articles that the laboring and illiterate Man may comprehend. This is a Religion suited to vulgar Capacities; And the state of Mankind in this World, destined to labour and travel.[68]

He continues on to chide the "Writers and Wranglers in Religion" who make it seem as if there were "no way into the Church, but through the Academy or Lyceum." He adds that most have no time for lengthy proofs and arguments: "Where the hand is used to the Plough, and the Spade, the head is seldom elevated to sublime Notions, or exercised in Mysterious reasonings." The common human can grasp plain propositions and short reasoning about that which is familiar to them; "Go beyond this, and you amaze the greatest part of Mankind."[69] Moreover, a rather interesting line of argument that Locke employs to emphasize the simplicity of the fundamentals is a comparison of Saint Paul to the other Apostles. While Paul was used mightily by the Lord, it was not until after the gospel was clearly promulgated. This was because often-times advanced learning, like that of Paul, can get in the way of a simple message.[70]

---

[68] Locke, *ROC*, 304–5.
[69] Locke, *ROC*, 305.
[70] Locke, *ROC*, 160.

The theme that fundamental articles are easy to determine due to their clarity and paucity is brought to the fore in Locke's *Vindication*. There he asserts that because of God's goodness and condescension, the Lord "proposed a new Law of Faith to sinful and lost Man, hath by that Law required no harder terms, nothing as absolutely necessary to be believed, but what is suited to Vulgar Capacities, and the Comprehension of Illiterate Men."[71] After asserting that it is not a derogation of Christianity to say that which is necessary to be believed is easily understood by all, he writes, "This I thought my self authorized to say by the very easie, and very intelligible Articles insisted on by our Saviour and his Apostles, which contain nothing but what could be understood by the *bulk of Mankind*." He then expresses puzzlement regarding Edwards's taking offense at his saying this. In seeming exasperation, he announces: "The making of Religions and Creeds I leave to others. I only set down the Christian Religion, as I find our Saviour and his Apostles preached it, and preached it to, and left it for the *Ignorant and unlearned Multitude*."[72] Some pages later he opines about the abundant clarity of the gospel:

> And at last, I think it may be doubted whether any Articles, which need mens Explications, can be so clearly and certainly understood, as one which is made so very plain by Scripture it self, as not to need any Explication at all. Such is this, That Jesus is the *Messiah*. For though you learnedly tell us, that *Messiah* is a Hebrew word, and no better understood by the Vulgar than *Arabick*; Yet I guess it is so fully explained in the New Testament, and in those places I have quoted out of it, that no body, who can understand any ordinary sentence in the Scripture, can be at a loss about it: And 'tis plain it needs no other Explication than what our Saviour and the Apostles gave it in their Preaching; so as they preached it men received it, and that sufficed to make them Believers.[73]

In other words, the fundamental article, Jesus is Messiah, is so clear that it does not even need anyone to explain it. No priest or pastor or theologian need explain or clarify this fundamental article. It requires little to no interpretation and is Scriptural pronouncement at its clearest.

---

[71] Locke, *Vindication*, 30.
[72] Locke, *Vindication*, 32.
[73] Locke, *Vindication*, 35–36.

He repeats much of the same sentiment in other works. In his *A Second Vindication*, in an address to Samuel Bold, he mentions that Christianity is suited to all conditions and capacities and is plain, simple, and reasonable.[74] And later in the same work, but in response to Edwards, he notes that it is due to God's goodness that He has made what is necessary for justification to be easy to understand.[75] He also argues with Edwards that, while he agrees that there are concomitant propositions related to the proposition Jesus is the Messiah, "no more is required to be believed concerning any Article, than is contain'd in that Article"[76] and that it stands to reason that necessary doctrines are proposed in the express words of Scripture.[77] In the *Essay*, in a section prior to one addressed above concerning God's equipping humans to judge religions for themselves, he writes of the common plight of most:

> These Men's Opportunity of Knowledge and Enquiry, are commonly as narrow as their Fortunes; and their Understandings are but little instructed, when all their whole Time and Pains is laid out, to still the Croaking of their own Bellies, or the Cries of their Children. 'Tis not to be expected, that a Man, who drudges on, all his Life, in a laborious Trade, should be more knowing in the variety of Things done in the World, than a Pack-horse, who is driven constantly forwards and backwards, in a narrow Lane, and dirty Road, only to Market, should be skilled in the Geography of the Country. Nor is it all more possible, that he who wants Leisure, Books, and Languages, and the Opportunity of Conversing with a variety of Men, should be in a Condition to collect those Testimonies and Observations, which are in Being, and are necessary to make out many, nay most of the Propositions, that, in the Societies of Men, are judged of the greatest Moment; or to find out Grounds of Assurance so great, as the Belief of the points he would build on them, is thought necessary. So that a great part of Mankind are, by the natural and unalterable State of Things in this World, and the Constitution of humane Affairs, unavoidably given over to invincible Ignorance of those Proofs, on which others build, and which are necessary to establish those Opinions: The greatest part of Men, having much to do to get the Means of Living, are not in a Condition to look after those of learned and laborious Enquiries.[78]

---

[74] Locke, *A Second Vindication*, xvi; cf. 85 86.
[75] Locke, *A Second Vindication*, 39; cf. 76–77.
[76] Locke, *A Second Vindication*, 101.
[77] Locke, *A Second Vindication*, 336.
[78] Locke, *Essay*, IV.xx.2 [IV.xix.2 in the third edition and earlier].

The above excerpt has a rather easy application. Most people do not have the opportunity to assent, in a proper fashion, to intricate theologies or systems of thought. Most humans do not have the leisure of the learned and thus many theologians and pastors should lower their (and God's) expectations of most of the parishioners.

Although not focused specifically on the fundamental articles, he does show God's concern for human frailty in his argument for the superiority of the delivery of moral teaching through special revelation. Locke thinks that the New Testament gives humans a morality superior to all the philosophers. He argues that even if all the moral precepts in the New Testament had been given at one time by various people and they were collected, there would still be an issue of authority. One would have to show his morals as authoritative from reason—and thus prove all of them through a mathematical-like demonstration from self-evident first principles—or from revelation—and thus the agent would have to show that he or she is a divine agent. But, even if the former could be done, most people do not have the time or capacity for proofs and so such authority would be to no effect. Thus, God in his mercy, delivers us a perfect system of morality through revelation. And anyone who is persuaded of Christ's (and his Apostles') authority must take all his commands as principles. No proof is required other than he said it. "All the Duties of Morality lye there clear, and plain, and easy to be understood. And here I appeal, whether this be not the surest, the safest, and most effectual way of teaching: Especially if we add this farther consideration; That as it suits the lowest Capacities of Reasonable Creatures, so it reaches and satisfies, nay, enlightens the highest."[79]

Others

The notion that God made the true faith simple, out of His care and concern for the vulgar, was also expressed by various of Locke's contemporaries. Although not focusing on fundamental articles per se, Gilbert Burnet notes in one of his works that Christianity is based upon the clear and extraordinary miracles indicating that Jesus is the foretold of and long-expected Messiah and that we should thus listen to all that he (and his Apostles) have to

---

[79] Locke, *ROC*, 269–84 [quotation, p. 184]. Cf. the discussion in Marko, "The Promulgation of Right Morals," and also Chapter 5.

say. The truth of His mission is unquestionable. "For any thing less will not be of weight to turn the scales in the opinion of any one, whether of an inferior or more exalted understanding . . . and there needs no assistance of learning, no deep thought to come to a certainty in it."[80] In other words, the proofs are more than sufficient for the educated and for the commoner. In another work he writes: "Religion being a design to recover and save Mankind, was to be so opened as to awaken and work upon all sorts of people: and generally men of a simplicity of Mind." That is why God needed to send such clear and "alarming Evidences."[81] In Burnet's minds, "Nothing [but Christianity] is more for the Interests of every man in particular."[82] What is more, not just its precepts are clear and plain, but its worship is "plain and simple." In the beginning of Christianity there were no secrets "but every thing was open to all *Christians*."[83] While appearing to affirm much traditional doctrine, he thinks that the theologians have not made things clearer but simply more complicated in their debates.[84] "But if Mysteries were received, rather in the simplicity in which they are delivered in the Scriptures, than according to the decantings of fanciful men upon them, they would not appear much more incredible, than some of the Objects of sense and perception."[85]

Samuel Bold maintains Locke's sentiments without much or any deviation. While God requires all to make fair endeavors into His word, more is expected from some and less from others:

> Peoples *Capacities, Opportunities,* and *Advantages* are very *various* and *different*. Many things may be *necessary* for some Christians to *believe,* which are not *necessary* to be believed by *others*; because some do attain to the knowledge of them, and a great many more may never attain to the knowledge of them, and this is not because of any *faulty omission* or *neglect* to use their *honest endeavours,* to understand what *Christ* hath made known to the World, but from *something else* which will not be *reckoned* to them for a *fault*.[86]

---

[80] Burnet, *Treatise*, 12.
[81] Burnet, *Some Passages*, 85–86; cf. Marshall, *John Locke, Toleration*, 709–11.
[82] Burnet, *Some Passages*, 93.
[83] Burnet, *Some Passages*, 95.
[84] Burnet, *Some Passages*, 104–6.
[85] Burnet, *Some Passages*, 107.
[86] Bold, *A Short Discourse*, 30.

In sum, what one finds in Scripture must be believed. Otherwise, a person is no Christian. That said, for those with less opportunity and/or gifts, it would be ridiculous to think that they will be held liable for not attaining to the same doctrinal specificity as those with learning and leisure. If it were, their low standing would be counted as a fault. Toward the end of the same work, he argues that it is not a blemish for Christianity to have so few articles but a blessing. "But the matter is so ordered, that nothing is made necessary to *constitute* a Person a Christian, but what the meanest of *Mankind* is capable of."[87]

The Reasonableness of the Fundamental Articles Given Expressly from the Messiah: Continuity of the Church and the Definition of a Christian

ROC and Its *Vindications*

In the final pages of *ROC* Locke asks and answers the question: To what purpose were the Epistles written if they were not necessary for justification (based on his assertion that the fundamental articles are promulgated in the gospels and Acts). He posits that because the Epistles were written to those who were Christians already, they could not teach them any fundamental articles or points necessary to justification.[88] In another place he writes the following:

> The Epistles therefore being all written to those who were already Believers and Christians, the occasion and end of writing them, could not be to Instruct them in that which was necessary to make them Christians. This 'tis plain they knew and believed already; or else they could not have been Christians and Believers. And they were writ upon Particular Occasions; and without those Occasions had not been writ; and so cannot be thought necessary to Salvation: Though they resolving doubts, and reforming Mistakes, are of great Advantage to our Knowledge and Practice. I do not deny, but the great doctrines of the Christian Faith are dropt here and there, and scattered up and down in most of them. But 'tis not in the Epistles we are

---

[87] Bold, *A Short Discourse*, 53. A similar concern was noted by Turretin, *Institutes of Elenctic Theology*, I.xiv.7; cf. I.xiv.13.

[88] Locke, *ROC*, 293–98; cf. Locke, *A Second Vindication*, 133–45.

to learn what are the Fundamental Articles of Faith, where they are promiscuously, and without distinction mixed with other Truths in Discourses that were (though for Edification indeed, yet) only occasional. We shall find and discern those great and necessary Points best in the Preaching of our Saviour and the Apostles, to those who were yet strangers, and ignorant of the Faith, to bring them in, and convert them to it.[89]

In short, one of the primary intents of the gospels and Acts is laying out the fundamentals as clearly as possible. That is not the intent of the Epistles. What is more, "If all, or most of the Truths declared in the Epistles, were to be received and believed as Fundamental Articles, what then became of those Christians who were fallen asleep?" Locke adds, "Most of the Epistles not being written till about Twenty Years after our Saviour's Ascension, and some after Thirty."[90] In other words, there were true believers in the faith who were not privy to the doctrinal content of the Epistles.

Locke is pressed by Edwards to defend his position on the justificatory non-necessity of the Epistles, which he does in *A Second Vindication*. To this end he points out that "The Primitive Church admitted converted Heathens to Baptism, upon the Faith contain'd in the Apostles Creed." Locke, using Tertullian for support, comments, "How little different the Faith of the Ancient Church was from the Faith I have mentioned."[91] So, in an open address to Edwards, he asks: does the Church of England, who also baptizes upon profession of the Apostles' Creed, baptize believers or no?[92]

Locke also presses back on four statements made by Edwards in *Socinianism Unmask'd* made in response to Locke's teaching on fundamentals: (1) believing that Jesus was the Messiah was only the first step of the Christian faith, (2) there is reason to think that there were other propositions proposed, (3) all parts of the faith do not happen in one portion of Scripture, and (4) Christianity was erected by degrees.[93] While Edwards thinks he has "satisfied" Locke's curiosity regarding why he rejects his minimal fundamentals, he is mistaken. Locke calls on Edwards to prove all of this beyond the several pages that he offered but then points out the unreasonableness of Edwards's claims. Focusing on Edwards's first point, Locke asserts

---

[89] Locke, *ROC*, 297–98; cf. Locke, *A Second Vindication*, 76–77. In the following pages of *ROC* he offers a taxonomy of the epistles based upon their characteristics and purpose.
[90] Locke, *ROC*, 300.
[91] Locke, *A Second Vindication*, 177–78.
[92] Locke, *A Second Vindication*, 178–79.
[93] Edwards, *Socinianism Unmask'd*, 74–79; Locke, *A Second Vindication*, 238.

that maintaining the one article—Jesus is the Messiah—is simply paving the way for the rest is tantamount to believing "That *Jesus* was the Person which was to teach them the true Religion, but that true Religion it self is not to be found in all their [his] Preaching."[94] Regarding the second point, Locke points out that three thousand were saved during Peter's short sermon in Acts and that none of Edwards's articles that go beyond Locke's short list are there. With the second and third points in mind, he asks, if all the necessary points for salvation are not set down in the histories of Christ, why are they called the gospels?[95] Locke does admit there are other propositions present in the gospels and Acts, like the crucifixion, death, and resurrection of Christ that must be believed; but, he argues, as stated earlier, that those propositions all are put forth to show Jesus is the Messiah: "For whatever is brought as an Argument to prove another Truth, cannot be thought to be the principal thing aimed at in that argumentation; though it may have so strong and immediate a connexion with the Conclusion, that you cannot deny it without denying even what is inferr'd from it, and is therefore the fitter to be an Argument to prove it." Therefore, and as stated earlier, Locke thinks such concomitant articles do not count as separate articles from the one, Jesus is the Messiah.[96]

The fourth point promulgated by Edwards is the most important as it builds upon the others. Edwards thinks that "*Christianity* was erected by degrees." He further notes that we are not to assume that all the present-day necessary doctrines were advanced in Jesus' time. Rather, "Not but that all that were necessary for *that time* were published: but some which were necessary for the *succeeding one* were not then discover'd, or at least not fully." He indexes that some were saved prior to even knowing Christ would die and rise.[97] One of Locke's main points against this idea is "that the Covenant of Grace in Christ Jesus had been but one, immutably the same" and so if the conditions change this immutable covenant cannot remain the same: "Every change of Conditions in my apprehension makes a new and another Covenant."[98]

---

[94] Locke, *A Second Vindication*, 250.
[95] Locke, *A Second Vindication*, 254–60.
[96] Locke, *A Second Vindication*, 268–69 [quotation, p. 269]; cf. 300–11. It is on p. 300 where Locke recognizes that Edwards might mean something different from him when they use the term "necessary" regarding fundamentals.
[97] Edwards, *Socinianism Unmask'd*, 78–79 [quotation, p. 78].
[98] Locke, *A Second Vindication*, 314.

Locke's *Letter* and Express "Fundamentals"

While Locke asserts that it would be peculiar for the Savior not to have preached the fundamental articles of the faith, he is, perhaps, nowhere clearer that fundamental articles of the faith must be "express" than in *A Letter Concerning Toleration*. There is no evidence that *ROC* was even an idea in his mind at the time. In the *Letter*'s "Postscript" he wants to answer the question: What qualifies religions as different (or actually being the same). His answer in brief is: "it is manifest that those who have one and the same Rule of Faith and Worship, are of the same Religion."[99] Muslims, who abide by the Alcoran, and Christians are obviously different religions, but so are Lutherans and Roman Catholics. Although the latter groups both identify themselves as followers of Christ, they are not the same religion: "because These [Lutherans] acknowledge nothing but the Holy Scriptures to be the Rule and Foundation of their Religion" while "Those [Roman Catholics] take in also Traditions and the Decrees of Popes, and of all three together make the Rule of their Religion."[100]

He then turns to comment on the notion of heresy. He defines heresy as being "a Separation made in Ecclesiastical Communion between men of the same Religion, for some Opinions no way contained in the Rule it self" or "That amongst those who acknowledge nothing but the Holy Scriptures to be their Rule of Faith, Heresie is a Separation made in their Christian Communion, for Opinions not contained in the express words of Scripture."[101] And there are two types of heresies in the latter case. The first type is when the greater part expels a smaller part "because they will not profess their Belief of certain Opinions which are not to be found in the express words of Scripture." The second type occurs, "When any one separates himself from the Communion of the Church, because that Church does not publickly profess some certain Opinions which the Holy Scriptures do not expressly teach"[102] Locke then briefly summarizes: "Both these are *Hereticks: because they err in Fundamentals, and they err obstinately against Knowledge.*"[103] He does not mean, here, that the fundamentals count as certain truths but rather that we *know* that they are unquestionably asserted

---

[99] Locke, *Letter*, 81.
[100] Locke, *Letter*, 82.
[101] Locke, *Letter*, 82.
[102] Locke, *Letter*, 83.
[103] Locke, *Letter*, 83.

in Scripture. Because many Christian doctrines are interpretations and opinions, to separate based on them is to err in fundamentals and against knowledge. Locke's assault on separations based on opinions and not express words of Scripture amounts to his charging these churches with having other authorities in addition to Scripture:

> And to make a Separation for such things as these, which neither are nor can be fundamental, is to become Hereticks. For I do not think there is any man arrived to that degree of madness, as that he dare give out his Consequences and Interpretations of Scripture as Divine Inspirations, and compare the Articles of Faith that he has framed according to his own Fancy with the Authority of the Scripture. I know there are some Propositions so evidently agreeable to Scripture, that no body can deny them to be drawn from thence; but about those therefore there can be no difference. This only I say, that however clearly we may think this or the other Doctrine to be deduced from Scripture, we not ought therefore to impose it upon others, as a necessary Article of Faith, because we believe it to be agreeable to the Rule of Faith; unless we would be content also that other Doctrines should be imposed upon us in the same manner; and that we should be compell'd to receive and profess all the different and contradictory Opinions of *Lutherans*, *Calvininst*, *Remonstrants*, *Anabaptists*, and other Sects, which the Contrivers of Symbols, Systems and Confessions, are accustomed to deliver unto their Followers as genuine and necessary Deductions from the Holy Scripture. I cannot but wonder at the extravagant arrogance of those Men who think that they themselves can explain things necessary to Salvation more clearly than the Holy Ghost, the Eternal and Infinite Wisdom of God.[104]

Many doctrines that form the basis of disagreement and separation are simply interpretations and opinions. They are epistemologically illegitimate bases upon which to base splits.

In *ROC*, he counted as fundamentals the propositions preached by Christ and the Apostles by which one is justified. Christians are obligated to accept the New Testament and anything that they think Scripture advances, based on their own thoughtful interpretations of it, as true if they really take Christ as king. Thus, the express propositions and one's thoughtful interpretation

---

[104] Locke, *Letter*, 84–85.

of the Bible are necessary in qualified senses. In the *Letter*, he appears not to have yet made a distinction between the two fundamentals noted in *ROC* and the other express words of Scripture, or the so-called fundamentals in the *Letter*. Instead, he seems to consider the New Testament functionally as a whole in the *Letter* and not functionally as a body compiled over a period of time as he does in *ROC*. Whatever the case, he is unequivocal in his desire that the fundamentals, either in the sense of the term used in *ROC* or the sense of the term in the *Letter*, are expressly in Scripture and that to give oneself unthoughtfully and unscrutinizingly to the interpretations of another, is to take that person as one's authority alongside of Scripture.

Lim's Study on Baxter: "Antient Simplicity" and "Scripture Sufficiency"

There are a number of similarities between the theological thinking of Richard Baxter, as presented in Paul Lim's recent study, and John Locke given above. Lim's thesis for one of his chapters in *In Pursuit of Purity, Unity, and Liberty* is: "As the issues of doctrinal unity and the limits of acceptable orthodoxy were hotly debated during the 1650s, he [Baxter] proposed a radical return to 'Scripture sufficiency' and pre-Nicene doctrinal purity, a view often interpreted by his high Calvinist opponents as similar to Socinianism."[105] What is more, Lim points out that Baxter was hardly alone in these convictions. John Davenant, Joseph Hall, and William Chillingworth, just to name a few, held the same positions and pre-dated Baxter.[106] Lim explains that in a time when confessions abounded to counter heterodoxy, Baxter instead believed that these confessions that were rife with non-scriptural language would confound the laity instead of giving them clarity.[107] For Baxter, the Bible was authoritative but God provided people with three symbols of ancient catholicity for their aid: the Lord's Prayer, the Ten Commandments or Decalogue, and the Apostles' Creed. All other creeds, were considered man-made by Baxter and, in the end, prove divisive.[108] In his 1658 *Judgment and Advice* he writes:

---

[105] Lim, *In Pursuit of Purity, Unity*, 157.
[106] Lim, *In Pursuit of Purity, Unity*, 164, 176–77.
[107] Lim, *In Pursuit of Purity, Unity*, 160.
[108] Lim, *In Pursuit of Purity, Unity*, 172.

the great cause of uncharitable censures and divisions, hath been our departing from the Antient simplicity of faith, and also from the sufficiency of the holy Scripture to be the Rule and Test of our Faith: And till we return to the Scripture sufficiency, and antient simplicity, there is no hope of the antient Christian Unity and Charity, while proud men thrust their own Opinions into the Churches Creed, or un-Church all that hold not such Opinions.[109]

For Baxter, the justificatory fundamentals did not go beyond the three ancient symbols all of which are found in Scripture or use Scriptural language and did not extend to the so-called ecumenical creeds of the ecumenical councils, the first six of which were typically accepted by Protestants. In the end, Lim proposes that "Baxter may be seen as a representative of the disciplinarian school, who, instead of doctrinal precision, sought to propose Scripture sufficiency and primitive purity of doctrine, combined with assiduous oversight and pastoral discipline."[110]

So, Locke was not alone in an emphasis on the need of fundamentals, in the sense used in the *Letter* and in the sense used by *ROC*, being expressly in Scripture. And he was not alone, even among those typically considered orthodox in the period, who would happily pass over the pronouncements of ecumenical councils in the test of orthodoxy. For many in the period, the definition of Christian and the fundamentals whereby one becomes a Christian do not change depending on the era.

Corollary: Toleration

Context

England had good reason to have a general feeling of unsettledness in the 1690s, given the number of doctrinal debates raging at the time. The Church of England was trying to come to grips with the impact of Unitarians and debate between Calvinists and Arminians, as well as the problem of

---

[109] Richard Baxter, *The Judgment and Advice of the Assembly of the Associated Ministers of Worcester--shire, Held at Worcester Aug. 6th 1658. Concerning the Endeavours of Ecclesiasticall Peace, and the Waies and Meanes of Christian Unity, which Mr. John Durey Doth Present; Sent unto Him in the Name, and by the Appointment of the Aforesaid Assembly* (London: Printed for T. Underhill, 1658), 4. Quoted by Lim, *In Pursuit of Purity, Unity*, 180.

[110] Lim, *In Pursuit of Purity, Unity*, 182.

non-conformity. It is not surprising, then, that debates on different doctrines had and would arise, some of which would evidence internal disagreement on these loci even within the individual sects. The late 1600s had no shortage of theological commentators on issues like justification, the Trinity, atonement, relationship of faith and reason, and, of course, fundamental articles.

The general state of religious unrest and desires for peace and toleration are common talking-points in the Locke–Limborch correspondences. In one letter, Locke writes, "I would wish the number of peace-seekers to increase daily, especially among the Reformed [Protestants], among who too many quarrels are engendered every day."[111] He also talks of the "captious Christians, who approve of nothing that is not their own" and "who measure the Christian religion with their own yardstick"[112] Locke and Limborch also regularly write of the intolerance of the Roman Catholic Church. And although it seems to be the paradigm of an intolerant sect, it is hardly the only one to be intolerant of dissenting religious opinions. To this effect, Locke, in writing to Limborch about the latter's book on the history of the Inquisitions, pens the following: "You do rightly in condemning persecution on account of religion in Romanists only. If you should pick out and stigmatize for its cruelty any particular sect among Christians you will be commended by the rest of them, though persecution is the same everywhere and plainly popish; for any church whatsoever lays claims in words to orthodoxy and in practice to infallibility."[113] And, Limborch, in commenting on the failed attempts churches have had in making peace, writes, "All make the cause of Christ and the Church their pretext; but if they were not seeking to further their own interests they would not impose unfair conditions of peace upon others or reject fair ones when offered to themselves."[114] Locke and Limborch also discuss the strife between the Presbyterians and Episcopalians.[115]

---

[111] John Locke, "L868. Locke to Philippus Van Limborch, 1/11 October [1686]," in *The Correspondence of John Locke*, vol. 3, ed. E. S. de Beer (Oxford: Oxford University Press, 1978), 43–45 [quotation, pp. 44–45].

[112] John Locke, "L964. Locke to Philippus Van Limborch, 13/23 September 1687," in *The Correspondence of John Locke*, vol. 3, ed. E. S. de Beer (Oxford: Oxford University Press, 1978), 270–72 [quotation, p. 271].

[113] John Locke, "L1473. Locke to Philippus Van Limborch, 29 February 1692," in *The Correspondence of John Locke*, vol. 4, ed. E. S. de Beer (Oxford: Oxford University Press, 1979), 399–403 [quotation, pp. 401–2].

[114] Philip Van Limborch, "L1283. Philippus Van Limborch to Locke, 15/25 April 1690," in *The Correspondence of John Locke*, vol. 4, ed. E. S. de Beer (Oxford: Oxford University Press, 1979), 55–60 [quotation, pp. 59–60].

[115] Philip Van Limborch, "L1101. Philippus Van Limborch to Locke, 27 January/6 February 1689," in *The Correspondence of John Locke*, vol. 3, ed. E. S. de Beer (Oxford: Oxford University Press, 1978), 542–44; John Locke, "L1127. Locke to Philippus Van Limborch, 12 April 1689," in *The Correspondence of John Locke*, vol. 3, ed. E. S. de Beer (Oxford: Oxford University Press, 1978), 596–601.

Also in their letters, one can observe quite easily the reason for their alarm: they are concerned with the peoples' liberties of conscience. In one letter to Limborch, Locke writes that nothing "should be imposed on the consciences of Christians except what is contained in the clear and express words of Holy Writ." He continues on, opining, "I should have readily believed that it would be so were not more attention paid to Orthodoxy of factions than to the simple truth of the Gospel."[116] In pondering what might come of the Prince of Orange's ascendancy in England, Limborch hopes that they may "see the emergence of complete toleration, by which no man's conscience may be forced even in the smallest degree"[117] Elsewhere, he writes:

> If, however, peace in the Church cannot be achieved amongst such determined adversaries [Presbyterians and Episcopalians], at least may so much restraint prevail amongst them all that each may willingly grant to another the liberty which he desire for himself, and that force be done to no man's conscience, of whatever persuasion he may be; for liberty is the right of all alike.[118]

Recall that liberty of conscience is so important for them, at the very least, for purposes of eternal salvation.

Something of the designs of *ROC* comes out in the Locke–Limborch discussion as well. Limborch writes to Locke that "For [by reading *ROC*] it will become clear that those things which are now insisted on by the majority as almost the sole foundation of Christianity are not included in the object of faith. This is the sole remedy for abolishing anathemas, schisms, and hatreds."[119] In reply, Locke comments that he hopes through the books that "the truth and foundation of the Christian religion tear up the roots of quarrels and schisms, so far as that is possible."[120]

---

[116] John Locke, "L1804. Locke to Philippus Van Limborch, 26 October 1694," in *The Correspondence of John Locke*, vol. 5, ed. E. S. de Beer (Oxford: Oxford University Press, 1979), 169–75 [quotation, p. 173].

[117] Philip Van Limborch, "L1158. Phillipus Van Limborch to Locke, 8/18 July 1689," in *The Correspondence of John Locke*, vol. 3, ed. E. S. de Beer (Oxford: Oxford University Press, 1978), 646–50 [quotation, p. 647].

[118] Limborch, "L1101," 543.

[119] Philip Van Limborch, "L2110. Philippus Van Limborch to Locke 14/24 July 1696," in *The Correspondence of John Locke*, vol. 5, ed. E. S. de Beer (Oxford: Oxford University Press, 1979), 665–71 [quotation, p. 668].

[120] John Locke, "L2126. Locke to Philippus Van Limborch, 3 September 1696," in *The Correspondence of John Locke*, vol. 5, ed. E. S. de Beer (Oxford: Oxford University Press, 1979), 694–97 [quotation, p. 696].

Locke and Toleration

Locke's *Letter* is well-known as an important work that promotes religious toleration. While Locke thought churches that split or excluded others for doctrines that require interpretation is heresy, he nonetheless speaks to those who are living in this unfortunate, fractured reality. Toleration is required and is the only salve. And perhaps once achieved, healing and unification can begin. In the first page of the *Letter*, he asserts, "I esteem that Toleration to be the chief Characteristical Mark of the True Church." On the very next, he writes, "It is in vain for any Man to usurp the Name of Christian, without Holiness of Life, Purity of Manners, and Benignity and Meekness of Spirit." He argues throughout the *Letter* that each religious society can rule within the bounds of their society but that their authority should not extend out to civil and worldly issues. For instance, in one place he writes:

> The end of a Religious Society (as has already been said) is the Publick Worship of God, and by means thereof the acquisition of Eternal Life. All Discipline ought therefore to tend to that End, and all Ecclesiastical Laws to be thereunto confined. Nothing ought, nor can be transacted in this Society, relating to the Possession of Civil and Worldly Goods. No Force is here to be made use of, upon any occasion whatsoever. For Force belongs wholly to the Civil Magistrate, and the Possession of all outward Goods is subject to his Jurisdiction."[121]

In short, limiting the reaches of the various religious societies will help create a country with liberty of conscience. More of this can be seen in his unpacking of the above statement. He argues that no church should be able to impose financial or bodily penalties in the cases of excommunication[122] and that no harm should come to one's civil enjoyment because one is part of a different church than that of the magistrate.[123] What is more, the boundaries between the churches and the civil government are immovable. They are not to overreach into the area of the other except for in unusual circumstances.[124] The Clergy cannot affect the worldly and civil well-being of any person[125]

---

[121] Locke, *Letter*, 17.
[122] Locke, *Letter*, 18–19.
[123] Locke, *Letter*, 20.
[124] Locke, *Letter*, 25.
[125] Locke, *Letter*, 25–26.

and the government cannot forcibly keep a man from bringing ruin upon himself.[126] If the arrangement were any different the consciences of many would be bound, most importantly in the area of eternal salvation.

The theme of toleration appears in Locke's *Essay* as well. He notes in his chapter on assent that those who have toiled to understand their doctrine and are past doubt are typically less imposing of others.[127] He actually likens peoples' assumptions of authority to dictate their opinions to others with little or no reasonable evidence to enthusiasm.[128] Thus Locke indicates an important connection in his *Essay*: the correlation between toleration and reasonableness. In the final pages of the *Essay*, Locke writes at length of those who fight over religion. He thinks that the doctrines over which many make a commotion, "they have no Thought, no Opinion at all." Perhaps in feigned repentance, he writes, "I must do mankind that Right, as to say, *There are not so many Men in Errours, and wrong Opinions, as is commonly supposed*."[129] He thinks that most of such people have never looked into the doctrinal matters over which they fight. He asserts, later in the section, "They are resolved to stick to a Party, that Education or Interest has engaged them in; and there, like the common Soldiers of an Army, shew their Courage and Warmth, as their Leaders direct, without ever examining, or so much as knowing the Cause they contend for."[130] Locke wonders why these people care so much about religion when they have never given any serious thought to it. He thinks it is simply because people will serve the leaders of a cause that benefits them. He ends the section with:

> Thus Men become Professors of, and Combatants for those Opinions, they were never convinced of, nor Proselytes to; no, nor ever had so much as floating in their Heads: And though one cannot say, there are fewer improbable or erroneous Opinions in the World than there are; yet this is certain, there are fewer, that actually assent to them, and mistake them for truths, than is imagined.[131]

His main thrust is that most do not walk around with strong religious opinions; they actually walk around with no opinions about religion. They

---

[126] Locke, *Letter*, 29–30.
[127] Locke, *Essay*, IV.xvi.4.
[128] Locke, *Essay*, IV.xix.2.
[129] Locke, *Essay*, IV.xx.18 [IV.xix.18 in the third edition and earlier].
[130] Locke, *Essay*, IV.xx.18 [IV.xix.18 in the third edition and earlier].
[131] Locke, *Essay*, IV.xx.18 [IV.xix.18 in the third edition and earlier].

have never thought about it. At best, they illegitimately decided to follow a particular authority or authorities for particular ends, few, if any, of which are religious. His immense concern for toleration is perhaps reflected in his essential conclusion of the *Essay* with the above excerpt (the next chapter, the very short "Of the Divisions of Science," seems more of a modern-day appendix than anything).

Similar statements concerning toleration are found in *ROC*. In the last two pages of that work, he mentions a justification controversy between the Dissenters and the Conformists. The congregations of the former claim to have the more learned leaders. Locke's response to that is: "But I ask them to tell me seriously, whether half their People have leisure to study? Nay, Whether one in ten of those who come to their Meetings in the Country, if they had time to study them, do or can understand, the Controversies at this time so warmly managed amongst them, about Justification, the subject of this present Treatise?" Locke even claims that he has talked to some of their teachers and they admit that they do not understand the controversy. He remarks what a shame it is: "And yet the points they stand on, are reckoned of so great weight, so material, so fundamental in Religion, that they divide Communion and separate upon them."[132]

Thus, it is not only in the *Essay*, but also in *ROC*, where Locke uses his final pages to push for religious toleration. This is perhaps not so surprising to those familiar with *ROC*, but those familiar primarily with the *Essay* have not duly recognized it. His concern for religious toleration not only creates a more civil and tolerant society, but it is, more importantly, necessary for individuals coming to their own personal and reasoned convictions about the gospel and thus the fates of their eternal souls. If leaders, civil and religious, are truly concerned for their people, they will be eminently concerned for their souls, and will thus give them room to have an opportunity, without discouragement, to take Christ as their King on the King's terms and not that of the leaders. Christians who have room to arrive at convictions themselves will be all the better for it. They will be better promulgators of the gospel and show the reasonableness and attractiveness of Christianity to non-believers because they have internalized Biblical principles through hard work. Then, there will be even more converts, and so on. And when this is done, it stands to reason, that society will be a better place.

---

[132] Locke, *ROC*, 306.

PART II
THE REASONABLENESS OF REVELATION

5
John Locke on the Necessity of Scripture Amidst the Innate Idea Controversy and the Rise of Deism

An apparent diastasis between two of John Locke's most noted works, *An Essay Concerning Human Understanding* (*Essay*) and *The Reasonableness of Christianity* (*ROC*), concerning the epistemology of moral principles has caught the attention of Locke scholars in recent generations.[1] In the former work, he lays out arguments against the innate ideas and principles tradition, and expressly against the thought of one of their number, Lord Herbert of Cherbury,[2] noting, among other things, that because we have faculties that can prove so-called innate principles to be certain, it is unlikely, therefore, that they are innate: "no less unreasonable would it be to attribute several Truths, to the Impressions of Nature, and innate Characters, when we may observe in our selves Faculties, fit to attain as easie and certain Knowledge of them."[3] Some think that, due to Locke's emphases on moral principles and human reason in the *Essay* and his professed desire elsewhere to produce a work demonstrating moral principles, his magnum opus is at least in part

---

[1] John Locke, *The Reasonableness of Christianity, as Delivered in the Scriptures*, 2nd ed. (London: Awnsham and John Churchil, 1696); cf. John Locke, *The Reasonableness of Christianity: As Delivered in the Scriptures*, ed. John C. Higgins-Biddle (Oxford: Clarendon Press, 1999). I have researched both and note the page numbers of only the 1696 second edition in the footnotes. John Locke, *A Vindication of the Reasonableness of Christianity, etc, from Mr. Edwards's Reflections* (London: Awnsham and John Churchil, 1695). This defense was published with the 1696 second edition of *ROC*. John Locke, *A Second Vindication of the Reasonableness of Christianity, etc.* (London: A. and J. Churchil, 1697); John Locke, *An Essay Concerning Humane Understanding*, 3rd ed. (London: Awnsham and John Churchil, 1695); John Locke, *An Essay Concerning Human Understanding*, ed. Peter H. Nidditch (Oxford: Clarendon Press, 1979). The 1695 third edition that existed at the writing of Locke's *ROC* and its two vindications has been consulted along with Nidditch's critical edition. John Locke, *A Letter Concerning Toleration*, 2nd ed. corrected (London: Awnsham Churchill, 1690).

[2] *Edward, Lord Herbert of Cherbury, De Veritate*, trans. Myrick H. Carré (Bristol: J. W. Arrowsmith, Ltd., 1937).

[3] Locke, *Essay*, I.ii.1.

a ground-clearing project toward fulfilling that desire.[4] Locke's *ROC*, however, which he claims to be ecumenical in thrust but in opposition to the natural religion of deism, stresses the need for divine revelation for ascertaining right moral principles. This seeming incongruity regarding Locke's differently described attainments of moral principles in his two works has perplexed some.[5] One noted scholar sums up the problem, asking, if Locke did not think morality demonstrable, as seems to be the case in *ROC*, why did he write the *Essay*?[6] The claim that Locke changed his position in the mid-1690s cannot be sustained inasmuch as to the end of his life, Locke maintained in all editions that moral principles can be proven and made certain.

Scholarship has responded to the apparent inconsistencies between the two works in different ways. The scholars who read Locke as religiously surreptitious (because corrosive) see this inconsistency as evidence that Locke appeals to the Bible (exoterically) while simultaneously trying to undercut its authority (esoterically). One scholar argues that Locke's *ROC* is a covert attempt to nudge his readers toward the fully natural theology promulgated by deism, the very position against which Locke claims to be debating in that

---

[4] Cf. Locke, *Essay*, I.ii.1; IV.iv.7. In the following letter Locke speaks of his desire to write a work demonstrating moral principles though he confesses the Gospels already contain "so perfect a body of Ethicks": John Locke, "L2059: Locke to William Molyneux, March 30 [c. April 5] 1696," in *The Correspondence of John Locke, vol. 5*, ed. E. S. de Beer (Oxford: Clarendon Press, 1979), 593–96. Also, those who view the *Essay* as a ground-clearing project most likely find further evidence for their position in the *Essay*'s "Epistle to the Reader." There Locke fashions himself as "*an Under-Labourer in clearing Ground a little, and removing some of the Rubbish, that lies in the way to Knowledge*."

[5] For example, John Dunn, *The Political Thought of John Locke: An Historical Account of the Argument of the 'Two Treatises of Government,'* (Cambridge: Cambridge University Press, 1969), 189–98; Richard Ashcraft, "Faith and Knowledge in Locke's Philosophy," in *John Locke: Problems and Perspectives*, ed. John W. Yolton (Cambridge: Cambridge University Press, 1969), 194–223. Ashcraft admits that he is not sure how these two works can be reconciled at all points. Others have made more headway in understanding the relationship between the two works. Victor Nuovo, *John Locke: The Philosopher as Christian Virtuoso* (Oxford: Oxford University Press, 2017), 216. For Nuovo, the *Essay* points to morality as humanity's proper business and the necessity of joining it with religion. This union of morality and religion was the thrust of *ROC*. Diego Lucci, *John Locke's Christianity* (Cambridge: Cambridge University Press, 2020), 27–28, 47. Lucci notes that *ROC* was written, in part, because "whereas he deemed morality demonstrable (at least in principle), he doubted the human capacity to *actually* demonstrate morality through the operation of natural reason" (28). J. T. Moore, "Locke on the Moral Need for Christianity," *The Southwestern Journal of Philosophy* 11 (1980): 61–68. Moore sees *ROC* as a salvaging of sorts of the *Essay*. He argues, however, that anyone who has cited reason vis-à-vis morality as a logical disjunction between the two works has overlooked an important subtlety: while morality is presented being *in fact* according to reason in the *Essay* it is presented as being above reason only *in effect* to most in *ROC*. In my estimation, this is consistent with Locke's assertion in the *Essay* and *ROC* that many people who do not have the time for *knowing* have recourse to *believing*.

[6] John Dunn asks the question: If he did not think morality demonstrable, why did he write the *Essay*? He argues that while Locke may not have achieved complete logical alignment of the two works, they do move toward the same practical ends: promoting individual and social morality and presenting God as their basis. Dunn, *The Political Thought*, 189–98, cf. 263–67.

work. On a related note, some find his ecumenical claims insincere and read *ROC* as being religiously sectarian.[7] Others take Locke's claims in *ROC*, such as his assertion that a moral society needs the Bible and the Christian faith, as sincere, although they acknowledge that there are inconsistencies between his two noted works.[8]

---

[7] The following are notable examples of those who read Locke as being religiously surreptitious: Steven Forde, "Natural Law, Theology, and Morality in Locke," *American Journal of Political Science* 45, no. 2 (April 2001): 396–409 [ref. pp. 407–8]; Leo Strauss, *Natural Right and History* (Chicago: The University of Chicago Press, 1953); Leo Strauss, *Persecution and the Art of Writing* (Chicago: The University of Chicago Press, 1952; Reprint, 1988); Michael S. Rabieh, "The Reasonableness of Locke, or the Questionableness of Christianity," *Journal of Politics* 53, no. 4 (November 1991): 933–57; Jonathan Donald Conrad, "Locke's Use of the Bible in: *The Two Treatises, The Reasonableness of Christianity*, and *A Letter Concerning Toleration*" (Ph.D. diss., Northern Illinois University, 2004); David Foster, "The Bible and Natural Freedom in John Locke's Political Thought," in *Piety and Humanity*, ed. Douglas Kries (Lanham: Rowman and Littlefield, 1997), 181–212. Foster's earlier claims are in the same vein as Conrad's. He concludes his essay with the suggestion that Locke rejects "crucial elements of the biblical teaching on God, property, and the family." See also: Nicholas Jolley, "Locke on Faith and Reason," in *The Cambridge Companion to Locke's "Essay Concerning Human Understanding,"* ed. Lex Newman (Cambridge: Cambridge University Press, 2007), 436–55; Michael Ayers, *Locke Volume 1: Epistemology* (New York: Routledge, 1991), 122. There is also a whole host of scholars that do not see Locke so much as surreptitious, as they do sectarian. They think that his appeals to Scripture as an authority are sincere but his conclusions in *ROC* are notably sectarian, even heterodox, thus exposing a narrow, yet still pro-positive-religious agenda. For the menagerie of views of these scholars and another argument against their lines of thinking from a different angle, as well as the more uniform line of thinking of those who read Locke as being religiously surreptitious in *ROC*, see also Chapter 3. It is conceivable that some might claim that Locke's works are insincere in the sense that all his biblical and theological incorporations are wholly superficial and neither positive nor negative toward Christianity. In other words, the incorporations are mere window-dressing perhaps to curry the favor of a largely Christian readership. Moreover, it is worthwhile noting that my categorization of scholars in Chapter 2 as falling into either the surreptitious, superficial, and vital categories are with respect to Locke's incorporation of a professed biblical faith. Here my categorizations of sincere (sincerely ecumenical) and sectarian fall out of Chapter 2's vital category because Locke's professed ecumenical design claims are of particular importance here. Thus Chapters 3 and 4 also have the same categorizations as this chapter. Many of the interlocutors of these three chapters (3, 4, and 5) are the same.

There is a work worthy of mention that has similar conclusions to my own, although presented in slightly exaggerated form: Manfred Svensson, "Locke, Toleration, and the Church," *Philosophy of Religion Annual* 15 (2016): 47–66. He rightly notes that Locke argued that the individual must be personally convicted of his or her doctrinal positions. But Svensson argues that Locke's works have erased the moral voice of the church and left it as a voluntary society associated merely with other-worldly goals (65). He also thinks that Locke's ecclesiastical stance offers a church bound to a doctrinal minimalism (53). Practically speaking, if dialogue regarding morals and disciplinary authority did not occur in the church, I am not sure one would ever want to attend, Locke included. While Svensson is correct that Locke is pushing back against an authoritarian church that can compel its people to do things against their conviction and conscience, he is incorrect in thinking that Locke negated the moral voice of the church in society. To do so would be incongruous with Locke's views of epistemology and pedagogy. Cf. Jonathan S. Marko, "The Promulgation of Right Morals: John Locke on the Church and the Christian as the Salvation of Society," *Journal of Markets and Morality* 19, no. 1 (2016): 41–59.

[8] In addition to the aforementioned scholars that have attempted to reconcile the two works, many Locke scholars approach his works as sincere articulations of his views: Nicholas Wolterstorff, "John Locke's Epistemological Piety: Reason is the Candle of the Lord," *Faith and Philosophy* 11, no. 4 (October 1994): 572–91; Stuart Brown, "Locke as Secret 'Spinozist': The Perspective of William Carroll," in *Disguised and Overt Spinozism Around 1700: Papers Presented at the International*

It appears, however, that scholarship on all sides has not sufficiently considered the implications of a few important consistencies between the *Essay* and *ROC* that point to them not being at odds, at least pertaining to the epistemology of morals. In both works, Locke opposes the innate principles tradition: while he explicitly enters the lists against Lord Herbert of Cherbury (1583–1648) and the innate principle tradition in the *Essay*, he does so implicitly in *ROC* when he discusses five advantages of Christ's advent, and thus advantages of revelation, in his offensive against the natural religion of the deists.[9] Also, in both he admits that morals are demonstrable and can be made certain and, further, insists that we tend to take our intellectual milieu for granted.

Arguably, Locke's belief that Christianity is epistemologically vital to the spread and maintenance of right morals in society is demonstrated by the mutual reinforcement between his argument against innate ideas and principles, which is most prominent in the *Essay*, and his conclusion in *ROC* that a great shift in moral thinking started with Christ's advent. Right moral principles, although demonstrable, are neither easily wrought nor innate but can seem to be so to the many who have taken for granted their Christian (or Christianized) milieu in which they have been raised, such as the deists. As a result, the removal of Scripture's position of authority from the public square will result in an inevitable decline in the quality and safety of it as it starts toward a morality of convenience. The conclusions of this chapter run counter to the frequent claims that Locke's advancement of the Christian faith is feigned or in some way intentionally divisive and establish an important logical link between two of Locke's greatest works. They further index why Locke did not alter the *Essay* based on what he wrote in *ROC* regarding the epistemology of moral principles.

Colloquium Held at Rotterdam, 5–8 October 1994, ed. Wiep Van Bunge and Wim Klever (New York: E. J. Brill, 1996), 213–34; Steven M. Dworetz, *The Unvarnished Doctrine: Locke, Liberalism, and the American Revolution* (Durham: Duke University Press, 1990); Greg Forster, *John Locke's Politics of Moral Consensus* (Cambridge: Cambridge University Press, 2005), 141–42; Alan P. F. Sell, *John Locke and the Eighteenth-Century Divines* (Cardif: University of Wales Press, 1997), 186–88; John C. Higgins-Biddle, Introduction to *The Reasonableness of Christianity: As Delivered in the Scriptures*, ed. John C. Higgins-Biddle (Oxford: Clarendon Press, 1999), xv–cxv.

[9] I am here claiming that Locke is targeting Lord Herbert and other innatist deists. By contrast, Higgins-Biddle and Lucci think that the later deists are the targets. Higgins-Biddle, Introduction, xxvii–xxxvii; Lucci, *John Locke's Christianity*, 22.

Historical Context: Two Theological Debates

The Innate Ideas Controversy

Of the many controversies in which Locke became a significant contributor, the most commonly cited is the controversy over innatism or nativism, the doctrine that humans are constituted in such a way, from their very beginnings, that they have, in some sense, ideas or principles impressed onto them.[10] Others maintained that humans should be likened to a smooth tablet, without such "innate" or "native" impressions. Such had been the argument since the time of the ancient Greek philosophers. The innatists or nativists could be divided into two groups (some scholars today dividing them even further): the naïve innatists or nativists, who held some position to the effect "that God wrote into or impressed upon the soul or mind at birth certain ideas or precepts (or a developed conscience capable of deciding what is right and wrong, independent of custom or learning) for the guidance of life and the foundation of morality, even though we do not become aware of these innate principles (or of the conscience) until maturity,"[11] and the dispositional or modified nativists who, although they might use such metaphorical language indicating an impression, would say more simply that we are in some way pre-disposed to assenting quickly to certain ideas or principles when presented.[12] Reformed theologian Francis Turretin, writing well before Locke's *Essay*, acknowledges the distinctions between the anti-innatists, naïve innatists, and dispositional innatists, rejecting the first two:

---

[10] Functionally speaking, I will make no distinction between innate ideas and principles although a distinction could be made. John W. Yolton, *John Locke and the Way of Ideas* (Oxford: Clarendon Press, 1968); Alan P. F. Sell, *John Locke and the Eighteenth-Century Divines: Prolegomena to Christian Apologetics* (Cardif: University of Wales Press, 1997); John E. Platt, "The Denial of the Innate Idea of God in Dutch Remonstrant Theology: From Episcopius to Van Limborch," in *Protestant Scholasticism in Essays in Reassessment*, ed. Carl R. Trueman and R. Scott Clark (Glasgow: Pater Noster Press, 1999), 213–26; Margaret Atherton, "Locke and the Issue over Innateness," in *Locke*, ed. Vere Chappell (Oxford: Oxford University Press, 1998), 48–59; Samuel C. Rickless, "Locke's Polemic against Nativism," in *The Cambridge Companion to Locke's "Essay Concerning Human Understanding,"* ed. Lex Newman (Cambridge: Cambridge University Press, 2007), 33–66; Keith Allen, "Ideas," in *The Oxford Handbook of British Philosophy in the Seventeenth-Century*, ed. Peter R. Antsey (Oxford: Oxford University Press, 2013), 329–48.

[11] Yolton, *John Locke and the Way of Ideas*, 29.

[12] This distinction between naïve and dispositional nativists or innatists is thoroughly imbedded into the scholarly literature. Yolton observes in *John Locke and the Way of Ideas*, that the dispositional innatists often described their position in the language of the naïve innatists. Yolton says this to defend Locke's attack on naïve innatism, a position his critics complain no one held. Further, whatever cannot be sensed will always be described analogously or by a representative metaphor. So, an attack on the naïve innatists does make an impact upon those who are of the dispositional variety.

> The question is not whether natural theology (which is such by act as soon as a man is born, as the act of life in one living or of sense in one perceiving as soon as he breathes) may be granted. For it is certain that no actual knowledge is born with us and that, in this respect, man is like a smooth tablet (*tabulae rasae*). Rather the question is whether such can be granted at least with regard to principle and potency; or whether such a natural faculty implanted in man may be granted as will put forth its strength of its own accord, and spontaneously in all adults endowed with reason, which embraces not only the capability of understanding, but also the natural first principles of knowledge from which conclusions both theoretical and practical are deduced (which we maintain).[13]

Thus, as Allen notes, acceptance or rejection of innate ideas is not the best line of demarcation to distinguish rationalists and empiricists.[14] The principles or ideas in dispositional innatism are in one sense a priori and in another a posteriori. As Turretin notes, they are "partly innate . . . and partly acquired."[15]

So many writers had attacked the naïve version prior to the publication of the *Essay*, that Yolton remarks it had been "thoroughly exploded by 1688."[16] Locke assailed all of nativism or innatism and he in turn was attacked by the likes of John Norris, a noted Platonist of sorts, and James Lowde, an incisive pastor-theologian. He was defended by Samuel Bold and others. Not all the dispositional innatists were precisely on the same page:

> Locke faced a number of philosophers who favored dispositional nativism, some on the grounds of universal assent (Lord Herbert), some on the grounds of universal assent "upon the free use of reason" (Stillingfleet), and some on grounds of universal assent "at the very first proposal" (Whichcote and More). In addition, Locke faced dispositional nativists who argued

---

[13] Francis Turretin, *Institutes of Elenctic Theology*, 3 vols., trans. George Musgrave Giger and ed. James T. Dennison, Jr. (Phillipsburg: P & R Publishing, 1992), I.iii.2. Turretin maintains that the anti-innatist position is Socinian: "Our controversy here is with the Socinians who deny the existence of any such natural theology or knowledge of God and hold that what may appear to be such has flowed from tradition handed down from Adam, and partly from revelations made at different times. The orthodox, on the contrary, uniformly teach that there is a natural theology, partly innate (derived from the book of conscience by means of common notions [*koinas ennoias*]) and partly acquired (drawn from the books of creatures discursively) . . ." (I.iii.4).
[14] Allen, "Ideas," 337.
[15] Turretin, *Institutes of Elenctic Theology*, I.iii.4.
[16] Yolton, *John Locke and the Way of Ideas*, 46.

that there are ideas (notably, relative, logical, and geometrical ideas) that "must needs spring from the active power . . . of the minds itself" because they could not be conveyed to the mind through the senses (More, and also Cudworth).[17]

This partial list does not even mention the more traditional theologians, like Turretin, and the Cartesians, who are reasonably described as dispositional nativists or innatists.

There were two notable issues associated with innate ideas that fueled adherence to innatism or nativism: belief in God and morality. Yolton explains that in the era, "the doctrine of innate knowledge was held, in one form or another, to be necessary for religion and especially for morality."[18] As a case in point, some, in the tradition of Melancthon and Calvin, maintained that such a doctrine was supported by Romans 1:18–21 and Romans 2:14–15, which they believed indicated that the idea of God and the principles of the natural law were in some way innate. While acceptance of innate ideas does not clearly demarcate rationalists and empiricists in this era, it did serve as a line between orthodoxy and orthopraxy in the minds of some, like the Reformed.[19] Many even thought that the loss of innateness amounted to atheism.[20] Some critics felt that Locke's assault on innate ideas left custom and tradition, or some other unsure footing, as the lone foundations of morality because they found no other alternative to innatism provided by his *Essay*.[21] In other words, they thought that Locke's *Essay* led to moral relativism.

Regarding Locke's targets, the only opponent that he expressly mentions is the innatist Lord Herbert of Cherbury.[22] But it is clear that he has other targets and other arguments for innatism, beyond those provided by Lord Herbert, in mind. Yolton points out that Locke is attacking both forms of innatism: "For Locke there were just two alternatives. Either ideas and principles are innate in the sense of full-blown and perfect ideas [naïve form], or they can be only tendencies which arise with experience [dispositional

---

[17] Rickless, "Locke's Polemic," 42. Rickless's list continues.
[18] Yolton, *John Locke and the Way of Ideas*, 29.
[19] Platt, "Denial of the Innate Idea."
[20] Sell, *John Locke*, 19.
[21] Yolton, *John Locke and the Way of Ideas*, 53–64.
[22] Although Lord Herbert of Cherbury's *De Veritate* was published in 1624, thus making him to be an unlikely candidate for repudiation, John Milner does defend Lord Herbert in *An Account of Mr. Lock's Religion* (London: Printed by J. Nutt, 1700). Cf. Yolton, *John Locke and the Way of Ideas*, 57. Thus, Lord Herbert was not completely out of fashion.

form]. The former is absurd and false, the latter trivial and of no consequence."[23] Although naïve innatism was no longer popular, Yolton convincingly demonstrates that many still adhered to naïve innatism, if not as their position, then at least in the way in which they often described and defended their dispositional form of it. For instance, Yolton writes the following of the Cambridge Platonists, who would be rightly denominated dispositional innatists: "The Cambridge Platonists developed this particular twist [the twist being 'only that such knowledge was implicit in the soul and merely required experience to elicit awareness of it'] to the theory with great care, showing at the same time an almost emotional attachment to the literal language of the naïve version."[24] Prominent thinkers of the church, like Edward Stillingfleet, were guilty of the same.[25] Margaret Atherton somewhat more recently argued that Locke was *also* attacking the Cartesians by arguing that "innate" is opposed to the nature of mentality. That is, "His position is that explanations in terms of innate ideas or principles can be rejected out of hand on grounds of incoherence. This is because he believes there is no way to have such mental states as ideas or principles except through being aware of them, so that the mark of the mental is that the mental states are conscious states." In other words, by virtue of the way Locke conceives of the nature of mentality, speaking of innate ideas or knowledge is akin to discussing unconscious awareness, an inherently contradictory label. Descartes and some of his followers thus delve into metaphysical speculation arguing for a hidden or unconscious structure to thought, while Locke shows little interest in metaphysics and, in fact, has no interest in proposing an alternative constructive program: "For Locke has no commitment at all to showing that his account of how we construct our ideas describes a system that is just as powerful as

---

[23] Yolton, *John Locke and the Way of Ideas*, 56. Keith Allen's summary of Locke's strategy of undermining both forms of innatism is somewhat different from Yolton's: "Locke argues essentially that the argument from universal consent either has a false premise, because the supposedly innate principles do not receive universal assent, or its conclusion is trivial, because it fails to distinguish the nativist's explanation of universal consent from the empiricist's, which appeals only to innate learning mechanisms and not innate principles or ideas" (Allen, "Ideas," 339). Samuel Rickless has recently given an impressive analysis of Locke's arguments: Rickless, "Locke's Polemic."

[24] Yolton, *John Locke and the Way of Ideas*, 39–40. Allen notes some of the differences among the Cambridge Platonists: "Whereas [Henry] More and [Ralph] Cudworth think that ideas in the soul are copies of the archetypes in God's mind, [John] Norris eliminates these intermediaries altogether, arguing that 'we see all things in God, or the Divine Ideas, that is, in the partial Representations of the Divine Omniformity'" (Allen, "Ideas," 337).

[25] Yolton, *John Locke and the Way of Ideas*, 36–39. For a very good and succinct taxonomy of innatists: Rickless, "Locke's Polemic."

that of the nativist, and he feels no need to say that he can explain whatever the nativist seeks to explain."[26]

Alan P. F. Sell offers two motivations for Locke entering the lists with so many thinkers, innatists and anti-innatists alike. First, Sell draws a connection between innate ideas and assent on account of authority or implicit faith (which Locke finds illegitimate), such as in the case of Roman Catholicism and enthusiasm. He argues that such authoritarianisms "not only rested upon innate principles, but, capitalizing upon the intellectual laziness of others, specified them and demanded allegiance to them." He directs the readers to places in the *Essay* where this motivation finds support: I.iv.12, 24, 23; IV.xx.10. Second, Sell argues, "Locke genuinely believed that what mattered in knowledge and certainty was established upon surer foundations than those provided by innate principles."[27] As already noted, Locke thought that morals were demonstrable.

The Rise of Deism or Natural Religion

One of the groups often overlooked in the innatism controversy in England at this time are the deists. The deists are mostly known for categorically rejecting claims of special revelation or the necessity of it for salvation. For those who accept special revelation, at least in theory, they would subordinate it to human reason, our predominant source of "divine revelation." One deist author defines natural religion as "the Belief we have of an Eternal Intellectual Being, and of the Duty which we owe him, manifested to us by our Reason, without Revelation or positive Law."[28] Moreover, the English deists are frequently presented as squaring off against the so-called orthodox divines in a battle of wits in England.[29] This, however, is a significant

---

[26] Atherton, "Locke and the Issues over Innateness," 58. This book will also describe other prominent ways Locke avoided metaphysical speculation. Cf. Jonathan S. Marko, "Why Locke's 'Of Power' Is Not a Metaphysical Pronouncement: Locke's Response to Molyneux's Critique," *Philosophy and Theology* 29, no. 1 (2017): 41–68.

[27] Sell, *John Locke*, 17–18.

[28] John Dryden, *An Essay on Natural Religion as Opposed to Divine Revelation*, in *A Summary Account of the Deists Religion: In a Letter to that Excellent Physician, the Late Dr. Thomas Sydenham. To Which Are Annex'd, Some Curious Remarks on the Immortality of the Soul; and An Essay by the Celebrated Poet, John Dryden, Esq; to Prove that Natural Religion Is Alone Necessary to Salvation, in Opposition to All Divine Revelation* (London: 1745), 1.

[29] Examples: Leslie Stephen, *History of English Thought in the Eighteenth Century*, vol. 1, 3rd ed. (London: Harbinger, 1962; 3rd ed. first published, 1902); John Herman Randall, Jr., *The Making of the Modern Mind* (New York: Columbia University Press, 1976; first published, 1926); James C. Livingston, *Modern Christian Thought*, 2nd ed., vol. 1 (Minneapolis: Fortress Press, 2006). A very

oversimplification:[30] those who are denominated orthodox argued among themselves, the deists were arguably smaller in number than might be assumed, and some mentioned in the narrative do not fit into the deist or orthodox categories.

There are two thinkers who are identified as major progenitors of the deist movement. One is England's Lord Herbert of Cherbury, who is known for his discussion and advancement of the idea that it is our God-given innate knowledge—specifically, five religious common notions—by which we adjudicate the legitimacy of so-called special revelation. The five common religious notions are: (1) there is a supreme God, (2) the sovereign deity ought to be worshipped, (3) virtue and piety are the most important aspects of our religious obeisance, (4) we must expiate our sins by repentance, and (5) there is reward or punishment after this life.[31] The other is René Descartes, whose dualism between extended substances and thinking substances eventually led to viewing the universe as a machine, and to the conclusion that God is either identical with the universe or he is wholly beyond the universal machine, playing the role of the great mechanic watching his invention run—the description often associated with deism.[32]

Locke is often incorporated into these narratives. While he is attempting to sway certain deists in his day from their stances regarding Christ and the necessity of revelation in *ROC*, there is another group of deists more often associated with Locke and whose writing careers are mainly in the eighteenth century: the so-called deist appropriators of the fundamental principles within Locke's *Essay*. The most noted are John Toland, Anthony Collins, and Matthew Tindal. Toland is known for bringing the deist controversy from smolder to flame and also for starting a years-long debate between Locke and Stillingfleet. His *Christianity Not Mysterious*, his most noted work, however,

---

helpful series of works, which does not succumb to uncareful dichotomies, is: Richard A. Muller, *Post-Reformation Reformed Dogmatics: The Rise and Development of Reformed Orthodoxy, ca. 1520 to ca. 1725*, 2nd ed., 4 vols. (Grand Rapids: Baker Academic, 2006).

[30] Cf. Marko, *Measuring the Distance*; Jonathan S. Marko, "Deism," *A Jonathan Edwards Encyclopedia*, ed. Harry S. Stout (Grand Rapids: Eerdmans, 2017), 136–38; Jonathan S. Marko, "The Brave New World of Discordant Voices into Which Jonathan Edwards Was Born," *A Collection of Essays on Jonathan Edwards*, ed. Robert Boss (Fortworth: Jonathan Edwards Society Press, 2017), 85–92; Jonathan S. Marko, "Reason and Revelation in Early Modern Protestantism," in *Encyclopedia of Early Modern Philosophy and Sciences*, ed. Dana Jalobeanu and Charles T. Wolfe (Cham: Springer, 2022), 1774–84.

[31] Herbert, *De Veritate*, 291–302.

[32] Colin Gunton, "Transcendence, Metaphor, and the Knowability of God," *Journal of Theological Studies* 31, no. 2 (Oct. 1980): 501–16 [pp. ref. are 507–8].

does not contain what are typically considered "deist" views but rather what are Locke's views with minor modifications. Collins seems to have been a close friend of and highly esteemed by Locke, but he would never touch the sophistication or notoriety of his mentor. Tindal wrote, *Christianity as Old as the Creation*, also known as the "Deists' Bible." While these three "deists" could comfortably be labeled as empiricists, that is not the case for all those deist contemporaries of Locke against whom he wrote. The innate idea tradition was alive and well during Locke's day not only in the church or among the Platonists or Cartesians but also among the subscribers to natural religion. In other words, the so-called deist movement eventually appropriated fundamental principles of the *Essay* even though it did not start with them.

Two examples of "deists" from the more rationalist strain pre-dating *ROC* and whose thoughts were most like the ones Locke was keen on dispatching are the author of *A Summary Account of the Deists' Religion*, Charles Blount (1654–1693), one of the most noted of the early deists, and the author of *An Essay on Natural Religion*, disputably, John Dryden.[33] While hardly identical, their works have some significant similarities. As expected, their respective offerings of the fundamentals or basics of deism or natural religion carry similar prominent themes: a Supreme Being, worship, repentance, obedience and morality, and rewards and punishments dispensed in the afterlife.[34] These correspond to the five religious common notions treated by Lord Herbert. What is more, both thinkers admit that at least some of the fundamentals are innate (The remaining ones would be capable of being teased out by unassisted, human reason).[35] In remarking upon the prevalence of the perceived need to appease God by those from all religions, the author of *An Essay on Natural Religion* says that it (which is at its core an admission of the necessity of sorrow and repentance) "is so agreed upon by all Men in all Ages" and "is not revealed, but innate, and a Part of Natural Religion."[36] Similarly, Blount writes, "for as there are immediate Propositions, to which

---

[33] Cf. John Dryden, *The Works of John Dryden, Volume II: Poems, 1681–1684* (Berkeley: The University of California Press, 1972), 360. For the opinion that the work in question was not penned by Dryden: Eugene R. Purpus, "Some Notes on a Deistical Essay Attributed to Dryden," *Philological Quarterly* 29 (January 1950): 342–49. He argues that the essay was not written by Dryden or Blount but another contemporary of Blount.

[34] Charles Blount, *A Summary Account of the Deists Religion: In a Letter to that Excellent Physician, the Late Dr. Thomas Sydenham. To Which Are Annex'd, Some Curious Remarks on the Immortality of the Soul; and An Essay by the Celebrated Poet, John Dryden, Esq; to Prove that Natural Religion Is Alone Necessary to Salvation, in Opposition to All Divine Revelation* (London: 1745), 1–4; Dryden, *An Essay*, 1–2.

[35] Blount, *A Summary Account*, 6; Dryden, *An Essay*, 3, 4.

[36] Dryden, *An Essay*, 4.

the Understanding (*sine discursu*) assents, as soon as proposed, so are there Things good and just which they will at first View, without Deliberation, approve of and chose also, (*viz.*) the Veneration of an Almighty invisible Being."[37] Finally, both are careful not to eschew Christianity.[38] They find biblical Christianity to have the same common core as deism, despite what self-professing Christians might claim. In fact, in his prefatory letter, written to Thomas Sydenham, Blount writes: "*However, undoubtedly, in our Travels to the other World, the common Road is the safest; and tho'* Deism *is a good Manuring of a Man's Conscience, yet, certainly, if sowed with Christianity, it will produce the most profitable crop.*" This likely should be understood as an acknowledgement of the respect that he has for the morality found in Jesus Christ and the Apostles.

Moreover, there is a pamphlet, *An Account of the Growth of Deism in England*, that is helpful in understanding what fueled the rise in natural religion. It was published on the heels of *ROC* and in it, its author, William Stephens, attempts to help the reader gain traction in the minds of those who have been or claimed to have been allured to natural religion. He notes that he surveyed many deists to determine the reason for their turn to this disconcerting movement. He cautions the reader that some so-called deists are feigning to be such and are actually "Men of loose and sensual Lives; and I make no wonder that they dislike the *Christian* Doctrine of Self-denial, and the severe threatenings against willful sinners." They have been encouraged to laugh at certain stories of the Bible, miracles, and revelation, and the like by reading Spinoza and Hobbes. They do not argue seriously but simply make jests when the topic of divine revelation is broached.[39]

There are, however, those who claim to be deists and who are more thoughtful than the aforementioned and struggle with real religious concerns, all of which Williams catalogues. They have turned their backs on organized religion but not morality. Some were taught how the Roman Catholic priesthood "was calculated for the Profit, Power and Honour" and other self-interests. Unfortunately, in the case of one young man interviewed, he, in following the controversy between Anglican Archbishop Laud and the Presbyterians, assessed that "both these *Protestant* Parties, under the pretence of Religion, were only grasping at *Power*, and that the Controversy at

---

[37] Blount, *A Summary Account*, 6.
[38] Cf. Blount, *A Summary Account*, 4; Dryden, *An Essay*, 10–11. They are by no means shy of critiquing the doctrines frequently found in the various Christian sects with which they disagree.
[39] Williams, *An Account*, 5.

bottom, was not whose Religion was best, but only what Sect of the *Clergy* should make the best Market of *the meer Lay-men*."[40] Williams also notes some related problems: the fractious and quarrelsome nature of the churches, the viciousness of some of the divines, and the impossibility of believing certain doctrines that the church requires for salvation but which are, at base, absurdities. Perhaps one of the most important issues that the author mentions, which is a misstep on the part of many who give up on Christianity in favor of a deistic outlook, is that they often wrongly identify priestcraft or hypocrisy of the clergy and Christ's teachings.[41]

In sum, then, histories of philosophy covering the rise of natural religion or deism in England often incorporate Locke. By some he is inserted as one of the orthodox opponents of the deists, who were, at the time, rather rationalistic. Others incorporate him into the narrative because it is his fundamental principles in the *Essay* that the most well-known, so-called deists of the next century appropriate. And so, from Lord Herbert of Cherbury to Matthew Tindal, the necessity of revelation for religion found itself under attack by a small movement of thinkers, all of whom stressed reason (sometimes to the negation of revelation) in religion but who did not agree on whether many of our religious principles came from within or without.

Locke's Assault on Innate Principles

Lord Herbert's Innate Principles

Locke's notion of the *tabula rasa* or blank slate, for which he gets so much attention, was hardly novel. Nearly a decade before Locke's birth, Lord Herbert of Cherbury, Locke's named interlocutor in his assault on innate ideas, writes in *De Veritate*: "Let us have done with the theory that asserts that our mind is a clean sheet, as though we obtained our capacity for dealing with objects from objects themselves. For while we can think of the mind as a closed book in so far as it is not open to objects, it cannot be justly called a clean sheet, as an appeal to consciousness, the final test concerning objects, shows."[42]

---

[40] Williams, *An Account*, 6.
[41] Cf. Williams, *An Account*, 19.
[42] Herbert, *De Veritate*, 132.

Some may find it strange that Lord Herbert would receive attention from Locke even though not being very current at the time. But while *De Veritate* was penned nearly 70 years before the 1690 publication of the first edition of the *Essay*, the *Essay* itself had been growing in the mind of Locke for a considerable length of time. And further, although perhaps Lord Herbert might have been an example that few intellectuals would have cared to defend in detail, he did have advocates in the 1690s and is still regarded by some as the "Father of Deism." At least the deist contemporaries of *ROC* share with Lord Herbert an acceptance of innate ideas in some sense, an enhanced role for reason in religion, and the elements or themes found in their respective lists of the fundamentals of natural religion. Whatever the case, Lord Herbert receives an explicit response to his thought in the *Essay* and an implicit one in *ROC*.

Lord Herbert of Cherbury's most noted treatment of common notions or innate ideas appears in the fifth chapter of *De Veritate*: "Common notions are so called because they are understood by all normal men, so long as their objects, whether they be things, terms or signs, remain constant."[43] Lord Herbert acknowledges that some notions that are commonly held are not necessarily common notions in the strict sense. We can identify a common notion as such if it has the following six characteristics. First, common notions or principles have priority, meaning that they serve as the givens in our discursive reasoning. Second, they are basic or are not derived from other notions; in short, they are independent. Third, they are universal, except in those with mental impairment, who are insane, or who have actively suppressed them. Fourth and fifth, respectively, they are certain and they have utility for our preservation in this world and the next. Finally, their truth is immediately seen.[44] The reason that these are grasped immediately and without the use of discursive reasoning is due to the fact that we have numerous faculties within called natural instincts that conform to these principles without. When we are confronted with some common notion, the associated faculty or natural instinct is activated, so to speak, and we are made instantaneously aware that we are confronted with truth. Both the expressions of these faculties that bring this awareness to the mind and the external notions themselves can both be referred to as common notions. So, the reader of *De Veritate* is informed in what sense common notions

---

[43] Herbert, *De Veritate*, 126.
[44] Herbert, *De Veritate*, 137–41.

can be said to be imprinted on our minds.⁴⁵ This description conforms to Rickless's identification of Lord Hebert as a dispositional nativist as opposed to a naïve one.

It is Lord Herbert's subsequent description of the five common religious notions that earns him the moniker, the Father of Deism. In short order, the five religious common notions are: (1) there is a supreme God; (2) the sovereign deity ought to be worshipped; (3) virtue and piety are the most important aspects of our religious obeisance; (4) we must expiate our sins by repentance; and (5) there is reward or punishment after this life.⁴⁶ These five notions are ultimately our religious authority and they stand in judgment over any purported revelation or doctrine constructed from it. He writes, "Every religion which proclaims a revelation is not good, nor is every doctrine which is taught under its authority always essential or even valuable."⁴⁷ Therefore, common notions afford us with the ability to definitively rule out some religious claims as legitimate. Everyone is responsible for his or her own beliefs and therefore God gave all normal people common notions by which to adjudge the various positive religions. Lord Herbert remarks, "I value these so highly that I would say that the book, religion, and prophet which adheres most closely to them is the best."⁴⁸ This is the foundation of the true catholic church. While Lord Herbert does not dismiss special divine revelation and expresses appreciation for it, such revelations must not contradict the common notions concerning religion if they are to be considered as such.⁴⁹

Locke's Assault

Locke's interaction with the teachings of innate principles or common notions does not immediately offer an explicit critique of Lord Herbert's thought. He opens his discourse with: "It is an established Opinion amongst some Men, That there are in the Understanding certain *innate Principles*; some primary Notions, Κοιναὶ ἔννοιαι [common notions], Characters, as it were stamped upon the Mind of Man, which the Soul receives in its very

---

⁴⁵ Herbert, *De Veritate*, 122–23.
⁴⁶ Herbert, *De Veritate*, 291–302.
⁴⁷ Herbert, *De Veritate*, 289.
⁴⁸ Herbert, *De Veritate*, 291.
⁴⁹ Herbert, *De Veritate*, 303, 312–13.

first Being; and brings into the World with it." He states that his goal is to "set down the Reasons, that made me doubt of the Truth of that Opinion, as an Excuse for my Mistake, if I be in one, which I leave to be consider'd by those, who, with me, dispose themselves to embrace the Truth, where-ever they find it."[50] Locke then embarks into his famed attempt at deconstructing teachings on innate ideas and principles. He starts with an analysis on speculative principles (e.g., whatever is, is and the law of non-contradiction) and from there moves to moral or practical principles. For both, he is adamant that even if principles have universal assent (and he does not think that any actually do) that does not prove them innate.[51]

Concentrating on speculative principles, he notes that the lack of awareness children and the uneducated have of them argues against their purported innateness. An apparent common response to such an observation is that these principles are there but that the souls of the aforementioned simply have not accessed them, to which Locke responds: "To say a Notion is imprinted on the Mind, and yet at the same time to say, that the mind is ignorant of it, and never yet took notice of it, is to make this Impression nothing."[52] If we allow some to assert that we do not have to be conscious of innate principles for us to know them or that one comes to know them when they come to a mature use of their reason, how might one separate acquired from innate principles?[53]

He finds the defense of innate moral principles even more dubious. Locke presents an array of objections to the identification of any moral principle as being innate. While acknowledging that he does think that moral principles are capable of certainty, it is not through intuition, but through a laborious logical demonstration, akin to mathematical proofs whose connections of one step to another are unquestionably certain.[54] When any moral principle is subject to doubt, our response, Locke remarks, is to provide a proof that comes by way of discursive reasoning. This alone is evidence on two counts that moral principles are not innate: that they are doubted strikes against them being such as does our natural proclivity to argue for them through logical proofs. Furthermore, if these moral principles were internalized, as the innate principle tradition thinks, one would always adhere to them. On a

---

[50] Locke, *Essay*, I.ii.1.
[51] Locke, *Essay*, I.ii.3. Recall, universal assent was an argument put forth by a variety of nativists or innatists.
[52] Locke, *Essay*, I.ii.5.
[53] Locke, *Essay*, I.ii.6–8.
[54] For example, Locke, *Essay*, I.ii.1; IV.iv.7; Locke, "L2059: Locke to William Molyneux," 593–96.

related note, moral principles that end in contemplation are not distinguishable from speculative principles. Moreover, Locke admits that nature has put within us the desire for happiness and the aversion to misery, but these are inclinations and not impressions of truth on the understanding.[55] Add to these objections above the great diversity of moral opinions throughout space and time. For instance, while not acceptable in his day or part of the world, there are peoples who have widely practiced the exposing of unwanted newborns.[56] The breaking of a rule does not argue that it is unknown, but "the *generally allowed breach of it any where*, I say, *is a Proof, that it is not innate.*"[57]

It is in the discussion of innate practical (or moral) principles that Locke pounces upon the five religious common notions as presented by Lord Herbert of Cherbury (whether Locke reads *De Veritate* with accuracy and charity will not be decided here).[58] Locke does admit that the five religious common notions are cogent and that a reasonable person will assent to them, although this hardly makes them innate. He notes first that if one were to abide by the marks of religious common notions that Lord Herbert actually employs, there would perhaps be hundreds more because none of the five religious common notions that he mentions have the six qualifying characteristics of innateness that he discusses. In opposition to these notions being innate, Locke's position is that the notion of God and his existence is derived and, further, that the remainder of Lord Herbert's so-called common notions concerning religion presuppose this reasoned idea of a supreme Deity, thus disqualifying the remaining four as being innate. Similarly, some of the religious common notions contain general ideas like sin, virtue, and piety that are arrived at through inductive reasoning that starts with specific ideas. The use of discursive reasoning, Locke argues, is evidence that these notions are not innate. But, if, for instance, the general concepts of vices and virtues were conceded by Locke to be innate as Lord Herbert seems to think, then there will be thousands of related, but more specific, rules and concepts that should also be admitted as being innate. In the end, however, Locke realizes that he has not definitively overturned Lord Herbert's teaching. His goal is

---

[55] Locke, *Essay*, I.iii.1–3.
[56] Locke, *Essay*, I.iii.6, 10–13.
[57] Locke, *Essay*, I.iii.12.
[58] His critiques below appear to show that he reads Lord Herbert more along the line of a naïve innatist. I do not see the relevance of that, however, for my overall argument for this chapter.

to cast a pall of doubt on it and have the reader realize that there are other ways—better ways—to account for the ascertainment of these principles.[59]

Locke does not only critique innate principles but tries to explain the prevalence of the concept. Nurses and authorities inculcate doctrines into us from before the time we have memories and in the days before we were critical thinkers: "for white Paper receives any Characters."[60] In short, we remember the moral principles with which we have been raised but we forget when or that we were taught them. Moreover, later in life, one might have reasons not to want to question their so-called innate tenets: doing so could result in the painful acknowledgment that they have abided by incorrect principles for a great portion of their lives and they may even have to part ways with members of their party (political group, religion, etc.).[61] It would then seem that ascertaining right moral principles requires humility, reflection, and the use of our reason to combat our prejudices, forgetfulness, and unreasoned, yet strong, apparent assent to questionable morals and principles.

Mutual Reinforcement between Locke's Assault on Innate Ideas and His Argument for the Need of Divine Revelation

What has been detailed so far, namely Locke's argument against innate ideas, and ensconced within that, his critique of Lord Herbert's teaching on religious common notions, is an important point of connection between the *Essay* and *ROC*. Regarding the latter work, this connection is found at its end. After a lengthy argument over justification that consumes most of the treatise (one is justified who: [1] believes in the one God, [2] believes Jesus is the Messiah, and [3] takes him as king),[62] he answers a few questions that the attentive reader might be asking, such as, What about those who have never heard the good news? Locke's response is that it becomes apparent to humans in the course of their lives that we have a general duty to employ our reason. Using it we have the potential to determine that there is a God and that there are some duties owed to him that we have not performed. And, a human, rightly applying reason, will notice that it is good and just when someone

---

[59] Locke, *Essay*, I.iii.15–19.
[60] Locke, *Essay*, I.iii.22–23 [quotation, I.iii.22].
[61] Locke, *Essay*, I.iii.25.
[62] Cf. Jonathan S. Marko, "Justification, Ecumenism, and Heretical Red Herrings in John Locke's *The Reasonableness of Christianity*," *Philosophy and Theology* 26, no. 2 (2014): 245–66. See also Chapter 3.

forgives one's own children and enemies upon their repentance, asking for pardon, and promising amendment. That person would be right to reason that our loving and merciful God would also forgive his children who likewise responded in the same way. Abiding by this reasoning one could be justified without the gospel.[63]

This evokes the entertainment of another question that a careful reader would likely ask: What need is there then of Christ's first coming? Locke notes that we cannot know every advantage but he proffers five: (1) awareness of the one and only true God, (2) revealing of our true duties toward him (i.e., morality), (3) eschewal of superstitious worship, (4) encouragement to a life of virtue and piety due to teachings about rewards and punishments that will be dispensed in the hereafter, and (5) assistance from the Holy Spirit.[64] This is another significant series of strikes against Lord Herbert of Cherbury's five religious common notions, although he or they are not mentioned. That is, the first four revealed advantages that Locke lists counter Lord Herbert's proposal that his five religious common notions—there is one supreme God, he ought to be worshipped, virtue and piety are due to God, the need of repentance, and the existence of an afterlife where one is rewarded or punished—are all innate. Because, however, Christ disabused us of polytheism and wrong morals and taught humanity that there was an afterlife, it would seem that none of Lord Herbert's common notions, all of which include one or more of those components, should be considered innate; rather, they should be considered derived. And it is difficult to imagine that the high degree to which the elements composing the advantages of Christ's advent in *ROC* match up with the elements of Lord Herbert's common religious notions is not intentional, especially given Locke's attack on his thought in the *Essay*. And in critiquing Lord Herbert's religious common notions, he is also critiquing the other rationalistic deists of the day.

Locke's defense of these advantages is largely from historical evidence, and he attempts to describe the epistemological reasons for these ancient circumstances. For instance, he draws the readers' attention to the prevalence of polytheism throughout the world before Christ—evidence against the idea of God being innate—and how monotheistic it became—whether Christian, Muslim, or Jewish—only subsequent to Christ's first coming. All one must do is turn to an ancient history book. He explains that there

---

[63] Locke, *ROC*, 254–57.
[64] Locke, *ROC*, 259–93.

was ample evidence to reason that there was one supreme God, and some of the Greek philosophers did, but a variety of factors worked against such reasoning: lust, carelessness, fear, priests who benefit from excluding reason from religion, etc.[65]

It is in his discussion of the second advantage, the revealing of morality, where he offers up his most concerted effort in arguing explicitly for the need for divine revelation and implicitly for the falsity of innate ideas. In fact, these two arguments are intertwined and mutually reinforcing. In addition, his chain of reasoning demonstrates the unlikelihood of being justified without the gospel and argues against the deistic claim that Christ is merely a restorer of natural religion. As he turns to argue for the soundness of his assertion of this advantage, Locke returns to his description of the general state of the world before Christ. Like the knowledge of the one true God, "This part of Knowledge, though cultivated with some care, by some of the Heathen Philosophers; Yet got little footing among the People." The priests actively suppressed the use of human reason and moral thinking for their own gain and few studied in the schools of the philosophers.[66] And the laws of the nations were expedient and largely based on convenience:

> So much *Virtue* as was necessary to hold Societies together; and to contribute to the quiet of Governments; the Civil Laws of Common wealths taught, and forced upon Men that lived under Magistrates. But these Laws, being for the most part made by such who had no other aims but their own Power, reached no farther than those things, that would serve to tie Men together in subjection; Or at most, were directly to conduce to the Prosperity and Temporal Happiness of any People.[67]

In short, the laws actually worked against attaining true moral principles; they offered only a moral veneer for society. Frequently, virtues were not promoted but forced, and, at best, the people were shown that obtaining them would offer a better temporal life.[68] What is more, Locke remarks that moralities differed from country to country and sect to sect, a piece of evidence also laid out against innate ideas in the *Essay* as established above.[69]

---

[65] Locke, *ROC*, 259–66. Cf. Blount, *An Account*, 5. Blount claims that the polytheists actually did know of one Supreme Being.
[66] Locke, *ROC*, 267.
[67] Locke, *ROC*, 268.
[68] Cf. Locke, *ROC*, 273, 278.
[69] Locke, *ROC*, 278.

In sum, then, a perusal of societies and their laws through history should make one doubt that moral principles are innate since most of the world throughout time lacked upright laws.[70]

If anyone were to attempt to confute the need of revelation and the unlikelihood of innate ideas, one would have to contend further with the following chain of reasoning offered by Locke. He invites the reader to compare the best pagan philosophers' teachings on morality with those of the Christians. He thinks that the difference in reasonableness between the two is staggering and asserts that the advantageous ingredient is, no doubt, the New Testament. "[A]s soon as they [the moral teachings of the Christian philosophers] are heard and considered, they are found to be agreeable to Reason."[71] He immediately points out that one should not suppose one would have arrived at these truths oneself just because one readily assents to them. Instead, experience shows us that:

> Every one may observe a great many truths which he receives at first from others, and readily assents to, as consonant to reason; which he would have found it hard, and perhaps beyond his strength to have discovered himself. Native and Original truth, is not so easily wrought out of the Mine, as we who have it delivered, ready dug and fashion'd into our hands, are apt to imagine.[72]

In context of *ROC*, this strikes at, among other things, the deists who claim Christ is simply the restorer of natural religion.[73] That is, it is not as if Christ came to humanity after a brief hiatus from the knowledge of true morality; rather there is nothing in history to conclude that individuals or communities knew all of the true moral principles found in the New Testament or were functionally capable of arriving at them.[74] One could also envision this

---

[70] Yolton notes, "The principles listed as innate are always formulations of the existing values of society." Yolton, *John Locke and the Way of Ideas*, 29; cf. Sell, *John Locke*, 18.
[71] Locke, *ROC*, 269.
[72] Locke, *ROC*, 269–70.
[73] Locke states several times that *ROC* was written to debate the deists: Locke, *ROC*, 1–2; Locke, *A Second Vindication*, xvii–xviii, 150–52, 376, 466; cf. 77–78.
[74] In Locke, *Treatises*, II.VIII.111, he writes of a "Golden Age" in history, after Adam and Eve, when people had "more Virtue" than they do now. There, the Golden Age is part of Locke's narrative, continued in the next paragraph, that the beginnings of peaceful government has always been by consent of the people. His thoughts promulgated here in *ROC* might be a development beyond his *Treatises*, but it is not necessarily so. As he is deducing what was likely the case, he is unable to actually do a comparison between post-Adamic, Golden Age morality and New Testament morality. An interesting comparison could be done between the Socinian views on the post-Adamic conveyance of morality (cf. Turretin, *Institutes of Elenctic Theology*, I.iii.4), the brief description of Locke's Golden

argument being leveled against the notion of innate ideas. Just as we should not assume that quick assent to a moral principle means that we could have determined it on our own, neither should we assume that it is innate because of our quick assent. Add to this our propensity to take the intellectual milieu in which we are raised and the moral principles delivered therein for granted. Those thinking that the New Testament was conveying no significant, new, moral instruction and thus not vital to society would hold this because they have not considered that their moral society, in which they had been raised and which had impressed right principles into them from an early age, is such because of the New Testament's influence. Because they overlook this societal influence, they might view the New Testament's moral principles, again, as being easily wrought by just about anyone or perhaps as innate.

Moreover, there is a further problem with systems of morality given before the time of Christ: the problem of authority. "Whatsoever should thus be universally useful, as a standard to which Men should conform their Manners, must have its Authority either from Reason or Revelation." To this Locke adds:

> He that any one will pretend to set up in this kind, and have his Rules pass for authentique directions, must shew, that either he builds his Doctrine upon Principles of Reason, self-Evident in themselves; and deduces all the parts of it from thence, by clear and evident demonstration: Or must shew his Commission from Heaven, that he comes with Authority from God, to deliver his Will and Commands to the World.[75]

In short, to be authoritative and thus obligatory the moral system must be shown to be indubitably certain or it must be shown to be revealed, such as the accompanying miracles that testify to the prophet's or Messiah's or apostle's divine agency.[76] So, Locke posits, even if all of the moral precepts promulgated in the New Testament had been collected from various other sources—a merely hypothetical situation—and put into one volume, one would still have this problem of authority. The people would have no

---

Age, and Matthew Tindal's historical narrative derived from *Christianity as Old as the Creation: or, The Gospel, a Republication of the Religion of Nature*, vol. 1 (London: 1730). Moreover, the *Treatises* and *ROC* might work well together here: the Golden Age is described in the *Treatises* and *ROC* describes the ages to which it gave way.

[75] Locke, *ROC*, 274–75.
[76] Locke, *ROC*, 276.

obligation to adopt it until the precepts were all demonstrated or testified to by a miracle from God.[77] What is more, and what shows revelation to be the superior form of conveyance, few would have the wherewithal to follow such logical chains of reasoning: "The bulk of mankind have not leisure nor capacity for Demonstration; nor can carry a train of Proofs; Which in that way they must always depend upon for Conviction, and cannot be required to assent to till they see the Demonstration."[78] In short, as he pronounces in the *Essay*, most are not afforded with the ability to know and therefore must believe.[79]

A few ironies in the scholarly literature focusing on *ROC* can now be pointed out. The very argument in *ROC* for the need for revelation in morality that is thought to be the most significant point of departure from the *Essay*, namely, regarding the claim in the latter that demonstration of moral principles is possible, is actually a continuation of his argument against innate principles that began in the *Essay* (and, as indicated, some of the historical evidence used for the five advantages in *ROC* is used against religious common notions advanced by Lord Herbert in the *Essay*[80]). What is more, Locke does not deny in *ROC* that demonstration of moral systems is possible. He in fact assumes such is the case in his remarks that only demonstration or clear evidence of divine revelation could make such a system obligatory.[81] It appears that Locke assumes that the attentive reader would make the connection between his argument against innate ideas and the argument for the need for revelation.

Perhaps the fact that he does not treat divine revelation until the end of the lengthy *Essay* has been a source of confusion. His treatments of revelation in both works, however, are consistent: as long as a purported divine revelation has the discernible marks of being from God they ought to trump that which has no certainty, but only probability. In the *Essay* he writes: "Whatsoever is divine *Revelation*, ought to over-rule all our Opinions, Prejudices, and Interests, and hath a right to be received with full Assent: Such a Submission as this of our *Reason* to *Faith*, takes not away the Land-marks of Knowledge."[82] Whereas divine revelation will overturn things which are in Locke's economy

---

[77] Locke, *ROC*, 271–72.
[78] Locke, *ROC*, 282.
[79] For example, Locke, *Essay*, IV.xx.2 [xix.2 in the third edition and earlier].
[80] Locke, *Essay*, I.iv.7ff.
[81] Note in his letter to Molyneux that he never dismisses the possibility of moral demonstration. It is assumed. Locke, "L2059: Locke to William Molyneux," 595. Cf. Moore, "Locke on the Moral."
[82] Locke, *Essay*, IV.xviii.10.

only belief—that which is based upon probability—it will not, because it is from God, overturn certain knowledge such as the law of noncontradiction or demonstrable principles of mathematics. Again, Locke is concerned in both works that people do not take their Christian milieu or any other moral environment that influenced them for granted. The explanation of revelation and its epistemological function is, in part, a means to this end.

In sum, there is mutual reinforcement between Locke's attempted offensive against the innate idea tradition, as varied as it is, and his argument for our need for revelation of morality (and other issues) in the *Essay* and *ROC*, respectively. Both, in effect, emphasize humans' tendency to take their Christian milieu, or whatever moral environment in which they are raised, for granted. Less important, but still relevant, the thought of Lord Herbert is used as a starting point in both.[83] And, Locke's claims of the possibility of moral demonstration spoken of in the *Essay* are not contradicted but assumed in *ROC*. It is the weakness of human moral reasoning, not its strength, with which he is much concerned in both works.[84]

The Church and the Christian as the Salvation of Society

Locke has a great interest in maintaining the Bible's status of authority. Because his argument for the need of revelation in morality and his argument against innate ideas work toward the same effect, and are symbiotic, the claims that Locke is surreptitious in *ROC*, regarding his affirmative statements of Scripture, are incorrect. Locke argued from the state of society before Christ. At worst, the governmental laws forced humans into subjection under those who wielded power; at best they helped people prosper and afforded them "Temporal Happiness."[85] The Bible has helped change all of this for the better.

---

[83] There are other interesting ironies between *ROC* and *De Veritate*. Both authors argue against implicit faith, that one cannot base one's religious thought on that of another. Herbert, *De Veritate*, 290. Both works have significant related ecumenical claims as well. Lord Herbert, *De Veritate*, 289–90. This is perhaps not so surprising given their religious and war-torn historical contexts. Cf. Livingston, *Modern Christian Thought*, 15.

[84] While I would not agree with Moore that *ROC* is a salvaging of the *Essay*, he does indicate that it seems Locke treats morals as according to reason in the *Essay* and in effect above reason in *ROC*. It is more accurate to say that many moral principles are treated as being effectively above reason prior to Christ's advent in *ROC*, but that they are viewed largely as being according to reason in England and Europe in the *Essay*. Cf. Moore, "Locke on the Moral."

[85] Locke, *ROC*, 268.

Where society had advanced in the civilized world, Locke gives credit to the Bible and Christ's first advent. If the Bible is removed from the public square as the highest personal authority of its citizens an inevitable decline will occur: the next generation might adopt a few non-biblical principles that seem reasonable enough to them; the subsequent generation will likely take those non-biblical principles for granted and they will be accepted as natural, and so on, until the civilized world is back where it was before Christ came. In the words of New Testament scholar Michael Green, "'Progressive morality' and 'progressive thinking' often go hand in hand with progressive deafness to the voice of God."[86] Of course there will be those like the Athenian philosophers, who stop the decline in their spheres of influence and even regain some ground; but Locke, as indicated above, points out the great gap in moral teachings between the Christian and pagan thinkers. With no revelation, there is no hope for wide-spread correct moral thinking. The only way to fully reap the benefits of God's law is to have Scripture as the societal authority. Natural law naturally acquired is helpful but, as shown above, it can only go so far. A by-product of the conversions from the evangelism of the Christians, lay and clergy alike, is a better life in society. Each new generation of Christians, who are truly following Scripture, *should* be continually propelling society forward and making it better.

That said, keeping Scripture in the hands and minds of professed Christians is very important and perhaps not all that easy. Locke takes issue with those who simply rely on the systematic thought of another and not Scripture in his second published defense of *ROC*: everyone "should be perswaded of the Truth of those Opinions he professes."[87] He further remarks:

> If the reading and study of the Scripture were more pressed that it is, and Men were fairly sent to the Bible to find their Religion; and not the Bible put into their hands only to find the Opinions of their peculiar Sect or Party, Christendom would have more Christians, and those that are, would be more knowing, and more in the right than now they are. That which hinders this, is that select bundle of Doctrines, which it has pleased every Sect to draw out of the Scriptures, or their own inventions, with an Omission of all

---

[86] Michael Green, *The Second Epistle of Peter and the Epistle of Jude: An Introduction and Commentary*, rev. ed. (Grand Rapids: Eerdmans, 1987), 185.
[87] Locke, *A Second Vindication*, 80, 84–85, 213, 214, 379–80, 400–1 [quotation, p. 380].

the rest ... Which in effect, what is it but to incourage [sic] ignorance, laziness, and neglect of the Scriptures?[88]

For Christians to be the best Christians they can be, they must have the Bible in their hands, not merely the opinions of another. Locke decries the practice of Christians basing their religious opinions on the opinions of another in both the *Essay* and *ROC*. Locke's stance in those works is that God has given each of us reason to employ and with which to answer questions for ourselves, especially in the very important spheres such as religion. Not to employ one's reason for oneself is an affront to God's design and a great cause of mischief in the world. At least in Locke's economy, one's assent to the truths in the Bible will be more tenaciously held (and legitimate) to by the Christian when assented from one's own persuasion and not simply the thoughts of another. The roots of such doctrines go deeper.[89] Thus, *ROC* is, in part, a call to the church and its leaders that they should change their practices.

While Locke thinks that Scripture and Christianity help to create and maintain a healthy society, his concern for personal discovery and reasonable conviction in religious matters help explain, in part, why Locke never advocates a "Christian state," where the church and state are co-mingled. Some of the ideas found in the *Essay* and *ROC* are also used by Locke in his *Letter* to argue for distinct jurisdictional boundaries between churches and the government. For instance, in the *Letter*, Locke also stresses the importance of the salvation of one's own soul, denominating it to be everyone's highest priority; thus, each person must do and believe that which he or she thinks obtains God's favor.[90] And as maintained in the *Essay* and *ROC*, Locke asserts in the *Letter* that religious beliefs and the performance of any accompanying duties are illegitimate if compulsory: "But true and saving Religion consists in the inward perswasion of the Mind; without which nothing can be acceptable to God. And such is the nature of the Understanding, that it cannot be compell'd to the belief of any thing by outward Force."[91] In other words, "Faith only, and inward Sincerity, are the things that procure acceptance with God."[92] What is more, Locke notes known instances where government officials have

---

[88] Locke, *A Second Vindication*, 211–12.
[89] Locke, *Essay*, IV.xx.17–18; *ROC*, 306; cf. *Essay*, IV.xvi.4; IV.xvii.19; IV.xx.2; IV.xx.7 [*Essay* IV.xx is IV.xix in the third edition and earlier].
[90] Locke, *Letter*, 57–58, cf. 33.
[91] Locke, *Letter*, 10.
[92] Locke, *Letter*, 37.

shown partiality to those of their own religious sects.[93] This may be in the spirit of other religions, but Locke is adamant that this is not the true spirit of Christianity: religious toleration is "the chief Characteristical Mark of the True Church" and anyone who is "destitute of Charity, Meekness, and Goodwill in general towards all Mankind, even to those that are not Christians, he is certainly yet short of being a true Christian himself."[94] Similar sentiments regarding this tolerant characteristic of Christianity are found throughout the *Essay* and *ROC*. As a result, the government ought to maintain an equitable disposition towards most religions, the exceptions being those religions having principles inherently "contrary to human Society, or to those moral Rules which are necessary to the preservation of Civil Society."[95]

Giving others space to employ their God-given faculties to contemplate Him and religion and demonstrating Christlikeness and its reasonableness in words and deeds is the way that true Christians should live. Christianity is an eminently moral, tolerant, and reasonable religion. In Locke's thinking, the imitation of Christ is the surest way to more converts and a healthier society.

---

[93] Locke, *Letter*, preface, 35–36.
[94] Locke, *Letter*, 1–2, cf. 6, 77.
[95] Locke, *Letter*, 64. For instance, the civil government is not to tolerate adherence to religions that oblige people to maintain a foreign power as their primary human authority. Otherwise, the government would be tolerating those willing to overthrow it (64–67).

6
John Locke on the Necessity of Miracles for Divine Revelation

Locke's prescribed acceptance of revelation (and thus for him Christianity) on the evidentiary basis of miracles and his apparent disregard for seriously defending that prescription have been a major problem of interpretation.[1] Leo Strauss and Straussian sympathizers conclude that Locke's construction of his entire platform for revelation and Christianity on the wobbly legs of the historical testimonies of miracles as evidence indexes his true thoughts about the Christian faith. They assert that Locke wrote in a time when one must exercise caution in writing against the ancient religion. Thus, a thinker like Locke would therefore purposely incorporate logical flaws, inconsistencies, and blatant oversights, "which are so obvious that they cannot have escaped the notice of a man of his rank and sobriety," in his treatments and alleged defenses of it.[2] In short, for the Straussians, Locke was covertly trying to undercut confidence in the Christian faith despite what he claims to be doing at face value; and his haphazard defense of miracles, or rather his lack of such a defense, is a case in point. Strauss's voice has lingered in Locke studies

---

[1] John Locke, *The Reasonableness of Christianity, as Delivered in the Scriptures*, 2nd ed. (London: Awnsham and John Churchil, 1696); John Locke, *The Reasonableness of Christianity: As Delivered in the Scriptures*, ed. John C. Higgins-Biddle (Oxford: Clarendon Press, 1999). Higgins-Biddle's critical edition of *ROC* is based, in part, upon the "Harvard copy" of *ROC*. The Harvard copy is a first edition *ROC* that contains Locke's notes, emendations, and corrections (cxxxiv). I have consulted both and note the page numbers of the 1696 second edition in the footnotes. John Locke, *A Vindication of the Reasonableness of Christianity, etc, From Mr. Edwards's Reflections* (London: Awnsham and John Churchil, 1695). This was published along with the 1696 second edition of *ROC*. John Locke, *A Second Vindication of the Reasonableness of Christianity, etc*. (London: A. and J. Churchil, 1697); John Locke, *An Essay Concerning Humane Understanding*, 3rd ed. (London: Awnsham and John Churchil, 1695); John Locke, *An Essay Concerning Human Understanding*, ed. Peter H. Nidditch (Oxford: Clarendon Press, 1979). Both named editions are consulted, and differences are noted. The changes made after the 1695 third edition are of particular interest as that was published in the same year as *ROC* and has absent the well-known chapter "Of Enthusiasm." That chapter discusses miracles further. John Locke, "A Discourse of Miracles," in *Posthumous Works of Mr. John Locke, etc.* (London: Printed by W. B. for A. and J. Churchill, 1706), 217–31.

[2] Leo Strauss, *Natural Right and History* (Chicago: The University of Chicago Press, 1953) [quotation, p. 220]; Leo Strauss, *Persecution and the Art of Writing* (Chicago: The University of Chicago Press, 1952; Reprint, 1988).

through the latter half of the twentieth-century and up to the present, and the position has gathered some followers.[3] Most scholars, however, notably John Dunn, Richard Ashcraft, Nicholas Wolterstorff, and Steven M. Dworetz, do not doubt the sincerity of Locke's professions of Christianity, despite significant problems in his works. Their reasons for doing so are varied.[4]

The majority of this latter group seriously wrestle with the manner in which Locke incorporates miracles into his religious epistemology. Of these, there are two distinct strands of scholarship: Locke's friendly critics and his sympathizers. The former sub-group consists of a number of philosophers, such as Nicholas Wolterstorff, Brian Mooney, Anthony Imbrosciano, Joseph Houston, and Paul Helm, to name a few. Wolterstorff articulates what he thinks are a few of the biggest problems with Locke's treatment of

---

[3] Michael S. Rabieh, "The Reasonableness of Locke, or the Questionableness of Christianity," *Journal of Politics* 53, no. 4 (November 1991): 933-57; Jonathan Donald Conrad, "Locke's Use of the Bible in: *The Two Treatises, The Reasonableness of Christianity*, and *A Letter Concerning Toleration*" (Ph.D. diss., Northern Illinois University, 2004). Conrad arrives at a tentative conclusion that would not be welcomed in the majority of Locke scholarship: that Locke "is an esoteric writer who may have been attempting to undermine the authority of the Bible while simultaneously appealing to it" (abstract). Cf. David Foster, "The Bible and Natural Freedom in John Locke's Political Thought," in *Piety and Humanity*, ed Douglas Kries (Lanham: Rowman and Littlefield Publishers, Inc., 1997), 181-212. His earlier claims are in the same vein as Conrad's. He concludes his essay with the suggestion that Locke rejects "crucial elements of the biblical teaching on God, property, and the family." Michael Ayers and Nicholas Jolley, while not asserting to my knowledge that Locke intentionally inserted logical inconsistencies, do think that Locke's *An Essay Concerning Human Understanding* properly understood is highly corrosive to Christianity. Nicholas Jolley "Locke on Faith and Reason," in *The Cambridge Companion to Locke's "Essay Concerning Human Understanding*," ed Lex Newman (Cambridge: Cambridge University Press, 2007), 436-55; Michael Ayers, *Locke Volume 1: Epistemology* (New York: Routledge, 1991), 122.

[4] John Dunn, *The Political Thought of John Locke: An Historical Account of the Argument of the 'Two Treatises of Government'* (Cambridge: Cambridge University Press, 1969); Nicholas Wolterstorff, "John Locke's Epistemological Piety: Reason is the Candle of the Lord," *Faith and Philosophy* 11, no. 4 (Oct 1994): 572-91; Richard Ashcraft, "Faith and Knowledge in Locke's Philosophy," in *John Locke: Problems and Perspectives*, ed. John W. Yolton (Cambridge: Cambridge University Press, 1969), 194-223; Stuart Brown, "Locke as Secret 'Spinozist': The Perspective of William Carroll," in *Disguised and Overt Spinozism Around 1700: Papers Presented at the International Colloquium Held at Rotterdam, 5-8 October 1994*, ed. Wiep Van Bunge and Wim Klever (New York: E.J. Brill, 1996), 213-34; Steven M. Dworetz, *The Unvarnished Doctrine: Locke, Liberalism, and the American Revolution* (Durham: Duke University Press, 1990); Greg Forster, *John Locke's Politics of Moral Consensus* (Cambridge: Cambridge University Press, 2005); Jonathan S. Marko, "The Promulgation of Right Morals: John Locke on the Church and the Christian as the Salvation of Society," *The Journal of Markets & Morality* 19, no. 1 (2016): 41-60; Jonathan S. Marko, "Justification, Ecumenism, and Heretical Red Herrings in John Locke's *The Reasonableness of Christianity*," *Philosophy and Theology* 26, no. 2 (2014): 245-66; Jonathan S. Marko, "Why Locke's 'Of Power' Is Not a Metaphysical Pronouncement: Locke's Response to Molyneux's Critique," *Philosophy and Theology* 29, no. 1 (2017): 41-68.

Interestingly, one recent scholar argues that Locke was more concerned with advancing theism as opposed specifically to Christianity: İsmail Kurun, *The Theological Origins of Liberalism* (New York: Lexington Books, 2016), ch. 5. I respond briefly to Kurun in Jonathan S. Marko, review of *The Theological Origins of Liberalism* by İsmail Kurun, *The Journal of Markets & Morality* 21, no. 2 (Fall 2018): 209-12; cf. Marko, "Promulgation of Right Morals." See also Chapters 4 and 5.

miracles: Locke does not say how much of an alleged revelation a corresponding miracle confirms, he does not carefully treat Hume's criticisms of the use of historical testimonies of miracles (which he should have anticipated), and he simply extracts the evidentiary use of miracles from the Bible to prove it as the word of God.[5] Even more recently, two friendly critics have pointed out what they think are inconsistencies in Locke's use of miracles and why they think his definition and description of what they are is wanting. They state clearly their assessment of the precariousness of the situation regarding the last point: "It is thus absolutely crucial for Locke's argument [for the reasonableness of revelation] that the notion of 'outward signs' be clear and unambiguous, for the whole edifice of our confidence in revelation is dependent upon it." They think Locke, in the end, is at a loss of how best to defend the existence and use of miracles.[6] Similarly, Joseph Houston thinks that the definition of miracles Locke provides in one of his works is confused and that Locke's incorporation of miracles indicates a "glaring slackness foreign to him."[7] Paul Helm is much less cutting in his assessment. Helm thinks Locke ends up collapsing all of the evidences for the divinity of Scripture into so-called external ones to avoid enthusiasm.[8] Alexander Broadie, while arguing that the Enlightenment is not unqualifiedly hostile to religion, posits that Locke does not make any reasonable attempt to defend the authority of Scripture in *The Reasonableness of Christianity* or *An Essay Concerning Human Understanding*. Building upon this claim, he

---

[5] Nicholas Wolterstorff, *John Locke and the Ethics of Belief* (Cambridge: Cambridge University Press, 1996), 132–33. Cf. Jonathan S. Marko, *Measuring the Distance between Locke and Toland: Reason, Revelation, and Rejection during the Locke–Stillingfleet Debate* (Eugene, OR: Pickwick Publications, 2017), 119.

[6] T. Brian Mooney and Anthony Imbrosciano, "The Curious Case of Mr. Locke's Miracles," *International Journal for Philosophy of Religion* 57, no. 3 (June 2005): 147–68 [quotation, p. 154]. They go on to say, "If it turns out that we can give no rationally compelling or even adequate account of the 'outwards signs' the reasonableness of assent and faith will thereby be diminished (if not completely shattered) by Locke's own light" (154). What is more, they think they have found a vicious circularity in Locke's use of miracles (165) to which Travis Dumsday responds (423–24 fn 11): Travis Dumsday, "Locke on Competing Miracles," *Faith and Philosophy* 25, no. 4 (October 2008): 416–24.

[7] Joseph Houston, *Reported Miracles: A Critique of Hume* (New York: Cambridge University Press, 1994), 33–48 [quotation, p. 48]. Houston thinks that the subjectivism in Locke's definition of miracles in *A Discourse on Miracles* is unnecessary (40). Houston concludes his work with the following: ". . . Yet he [Locke] does not explain how or on what basis the all-important appeal to miracle-reports can justify our high confidence that miracles, and consequently, that trustworthy revelations, have occurred . . . If our believings in revelation are to be responsible, rational, as Locke wishes, we surely need from him further help, more light. If he meant to attach certainty in God to his revelation then we would accuse him of a glaring slackness foreign to him" (48).

[8] Paul Helm, "Thomas Halyburton and John Locke on the Grounding of Faith in Scripture," in *Reformed Orthodoxy in Scotland: Essays on Scottish Theology, 1560–1775*, ed. Aaron Clay Denlinger (London: Bloomsbury T&T Clark, 2015), 213–30.

argues that Locke assumes the authority of Scripture in the former and that Locke's position in the latter is that if reason is essentially neutral in its assessment of some alleged revelation, one is permitted to follow the lead of one's own "spirit." Similar to Helm, Broadie believes that Locke is doing his best to avoid a religious epistemological position that is open to the charges of enthusiasm.[9]

The other sub-group, the sympathizers, appears less alarmed and critical of Locke's incorporation of miracles and defense of them in his religious epistemology. This is in large part due to their having studied Locke in his intellectual and social context. R. M. Burns's study of Locke in this regard is paradigmatic. He places Locke among other so-called moderate empiricists, who approach the incorporation of miracles in a not unsimilar way. He argues that they, Locke included, did not accept testimonies of miracles in a simplistic manner. Instead, they employed a context principle: the judgment of whether or not something is a miracle from God is a "gestalt judgment" based on the situation in which the miracle occurs.[10] J. J. MacIntosh, following in the path of Burns, also seems unphased by the shortcomings in Locke's treatment of miracles. He argues that Boyle, another moderate

---

[9] Alexander Broadie, "Philosophy, Revealed Religion, and the Enlightenment," in *The Oxford Handbook of British Philosophy in the Eighteenth Century*, ed. James A. Harris (Oxford: Oxford University Press, 2013), 621-37. It does seem that by "revelation," Broadie has, at least, Scriptural passages in mind. This was not completely clear throughout his otherwise well-composed essay.

[10] R. M. Burns, *The Great Debate on Miracles: From Joseph Glanvill to David Hume* (Lewisburg: Bucknell University Press, 1981). Craig Keener leans on Burns's analysis of Locke in his two volume work: *Miracles: The Credibility of the New Testament Accounts*, 2 vols. (Grand Rapids: Baker Academic, 2011), 1:26 fn 36, 1:153 fn 275. Cf. Dorothy Coleman. "Baconian Probability and Hume's Theory of Testimony," *Hume Studies* 27, no. 2 (November 2001): 195-226. This last work focuses on the connection between Bacon and Hume, but there are potential implications for Burns's overall study. Cf. Peter Harrison, "Miracles, Early Modern Science, and Rational Religion" *Church History* 75, no. 3 (September 2006): 493-510. This work is temporally broader than Burns's work. Harrison offers a narrative that shows how movements in history (the Reformation, waning influence of Aristotelianism, and the concurrent rise of empiricism) pushed the historical testimonies of miracles to the fore as an evidentiary basis for the authority of Scripture and the epistemological justification of Christianity. He helpfully points out that natural philosophy or science was not the trusted discipline it is today and thus, "It was partly by proving their religious usefulness that these new forms of knowledge gradually achieved a measure of social legitimacy. The attempt to establish the religious utility of science had the unintended consequence of transforming religion itself, and was one factor in the creation of modern 'religion'" (510). Cf. M. A. Stewart, "Revealed Religion: The British Debate," in *The Cambridge History of Eighteenth-Century Philosophy*, vol. 2, ed. Knut Haakonssen, 683-709 (Cambridge: Cambridge University Press, 2006). Stewart's work is a nice chronological survey of the major British thinkers involved in the debate over the place and value of miracles in the epistemological justification of religion. He argues that Hume does appropriate Locke's fundamental epistemology but where they majorly differ is the potential utility of historical testimonies of miracles in justifying religious belief: Locke admits quality of a testimony as a factor, while Hume does not. For Locke, the quality of testimony can trump the quantity of experiences of natural laws working flawlessly and without interruption (697-98).

empiricist, employs miracles into his religious epistemology more persuasively than does Locke.[11] Victor Nuovo, building upon Burns, thinks scholarship has given too much attention to issues related to Locke's reliance on miracles to prove the divinity of Scripture at the expense of sufficiently appreciating a particular evidence of divinity touted by Locke: the excellency of Scripture. He contends that Locke argues that the Bible not only compels people to be concerned with morality by virtue of its reasonable teachings on one divine Law-giver and the afterlife, but it also gives us the best morality![12] Greg Forster also recently added his voice to those that downplay the problem of miracles in Locke. He posits that a rigorous defense of the historical testimonies of miracles as an evidentiary basis of the divinity of revelation would be overkill to an audience that is vastly Christian.[13] And in response to those who claim Locke is guilty of circular reasoning—that is, that Locke takes miracles as a mark of divinity of Scripture from the Bible and then uses biblical testimonies of them to argue that they prove the Bible is the word of God—Forster notes, "Its [the *Essay*'s] argument for basing faith on miracles arises from the imperative for rational regulation of all beliefs, which is not a specifically Christian concern."[14] And, Travis Dumsday, whose study is not as historically contextualized as the others, argues that, given Locke's monotheistic intellectual milieu and despite the many criticisms, his *A Discourse on Miracles* is rather helpful and well thought out.[15]

In this chapter I will argue that Locke is just one of many Christian theologians in the era with a strong emphasis on the evidentiary utility of the historical testimonies of miracles for proving the divinity of Scripture.[16] But,

---

[11] J. J. MacIntosh, "Locke and Boyle on Miracles and God's Existence," in *Robert Boyle Reconsidered*, ed. Michael Hunter (Cambridge: Cambridge University Press, 1994), 193–215.

[12] Victor Nuovo, "Chapter 3: Locke's Proof of the Divine Authority of Scripture," in *Philosophy and Religion in Enlightenment Britain: New Case Studies*, ed. Ruth Savage (Oxford: Oxford University Press, 2012), 57–76; Nuovo, *John Locke: The Philosopher*, 233–35. Cf. Lucci, *John Locke's Christianity*, 49–50, 58–67.

[13] Forster, *John Locke's Politics*, 141–42.

[14] Forster, *John Locke's Politics*, 136.

[15] Dumsday, "Locke on Competing Miracles."

[16] John Tillotson and John Locke were friends and dialogued. It is possible that Locke shared some of Tillotson's more specific views regarding miraculous confirmation of revelation. John Tillotson, *Fifteen Sermons on Various Subjects*, ed. Ralph Barker (London: Ri. Chiswell, 1703). Of importance here are three sermons: "Sermon XI: Of the Miracles Wrought in Confirmation of Christianity," 301–42, "Sermon XII: Of the Miracles Wrought in Confirmation of Christianity," 343–70, and "Sermon XIII: Of the Miracles Wrought in Confirmation of Christianity," 371–96. Most of the sermons in the aforementioned work focus on the nature and relationship of faith, reason, revelation, and the Holy Spirit. John Toland appeared to follow and understand the works of both John Locke and John Tillotson, though the former to a much greater extent. His most noted work largely appropriates the religious epistemology of John Locke. John Toland, *Christianity Not Mysterious: or, A Treatise Shewing, That There Is Nothing in the Gospel Contrary to Reason, Nor Above It: And That*

for those who reject miracles as such an evidentiary basis and the need for special revelation, such as the deists,[17] Locke asks them to consider: (1) the reasonableness of revealing Scripture as Locke thinks God did; and (2) the extraordinary advancement in right morality between Christ and the best thinkers preceding Him. The former consideration, the reasonableness of God using miracles, has to do in part with the ease of legitimate assent to the Christian faith that miracles provide for the poor and uneducated, a heretofore untreated element in the Locke-miracles discussion, and also a factor that I contend solidified the importance he continued to give to miracles in his works, notwithstanding any problems with incorporating them.

Historical Context: The Use of Historical Testimonies of Miracles as an Evidentiary Basis for the Divinity of Scripture in Locke's Era

Marks of Divinity in the Protestants

The use of evidences for the divinity of Scripture varied in Locke's era. For the Reformed scholastics, the Holy Spirit's work was key to the conviction of the divinity of Scripture, and the evidences were helpful but not ultimately

---

No Christian Doctrine Can Be Properly Call'd a Mystery, 2nd ed. enlarged (London: Printed for Sam. Buckley, 1696). Cf. Marko, *Measuring the Distance*.

There are other works that prove helpful for setting the historical-theological context in which Locke wrote: Richard A. Muller, *Post-Reformation Reformed Dogmatics: The Rise and Development of Reformed Orthodoxy, ca. 1520 to ca. 1725*, 2nd ed., 4 vols. (Grand Rapids: Baker Academic, 2003); Francis Turretin, *Institutes of Elenctic Theology*, 3 vols., ed. James T. Dennison, Jr. and trans. George Musgrave Giger (Phillipsburg: P & R Publishing, 1992); Philip Van Limborch, *A Compleat System, or Body of Divinity, Both Speculative and Practical, Founded on Scripture and Reason*, trans. William Jones (London: 1702); John Owen, *The Works of John Owen*, 16 vols., ed. William H. Goold (Carlisle, PA: Banner of Truth Trust, 1966); Benedict de Spinoza, "On Miracles," in *Theological-Political Treatise*, ed. Jonathan Israel and trans. Michael Silverstone and Jonathan Israel (New York: Cambridge University Press, 2007), 81–96.

[17] Charles Blount, *Miracles, No Violations of the Laws of Nature* (London: Printed for Robert Sollers, 1683); Charles Blount, *A Summary Account of the Deists Religion: In a Letter to that Excellent Physician, the Late Dr. Thomas Sydenham. To Which Are Annex'd, Some Curious Remarks on the Immortality of the Soul; and An Essay by the Celebrated Poet, John Dryden, Esq; to Prove that Natural Religion Is Alone Necessary to Salvation, in Opposition to All Divine Revelation* (London: 1745); John Dryden, *An Essay on Natural Religion as Opposed to Divine Revelation* in *A Summary Account of the Deists Religion: In a Letter to that Excellent Physician, the Late Dr. Thomas Sydenham. To Which Are Annex'd, Some Curious Remarks on the Immortality of the Soul; and An Essay by the Celebrated Poet, John Dryden, Esq; to Prove that Natural Religion Is Alone Necessary to Salvation, in Opposition to All Divine Revelation* (London: 1745).

unassailable without the Spirit's tutelage. And the authority of Scripture, they argued, does not depend upon the proclamation of the church, as the Roman Catholics evidently contended (or any other human authority, for that matter). The Post-Reformation Reformed and the earlier Reformers were of one mind on these counts.[18] To these ends, Turretin, with whose works Locke was familiar, writes, "The Bible proves itself divine, not only authoritatively and in the manner of an artless argument or testimony ... [but it] also proves itself divine ratiocinatively by an argument artfully made from the marks which God has impressed upon the Scriptures and which furnish indubitable proof of divinity."[19] Muller's study of the divinity of Scripture points out that the Reformed "insist on the inseparability of Word and Spirit and deny that this testimony is a private revelation of any sort."[20] (It is perhaps worth noting that the Reformed position on illumination does not fit as neatly into Locke's description of enthusiasm in the *Essay*, as Helm thinks.[21]) Scripture is self-authenticating or self-evidencing through its marks, but one will not hear the Father and Christ speaking through Scripture and have true conviction of the divinity of it without the Holy Spirit's personal work.[22] Thus, the marks or evidences are primarily useful for building up the faith of the believers and have limited apologetic use by themselves.[23]

It was common for the Reformed to discuss both internal and external evidences or marks of divinity. The first belong to Scripture itself and the latter has to do with God's works related to Scripture. Although not uniform in categorization, Muller lists no less than eight common internal marks such as the "truth and sublimity of its doctrine, especially so in comparison to human teaching," "the purity, holiness, and righteousness of biblical teaching," the harmony of Scripture's many parts, its overall end, divine attestation throughout Scripture, prophetic and promissory fulfillments, "simplicity and majesty of style," and the efficacy of Scripture. These are held as being of greater importance than the external evidences. Of the lesser evidences, Muller lists four: antiquity and preservation of the texts of Scripture, character of the authors, miracles in the Old and New Testaments, and human testimony.[24]

---

[18] Muller, *PRRD*, vol. 2, 266–65.
[19] Turretin, *Institutes of Elenctic Theology*, II.iv.6.
[20] Muller, *PRRD*, vol. 2, 266–67.
[21] Cf. Helm, "Thomas Halyburton and John Locke," 220; Locke, *Essay*, IV.xix.5–7. In those sections, "enthusiasm" involves an alleged immediate revelation unsupported by reason or revelation.
[22] Muller, *PRRD*, vol. 2, 266.
[23] Muller, *PRRD*, vol. 2, 281–83.
[24] Muller, *PRRD*, vol. 2, 270–81.

The brief treatment of Scripture's divinity by the noted Dutch Remonstrant Philip Van Limborch, a close friend, interlocutor, and confidant of Locke, carries some of the same elements as found in the Reformed. Although he acknowledges up front that one with an honest and humble mind would readily admit the truth and divinity of the writings of Scripture, he notes that he must spend time to show the integrity of the historiography therein because of the many of perverse mind that had arisen in that age. He spends half of the chapter on Scripture's authority, arguing that the authors were reliable witnesses who had nothing to gain, but everything to lose, including their souls, if they knowingly promulgated lies. He abruptly ends that treatment by listing the following arguments for accepting the divinity of the New Testament: (1) the preachers of the doctrine in Scripture claim to have received it from God; (2) their doctrines were confirmed by miracles; (3) "Because Jesus Christ, the Author of the doctrine, confirm'd it by his Resurrection from the Dead, and Ascension into Heaven"; (4) the historical narrative of the New Testament and its doctrine "have in their own nature the Character of Divinity stamp'd upon them: The one relating such wonderful Effects as we could never have known but by a Revelation from God; and the Other exhibiting such Precepts to be done, and such Promises to move us to Practice of them, as none but God could prescribe or propose to us"; (5) the amazing efficacy of this doctrine, especially considering the persons who promulgated it and overcame very powerful opposition; and (6) the Apostles are conscientious enough to make a distinction between commands given to them by the Lord and their own private opinions. It is by these marks that Limborch claims that we should know that the books of the Bible were the inerrant, Spirit-directed, written will of God, penned by holy men.[25]

It is perhaps worthwhile noting a few other observations regarding Limborch's treatment of the marks of divinity. While the list of evidences he incorporates is not as lengthy or detailed as some of the lists used by his Reformed colleagues, he still uses several of what the Reformed would call internal and external evidences. Limborch's treatment, comparatively, has a more evidentialist flavor. It focuses wholly on arguments or evidences. Arguments of divine inspiration aside, he initially argues for the moral probability or certainty of the trustworthiness of the writings of the Apostles. His discussion of the Holy Spirit's role in conviction of the divinity and authority of Scripture is only implicit in his chapter once he begins his treatment of

---

[25] Limborch, *A Compleat System*, 7–11.

the above six evidences and thus ends the discussion of the reasons that the authors of Scripture were "Eye and Ear-witnesses of, and had all the Evidence for" what they wrote and that they would not write anything else but truth.[26] It is not until later in the book that he expressly discusses the Holy Spirit's sufficient and resistible grace in faith and repentance. Also, he, too, is interested in attacking the views of the Roman Catholic Church: "From hence likewise it is plain that the *Authority* of the Holy Scripture depends upon the Truth and Divinity of it, and not upon the *Tradition of the Church*, as the *Romanists* contend."[27]

The Rise of the Use of Miracles in the Moderate Empiricists and Probability Arguments in Theology

R. M. Burns's work on the miracles-related debates in England in the Enlightenment era explains how those he identifies as the "moderate empiricists" (moderate in comparison to the positivistic empiricism promulgated by Hume) came to emphasize the use of miracles as an evidentiary basis of Scripture's divinity to an even greater extent than did those like "traditional" theologians. He posits that Cartesian philosophy arose in response to the New Pyrrhonists, skeptics, who thought real knowledge must be certain beyond any sort of doubt. Descartes agreed and developed a kind of rationalism that attempted to eschew all doubt. Burns believes that this episode in the history of philosophy gave rise to the so-called egocentric predicament, where one sees oneself as epistemologically bounded by one's own experience. Moderate empiricists, like Newton, Boyle, Locke, and Glanvill, found this philosophical outlook to be too constraining because metaphysical or mathematical certainty was not feasibly attainable in many areas. Thus, they placed great reliance on the utility of moral probability judgments based on the reported observations of others and would happily settle in most instances for the resultant moral certainty. To them, science was a communal project and thus the scientist avoided putting his or her own experience above that of another. What is more, they were loath to adopt any sort of *a priori* methodology as Descartes had done. The omnipotence of God, a major presupposition of these early scientists, made the claims of

---

[26] Limborch, *A Compleat System*, 8.
[27] Limborch, *A Compleat System*, 11.

miracles rather reasonable: if revelation cannot be adjudicated by its content alone (if it could, why would we need it), it must have external credentials like miracles or prophecy, which are all easily executed by God.[28] All of this proved conducive to putting a higher emphasis on the historical testimonies of miracles than had been done in the theologians of an earlier age. In the end, Burns asserts that they were largely concerned with being reasonable as opposed to rational in a Cartesian sense.[29]

Drawing on other scholarship, Burns further argues that using moral probability arguments in theology came from two sources. First, as already noted, many of the first moderate empiricists were Christians, some of whom would occasionally write theological works in which they would employ moral probability arguments. Second, some Protestants, initially to combat the pyrrhonist attacks of the Roman Catholics, employed probability arguments. They increasingly recognized that one cannot have metaphysical certainty in most areas in religion and thus moral or practical certainty is all for which one could hope.[30]

The group of Protestants that Burns references cannot, however, be too large because many of the Protestants did not think that certainty was only of the moral or metaphysical varieties. Most were adamant that the Holy Spirit is involved with the subjective apprehension of Scripture's divinity.[31] Turretin acknowledges that while "The Scriptures do not possess metaphysical certainty," they do possess theological certainty that is above moral certainty. He argues that theological certainty must be more assured because "otherwise our faith would not be more certain than any historical assent given to human writings. But they have a theological and infallible certainty, which cannot possibly deceive the true believer illuminated by the Spirit of God."[32] Even Limborch appears to own something higher than moral probability. As already mentioned above, he spends the first half of his treatment

---

[28] This does not appear to be a completely accurate assessment by Burns. Locke seems to argue in *ROC* that many biblical prescriptions are recognized as being reasonable as soon as they are understood though many realize the improbability of humans arriving at the prescriptions on their own abilities. In other words, they are not technically above reason, but they are functionally so. Thus, there are instances where we might not technically be able to recognize revelation as such due to the lack of external testimonies such as miracles, though we would be able to adjudicate it as true or likely so. Cf. J. T. Moore, "Locke on the Moral Need for Christianity," *The Southwestern Journal of Philosophy* 11 (1980): 61–68; Marko, "The Promulgation of Right Morals," 55 en 6. Moore's work is briefly discussed there. See also Chapter 5.

[29] Burns, *The Great Debate*, chs. 1 & 2.

[30] Burns, *The Great Debate*, 38–46.

[31] Muller, *PRRD*, vol. 2, 283.

[32] Turretin, *Institutes of Elenctic Theology*, II.iv.22.

of the divinity of Scripture offering what amounts to a probabilistic argument that the New Testament can be trusted or is morally certain. But his description of faith thereafter appears to extend beyond that simple moral certainty. And, in his chapter on "Divine Vocation," he writes, "The Internal Vocation is that which is done by the Spirit of God, which influences the Hearts of Men, moving, exciting and stirring them up to obey the outward Call made to them by the word of God."[33] God's evangelical grace never operates apart from the Word and it is sufficient to move one to faith and repentance although one may resist.[34] Limborch, like all non-Pelagians, admits something beyond mere rational, moral probability in inducing one to saving faith.

Despite some minor overstatements in the work of Burns, it does provide a coherent framework to understand how probability arguments and a new emphasis on external evidences, especially testimonies of miracles, came increasingly to the fore in the 1600s. And it is this emphasis on testimonies of miracles in some quarters of Christianity that drew so much scrutiny of them by antagonists.[35] The more traditional theologians in the 1600s were not as open to such attacks.[36]

Lockean-Era Theologians on Miracles

Benedict de Spinoza's attack on miracles in 1670 might offer evidence of how prominent the use of historical testimonies of miracles associated with Scripture had become among some lay, clerical, and/or academic circles in Europe. Charles Blount's republication of Spinoza's counterargument and those of others in his *Miracles, No Violations of the Laws of Nature* is perhaps similar evidence of the same phenomenon in England. In his *Theological-Political Treatise*, Spinoza defines miracles as being "nothing other than a phenomenon whose natural cause cannot be explained on the pattern of some other familiar thing or at least cannot be so explained by the narrator or reporter of the miracle."[37] Spinoza thinks that the existence and providence

---

[33] Limborch, *A Compleat System*, 412.
[34] Limborch, *A Compleat System*, 414-15.
[35] Burns, *The Great Debates*, 11-14.
[36] Muller, *PRRD*, vol. 2, 283-85. He discusses the decline of orthodoxy and the eventual conflation by some of moral and theological certainty.
[37] Spinoza, "On Miracles," §5. Later in the section, he writes "a miracle is something whose cause cannot be explained from the principles of the natural things known to us by the natural light of reason."

of God can be inferred from the fixed and immutable order of nature that we observe. Therefore, if anything, instead of producing belief, miracles, if they were real, should cause doubts![38] What is more, if miracles were real, he thinks they only reveal a limited and fixed power because the miracles, however grand they are, are limited. Thus, again, miracles, rationally speaking, do not offer positive evidence for an almighty deity.[39] All of this somewhat comports to one of Burns's claims. In reference to a writing from Thomas Sprat, early official of the Royal Society in England, Burns writes, "already in 1667 this notion [that we would not be obliged to believe Christ without His miracles] was being regarded as axiomatic [at least among moderate empiricists], and the presumption of the indispensability of miracles in a truly revelatory situation remained unquestioned throughout the period under discussion."[40]

While it would be expected that a Reformed theologian like John Owen would not find the historical testimonies of miracles as effecting true faith, his explicit and recurrent disdain of using historical testimonies of miracles as proof of the divinity of Scripture is perhaps additional evidence for how prominent they had become by the latter half of the seventeenth century in England. He does not list miracles as an external mark of the divinity of Scripture. Among the external markers that he finds worth mentioning are the antiquity of Scripture, its preservation, the design of the whole and parts that "hath an impress on it of divine wisdom and authority," the testimony of the church, and the success of the doctrine.[41] Immediately afterwards, in discussing the insufficiency of the moral certainty that results from external arguments, he does mention miracles. He admits that Jesus and other biblical figures "wrought miracles in confirmation of their own divine mission and of the doctrine which they taught." Nonetheless, there is no example of biblical figures using miracles to produce faith in the word of God as such. Christ produced His miracles in front of those already convinced of the divinity of the Old Testament. Additionally, the Apostles' miracles were done prior to the writing of the New Testament and thus not performed to prove the

---

[38] Spinoza, "On Miracles," §6.
[39] Spinoza, "On Miracles," §8.
[40] Burns, *The Great Debates*, 18.
[41] Owen, *Works*, vol. IV, 20-47. The third mark Owen lists would be considered an internal mark of divinity by many and not external as Owen has identified it. As noted above, the Reformed were not uniform in the way that they denominated an evidence to be "internal" or "external." Cf. Muller, *PRRD*, vol. 2, 270.

divinity of it.[42] Owen later notes that Scripture is clear that the most blatant miracles will not convince one who will not submit to the authority of God.[43] What is more, he argues that the *biblical* historical testimonies of miracles are not worthwhile employing because people will only believe those reported accounts if they believe Scripture to be true. The so-called "tradition" of testimonies of miracles not passed down through Scripture in confirmation of Christianity is of little value because humans are dubious and are prone to exaggeration. He notes that to be obliged to believe something because it has been passed down by one's forefathers would mean that some would be obliged, perhaps, to believe the claims of the divinity of the Koran due to a similar, competing tradition or that there were no miracles based on another tradition that claimed as much. Due to all these considerations, one has no true grounds in tradition upon which to claim the divinity of Scripture.[44]

By contrast, Archbishop John Tillotson is an example of a theologian contemporary with Locke who held that miracles were a very reasonable way for God to confirm His revelation. He clearly outlines his position in a sermon entitled, "Of the Miracles Wrought in Confirmation of Christianity." In the sermon, the good archbishop discusses two issues: (1) "That Miracles are a Divine Testimony given to a Person or Doctrine"; and (2) "That God gave this Testimony to the Apostles, and first Preachers of Christianity, in a very eminent manner."[45] He offers a brief definition of miracles that he subsequently unpacks: "The shortest and plainest description I can give of it, is this, that it is a supernatural Effect evident and wonderful to sense." He notes that there are different kinds of supernatural events: there are those that are simply supernatural in themselves, like someone's resurrection, and effects that are supernatural in their manner, but which nature could do over a much longer period of time, like healings.[46] Miracles must, in Tillotson's mind, be

---

[42] Owen, *Works*, vol. IV, 48–49. He writes, "Their doctrine, therefore, materially considered, and their warranty to teach it, were sufficiently, yea, abundantly confirmed by them [miracles]. But divine revelation, formally considered, and as written, was left upon the old foundation of the authority of God who gave it" (48).

[43] Owen, *Works*, vol. XVI, 317–18.

[44] Owen, *Works*, vol. XVI, 330–32. There are two additional notes worth mentioning. First, in Locke's *A Discourse on Miracles*, he asserts that only the Jews and Christians claim the use of miracles as the credentials of a divine messenger. Muhammed, he says, did not make claims to miracles. He thinks the historical claims of the Zoroastrians and Hindus are too obscure and fabulous to take seriously (220–21). So, Locke is aware of such attacks on the utility of miracles, as Owen makes, and believes them to be without merit. Second, Owen, after noting other strategies of arguing for the divinity of Scripture, asserts that there is not "any public or private authority of man or church, tradition or otherwise," but only Scripture itself that can truly attest to its divinity (335).

[45] Tillotson, "Sermon XI," 308.

[46] Tillotson, "Sermon XI," 309–10.

"nothing else but a thing wonderful to the sense; and the very end and design of it, is to be a sensible proof and conviction to us of some thing which we do not see." Thus, the transubstantiation of the Roman Catholics is not a miracle. If it were, then anyone could claim non-evident miracles whenever they desired.[47]

Tillotson gave a more prominent role to miracles than the Reformed theologians, but he also found other factors to be of importance to help identify the miracle and the associated doctrine or agent as being from God. He writes, "That the entire Proof of the Christian doctrine or Religion, consists of many Considerations, which taken together, make up a full Demonstration of the Truth of it, when perhaps no one of them, taken singly and by it self, is a convincing and undeniable proof."[48] Thus, while the precepts of Christianity are highly reasonable, that alone does not mean that they are from God.[49] And, if there is some teaching (or someone) associated with a miracle, but the thing propounded is "so unreasonable and absurd, so unworthy of God, and so contrary to the natural notions which men have of him, that no Miracles can be sufficient to give confirmation to it."[50] Later he writes:

> But yet Miracles are the principal external Proof and Confirmation of the Divinity of a Doctrine. I told you before, that some Doctrines are so absurd, that a Miracle is not a sufficient proof of them: but if a Doctrine be such as is no ways unworthy of God, nor contrary to those notions of him, Miracles are the highest Testimony that can be given to it, and have always been owned by Mankind for an evidence of inspiration.[51]

He goes on to find support for these claims from Scripture. Moreover, Tillotson asserts that the more fantastic, unquestionable, public, and numerous miracles are, the more credible reports of them will be. And, while God may allow a demon to perform a miracle for a false prophet, there is always sufficient marks to dismiss the associated doctrine and human agent: either the doctrine propounded will be ridiculous or the doctrine testified to is contrary to a doctrine with far greater confirmation.[52] In sum, then, for Tillotson, miracles are the principal evidence of a doctrine or agent being

---

[47] Tillotson, "Sermon XI," 315–17.
[48] Tillotson, "Sermon XI," 318.
[49] Tillotson, "Sermon XI," 319.
[50] Tillotson, "Sermon XI," 321.
[51] Tillotson, "Sermon XI," 322–23.
[52] Tillotson, "Sermon XI," 325–31.

from God, but still to acknowledge the miracle as being from God we must consider "in what Circumstances, and with what Cautions and Limitations they are so."[53]

Despite his unmerited reputation for being one of the most important deists of the day, John Toland, author of *Christianity Not Mysterious*, is another thinker who finds notable utility in miracles. (Admittedly, he does seem to deny present-day miracles, but he gives biblical arguments for that position.[54]) For one, Jesus Christ used them as confirmation to the Jews of His authority despite all of the marks of the Messiah that could be reasonably observed regarding Jesus in light of the Old Testament.[55] There are even examples in the Bible of people waiting for miraculous confirmation before presuming the message that they received was from God.[56] What is more, Toland offers a definition of a miracle: "*is some Action exceeding all humane Power, and which the Laws of NATURE cannot perform by their ordinary Operations.*"[57] He clarifies this a bit later on, noting if someone can determine how a miracle was performed, then it is no miracle and "Miracles are produc'd according to the Laws of Nature, tho above its ordinary Operations, which are therefore supernaturally assisted."[58] In other words, miracles are not events in which natural laws are stalled or temporarily ceased, but rather observable events in nature where supernatural forces break into the created, natural order: "The Order of Nature is not alter'd, stopp'd, or forwarded, unless for some weighty Design becoming the Divine Wisdom and Majesty." Like Tillotson, he asserts "that no *Miracle* is ever wrought without some special and important End . . . Nor is there any *Miracle* mention'd in the *New Testament*, but what serv'd to confirm the Authority of those that wrought it, to procure Attention to the Doctrines of the *Gospel*, or for the like wise and reasonable Purposes."[59] He does not, however, believe, like Tillotson, that God would allow competing miracles. He simply thinks God will not allow an actual disruption to the universal order unless it is for the benefit of the unbeliever.[60]

---

[53] Tillotson, "Sermon XI," 335.
[54] Marko, *Measuring the Distance*, ch. 4.
[55] Toland, *Christianity Not Mysterious*, 46–48.
[56] Toland, *Christianity Not Mysterious*, 43–48.
[57] Toland, *Christianity Not Mysterious*, 144.
[58] Toland, *Christianity Not Mysterious*, 150.
[59] Toland, *Christianity Not Mysterious*, 146–47.
[60] Toland, *Christianity Not Mysterious*, 147–49.

Toland, although putting a notable emphasis on miracles, hardly has this as his only evidence. So, while both Toland and Tillotson find miracles as indispensable to prove the divinity of Scripture, there are other evidences both thinkers declare as well. Toland writes the following in his argument that it is not by the Church (or simply by miracles) that we know that Scripture is divine, but rather its qualities or certain marks:

> But if we believe the *Scripture* to be Divine, not upon its own bare Assertion, but from a real Testimony consisting in the Evidence of the things contain'd therein; from undoubted Effects, and not from Words and Letters; what is this but to prove it by *Reason*? It has in it self, I grant, the brightest Characters of *Divinity:* But 'tis *Reason* finds them out, examines them, and by its Principles approves and pronounces them sufficient; which orderly begets in us an Acquiescence of *Faith* or Perswasion.[61]

Toland goes on to list other evidences of divinity. So, marks of divinity are more diverse than just miracles: the effects that Scripture has on its adherents, the characters of its protagonists, and more.[62]

Both Tillotson and Toland appear to be essentially employing the context principle: the idea that identifying a supposed miracle as being from God (or, more importantly, the associated divine doctrine as being such) depends upon a gestalt judgment of an overall view of the situation in which the miracle occurred (or in which the doctrine was promulgated). As noted above, Burns, MacIntosh, and Nuovo defend Locke's use of miracles by pointing out his use of the context principle as opposed to a crass acceptance of divine revelation as such based merely on historical testimonies of miracles. And, when one is employing the context principle, the associated miracle apparently is one reported from without or within Scripture (the distinction Owen expressly makes), although there are most likely far more trusted examples of the latter. Some in the era would likely find utility in the attestation of the resurrection of Christ from purportedly quality extant copies of the works of Josephus, for instance, in addition to those from the apostles' works. On a related point, Locke even admits the possibility of modern-day revelation and concomitant miracles, both of which obviously would be beyond those found in the Protestant canon. Thus, it seems the testimonies of miracles for

---

[61] Toland, *Christianity Not Mysterious*, 33–34.
[62] Toland, *Christianity Not Mysterious*, 34.

many in the era are simply an indication that the testifier of an alleged divine message was not deceived or self-deceiving. Moreover, both Tillotson and Toland, in the works by them that I have addressed, do not explicitly incorporate illumination or assistance of the Holy Spirit into the conviction process. Tillotson does, however, elsewhere, but I am not aware if Toland ever does.[63]

Limborch has much to say about miracles as well. He offers the following in his *A Compleat Body of Divinty*: "all those Operations which are not only above the Power, but also contrary to the ordinary Course and the fix'd Laws of Nature." To deny them is to ignorantly identify the power of God and the power of nature. Miracles are the "clearest and brightest Notices we have of the Nature as well as Existence of God." In contrast to Spinoza and Blount, he thinks that miracles are a sufficient proof of the existence of God: "and that therefore the Miracles wrought by *Moses* and others before Christ, as well as those wrought by him, are a sufficient Demonstration of a Power above Nature, and prove the existence of God; the Belief whereof is the Foundation of all Religion."[64] Moreover, regarding the ways in which Christ's doctrine is proved, he asserts, "The first and chiefest of them is by Miracles, which are an unquestionable Sign of the Divine Mission." And the nature of Christ's miracles put them beyond dispute: (1) all of them were observable to the senses; (2) they exceeded the power of nature; and (3) none of His miracles tended "to the Subversion of any Doctrine, approv'd by God formerly by sufficient Miracles." All false prophets are capable of producing are lying wonders of Satan that will fail in one of these ways.[65] What is more, God the Father used miracles "in order to establish his [Jesus'] Authority among Men, and to testify that he was his true Son."[66]

In sum, then, there is ample evidence of a movement away from the more traditional Protestant treatment of the divinity of Scripture. Miracles, which were not the primary pieces of evidence for the divinity of Scripture among the scholastics of the day, not to mention the Reformers of the previous

---

[63] For example, Tillotson, *Fifteen Sermons*, 140-2. Cf. Toland, *Christianity Not Mysterious*, 33, 45. On the latter referenced page, Toland writes: "I am not ignorant how some boast they are strongly perswaded *by the illuminating and efficacious Operation of the Holy Spirit*, and that they neither have nor approve other Reasons of their FAITH." He is not necessarily attacking those who claim to be illuminated by the Holy Spirit but rather those who approve of no other reason than that. I think it is likely that his reticence to make a clear pronouncement about the Holy Spirit's operation on believers is influenced by his close reading of Locke. Cf. Marko, *Measuring the Distance*, ch. 4. It is important to mention that Locke does not incorporate his chapter "Of Enthusiasm" until the fourth edition of the *Essay*, years after the publication of Toland's work.
[64] Limborch, *A Compleat System*, 4-5.
[65] Limborch, *A Compleat System*, 272-73.
[66] Limborch, *A Compleat System*, 274.

century, came to the fore in arguments used by moderate empiricists and evidentialist theologians by the late 1600s. If they were not the primary evidence, they at least became an indispensable component to a cumulative argument. And a concurrent de-emphasis (or perhaps for some, negation) of the illumination or the assistance of the Holy Spirit perhaps put even more evidentiary weight on miracles. But this increased reliance on miracles, as understandable as it may be given the operating tendencies of the moderate empiricists, with their Christian presuppositions, and the evidentialist theologians of different kinds, made these reported, divine events the focus of increased scrutiny by those antagonistic toward Christianity.

Locke's Writings on Miracles

Miracles, Testimonies, and Their Reasonable Evidentiary Use in *An Essay Concerning Human Understanding*

In *An Essay Concerning Human Understanding* (*Essay*), Locke discusses the use of miracles as an evidentiary basis for alleged revelation in the closing chapters. In his chapter on "Degrees of Assent," after he has discussed varying levels of intensity in belief, he turns his attention to miracles.[67] Regarding particular matters of fact, he had said that the highest level of assurance (but still not technically "certain") was the following: "Where any particular thing, consonant to the constant Observation of our selves and others, in the like case, comes attested by the concurrent Reports of all that mention it, we receive it as easily, and build as firmly upon it, as if it were certain Knowledge."[68] Paragraphs later he reaffirms the sentiments of this statement but writes:

> yet there is one Case, wherein the strangeness of the Fact lessens not the Assent to a fair Testimony given of it. For where such supernatural Events are suitable to ends aim'd at by him, who has the Power to change the course of Nature, there, under such Circumstances, they may be the fitter to

---

[67] Much of this analysis was first done in Marko, *Measuring the Distance*, especially, chapter 3. At the risk of being read as contradicting myself or overturning what I first thought, some of the complexities there are not repeated here or are muted. I thought it necessary for the manageability of this chapter. The most prominent aspect not covered in its fullness here is the complex discussion on the internal marks of Scripture. There are definitely, however, some new discoveries and connections made in this sub-section.

[68] Locke, *Essay*, IV.xvi.6.

procure Belief, by how much the more they are beyond, or contrary to ordinary Observations. This is the proper Case of *Miracles*, which well attested, do not only find Credit themselves; but give it also to other Truths, which need such Confirmation.[69]

In other words, one should not rule out miracles by God, but actually expect Him to do or have done them for appropriate ends (as rare as they might be). Locke does not think there is a much better way for God to get our attention. One should not conclude that Locke is guilty of a contradiction in allowing that generally the strangeness of an event or claim detracts from assurance, but in the case of miracles improves it. First, the more astounding the event is the less it would seem that the reporter was mistaken about it being a miracle. Second, Locke would say that most of the things that we assent to near certainty are often trivial matters. The most important matters require more attention, and what more important matter is there than the eternal state of one's soul![70]

Locke says even more about this seeming discrepancy in the next section. He notes that God will not deceive or be deceived. A testimony from God "carries with it Assurance beyond Doubt, Evidence beyond Exception." Our assent to this revelation "absolutely determines our Minds, and as perfectly excludes all wavering as our Knowledge it self . . . So that Faith is a setled and sure Principle of Assent and Assurance, and leaves no manner of room for Doubt or Hesitation." But, for most, especially those not privy to the original confirming event, "we must be sure, that it be a divine Revelation, and that we understand it right," lest we fall into the errors of the enthusiasts. He then notes, "If the evidence of its being a Revelation, or that this its true Sense be only on probable Proofs, our Assent can reach no higher than an Assurance or Diffidence, arising from the more, or less apparent Probability of the Proofs." But before one thinks Locke is backtracking or qualifying his earlier statement away, one must consider this might be aimed at enthusiasts, with respect to what they consider to be revelation ("If the evidence of its being a Revelation"), and those who rightly believe the Bible as the word of God, but foist the burdens of their own, at best, probable interpretations on others ("or that this its true Sense be only on probable Proofs"). Besides, he ends the section with the following: "But of Faith, and the Precedency it ought to have

---

[69] Locke, *Essay*, IV.xvi.13.
[70] Locke, *Essay*, IV.xiv.2; IV.xvi.3, 6; IV.xx.3. Cf. Marko, "Why Locke's Response."

before other Arguments of Perswasion, I shall speak more hereafter, where I treat of it, as it is ordinarily placed, in contradistinction to Reason; though in Truth, it be nothing else but an Assent founded on the highest Reason."[71]

Locke picks up the topic of faith in revelation after a lengthy chapter on reason. Although he had earlier asserted that faith is simply a function of reason, in this chapter he writes of them distinctly, the former dealing only with natural issues and the latter dealing with purportedly revelatory matters. There he states that "*no Proposition can be received by divine Revelation*, or obtain the Assent due to all such, *if it be contradictory to our clear intuitive Knowledge*." To allow this would be to overturn the very principles of reason itself, with which we come to believe.[72] However, when our conclusions from natural reason are only probable or, as it were, natural belief, it must concede to faith:

> But since GOD in giving us the light of *Reason* has not therefore tied up his own Hands from affording us, when he thinks fit, the light of *Revelation* in any of those Matters, wherein our natural Faculties are able to give a probable Determination, *Revelation*, where God has been pleased to give it, *must carry it, against the probable Conjectures of Reason*. Because the Mind, not being certain of the Truth of that it does not evidently know, but only yielding to the Probability that appears in it, is bound to give up its Assent to such a Testimony, which, it is satisfied, comes from one, who cannot err, and will not deceive.[73]

He says something similar a couple of sections later after he notes that faith cannot overturn certain knowledge: "Whatsoever is divine *Revelation*, ought to over-rule all our Opinions, Prejudices, and Interests, and hath a right to be received with full Assent."[74]

The next chapter in the *Essay* is "On Enthusiasm," where Locke continues to explicitly discuss miracles. In it he says that if God wants us to assent to something he will evidence it to us through natural means or "by some Marks which Reason cannot be mistaken in."[75] In the next section, he asserts that if an alleged revelation is conformable to natural reason or the Word of

---

[71] Locke, *Essay*, IV.xvi.14.
[72] Locke, *Essay*, IV.xviii.5.
[73] Locke, *Essay*, IV.xviii.8.
[74] Locke, *Essay*, IV.xviii.10.
[75] Locke, *Essay*, IV.xix.14.

God [i.e., attested revelation] it is safe to receive it as a revelation. But, if there is no miracle and the supposed revelation does not apparently comport with the conclusions of natural reason or Scripture, then it cannot be accepted as such. He then points to Moses and Gideon who both required miracles to confirm the revelations that they had received from God.[76] He does not deny that God enlightens our minds in apprehending truths and influences us by the Holy Spirit without any sign. Again, he states, as long as the enlightened truth is conformable to reason or Scripture, it can be taken as revelation:

> Where the Truth imbraced is consonant to the *Revelation* in the written word of GOD; or the Action conformable to the dictates of right *Reason* or Holy Writ, we may be assured that we run no risque in entertaining it as such, because though perhaps it be not an immediate Revelation from GOD, extraordinarily operating on our Minds, yet we are sure it is warranted by that Revelation which he has given us of Truth.[77]

Thus, there appears to be an argument regarding the reasonable acceptance of revelation with miraculous testimonies in the last few chapters of Book IV of the *Essay*. First, it is evident that Locke found that a revelation can be accepted as such if it is not contrary to certain knowledge and other, but better-attested revelation. If it is beyond both—that is, it introduces something wholly new or contrary to naturally wrought probability or argumentation—then it must have a miracle or miracles testifying to it. In answer to the problem of putting so much confidence in miraculous testimonies that are no more than historically or morally probable, some guess can be made at what Locke would say. He thought that based on our weakness—we have so few occasions to have knowledge and certainty in a variety of areas and thus are required to assent to so many propositions—it is reasonable that God reveals things, especially regarding His will and the way to salvation, and helps us the way that He does. Thus, regardless of whether testimonies are technically only probable, they are very good in the case of Christianity. If one agrees with Locke on the reasonableness of God's revelatory process and that the Bible is from Him, one's approach to Scripture must necessarily change. One will approach it being prepared to have what otherwise would be naturally formed beliefs overturned, however sure we feel about those beliefs. Each proposition of

---

[76] Locke, *Essay*, IV.xix.15.
[77] Locke, *Essay*, IV.xix.16.

Scripture is not treated as historically probable or merely morally certain, and thus overturnable by what would seem to be a more naturally reasonable conclusion. The entirety of Scripture thus is approached with more surety than one's weak operations. In fact, the very next chapter of the *Essay* is "Of Wrong Assent, or Error," where he enumerates the ways in which we reason wrongly or the many instances where our passions, biases, prejudices, laziness, and the like, keep us from reasoning well and rightly concluding.

In brief, in his chapter on assent, Locke discusses miracles. He then moves on to discuss reason and then the precedence that revealed faith ought to have over natural belief. This is followed by his chapter on enthusiasm, where he discusses, among other things, the need for miracles. Then, he essentially ends the *Essay* with a chapter where the unguided mind so often goes wrong. All the major elements in this line of argument are present in *The Reasonableness of Christianity*.

Locke also makes room for the idea of illumination. He allows that the Holy Spirit might assist our reasoning abilities. In answer to why he might not just come out and own something akin to the notion of illumination, theological certainty, or the like, a few things might be said. He might simply be undecided about what precisely the Holy Spirit does or how and how frequently He helps us; or, it simply is beyond the scope and designs of the *Essay*. It does fall in line with Locke's reluctance to make metaphysical pronouncements as I have argued elsewhere.[78] With all of these questions unanswered, as his last few chapters of the *Essay*, especially "Of Enthusiasm," stand, it appears that Locke's treatment of revelation, contrary to the assessments of some, actually makes space for Reformed Christians, who will speak of the Holy Spirit's work as the primary reason for their faith but not at the expense of all other evidences. That is, that to which they assent is simply Scripture itself, one of two sources (the other being natural reason) to which allegedly enlightened truths without a miracle must be conformable to be permitted to be considered from God in Locke's economy. Of course, the Reformed did not think of illumination as a personal revelation.[79] And, Locke, in "Of Enthusiasm," at least acknowledges a distinction used by some between immediate revelation and the Holy Spirit's illuminating work: "In what I have said I am far from denying, that GOD can, or doth sometimes enlighten Mens [sic] Minds in the apprehending of certain Truths, or excite them to

---

[78] Marko, "Why Locke's 'Of Power.'"
[79] Muller, *PRRD*, vol. 2, 266-67.

Good Actions by the immediate influence and assistance of the Holy Spirit, without any extraordinary Signs accompanying it."[80] It is very understandable why so many have read the aforementioned chapter as being, in part, an attack on Reformed thought: Locke is clearly an empirical-evidentialist and desires to cast doubts on innate notions.[81] But, unless Locke's understanding of Reformed thought was inaccurate, the attacks, specifically against the so-called enthusiasts, do not seem to cut to the heart of the Reformed claims.

Miracles, Testimonies, and Their Reasonable Evidentiary Use in *The Reasonableness of Christianity*

Locke discusses miracles throughout *The Reasonableness of Christianity*. Locke asserts that there is a three-fold declaration of Christ as Messiah in the Gospels: (1) miracles, (2) phrases and circumlocutions that signified or intimated his coming, and (3) the plain and direct address by the Messiah. He thinks that Jews expected Christ to be a great miracle worker and justified their belief in him based on that.[82] And, after Christ's ascension, the Apostles confirmed "that Doctrine [the resurrection of Christ] by the Miracles which the Holy Ghost impowered them to do."[83]

Locke does offer some general comments on God's use of miracles. First, working supernatural events is within his power and He does it to draw attention to Himself (or His message or messengers). Second, they, reasonably speaking, will be rare. To both points he writes:

> Yet his Wisdom is not usually at the expence of Miracles (if I may so say) but only in cases that require them, for the evidencing of some Revelation or Mission to be from him. He does constantly (unless where the confirmation of some Truth requires it otherwise) bring about his Purposes by means operating according to their Natures. If it were not so, the course and evidence of things would be confounded; Miracles would lose their name and force, and there could be no distinction between Natural and Supernatural.[84]

---

[80] Locke, *Essay*, IV.xix.16.
[81] Cf. Muller, *PRRD*, vol. 2, 268.
[82] Locke, *ROC*, 54–59; cf. 77, 79–147. Discussions or mentions of Jesus' miracles are sprinkled throughout these pages.
[83] Locke, *ROC*, 178.
[84] Locke, *ROC*, 161.

Thus, if miracles were frequent, our natural notices would be greatly devalued as we would not know when something is natural or supernatural and the same goes for the cases involving miracles. What is more, God and Jesus, during His mission, used miracles sparingly. Jesus did not put himself in situations where he would need miracles to escape, for instance. Besides, if he were to do too many miracles, he would have gained such a large following that he would have so many followers desiring to set him up as king that he would have been charged by Pilate of sedition.[85]

Locke writes further of the reasonableness of God's revelatory *modus operandi* near the end of the book within his discussion of the five advantages that he discusses pertaining to Jesus Christ's arrival. The first advantage is belief in the one, true God. Although belief in God is rationally demonstrable, due to the corruption of people and their religious leaders, polytheism had before prevailed. The second advantage is clear identification and explanation of true morality. Again, although Locke thinks morality demonstrable or at least somewhat accessible by lesser minds, right thinking in morality was universally weak. The third advantage is Christ's teaching of true worship. As opposed to the pomp and circumstance that attended pagan worship, Christ taught that application of the mind and sincerity of heart is what God requires. The fourth advantage is Christ's teaching on the afterlife and that one would receive rewards and punishments. This was impetus to lead a virtuous life and an idea that was not assured in the minds of most. And the fifth advantage was the Holy Spirit. We are encouraged by the promise of the assistance of the Holy Spirit.[86] Moreover, Victor Nuovo believes there to be ample evidence within these advantages that Locke did not use miracles in the unsophisticated manner that some claim he does. He thinks that these advantages, at least the first, second, and fourth, are evidence of the excellency of Scripture. Its morality is great and the belief in one God who punishes and rewards in the afterlife compels people to pay attention to it.[87]

That said, it is within his discussion of the second advantage where he describes the reasonableness of God's revelation. It was Locke's belief that one could demonstrate the true system of moral principles. Even though he maintained that notion in *ROC*, he admits there, as he did in one of his letters, "That 'tis too hard a thing for unassisted Reason, to establish Morality

---

[85] Locke, *ROC*, 161–64.
[86] Locke, *ROC*, 259–93.
[87] Nuovo, "Locke's Proof."

in all its parts upon its true foundations; with a clear and convincing light."[88] He asserts that it is more expedient and surer for one sent from God with authority to reveal humans' duty than to leave them to discover it by long deductions of reason.[89] As moral principles are capable of certainty, a philosopher would need to make his or her standard of morality mandatory by demonstrating it from reason or by showing that he is from God: "must shew, that either he builds his Doctrine from Principles of Reason, self-Evident in themselves; and deduces all the parts of it from thence, by clear and evident demonstration; Or must shew his Commission from Heaven, that he comes from the Authority from God, to deliver his Will and Commands to the World."[90] A little later he acknowledges that even if ethics has the proper demonstrable foundation, most people do not have the time or the ability to follow long trains of reasoning. One might as well expect the typical person to be a perfect mathematician. Instead, they are given simple commands testified to by divine miracles. "The greatest part cannot know, and therefore they must believe." In other words, revelation, which can deliver simple to understand commands without long deductions of reason to make them obligatory, is the best and most reasonable way for God to reveal his morality taking into consideration the human situation and limitations.[91]

A charitable read of Locke's *ROC*, especially amidst the five advantages, yields all or most of the aforementioned internal evidences Muller offers: "truth and sublimity of its doctrine, especially so in comparison to human teaching," "the purity, holiness, and righteousness of biblical teaching," the harmony of Scripture's many parts, its overall end, divine attestation throughout Scripture, prophetic and promissory fulfillments, "simplicity and majesty of style," and the efficacy of Scripture. For instance, regarding the efficacy, Locke mentions how polytheism was practically eradicated wherever Christ went.[92] Regarding its truth and sublimity, he writes of New Testament morality:

> Though as soon as they are heard and considered, they are found to be agreeable to Reason; and such as can by no means be contradicted. Every

---

[88] Locke, *ROC*, 268; John Locke, "L2059: Locke to William Molyneux, March 30 [c. April 5] 1696," in *The Correspondence of John Locke*, vol. 5, ed. E. S. de Beer (Oxford: Oxford University Press, 1979), 593–96; cf. Locke, *Essay*, I.ii.1; IV.iv.7; Marko, "Promulgation of Right Morals," 42.
[89] Locke, *ROC*, 269.
[90] Locke, *ROC*, 274–75.
[91] Locke, *ROC*, 282.
[92] Locke, *ROC*, 263–64.

one may observe a great many truths which he receives at first from others, and readily assents to, as consonant to reason; which he would have found it hard, and perhaps beyond his strength to have discovered himself.[93]

ROC also explicitly advances the same acceptance of revelation ahead of all probable, naturally formed beliefs. After mentioning some of the miracles done by Christ, Locke writes:

> To one who is once perswaded that Jesus Christ was sent by God to be a King, and a Saviour of those who do believe in him; All his Commands become Principles: There needs no other Proof for the truth of what he says, but that he said it. And then there needs no more but to read the inspired Books, to be instructed: All the duties of Morality lye there clear, and plain, and easy to be understood.[94]

While the interpretation might be less clear in other parts, the position that God said it still holds. The more obscure parts of Scripture do not lose their advanced standing. We are to "receive all parts of Divine Revelation, with a docility and disposition prepared to imbrace, and assent to all Truths coming from God; And submit his mind to whatsoever shall appear to him to bear that Character."[95] And if he cannot understand a text or render several texts consistent with one another, he ought to simply suspend his opinion, at least for a time.[96]

Thus, in *ROC*, we see the same general argument for the reasonableness of God using miracles as evidence of the divinity of Scripture as is inferable from the *Essay*. In *ROC* it is more explicit. In *ROC*, too, one can see the same advanced standing that revelation receives in the *Essay*; and again, it is more explicit in *ROC*. One notable difference is the presentation (or perhaps much clearer presentation) of the internal marks of Scripture. There are more in *ROC* than anyone has indicated. Nevertheless, Locke does put a high emphasis on miracles as a mark of divinity, at least compared to the Reformed.

---

[93] Locke, *ROC*, 269-70.
[94] Locke, *ROC*, 283-84.
[95] Locke, *ROC*, 303-4.
[96] Locke, *ROC*, 304.

Miracles, Testimonies, and Their Reasonable Evidentiary Use in "A Discourse on Miracles"

Locke offers a definition of miracles in his "A Discourse on Miracles" ("Discourse"): "A Miracle then I take to be a sensible Operation, which being above the comprehension of the Spectator, and in his Opinion contrary to the establish'd Course of Nature, is taken by him to be Divine."[97] He further states, "He that is present at the fact, is a Spectator: He that believes the History of the fact, puts himself in the place of a Spectator." He immediately acknowledges two complaints that critics will have. First, some will complain that he makes what is and is not a miracle depend upon the opinion of the spectator: "That hereby what is a Miracle is made very uncertain; for it depending on the Opinion of the Spectator, that will be a Miracle to one which will not be so to another." For Locke, this is of no force, because he is doubtful one could produce a better definition.[98] It is not until the end of the "Discourse" that he more clearly explains that it is too difficult to know what occurrences clearly go against fixed laws and whether or not only God is capable of performing the event.[99] Because revelation (and miracles are a type of revelation) is to surpass our natural reason in some way and all of natural philosophy is a posteriori, it is futile to conjecture an exhaustive list of the characteristics of a miracle. (Someone like Spinoza would claim them to be naturally occurring phenomena that simply cannot yet be explained. That mere assertion could not be rebutted with metaphysical certainty unless one perfectly and demonstrably understood the physical order.) The second objection is that the subjective element of his definition opens up the possibility of something wholly natural being taken as a miracle, and, as a result, invalidating the use of miracles as a mark of divinity. He does not think that this is a concern if miracles are rightly considered: "To know that any Revelation is from God, it is necessary to know that the Missenger [sic] that delivers it is sent from God, and that cannot be known but by some credentials given him by God himself."[100] It is to these credentials that Locke turns.

He considers polytheistic and monotheistic religions in succession. He notes that polytheistic religions had no use for miracles as none of their

---

[97] Locke, "A Discourse of Miracles," 217.
[98] Locke, "A Discourse of Miracles," 217–18.
[99] Locke, "A Discourse of Miracles," 230–31.
[100] Locke, "A Discourse of Miracles," 218.

supposed deities were concerned with marking themselves out as the only one. He remarks how well the devil blinded these people who adhered to polytheism that was neither derived from reason nor had a sure foundation in revelation. The notion of miracles makes the best sense in religions that suppose only one God. But of the monotheistic religions, only the Jews and Christians claim miracles, and those confirm each other.[101] Locke thus thinks miracles are the eminently reasonable way for God to mark his messengers. He knows he will still have objectors and critics but writes, "For every rational thinking Man must conclude as *Nicodemus* did, *We know that thou art a teacher from God, for no Man can do these signs which thou dost, except God be with him.*"[102] Locke recognizes that they might not be convinced by a singular miracle but they ought to be by miracle upon miracle.[103]

Locke turns to the question, "what shall be a sufficient inducement to take any extraordinary Operation to be a Miracle" of God?[104] His response is, "And to this I answer, the carrying with it the Marks of a greater power than appears in opposition to it." He explains that if there are ever two competing, alleged divine agents it is reasonable to presume that God will not be outdone and will always give His agent the greatest miracle or miracles: "wherever there is an opposition, and two pretending to be sent from Heaven clash, the signs which carry with them the evident marks of a greater Power, will always be a certain and unquestionable evidence that the Truth and Divine Mission is on that side on which they appear."[105] This is reasonable because although no one knows "the uttermost Power of natural Agents or created beings" it is obvious that God always can exceed their works.[106] This was the case with Moses versus the priests of Pharaoh. It is the case with Jesus Christ at present: nothing has arisen to realistically oppose him.[107] In fact, "that wherever the Gospel comes, it prevails to the beating down the strong Holds of *Satan*, and dislodging the Prince of the Power of Darkness, driving him away with all his living wonders; which is a standing Miracle, carrying with it the Testimony of Superiority." In other words, the power of the gospel and the Christian faith is a present-day miracle.[108]

---

[101] Locke, "A Discourse of Miracles," 219-21.
[102] Locke, "A Discourse of Miracles," 221.
[103] Locke, "A Discourse of Miracles," 222.
[104] Locke, "A Discourse of Miracles," 222.
[105] Locke, "A Discourse of Miracles," 223.
[106] Locke, "A Discourse of Miracles," 226 [quotation, 227-29].
[107] Locke, "A Discourse of Miracles," 224-25.
[108] Locke, "A Discourse of Miracles," 225.

Locke does assert some additional qualifications to adjudicate an alleged divine miracle. These qualifications are the basis of the context principle pointed out by Burns. First, "That no Mission can be look'd on to be Divine, that delivers any thing derogating from the Honour of the one, only, true invisible God, or inconsistent with natural Religion and the rules of Morality."[109] Second, "That it cannot be expected that God should send any one into the World on purpose to inform Men of things indifferent, and of small moment, or that are knowable by the use of their Faculties." Doing so would detract His majesty and contribute to our laziness.[110] Third, the revelation must be "of some supernatural Truths relating to the Glory of God, and some great concern of Men."[111]

Thereafter, he again discusses the reasonableness of God using miracles as the evidentiary basis for identifying a message or messenger as being from Him and how this is also prescribed in Scripture itself. He writes, "For these supernatural signs being the only means God is conceived to have to satisfie Men as rational Creatures of the Certainty of any thing he would reveal, as coming from himself, can never consent that it should be wrested out of his hands, to serve the Ends and establish the Authority of an inferior agent that rivals him."[112] Although not mentioning the following, his views on the utility of miracles is in line with his position on much of revelation being beyond our abilities of discovery. Miracles are an efficient way to parse through competing revelations both of whose content is beyond our discovery or discernment. Jesus and Moses performed miracles for the unbelief of the Jews.[113] Toward the end of the "Discourse," Locke asserts, "For Miracles being the Basis on which divine Mission is always establish'd, and consequently that Foundation on which the Believers of any divine Revelation must ultimately bottom their Faith."[114] There is no better way to indicate his message and messengers than God providing a mark or marks so seemingly supernatural along with an appropriate message—appropriate based on the nature of the message indicated above through three points. Locke can think of nothing better or more convincing.

In sum, Locke thinks that miracles are a very reasonable way for God to get our attention and identify His divine agents. This assertion is amply defended

---

[109] Locke, "A Discourse of Miracles," 226.
[110] Locke, "A Discourse of Miracles," 226-27.
[111] Locke, "A Discourse of Miracles," 227.
[112] Locke, "A Discourse of Miracles," 227-28.
[113] Locke, "A Discourse of Miracles," 228-30.
[114] Locke, "A Discourse of Miracles," 230.

in three of his works. There is no more suitable way to make his revelation obligatory. Still, it is rather clear that miracles are hardly the only traditional evidence of divinity that Locke incorporates. What is more, Locke believes one who is following Christ will submit to His Scripture, approaching it prepared to have anything that is technically only assent overturned by it.

Ease of Assent for the Poor and Uneducated

One of the reasons Locke leans so much on the historical testimonies of miracles as an evidentiary basis for accepting the divinity of the Bible is that legitimate assent to the gospel would be possible for more people. This view is most clearly expressed in *ROC* and its vindications. There he argues that God shows a distinct concern for the uneducated and illiterate in the simplicity of the Christian faith, its deliverance, and its accompanying proof.

As discussed in Chapters 3 and 4, Locke promulgated the notion in *ROC* that the simplicity of the message of salvation was highly reasonable based on the state of most of humans through history. In the opening pages of *ROC*, he calls the Bible "a Collection of Writings designed by God for the Instruction of the illiterate bulk of Mankind in the way to Salvation."[115] Throughout most of *ROC* he laboriously makes the argument, from abundant biblical evidence and exposition, that there are only two fundamental articles of faith and one thing people must do: they must be monotheists, they must believe that Jesus is the Messiah of which the Old Testament foretold, and they must take Christ as King.[116] He proves throughout *ROC* that this is what Jesus and His Apostles repeat in the Gospels and Acts over and over. That was it. Of course, this meant believing anything one was convinced that was promulgated in the New Testament and the Old Testament; but doing so was concomitant with the two fundamental articles and a major aspect of taking Christ as king.[117] He defends this simplicity of the Christian faith on the reasonable character of God:

> He gave him Reason, and with it a Law . . . But considering the frailty of Man, apt to run into corruption and misery, he promised a Deliverer, whom

---

[115] Locke, *ROC*, 2.
[116] Cf. Marko, "Justification, Ecumenism."
[117] Cf. Marko, "Justification, Ecumenism."

> in his good time he sent; And then declared to all Mankind, that whoever would believe him to be the Saviour promised, and take him now raised from the dead, and constituted the Lord and Judge of all Men, to be their King and Ruler, should be saved. This is a plain intelligible Proposition; And the all-merciful God seems herein to have consulted the poor of this World, and the bulk of Mankind. These are Articles that laboring and illiterate Man may comprehend. This is a Religion suited to vulgar Capacities; And the state of Mankind in this World, destined to labour and travel . . . The bulk of Mankind have not leisure for Learning and Logick, and superfine distinctions of the Schools. Where the hand is used to the Plough, and the Spade, the head is seldom elevated to sublime Notions, or exercised in mysterious reasonings. 'Tis well if Men of that rank (to say nothing of the other Sex) can comprehend plain propositions, and a short reasoning about things familiar to their Minds, and nearly allied to their daily experience. Go beyond this, and you amaze the greatest part of Mankind: And may as well talk *Arabick* to a poor day Labourer, as the Notions and Language that the Books and Disputes of Religion are filled with, and as soon you will be understood.[118]

For Locke, it is simply reasonable, based on the simplicity of most of humankind, due to their station in life, and what we think about God, that He would make the way of salvation simple and easy. Locke ends *ROC* with the following: "And if the poor had the Gospel preached to them, it was, without doubt, such a Gospel, as the poor could understand, plain and intelligible: And so it was, as we have seen, in the Preachings of Christ and his Apostles."[119]

Locke was also convinced that simplicity is necessary for simple people because they had to be convinced of the gospel of Christ through legitimate means. In other words, they must be able to cull the gospel message on their own, lest they illegitimately take an authority's word for it. In reply to Protestants, some whom thought Locke's fundamentals too scanty, he writes:

> Whenever Men take upon them to go beyond those Fundamental Articles of Christianity, which are to be found in the Preachings of our Saviour and his Apostles, where will they stop? Whenever any Set of Men will require

---

[118] Locke, *ROC*, 304-6.
[119] Locke, *ROC*, 307.

more as necessary to be believed to make Men of their Church, *i.e.* in their sense Christians, than what our Saviour and his Apostles propos'd to those, whom they made Christians, and admitted into the Church of Christ; however they may pretend to recommend the Scripture to their People, in effect no more of it is recommended to them, than just comports with what the Leaders of that Sect have resolved Christianity shall consist in.[120]

He goes on to argue that such sects that do not send their people to Scripture or do so only to confirm their particular church's doctrinal system are guilty of advancing implicit faith just as they accuse the Church of Rome of doing: "And therefore, I have often wonder'd to hear Men of several Churches so heartily exclaim against the implicit Faith of the Church of *Rome*; when the same implicit Faith is as much practiced and required in their own, though not so openly professed, and ingenuously owned there."[121] In short, he thinks most churches have required implicit faith in themselves as authorities. In the *Essay*, he similarly argues that assent based on arguments from authority, especially in important matters, is illegitimate.[122]

Most important for our purposes here, however, historical testimonies of miracles are also a simple and, to Locke, reasonable way to help convince someone of the divinity of Scripture, and thus the gospel. Previously, I showed that Locke thought that because most people do not have time or capacity for long deductions of reason it was more expedient for God to reveal morality with clear marks of divinity, namely miracles, to make it obligatory. God could have given us long, demonstrable proofs to make true morality obligatory but that would be lost on most of humankind. How much more do these arguments stand for the case of the illiterate and poor, with little to no education? He says as much in the penultimate paragraph of the "Discourse," where he is defending his defining of a miracle as not something objectively beyond the power of all creatures, but as something we take to be beyond the ordinary course of nature and divine:

> This perhaps, as it is the plainest, so it is also the surest way to preserve the Testimony of Miracles in its due force to all sorts and degrees of People. For Miracles being the Basis on which divine Mission is always establish'd,

---

[120] Locke, *A Second Vindication*, 216.
[121] Locke, *A Second Vindication*, 217-18.
[122] Locke, *Essay*, II.xxi.67-68, IV.xv.6, IV.xx.18; cf. Marko, *Measuring the Distance*, 74-75, 84-85.

and consequently that Foundation on which the Believers of any divine Revelation must ultimately bottom their Faith, this use of them would be lost, if not to all Mankind, yet at least to the simple and illiterate (which is the far greatest part) if Miracles be defin'd to be none but such divine Operations as are in themselves beyond the power of all created Beings."[123]

Few could hope to use the notion of miracles as defense if one had to try to argue why they think that the event is only within the power of God. The uneducated and illiterate could not so argue, and that would be taking away the surest and most expedient mark of divinity. They of course could look at the other internal marks and external marks, but that requires some erudition. Miracles are simple. If the faith and its acceptance is not simple, who could be saved?

The Unnatural Advancement of Morality

Locke is clear that he wrote *ROC*, in part, to counter the positions of the deists.[124] In the opening pages of his treatise, he writes of those who "so made Jesus Christ nothing but the Restorer and Preacher of pure Natural Religion; thereby doing violence to the whole Tenor of the New Testament."[125] A prominent emphasis in *ROC* is that Christ cannot be viewed as simply a preacher of pure natural religion. Although reasonable, the message of Christianity had to be revealed for our salvation. Now he does admit that it is conceivable that one could determine, using their God-given reason without revelation, that there is only one God, that we require forgiveness, that we should trust that He is merciful, that he has determined a way for atonement, and that if we repent we will be forgiven.[126] But what he goes on to say regarding the aforementioned five advantages, arriving at such a determination is highly improbable. Polytheism was accepted everywhere and the priests and the world's government's kept people from employing their reason, not to mention all the weaknesses of humans that keep us from reasoning well.[127]

---

[123] Locke, "A Discourse," 230.
[124] Cf. Marko, "Promulgation of Right Morals." See also Chapter 5.
[125] Locke, *ROC*, 2.
[126] Locke, *ROC*, 254-57.
[127] Locke, *ROC*, 259-93.

What is more, he makes it quite clear that it is difficult to call Jesus Christ the *restorer* of natural religion. Regarding the state of morality prior to Christ, Locke writes, "Next to the Knowledge of one God . . . A clear *knowledge of their Duty* was wanting to Mankind. This part of Knowledge, though cultivated with some care, by some of the Heathen Philosophers; Yet got little footing among the People."[128] Again, the governments and polytheistic priests were no help. Locke says that in these pagan times and places, "Religion was every where distinguished from, and preferred to *Virtue*." And he states that while virtue was necessary to hold the societies together, the laws were not aimed toward achieving virtue among the people, "But these Laws, being for the most part made by such who had no other aims but their own Power, reached no farther than those things, that would serve to tie Men together in subjection." He adds that these civil laws, in the best cases, "were directly to conduce to the Prosperity and Temporal Happiness."[129] Locke is convinced that "*Natural Religion* in its full extent, was no where, that I know, taken care of by the force of Natural Reason."[130] He goes on to discuss the difficulties of coming up with morality, not just in the case of the uneducated.[131] In sum, it is difficult, in Locke's studies, to call Christ the *restorer* of natural religion, when it was nowhere obeyed in the time before Him.

An argument woven through his description of the five advantages is that morality had a great advancement because of Christ. Wherever Christ's preaching went polytheism was eradicated and people were much more convinced of an afterlife and thus had an impetus to pay attention to their moral obligations toward God. More to the point, Locke articulates a contrast between pre- and post-Christ morality:

> We see how unsuccessful in this, the attempts of Philosophers [to prove their moral systems] were before our Saviour's time. How short their several Systems came of the perfection of a true and compleat *Morality*, is very visible. And it, since that, the Christian philosophers have much outdone them; yet we may observe, that the first knowledge of the truths they have added, are owing to Revelation: Though as soon as they are heard and considered, they are found to be agreeable to Reason; and as such can by no means be contradicted.[132]

---

[128] Locke, *ROC*, 267.
[129] Locke, *ROC*, 268.
[130] Locke, *ROC*, 268.
[131] Locke, *ROC*, 268–69.
[132] Locke, *ROC*, 269.

He asserts that if one were to "collect all the Moral Rules of the Philosophers, and compare them with those contained in the New Testament, will find them to come short of the *Morality* delivered by our Saviour, and taught by our Saviour, and taught by his Apostles," who Locke points out were "A Colledge made up for the most part of ignorant, but inspired Fishermen."[133] He goes on to list numerous philosophers who will offer some moral truths with an admixture of error.[134] In fact, he argues that he does not even think all of the moral precepts of the New Testament are in all the philosophers: "But such a Body of *Ethicks*, proved to be the Law of Nature, from principles of Reason, and reaching all Duties of Life; I think no body will say the World had before our Saviour's time."[135] Although, beside the point and intimated above, he notes that even if this "Body of *Ethicks*" did not exist it still would not be obligatory until it is proven demonstrably by reason or shown to be by revelation.[136] In what follows, he repeats some of his points, such as the superiority of Christ's morality, but adds a few others such as, "The Rules of Morality were in different Countries and Sects, different." Natural reason, even of the philosophers, was no cure for the differences and defects therein and the promulgated morality never stood on its true foundations.[137]

Locke augments his argument for the unnatural advancement of morality by Christ, by continually pointing out how difficult true morality is to arrive at despite it often being very easy to accept: "Every one may observe a great many truths which he receives at first from others, and readily assents to, as consonant to reason; which he would have found it hard, and perhaps beyond his strength to have discovered himself." He adds, "Native and Original truth, is not so easily wrought out of the Mine, as we who have it deliver'd, ready dug and fashion'd into our hands, are apt to imagine."[138] He points out that we often stand on the accomplishments of those who have gone before: "He that Travels the Roads now, applauds his own strength and legs ... little considering how much he ows to their pains, who cleared the Woods, drained the Bogs, built the Bridges, and made the Ways passable."[139] Furthermore, Locke adds to this line of argumentation the issue of our taking for granted the ideas and principles with which we were raised:

---

[133] Locke, *ROC*, 271.
[134] Locke, *ROC*, 271-73.
[135] Locke, *ROC*, 273.
[136] Locke, *ROC*, 274-75.
[137] Locke, *ROC*, 278, cf. 268.
[138] Locke, *ROC*, 269-70.
[139] Locke, *ROC*, 280.

> A great many things which we have been bred up in the belief of from our Cradles, (and are Notions grown Familiar, and as it were Natural to us, under the Gospel,) we take for unquestionable obvious Truths, and easily demonstrable; without considering how long we might have been in doubt or ignorance of them, had Revelation been silent. And many are beholden to Revelation, who do not acknowledge it.[140]

In other words, we often take our intellectual milieu for granted, and in Locke's day, Christian principles and ideas were a major part of it. Arguably, the deists have taken for granted the Christian, moral, intellectual milieu in which they have been raised and thus lack the proper admiration or amazement of what the New Testament has delivered with respect to morality. New Testament morality seems facile to them because they have been raised in it.[141]

This type of comparison between the excellency of the New Testament and pre-Christ philosophers that Locke posits is nothing new. This would fit within Muller's list of the marks of the divinity of Scripture: "the purity, holiness, and righteousness of biblical teaching" and its superiority to human teaching.[142] Based on what was drawn out in the previous sections, it is no surprise that Locke does incorporate internal evidences, in addition to miracles in arguing for the divinity of Scripture. But this argument, outlined immediately above, is interesting because, while it incorporates some of the traditional internal elements of, or arguments for, the divinity of Scripture, it also incorporates arguments or elements that could be considered, at least in part, external: comparison of the purity of morality of the New Testament as compared to the best non-Christian ethical thinking in history and the extraordinary effects Christ and His apostles had through the world. These two can remain distinct or be combined. Whatever the case, the unnatural advancement of morality points any readers he has who are skeptical of miracles not immediately to miracles, but it directs them to a historical comparison. He believes readers will honestly acknowledge how astounding the New Testament's morality is once they make the comparison for themselves.

---

[140] Locke, *ROC*, 280-81.
[141] Marko, "Promulgation of Right Morals." See also Chapter 5.
[142] Muller, *PRRD*, vol. 2, 271-73.

Conclusions

Locke thought that the use of miracles by God to identify his messages and messengers was eminently reasonable. He emphasized the historical testimonies of miracles as an evidentiary basis for the divinity of Scripture, as had many others, beyond the more traditional theologians. At least for Locke, part of the reason he thought the use of them to be so reasonable was that this was one of the easiest marks of divinity that the poor and uneducated could recognize as such. And although he continued to use miracles as an important part of his religious epistemology, as did others, he recognized that others eschewed miraculous testimonies. To those thinkers, especially the deists, Locke uses, in addition to his incorporation of internal marks of divinity in *ROC*, other external evidences, such as the unnatural advancement of morality that the New Testament gave us beyond the pre-Christ philosophers. Such evidences pointed deists not immediately to miracles but to the history and ancient philosophy books.

While he and others of the era do emphasize miracles more than do the orthodox, Locke, again, is not wholly reliant on miracles, although he does acknowledge that they are necessary for most. It could be an interesting project to see if the marks of divinity readily inferable from *ROC* were readily inferable from his other works.

Another characteristic of Locke's works is that he will assert that we are assisted by the Holy Spirit, but he refuses to say much more or conjecture how the Spirit might help. In fact, the Holy Spirit is one of the five advantages of Christ's advent. This does not appear to be mere lip service. Lack of metaphysical conjecture perhaps points to the empirical mindset of Locke or at least an attempt to be ecumenical or keep focused on the basics. How the Holy Spirit acts upon us in various circumstances is a highly charged issue separating many of the sects. Christians can at least agree on the fact that they are assisted.

Another important point drawn out of this study is Locke's answer to those who would argue how Scripture can be viewed as more than historically probable or morally certain. Again, if one agrees with Locke on the reasonableness of God's revelatory process and that the Bible is from Him, one's approach to Scripture must necessarily change. One will approach it being prepared to have what otherwise would be naturally formed beliefs overturned, however sure we feel about those beliefs. Each proposition of Scripture is not treated as historically probable or merely morally certain, and thus overturnable by what would seem to be a more naturally reasonable conclusion. The entirety of Scripture thus is approached with more surety than one's weak operations.

And finally, given the background of the use of miracles in Locke's era, it is difficult to see why so many scholars are concerned about Locke's emphatic incorporation of miracles as the clearest indicator of divinity. Perhaps for the evidentialist he is too quickly showing his hand. But without miracles what is left in Christianity? As C. S. Lewis commented, "If they [miracles] have occurred, they have occurred because they are the very thing this universal story is about... They are precisely those chapters in this great story on which the plot turns."[143]

---

[143] C. S. Lewis, *Miracles: A Preliminary Study* (San Francisco: Harper Collins, 2000), 157.

PART III

PARALLELS IN LOCKE'S LARGER CORPUS

7
John Locke and the "Free Will" Controversies
Why "Of Power" Is Not a Metaphysical Pronouncement

Locke's chapter "Of Power," his most thorough-going treatment of the topic of human free will and the most revised part of *An Essay Concerning Human Understanding* (*Essay*), has been extensively treated through numerous articles and books in recent decades. The oft rehearsed narrative of the development of his chapter goes something like this: Locke's first edition version of "Of Power" was found to be wanting in terms of clarity and detail; one critic was William Molyneux, who, in a 1692 letter to Locke, pointed out some deficiencies of the chapter; this letter, at least in part, prompted Locke significantly to refine and expand "Of Power" in the 1694 second edition, adding to it, among other things, a discussion of our power of suspension; Locke then made less drastic yet intriguing alterations in the 1700 fourth and 1706 fifth (posthumous) editions.[1] The precise effect of each updated edition has

---

[1] Editions of the *Essay*: John Locke, *An Essay Concerning Humane Understanding*, 1st ed. (London: Printed for Tho. Basset, 1690); 2nd ed. (London: Printed for Awnsham and John Churchil and Samuel Manship, 1694); 3rd ed. (London: Printed for Awnsham and John Churchil and Samuel Manship, 1695); 4th ed. (London: Printed for Awnsham and John Churchil and Samuel Manship, 1700); 5th ed. (London: Printed for Awnsham and John Churchil and Samuel Manship, 1706); critical edition, ed. Peter H. Nidditch (Oxford: Clarendon Press, 1979). From here onward, I will be quoting from the critical edition and will note any important variances from the second through fifth editions. When referencing a section from book II, chapter xxi, "Of Power," I will parenthetically reference only the section number. The correspondences between John Locke and William Molyneux with which I am concerned, in chronological order, are: William Molyneux, "L1579. William Molyneux to Locke, 22 December 1692," *The Correspondence of John Locke*, vol. 4, ed. E. S. de Beer (Oxford: Clarendon Press, 1979), 599–602; John Locke, "L1592. Locke to William Molyneux, 20 January 1693," *The Correspondence of John Locke*, vol. 4, ed. E. S. de Beer (Oxford: Clarendon Press, 1979), 623–28; William Molynuex, "L1622. William Molyneux to Locke, 18 April 1693," *The Correspondence of John Locke*, vol. 4, ed. E. S. de Beer (Oxford: Clarendon Press, 1979), 667–69; John Locke, "L1643. Locke to William Molyneux, 15 July 1693," *The Correspondence of John Locke*, vol. 4, ed. E. S. de Beer (Oxford: Clarendon Press, 1979), 700–1; John Locke, "L1655. Locke to William Molyneux, 23 August 1693," *The Correspondence of John Locke*, vol. 4, ed. E. S. de Beer (Oxford: Clarendon Press, 1979), 719–23; William Molyneux, "L1763. William Molyneux to Locke, 28 July 1694," *The Correspondence of John Locke*, vol. 5, ed. E. S. de Beer (Oxford: Clarendon Press, 1979), 92–93. Other pertinent works of Locke during this period: John Locke, *The Reasonableness of Christianity, as Delivered in the Scriptures*, 2nd ed. (London: Printed for Awnsham and John Churchil,

frequently served as the backdrop for the many studies aimed at deciphering what Locke's pronouncement is on the metaphysical question of human freedom. Some scholars have claimed that Locke is defending a form of necessitarianism more sophisticated than that of Thomas Hobbes, while others, contrary to that popular opinion, defend their portrayal of a metaphysically libertarian Locke.[2] Still others maintain that Locke is trying to avoid the metaphysical free will question altogether. James Harris argues that Locke is attempting to offer a description, in every edition, that is "true to the experience of freedom, to the experience of what deliberation and choice-making

---

1696). To it is appended Locke's first vindication of the book, *A Vindication of the Reasonableness of Christianity, etc.* His second vindication is John Locke, *A Second Vindication of the Reasonableness of Christianity, etc.* (London: Printed for A. and J. Churchil, 1697). The first is a theological treatise and the latter two are defenses of it.

[2] By necessitarian I mean the general position held by Thomas Hobbes that our actions are necessary effects of external antecedent causes. By libertarian, I intend to refer to the position held by John Bramhall (or ones similar to it) that humans are agents who, though influenced by conditions outside of their control, are self-determining and free in their choices. For an overview of the Hobbes–Bramhall debate: Vere Chappell, Introduction in *Hobbes and Bramhall on Liberty and Necessity*, ed. Vere Chappell (Cambridge: Cambridge University Press, 1999), ix–xxiii [definitions of necessitarianism and libertarianism above—and other related positions—from p. xi]. Cf. J. Mark Beach, "The Hobbes–Bramhall Debate on the Nature of Freedom and Necessity," in *Biblical Interpretation and Doctrinal Formulation in the Reformed Tradition*, ed. Arie C. Leder and Richard A. Muller (Grand Rapids: Reformation Heritage Books, 2014), 231–61.

Locke has been most often framed as a necessitarian. For example, James O'Higgins, *Determinism and Freewill: Anthony Collins' "A Philosophical Inquiry Concerning Human Liberty" Edited and Annotated with a Discussion of the Opinions of Hobbes, Locke, Pierre Bayle, William King and Leibniz* (The Hague: Martinus Nijhoff, 1976), 11–12. James O'Higgins calls Locke a "psychic determinist" in the *Essay*'s first edition. While noting that there are multiple ways to understand the suspension of the will added in the second edition and its import, O'Higgins concludes, "Locke's final position, therefore, might not have been one of complete psychic necessity" (12). Vere Chappell, "Locke on the Suspension of Desire," *John Locke: An Essay Concerning Human Understanding in Focus*, ed. Gary Fuller, Robert Stecker, and John P. Wright (London: Routledge, 2000), 236–48. Chappell is more definitive than O'Higgins in this work: "Locke, however, holds that everything that happens, including free human actions, is causally determined. So, Locke is a compatibilist with respect to freedom and determination, just as Hobbes is" (236–37). Samuel C. Rickless, "Locke on the Freedom to Will," *The Locke Newsletter* 31 (2000): 43–67; Samuel Rickless, "Locke on Active Power, Freedom, and Moral Agency," *Locke Studies* 13 (2013): 33–55; Samuel Rickless, "Will and Motivation," *The Oxford Handbook of British Philosophy in the Seventeenth Century*, ed. Peter R. Antsey (Oxford: Oxford University Press, 2013), 393–414. Rickless reads Locke also as a "compatibilist." Gideon Yaffe, *Liberty Worth the Name: Locke on Free Agency* (Princeton: Princeton University Press, 2000), 4–5. Gideon Yaffe, "Locke on Refraining, Suspending, and the Freedom of the Will," *History of Philosophy Quarterly* 18, no. 4 (October 2001): 373–91. J. P. Moreland and William Lane Craig, *Philosophical Foundations for a Christian Worldview* (Downers Grove: IVP Academic, 2003), 269. Craig and Moreland call Locke a "classical compatibilist." This last work is not representative of an in depth treatment but is an example of Locke being commonly framed as a necessitarian or determinist.

Some maintain that he is a libertarian. For example, Peter A. Schouls, *Reasoned Freedom: John Locke and the Enlightenment* (Ithaca: Cornell University Press, 1992), 117–44. Schouls is distinctive for two reasons. First, he confidently asserts his position regarding Locke's chapter "Of Power." Second, and more importantly, he reads Locke as being a libertarian. Schouls's idea is that Locke is a libertarian from the very first edition of the *Essay* (119).

are actually like" and not to answer the question of liberty versus necessity as Hobbes and Bramhall had attempted a few decades prior.³ One could also conceivably claim that Locke switched views, even more than once, through the various editions, or that he was confused.⁴

It is important to note that Molyneux's oft referenced critique from his December 1692 letter is not merely metaphysical but also theological:

> The Next place I take Notice off as requiring some Farther Explication is Your Discourse about Mans Liberty and Necessity. this Thread seems so wonderfully fine spun in your Book, that at last the Great Question of Liberty and Necessity seems to Vanish. and herein you seem to make all Sins to proceed from our Understandings, or to be against Conscience; and not at all from the Depravity of our Wills. Now it seems harsh to say, that a Man shall be Damn'd, because he understands no better than he does.⁵

Molyneux thinks that the question of metaphysical human free will disappears in Locke's chapter and that therein the damned are portrayed as being such because of their lack of understanding and not depravity. The most noted change found in the second edition, Locke's incorporation of the suspension of the execution and satisfaction of any of the mind's desires, is frequently acknowledged as a response to the above critique. Scholarship tends to focus, however, on the metaphysical import of this and other changes and not the theological implications.⁶

---

³ James A. Harris, *Of Liberty and Necessity: The Free Will Debate in Eighteenth-Century British Philosophy* (Oxford: Oxford University Press, 2005). See the introduction and the first chapter for his treatment of Locke [quotation, p. 20]. More recently Antonia LoLordo also argued for "metaphysical neutrality." She engaged in an intriguing back and forth with Samuel Rickless (referenced above). Antonia LoLordo, *Locke's Moral Man* (Oxford: Oxford University Press, 2012); Antonia LoLordo, "Reply to Rickless," *Locke Studies* 13 (2013): 55–64. I will be arguing for a metaphysically neutral reading of Locke as well but from a different angle than LoLordo.

⁴ Samuel Clarke, *Remarks upon a Book Entituled, A Philosophical Enquiry Concerning Human Liberty* (London: 1717); Anthony Collins, *A Philosophical Inquiry Concerning Human Liberty*, 2nd ed., corrected (London: 1717). Samuel Clarke and Anthony Collins, in their liberty-necessity debate, are critical of Locke but their criticisms are not completely clear. Clarke says that Locke was "much perplexed" in his discussion of the doctrine of suspension (23). It is not clear if he thought Locke was confused and knew it or confused and did not know it. Regarding suspension, Collins either disapproves of the way the doctrine of suspense can be read or because he thinks Locke is actually attempting to allow for instances of libertarian freedom (39–40). Cf. Jonathan S. Marko, "Revisiting the Question: Is Anthony Collins the Author of the 1729 *Dissertation on Liberty and Necessity*?," *Philosophy and Theology* 22, nos. 1 & 2 (2010): 77–104; Jonathan S. Marko, *Measuring the Distance between Locke and Toland: Reason, Revelation, and Rejection during the Locke-Stillingfleet Debate* (Eugene: Wipf & Stock, 2017).

⁵ Molyneux, "L1579. William Molyneux to Locke," 600–1.

⁶ The theological aspects of "Of Power" have not been completely eschewed by scholarship, who are likely more interested in investigating what the chapter has to say to a broader audience. For

It is my contention here that "Of Power" is not a metaphysical pronouncement but more along the lines of what those like Harris portray it to be: a description of our experience of freedom of the will. It is also prescriptive because it is descriptive of the right use of the will. All of this is due to two key pieces of evidence, which, interestingly, are responses to Molyneux's critique: (1) an admission by Locke in his correspondence: he is attempting to avoid metaphysical pronouncements, at least partly, because trying to reconcile divine and human agency is too difficult; and (2) the theological message of "Of Power"—the truly free agent is reasonable, and the truly reasonable agent will have her eyes fixed on the afterlife, thus aiming for herself to be a slave and determined, therefore, by her ever-cultivated desire for righteousness and not by her fleshly desires—and his development of it throughout the chapter eludes sectarian categorization by the avoidance of theological issues that are not unrelated to the metaphysical question of human free agency. To frame his chapter otherwise makes him out to be a theological novice or, perhaps, unconcerned with the religious background of his readership.

I will lay out my argument in two parts, one for each of the two key pieces of evidence. But, prior to that, I will provide a historical overview to situate Locke's chapter amidst the multivalent free will controversies of the era. This will show the complexity of the discussions that goes beyond many insular modern-day ones that can be categorized as being "philosophical" or "theological."

---

example, Chappell, "Locke on the Suspension of Desire." Chappell notes that there is something religiously significant about "Of Power." He writes, "Freedom, I think Locke thinks, is a power granted us by God for a certain purpose, namely, that we might achieve rationality and thence moral rectitude in our actions. There are other things that we can do with this power—sin, for example—but its proper goal is rational action" (246–47). Yaffe, *Liberty Worth the Name*. Yaffe's work goes the furthest in commenting on the theological message of "Of Power." He writes, "We have freedom of action, if we have it, only because we are persons. But, as I've mentioned already, a free agent isn't just active in the production of her conduct; she does not merely escape being a victim of circumstance, she also escapes herself; she is not a slave to her own parochialisms and peculiarities" (139). This is somewhat similar to the theological message that I have culled from "Of Power."

Also, Locke was familiar with the theologies of Francis Turretin and John Calvin. John C. Higgins-Biddle, Introduction to *The Reasonableness of Christianity: As Delivered in the Scriptures*, ed. John C. Higgins-Biddle (Oxford: Clarendon Press, 1999), xv–cxv, xxvi, xl. John Calvin, *Institutes of the Christian Religion*, trans. Henry Beveridge (Grand Rapids: Eerdmans, 1989); Francis Turretin, *Institutes of Elenctic Theology*, 3 vols, trans. George Musgrave Giger, ed. James T. Dennison, Jr. (Phillipsburg: P&R Publishing). It appears that Locke would not often find himself in agreement with them on a variety of theological points, but he at least knows how they would object to his personal theological and philosophical convictions on a range of topics.

Historical Context: The Multivalent Free Will Controversies and Issues of the 1600s

Introduction

The mention of "free will" at the focal point of controversies and discussions in the seventeenth century requires disambiguation. While various common threads of so-called free will notions can be distinguished, they were not often separately treated. For instance, consider the title of Thomas Hobbes's first published reply to John Bramhall that sparked one of the biggest free will debates in the mid-1600s: *Of Libertie and Necessitie: A Treatise, Wherein All Controversie Concerning Predestination, Election, Free-Will, Grace, Merits, Reprobation, etc. Is Fully Decided and Cleared.* Therein are promises of discussions involving metaphysics, divine sovereignty vis-à-vis human agency, and the way and means of salvation. A series of questions and distinctions associated with the term free will were debated in Locke's era and belong to the background of his thought. The question of liberty and necessity in our choices and the question of the need and nature of grace in response to God's redemptive call (and perseverance until the end) are fundamental to the scope of topics involved in and impacted by free will discussions. A further question concerns suspension of judgment as argued by Nicolas Malebranche, with whose works Locke was acquainted, that is similar in some important ways to Locke's treatment of the same issue. At the very least, it shows Locke was hardly original in his incorporation of suspension. Malebranche's treatment, as Harris has argued regarding Locke's treatment, is explanatorily helpful without fixating on the points of debate in the liberty-necessity controversy between Hobbes and Bramhall.

There are also two important cautions to be noted. First, in the seventeenth century, theology and philosophy were not easily separable. Second, there are certain assumptions of the older scholarship that have recently been challenged. For instance, there has long existed the notion that the only metaphysical options for Christian theologians are compatibilism or libertarianism. A related assumption is that intellectualism implies determinism and that Calvinism and determinism go together. Both assumptions have been questioned in recent scholarship.[7]

---

[7] Richard A. Muller, *Divine Will and Human Choice: Freedom, Contingency, and Necessity in Early Modern Reformed Thought* (Grand Rapids: Baker Academic, 2017); *Reformed Thought on Freedom: The Concept of Free Choice in Early Modern Reformed Theology*, ed. William J. Van Asselt,

Traditional Theological Elements Pertinent or Central to Free Will Discussions

There are a number of different theological doctrines associated with the debates over free will. God's providence understood as the preservation, concurrence, and guidance of creation based upon His foreordination (or His decrees) and His concomitant foreknowledge are all interconnected theological doctrines associated with discussions and debates over the sense of our freedom vis-à-vis divine sovereignty.

Whenever early modern philosophical conversations start to bear upon the issue of eternal salvation of individuals, historians of philosophy understandably tend to tread lightly and pull back from giving overly specific commentary. Soteriological free will is, in the minds of many theologians, the main thread or concern of the multivalent free will conversations: the other discussions are a prelude to or support to it. But this soteriological thread is itself divisible into other strands, one pertaining to God's sovereignty that ultimately faces the question of election of some souls to everlasting felicity and life and reprobation of others to everlasting torment and death.

The major debate associated with this strand concerned the Molinist doctrine of middle knowledge.[8] This debate began in the Roman Catholic Church but quickly made its way into the Protestant tradition in the thought of Jacob Arminius. In Thomism and according to many of the Reformed, God has two kinds of knowledge: natural knowledge and free knowledge. The former is God's exhaustive knowledge of Himself and all possibilities. His free knowledge pertains to what God has determined to bring into actuality.[9] Even

---

J. Martin Bac, and Roelf T. te Velde (Grand Rapids: Baker Academic, 2010). The *Westminster Confession*, one of the most noted confessions lying squarely within the Reformed tradition, professes: "Although, in relation to the foreknowledge and decree of God, the first Cause, all things come to pass immutably, and infallibly: yet, by the same providence, He ordereth them to fall out, according to the nature of second causes, either necessarily, freely, or contingently." *Westminster Confession* (Glasgow: Free Presbyterian Publications, 1994), 5.2.

[8] Cf. F. L. Sheerin, s.v. "Scientia Media," *New Catholic Encyclopedia*, 2nd ed, vol. 12, ed. Thomas Carson and Joann Cerrito (Farmington Hills, MI: Gale, 2003), 821–22; William Lane Craig, "Middle Knowledge: A Calvinist-Arminian Rapprochement?," in *The Grace of God and the Will of Man*, ed. Clark H. Pinnock (Grand Rapids: Zondervan, 1989), 141–64.

[9] Richard A. Muller, *PRRD*, vol. 3, 406–31; Richard A. Muller, "Grace, Election, and Contingent Choice: Arminius's Gambit and the Reformed Response," in *The Grace of God, the Bondage of the Will, Vol. 2: Historical and Theological Perspectives on Calvinism*, ed. Thomas R. Schreiner and Bruce A. Ware (Grand Rapids: Baker Books, 1995), 251–78 [reference, pp. 264–69]. Molina used the terms "natural," "middle," and "free." The corresponding Thomist terms are "knowledge of simple intelligence" and "knowledge of vision."

with the admittance that this movement from possibility to actuality does not produce metaphysical human *patients* as Hobbes would have it, it still brought up a number of difficulties regarding the fact and existence of things that are not seemingly logically necessary or which God need not allow but does: evil, the fall, sin, hell, damnation, etc.[10] Molina posited the notion of middle knowledge in response to these difficulties and would even argue that certain passages of Scripture demanded it.[11] Sheerin defines middle knowledge or *scientia media* as "that knowledge by which God, prior to any absolute decree, but not without the supposition that He would decree, infallibly perceives free futurible acts of creatures. He knows what a man would do in any circumstances if He would decree to concur in them, before He makes any absolute decree establishing the situation."[12] Contingent free choices are outside of the divine willing.[13] Proponents of middle knowledge argued that this understanding significantly shifted responsibility for evil and damnation to radically free creatures, and thus made better biblical sense.[14] It also delimited the options of possibilities that could be actualized because of the radically free and divinely "foreseen" choices of finite moral agents.[15]

Debate between the Thomists and Molinists was settled by papal decree in 1607, making space for Molinism within the pale of orthodoxy.[16] The parallel

---

[10] Stanglin and McCall depict well Arminius's pastoral attraction to middle knowledge. Keith D. Stanglin and Thomas H. McCall, *Jacob Arminius: Theologian of Grace* (New York: Oxford University Press, 2012). Cf. Richard A. Muller, *God, Creation, and Providence in the Thought of Jacob Arminius: Sources and Directions of Scholastic Protestantism in the Era of Early Orthodoxy* (Grand Rapids: Baker, 1991), 255-68.

[11] See Kirk R. MacGregor, *Luis de Molina: The Life and Theology of the Founder of Middle Knowledge* (Grand Rapids: Zondervan, 2015), 80-84 et passim.

[12] Sheerin, "Scientia Media," 821.

[13] Cf. Muller, *Divine Will and Human Choice*, 263. Preceding scholastics maintained such claims amounted to an ontological absurdity because contingency is dependent on divine willing.

[14] Cf. Craig, "Middle Knowledge," 141-64.

[15] There were two notable strains of middle knowledge incorporation early on in the Roman Catholic debates. Luis de Molina thought that God foresaw what all free and fallen creatures would do with His sufficient grace or grace sufficient to respond appropriately to the offer of salvation and persevere in it. Francisco Suárez deviated from Molina's position. He "held that while all are given grace sufficient for salvation, God elected some for salvation and subsequently discovered what graces would be successful in bringing about the free consent of the elect individuals." These graces were not irresistible or infallible in and of themselves. God knew, rather, by His middle knowledge, how He would arrive infallibly at his desired effects: the election of particular individuals. This was perhaps construed as middle way between Thomistic and Molinistic soteriologies and has come to be known as Congruism. Jonathan S. Marko, "Early Modern Discussions of Grace," in *Encyclopedia of Early Modern Philosophy and Sciences*, ed. Dana Jalobeanu and Charles T. Wolfe (Cham: Springer, 2022), 770-81; Cf. Craig, "Middle Knowledge."

[16] Thomas Ryan, s.v. "Congregatio de auxiliis," *New Catholic Encyclopedia*, 2nd ed., vol. 4, ed. Thomas Carson and Joann Cerrito (Farmington Hills, MI: Gale, 2003), 110-13. MacGregor, *Luis de Molina*, 228-42; cf. Guido Stucco, *The Catholic Doctrine of Predestination from Luther to Jansenius* (Bloomington: Ex Libris, 2014), 155-218.

debate in the Reformed Churches over the synergistic teachings of Arminius, who had appropriated the Molinist doctrine of middle knowledge, was settled by the expulsion of Arminius' followers, the Remonstrants, by the Synod of Dordrecht (1618–1619).[17] The importance of this debate for later theology and philosophy lies in the association of Molinism with Armninian thought, as evidenced in the views of John Bramhall in debate over human freedom with Thomas Hobbes.[18]

The Hobbes–Bramhall Debate's Foci

The Hobbes–Bramhall debate on liberty is the most noted free will debate in Locke's period from histories of philosophy.[19] In fact, Locke is typically framed as responding to it, at least in part, with his chapter "Of Power." One philosophical historian, William Rowe, opens one of his articles noting that "John Locke [unsuccessfully] tried to lay to rest the controversy over free will by directing attention to the question whether we are free to *do* what we will, while pushing into the background the more fundamental question of

---

[17] Cf. Keith D. Stanglin, "Scientia Media: The Protestant Reception of a Jesuit Idea," in *Beyond Dordt and De Auxiliis: The Dynamics of Protestant and Catholic Soteriology in the Sixteenth and Seventeenth Centuries*, ed. Jordan Ballor, Matthew Gaetano, and David Sytsma (Leiden: Brill, 2019), 148–68; Richard A. Muller, "Arminius's 'Conference' with Junius and the Protestant Reception of Molina's Concordia," in *Beyond Dordt and De Auxiliis: The Dynamics of Protestant and Catholic Soteriology in the Sixteenth and Seventeenth Centuries*, ed. Jordan Ballor, Matthew Gaetano, and David Sytsma (Leiden: Brill, 2019), 103–26.

[18] Beach, "The Hobbes–Bramhall Debate," 234, 241–42.

[19] The first work in the Hobbes-Bramhall debate, which was penned by Bramhall, was not published alone in the course of the debate. Vere Chappell has published it in a stand-alone form: "Bramhall's Discourse of Liberty and Necessity," in *Hobbes and Bramhall on Liberty and Necessity*, ed. Vere Chappell (Cambridge: Cambridge University Press, 1999), 15–42. The gist of it can be inferred from Hobbes's response to it and it is published completely in Bramhall's first published book in the debate. This first publication of Bramhall follows the outline of his original work; in each portion of it, he first gives a piece of the original, Hobbes's published response to it, and his response to Hobbes. The following are the publications comprising the Hobbes-Bramhall debate in order of publication: Thomas Hobbes, *Of Libertie and Necessitie: A Treatise, Whererin All Controversie Concerning Predestination, Election, Free-will, Grace, Merits, Reprobation, etc. Is Fully Decided and Cleared, in Answer to a Treatise Written by the Bishop of London-derry, on the Same Subject* (London: Printed by W. B. for F. Eaglesfield, 1654); John Bramhall, *A Defence of True Liberty from Ante-cedent and Extrinsicall Necessity, Being an Answer to a Late Book of Mr. Thomas Hobbs of Malmsbury, Intituled, A Treatise of Liberty and Necessity* (London: Printed for John Crook, 1655); Thomas Hobbes, *The Questions concerning Liberty, Necessity, and Chance. Clearly Stated and Debated between Dr. Bramhall Bishop of Derry, and Thomas Hobbes of Malmsbury* (London: Printed for Andrew Cook, 1656); John Bramhall, *Castigations of Mr. Hobbes: His Last Animadversions, in The Case Concerning Liberty, and Universal Necessity. With an Appendix concerning The Catching of Leviathan, or the Great Whale* (London: Printed by E. T. for J. Crook, 1658).

whether we are free to *will* what we will."²⁰ Rowe is not alone framing Locke as the first major respondent of sorts to the Hobbes–Bramhall debate.²¹

The debate began as a private one, instigated and moderated by a mutual acquaintance of the two thinkers, the Marquess of Newcastle, in 1645. An acquaintance of Hobbes published his critique of Bramhall's original written response, without the former's permission in 1654: *Of Liberty and Necessity*. Bramhall fired back by publishing *A Defence of True Liberty from Antecedent and Extrinsical Necessity* in 1655. Two more books were published in this controversy: Hobbes's *The Questions Concerning Liberty, Necessity, and Chance*, published in 1656, and Bramhall's *Castigations of Mr. Hobbes*, published in 1658. The different training and interests of the two thinkers are, in part, what makes the debate so interesting. Bramhall was a fairly traditional scholastic theologian and Hobbes was a philosopher with various unorthodox views. Accordingly, their terminology is markedly different, with Hobbes anticipating modern philosophical usage and Bramhall posing arguments in a way unfamiliar to those schooled only in contemporary philosophy.

Hobbes's definition of liberty is simply freedom from external impediments from doing what we will to do. He gives a number of alternative definitions, perhaps the most noted of which is in *Of Liberty and Necessitie*: "*Libertie is the absence of all the impediments to action that are not contained in the nature and instrinsecal qualitie of the Agent.*"²² He goes on to exposit his own definition by an analogy involving a river: a river is also said to have liberty to descend by its channel because there is no impediment that stops it from so doing. People never say that it has the liberty to ascend because the impediment to do that is within the nature of the water or is intrinsical. He then shifts to another illustration to complete his thought: "So also we say, that that is tied wants the *libertie* to go, because the impediment is not in him, but in his bands, whereas we say not so of him that is sick or lame, because the impediment is in himself."²³ Hobbes advocates simply what scholastics of the era would have called freedom from coaction or coercion.²⁴ This stance

---

²⁰ William L. Rowe, "Causality and Free Will in the Controversy between Collins and Clarke," *Journal of the History of Philosophy* 25, no. 1 (January 1987): 51–67.

²¹ Harris, *Of Liberty and Necessity*; O'Higgins, *Determinism and Freewill*. Both these important historical treatments frame Locke as the next major respondent to the free will debates after Hobbes and Bramhall (at the very least, in the British context).

²² Hobbes, *Of Liberty and Necessity*, 69–70.

²³ Hobbes, *Of Liberty and Necessity*, 70–71.

²⁴ Cf. Richard A. Muller, s.v. "*libertas a coactione*," *Dictionary of Latin and Greek Theological Terms: Drawn Principally from Protestant Scholastic Theology*, 2nd ed. (Grand Rapids: Baker Academic, 2017). Samuel Rickless has an interesting discussion on the three definitions Hobbes

does not necessitate metaphysical determinism or necessitarianism by itself, however.

His necessitarianism becomes evident within the same section in *Of Libertie and Necessitie*—"My Opinion about Libertie and Necessitie." There he conceives of an action being voluntary as one that follows the last and strongest appetite or desire, or in this instance, what Hobbes calls "will," that was arrived upon through the deliberation of a succession of contrary desires (which, not being the last and strongest, cannot be called wills but intentions or inclinations). He further argues that humans are not self-moved, but their initial actions are initiated from outside. Hobbes's point is that the cause of the will or last desire cannot be the will itself.[25] What is more, he denies that there is any sense to speak of necessary causes—causes that necessarily produce an effect—versus "sufficient causes"—causes "to which nothing is wanting that is needfull to producing the effect"—because they are the same.[26] If the sufficient cause does not bring about its effect it cannot, by Hobbes's reasoning, be called sufficient. On a related note, he thinks that the "Ordinary *Definition* of a *free Agent*"—"*That a free Agent is that, which when all things are present which are needful to produce the effect, can nevertheless not produce it*"—is inherently contradictory. Ensconced within this definition is a nonsensical naming as sufficient a cause that does not produce its effect. In Vere Chappell's words, "Hobbes is a determinist: he thinks that everything that happened, including human action, is the necessary effect of antecedent causes." And because he conceives of "liberty" as being consistent with necessity, in Chappell's estimation, Hobbes is what scholars today would call a compatibilist.[27]

John Bramhall is fairly traditional in his treatment of free choice. In one place he writes: "By liberty, I do understand neither a liberty from sin, nor a liberty from misery, nor a liberty from servitude, nor a liberty from violence, but I understand a liberty from necessity or rather from necessitation, that is an universal immunity from all inevitability and determination to one."[28] He goes on to offer the positive explanation of what he understands liberty to be: liberty of contradiction or exercise and liberty of contrariety

---

offers for liberty and he believes that Hobbes *intends* them all to be consistent. Rickless, "Will and Motivation," 402–3.

[25] Hobbes, *Of Libertie and Necessitie*, 65–72.
[26] Hobbes, *Of Libertie and Necessitie*, 72.
[27] Chappell, Introduction, x.
[28] Bramhall, *Defence*, 17.

or specification. The former refers to our supposed ability to accept or reject something. The latter builds upon the former and refers to our broader ability not only to accept or reject something but to accept something else in the place of what action was initially under consideration.[29] He later specifies "that the proper act of liberty is election, and election is opposed, not only to coaction, but also to coarctation or determination to one."[30] Proper liberty involves election or choice that is not unduly influenced or forced and that is not determined or necessitated. What is more, Bramhall notes that free acts in the truest sense occur when agents act based upon an understanding of the end of the action wrought through deliberation. He is not conceding, however, that all other elections or chosen actions by a person that do not meet this deliberative criteria are necessary.[31] Also, he maintains that the agent is self-determining, a common notion maintained by scholastics and in opposition to Hobbes's position.[32]

Bramhall makes statements regarding the near universal acceptance of liberty, as he generally understands it. In reference to Hobbes's rejection of liberty of contradiction and contrariety, Bramhall notes that those two senses of liberty are "so true, so necessary, so generally received, that there is scarce that writer of note, either Divine or Philosopher, who did ever treat upon this subject, but he useth it."[33] Now, of course, Bramhall does allude to some determinists like the Neo-Stoics,[34] but he is surprised by Hobbes's rejections. Earlier he had even noted that the "greatest opposers of our liberty, are as earnest maintainers of the liberty of *Adam*."[35] Although the "opposers" to which he is alluding are probably the Reformed, he points out that even they—whoever they are—maintain the true liberty of Adam.

What Bramhall has said regarding freedom and its pervasiveness in his era reflects issues in Muller's recent, *Divine Will and Human Free Choice*, where he argues that the Reformed orthodox espoused liberty of contradiction and liberty of contrariety and assumed that humans have potency to multiple effects even though God decreed from eternity past what they would

---

[29] Bramhall, *Defence*, 17–18.
[30] Bramhall, *Defence*, 158.
[31] Bramhall, *Defence*, 40.
[32] Bramhall, *Defence*, 4.
[33] Bramhall, *Defence*, 21.
[34] Chappell, *Hobbes and Bramhall*, 6–7. See the series of footnotes referencing Lipsius on these pages. He is one of the most noted so-called Neo-Stoics of the era. Cf. John Sellars, "Stoic Fate in Justus Lipsius's *De Constantia* and *Physiologica Stoicorum*," *Journal of the History of Philosophy* 52, no. 4 (October 2014): 653–74.
[35] Bramhall, *Defence*, 53; cf. 19.

freely decide to do in the moment. In other words, the world is contingent—it could have been different—and humans maintain the *power* to do alternative actions although only the action that God has decreed the human will freely choose is actualizable. This makes sense of Bramhall's statements about the dearth of notable divines or philosophers who are necessitarians in his era: he may not have read the Reformed or the Reformers as determinists either. Hobbes's position on liberty and necessity is not unique, but it was hardly common.

Faculties and Free Will

The Hobbes–Bramhall debate and practically every other discussion in the era on human freedom also involved another thread of discussion: the role and interaction of the psychological faculties involving free choice. Traditionally, the discussions surrounded the interaction of the intellect and the will and the distinction between intellectualism and voluntarism. Typically in both, the intellect and will have a major role, but in the former, the intellect plays a comparatively larger role in the election process, and the will does so in the latter. In the intellectualism of Thomas Aquinas, who is often referenced as a paradigmatic intellectualist, "the intellect has priority over the will not only because it is the faculty that renders deliberative judgment but also because it is an active power capable of self-motion."[36] The intellect is, relatively, a cause unto itself. The will, in Aquinas, is an appetitive power that is relatively passive, and which accepts or rejects the objects presented to it from the intellect. While the will ultimately makes a non-necessitated choice, the most important basis of freedom is the intellect. Nonetheless, the priority of the intellect does not lead to determinism as is commonly thought. For one, the will is not necessitated.[37] Also, "the judgment of reason about contingent or possible things is itself contingent: it does not follow as a necessary conclusion from necessary principles."[38] By contrast, in voluntarism emphasis is placed on the will. For instance, in Scotistic thought, in the act of choosing, the will has the ability to create its own order of objects. In fact, the will can ignore the

---

[36] Muller, *Divine Will and Human Choice*, 133.
[37] Muller, *Divine Will and Human Choice*, 134–35.
[38] Muller, *Divine Will and Human Choice*, 135. Muller goes on to argue not only that Aquinas is not a compatibilist but that he is not a libertarian either, at least not in the way that those two terms are typically construed.

judgment of the intellect. And it seemed that Scotus was concerned that if the will depended upon anything "causally prior to the will," like the ordering of objects and determinations of the intellect, then the will would not be free.[39]

Some seventeenth-century thinkers had a distaste for what some have called the hypostatization of the faculties. That is, some found the scholastic tendency to talk about the agent's faculties as agents themselves to be confusing and potentially misleading. The Cambridge Platonist, Ralph Cudworth was one of those. Borrowing from the structure of the soul from Plato's *Republic*, he framed the faculty that he called the "hegemonic" as the central aspect of the self that ruled the soul.[40] Although appreciating the difficulty of completely avoiding such anthropomorphization of human faculties, Locke also noted the confusion that it created.

Two other issues ought to be noted that are pertinent to free will discussions and human mental faculties: issues of suspension of the will or judgment and weakness of the will. Suspension is simply the ability of the agent to put off a definitive decision until later. Some will deny that it can be identified as a suspension because clearly the agent *decided* to forego a particular action in the moment. Some determinists point out that this is not an iron-clad demonstration that a particular thinker was libertarian. Moreover, the issue of the weakness of the will is whether it is possible that we knowingly will what is not the best choice. These issues have already been broached in the Lockean narrative involving the various editions of the *Essay*'s chapter "Of Power." In the first edition, Locke appeared to frame people as always choosing the greatest perceived good, resulting in Molyneux's critique that Locke makes it appear that people are damned for not understanding better than they do. In the second edition, Locke incorporates the doctrine of suspension to correct that presentation and show why people so often choose what they concede is not the best choice.

Malebranche's Liberty and Suspension

Although the controversies in which Malebranche and Locke were involved are typically discussed separately, Malebranche against Antoine Arnauld[41]

---

[39] Muller, *Divine Will and Human Choice*, 159–60.
[40] Rickless, "Will and Motivation," 403–6.
[41] For helpful commentary and introduction to the Arnauld–Malebranche debate: Denis Moreau, "The Malebranche-Arnauld Debate," in *The Cambridge Companion to Malebranche*, ed. Steven Nadler (Cambridge: Cambridge University Press, 2000), 87–111; Elmar Kremer, "Antoine Arnauld," in *The*

and Locke against Edward Stillingfleet,[42] there is a connection between Locke and Malebranche that can be pursued. Paul Schuurman has examined Locke's response to Malebranche's concept of vision in God and has pointed out that Locke's definition of ideas borrows from Malebranche.[43] Specifically, there are similarities in the way that Malebranche incorporates the notion of suspension into his account of human freedom. He offers an intelligible treatment of free will that incorporates suspense, that like Locke's, need not be read as engaging the debate over liberty and necessity.[44] Malebranche, like Locke, seems to negate hypostatization of the faculties as much as possible. Both thinkers focus on the "mind" as the agent in their free will treatments. There are, moreover, significant differences between Locke's and Malebranche's views. For one, Locke's "Of Power" is far different from *Nature and Grace*: the former is largely philosophical and the latter theological. Furthermore, Locke, although clearly concerned with the notion of eternal salvation, does not discuss divine grace; whereas Malebranche's treatment of liberty and suspension is imbued with it. So, the over-arching goals and aims of their respective works are notably different and their concentration on so-called graces are antipodal.

The aim of Malebranche's treatment "Concerning Liberty" appears to be his response to a similar question what Molyneux thinks Locke's incorporation of suspension resolves: how might some be contented with our current existence and goods as opposed to the goods and joys of heaven?[45] Malebranche maintains that our desire for good in general is invincible and that is wherein we find the roots of our liberty.[46] But this invincibility is also related to the root of our problem: loving goods. This poses a problem

---

Stanford Encyclopedia of Philosophy, ed. Edward N. Zalta (2018) https://plato.stanford.edu/archives/sum2018/entries/arnauld/. Cf. Nicolas Malebranche, *Nature and Grace* in *Father Malebranche: His Treatise Concerning Search after Truth. The Whole Work Complete. To Which Is Added the Author's Treatise of Nature and Grace: Being a Consequence of the Principles Contained in the Search*, 2nd ed., corrected, trans. T. Taylor (London: Printed by W. Bowyer for Thomas Bennett, 1700).

[42] For introduction to the Locke–Stillingfleet debate: Jonathan S. Marko, *Measuring the Distance between Locke and Toland: Reason, Revelation, and Rejection during the Locke–Stillingfleet Debate* (Eugene: Pickwick, 2017), 13–60; Jonathan S. Marko, "The Locke-Stillingfleet Controversy," *Encyclopedia of Early Modern Philosophy and Sciences*, ed. Dana Jalobeanu and Charles T. Wolfe (Cham: Springer, 2022), 1138–44, https://doi.org/10.1007/978-3-319-20791-9_358-1.

[43] Paul Schuurman, "Vision in God and Thinking Matter: Locke's Epistemological Agnosticism Used Against Malebranche and Stillingfleet," in *Studies on Locke: Sources, Contemporaries, and Legacy*, ed. Sarah Hutton and Paul Schuurman (Dordrecht: Springer, 2008), 177–93.

[44] Cf. Elmer J. Kremer, "Malebranche on Human Freedom," in *The Cambridge Companion to Malebranche*, ed. Steven Nadler (Cambridge: Cambridge University Press, 2000), 190–219.

[45] Malebranche, *Nature and Grace*, III.7.

[46] Malebranche, *Nature and Grace*, III.2–3.

because there is true happiness, found in God, and there are the lesser goods, or seeming causes of pleasure, toward which we find ourselves drawn.[47] In fact, "there are Moments in which Passion takes away all Liberty from the Mind, and that it always lessens it."[48] What is more, we do not love the toilsome burden of examining goods prior to enjoying them but rather the enjoying of the goods.[49]

Malebranche asserts that there are infinite degrees of liberty among humans.[50] On the one hand, there is the person who is practically enslaved to fleeting pleasures. There are souls whose "Pleasure being ill-grounded, unjust, and deceitful, immediately disquiets and molests her, because she desires to be solidly and truly happy." "Thus the Love of the True Good excites in her new Desires for fresh Goods; and whilst she constantly changes her Pursuit, all her Life, and her whole Happiness on Earth, consists in a continual Circulation of Thoughts, Desires, and Pleasures." In short, there are those who voraciously jump from one ephemeral pleasure to the next, never to be satisfied: "But this is the State of a Man whose Understanding is so weak as daily to mistake the false for the true Good; and whose Heart is so corrupt as to betray and sell it self to every thing it is touch'd with, to the Good which gives it an actual Sense of the Most sweet and agreeable Pleasures."[51] By contrast, there is the case of Adam, who was originally too cautious to be intoxicated by pleasures: "Thus the perfectest Liberty is that of Minds, which can at all times overcome the greatest Pleasures: of Minds, to which no Motion towards particular Goods is ever irresistible." But this latter, lofty extreme, was the case prior to the fall and corruption.[52]

Malebranche thinks that God has designed us as such to be able to overcome our weaknesses and move toward the disposition of Adam:

> To our distinct understanding the Inequality which is found in the Liberty of different Persons, we must observe, that every Man perfectly reasonable, perfectly free, and who would be truly happy, may, and ought, upon the Presence of any Object which gives him the sense of Pleasure, suspend his Love, and carefully examine whether this Object be the true Good, or whether the Motion which carries him towards it exactly comport with that

---

[47] Malebranche, *Nature and Grace*, III.4–5.
[48] Malebranche, *Nature and Grace*, III.7.
[49] Malebranche, *Nature and Grace*, III.8.
[50] Malebranche, *Nature and Grace*, III.10.
[51] Malebranche, *Nature and Grace*, III.8.
[52] Malebranche, *Nature and Grace*, III.9.

which leads him to the true Good: Otherwise he would love by Instinct, and not by Reason; and if he could not suspend the Judgment of his Love, before he examin'd it, he would not be perfectly free.[53]

In other words, true freedom comes from our ability not to be determined by our thoughtless pleasures, passions, and desires. True freedom is sourced in being able to engage the power or faculty of reason to examine the goods as soberly as we can in the present moment. He notes, "This Power of suspending the Judgment, which is the actual Rule of Love; this Power, which is the Principle of our Liberty, and by which Pleasures are not always invincible, is very much weaken'd since Sin, though not quite destroy'd."[54] We can in fact build up this liberty. Even the weakest of souls can build up this liberty. In fact, it is the "chief Duty of our Minds."[55] One can start with building self-control and will increasingly find it easier to suspend their judgment and they will concomitantly be more sensible to the whispers of reason.[56] What is more, by comparing sensible goods to the "indelible Idea of the Supreme Good" one can come to "relish" the "Sovereign Good."[57] "Liberty thus insensibly increasing, and perfecting it self by Exercise, and the Assistance of Grace, we may at last put our selves in a Capacity of performing the most difficult Commandments."[58] All of these elements drawn out from *Nature and Grace* have analogues in Locke's "Of Power."

Final Comments on Locke's Context

There are a few important observations regarding Locke's milieu to bring to the fore before proceeding, some alluded to above. First, scholasticism was still very much alive in the era of Locke's philosophizing and theologizing. In fact, Locke debated prominent scholastics in his day. He was not ignorant of that methodology and approach to theology and philosophy. Second, as has been well-indexed by Stephen Hampton, the Anglican Church of which Locke was a part was hardly uniform regarding the doctrinal positions of

---

[53] Malebranche, *Nature and Grace*, III.12.
[54] Malebranche, *Nature and Grace*, III.13.
[55] Malebranche, *Nature and Grace*, III.15.
[56] Malebranche, *Nature and Grace*, III.16.
[57] Malebranche, *Nature and Grace*, III.6. Malebranche uses the word "goûter" that is translated as "relished." Locke frequently uses this term in his chapter.
[58] Malebranche, *Nature and Grace*, III.16.

its theologians and pastors and doctrinal specificity they were comfortable with in their writings.[59] In fact, Locke himself is an adherent of toleration and not comprehension, the former being a person who thought Christian traditions beyond the ecclesiastical and theological bounds of the then-present Anglican Church should be societally and politically tolerated and the latter being one who thought instead that the pale of orthodoxy of the Church of England ought to be expanded to comprehend more positions on various topics.[60] Third, given the combative air of British theology and the complexities of free will discussions, cautious thinkers such as Locke would have good reason to be wary in treating such a large topic. Fourth, and closely related to the preceding observation, based on Locke's political interests, liberty from coaction would be an important aspect of free will to highlight in addition to his concerns about eternal salvation. If the government restrains or hinders people from searching out questions of religion, their salvation is put in peril. At one place, toward the end of the *Essay*, he notes that those who live in restrictive countries, "where Men are forced, at a venture, to be of the Religion of the Country," compared to the poor laborers of relatively free countries, "are as far, nay farther from the *Liberty and Opportunities of a fair Enquiry*."[61]

Locke's Admission of Avoidance of Metaphysical Pronouncement

James Harris's Argument from *Of Liberty and Necessity*

Of Liberty and Necessity: The Free Will Debate in Eighteenth-Century British Philosophy was published in 2005 by James Harris. As the subtitle indicates, the book is not merely about Locke. Harris's first chapter focuses upon "Of

---

[59] Stephen Hampton, *Anti-Arminians: The Anglican Reformed Tradition from Charles II to George I* (Oxford: Oxford University Press, 2008).
[60] John Locke, *A Letter Concerning Toleration*, 2nd ed. corrected (London: Awnsham Churchill, 1690); Diana Stanciu, "Arminian Toleration, Irenicism and Latitudinarianism in Cudworth's Letters to Van Limborch: Text and Contect," *Lias* 40, no. 2 (2013): 177-209; G. A. J. Rogers, "Locke and the Latitude-Men: Ignorance as a Ground of Toleration," in *Philosophy, Science, and Religion in England 1640-1700*, ed. Richard Kroll, Richard Ashcraft, and Perez Zagorin (New York: Cambridge University Press, 1992), 230-52; John Marshall, "John Locke and Latitudinarianism," in *Philosophy, Science, and Religion in England 1640-1700*, ed. Richard Kroll, Richard Ashcraft, and Perez Zagorin (New York: Cambridge University Press, 1992), 253-82.
[61] Locke, *Essay*, IV.xx.4

Power" from three different angles: an exposition of it, a discussion of its various revisions, and a treatment of its reception by the subsequent generation. Harris thinks that in Locke's chapter, "He intends to be true to the experience of freedom, to the experience of what deliberation and choice-making are actually like."[62] Harris notes that while Locke "is resistant to the idea that freedom consists in the indifference of the will to the deliverances of the understanding"[63] (according to Harris, not a very popular type of what could be called libertarian freedom), "Locke appears not to want to address the metaphysical—and theological—problems surrounding freedom at all."[64] So, Locke is not trying to defend a more nuanced view of Hobbes's necessitarianism or Bramhall's libertarianism, although he does not approve of libertarian views of human free will where the will and reason are unlinked.

Harris discusses each of the editions of "Of Power" in order. He frames the first edition as a promulgation of freedom of action. He captures the primary thrust of Molyneux's critique: "Locke has recoiled all the way from the indifference of the will to a position where choice, and with it the freedom that confers responsibility and liability, threatens to be subsumed by the operations of the understanding." He adds, "We do not choose to believe what the understanding represents to us as true; so, if the understanding is what determines our actions, it looks as though, by the same token, we cannot really be said to choose to act as we do." In the end it appears that people are punished, therefore, for not understanding better than they do or for not being better reasoners than they actually are.[65] Harris explains how some of the additions to the second edition appear to be provocatively libertarian, such as Locke's introduction and incorporation of the so-called power of suspension, but upon closer inspection prove not to be such. Again, Locke is attempting to capture and depict our human experience as personal and free agents. There is more to freedom than freedom from external restraint (freedom of action). There is also something internal, something psychological as it were, that is part of our experience of freedom.[66] Harris also explains how the later editions' revisions comport with Locke's approach to the second edition as just outlined.

---

[62] Harris, *Of Liberty and Necessity*, 20.
[63] Harris, *Of Liberty and Necessity*, 19.
[64] Harris, *Of Liberty and Necessity*, 21.
[65] Harris, *Of Liberty and Necessity*, 26.
[66] Cf. Harris, *Of Liberty and Necessity*, 30–31.

Harris demonstrates that the chapter need not be read metaphysically and is best not read that way. He points out that there is no explicit argument for or against necessitarianism or libertarianism (other than the so-called liberty of indifference). He reasons that passages often purported to show Locke's necessitarianism are open to interpretation. Harris paints Locke as "a *cautious* philosopher, one who shies away from clear and decisive pronouncements," a claim that one familiar with Locke is hard pressed to deny.[67] He also directs the readers' attention to projects contemporaneous to Locke's that discuss free will in a metaphysically neutral way.[68]

Evidence from the Locke–Molyneux Correspondence that Supports the Theory that He Is Attempting to Avoid Metaphysical Pronouncements

Locke's reply to Molyneux in a letter dated July 16, 1692 is important. It is odd that it has not been more prominent in the scholarly discussions. Locke writes: "I do not wonder to find you think my discourse about liberty a little too fine spun, I had so much that thought of it my self, that I said the same thing of it to some of my friends before it was printed, and told them that upon that account I judg'd it best to leave it out, but they persuaded me to the contrary." Locke appears to appreciate Molyneux's discomfort with the chapter. But more importantly, in the missive, Locke appears to confess that he is trying to avoid venturing into a metaphysical discussion:

> When the connection of the parts of my subject brought me to the consideration of power, I had no design to meddle with the question of liberty, but barely pursued my thoughts in the contemplation of that power in man of choosing or preferring, which we call the will, as far as they would lead me without any the least bypass to one side or other; or if there was any leaning in my mind, it was rather to the contrary side to that where I found myself at the end of my pursuit. But doubting that it bore a little too hard upon man's liberty, I shew'd it to a very ingenious but professed Arminian, and desired him, after he had consider'd it, to tell me his objections if he had any, who frankly confessed he could carry it no farther.[69]

---

[67] Harris, *Of Liberty and Necessity*, 21.
[68] Harris, *Of Liberty and Necessity*, 23.
[69] John Locke, "L1592. Locke to William Molyneux," 625.

Locke here admits his desire not to be entangled in the metaphysical debate over liberty, and that in an earlier draft of "Of Power" felt that he leaned too heavily to the side of the necessitarians. This prompted him to consult a professed Arminian, presumably a metaphysical libertarian. At the very least, this person appears to have not thought that "Of Power," charitably read, definitively offends his or her metaphysical views.[70]

There is more in the letter that points toward Locke's aim of staying metaphysically neutral in his second edition. He notes, "I confess, I think there might be something said, which with a great many men would pass for a satisfactory answer to your objection; but it not satisfying me, I neither put it into my book, nor shall now in my letter." Perhaps Locke has some idea of how he might respond to the metaphysical question, but he does not desire to include that in the second edition of the *Essay*. Then, after requesting that Molyneux point out any other errors to him so that he can "reform it," Locke states:

> But if you will argue for or against liberty, from consequences, I will not undertake to answer you. For I own freely to you the weakness of my understanding, that though it be unquestionable that there is omnipotence and omniscience in God our maker, and I cannot have a clearer perception of any thing that I am free, yet I cannot make freedom in man consistent with omnipotence and omniscience in God, though I am as fully perswaded of both as of any truths I most firmly assent to. And therefore I have long since given off the consideration of that question, resolving all into this short conclusion, That if it be possible for God to make a free agent, then man is free, though I see not the way of it.[71]

Locke states that if Molyneux attempts to demonstrate "Of Power" to be promoting liberty or necessity from the consequences of his argument, he will make no reply. In the latter part of the excerpt, however, he shifts his focus. Whereas he previously indicated that he had attempted to avoid the metaphysical question, which was partially the source of Molyneux's consternation with "Of Power" in the *Essay*'s first edition, it appears that he is now giving a private pronouncement, without any intention of making a published declaration. There are two things he knows: (1) God is omnipotent

---

[70] John Locke, "L1592. Locke to William Molyneux," 625 fn 2. E. S. de Beer indicates that the Armininan is Jean Le Clerc.
[71] John Locke, "L1592. Locke to William Molyneux," 625–26.

and omniscient; and (2) that he perceives that human beings have metaphysical freedom of choice. Yet he cannot reconcile God's sovereignty with human freedom of choice. Acknowledging his inability to argue that humans have metaphysical freedom without detracting from God's sovereignty, Locke inclines toward non-necessitarian freedom and throws up his hands at continuing the metaphysical question any further.[72]

Locke says something similar to this in the *Essay* IV.xvii.10. In the section he is asserting that our reason becomes puzzled or confused because of the imperfect ideas that we have. The second and final example of such an issue of puzzlement that he posits is that of free created agents in light of the idea of God: "Thus, we having but imperfect *Ideas* of the Operations of our Minds, and of the Beginning of Motion or Thought how the Mind produces either of them in us, and much imperfecter yet, of the Operation of GOD, run into great Difficulties about free created Agents, which Reason cannot well extricate it self out of." Again, Locke acknowledges the seeming impossibility of the human intellect answering the metaphysical question of liberty. This would be an odd example to use in book IV of the *Essay* if he were promulgating a metaphysical answer to the question in "Of Power" in book II.[73]

The very fact that Locke is a professed theist who knows that God is omnipotent and omniscient, as indicated in the *Essay*, his correspondence, and throughout his works, makes approaching "Of Power" as a metaphysical pronouncement all the more precarious. However one resolves the question of metaphysical human free agency, one is still left with the question how that metaphysical human freedom is meaningful in light of divine agency. For instance, Francis Turretin, a theologian with whom Locke was familiar, asks the question: "How can the concourse of God be reconciled with the contingency and liberty of second causes—especially of the will of man?" In speaking of the difficulty of the question, Turretin writes:

> These two things we derive most clearly from Scriptures: that the providence of God concurs with all second causes and especially with the human will; yet the contingency and liberty of the will remain unimpaired. But how these two things can consist with each other, no mortal can in this

---

[72] Recall, Bramhall identifies adherents of liberty as being broader than what contemporary scholars would identify as libertarian. Thus, I have labeled Lock's inclinations as non-necessitarian.
[73] It is worthwhile noting that this quotation was changed to its present state in the second edition. So, Locke was aware of this section's content and altered it along with "Of Power." Cf. IV.xvii.4.

life perfectly understand. Nor should it seem a cause for wonder, since he has a thousand ways (to us incomprehensible) of concurring with our will, insinuating himself into us and turning our hearts, so that by acting freely as we will, we still do nothing besides the will and determination of God.[74]

If God foreordains all that comes to pass why is God not morally responsible for all that comes to pass? How can any position on human free agency be considered such in light of this powerful God? Orthodox Reformed teaching regarded God as the primary cause and humans as secondary causes, arguing a dual causality and the divine concurrence in all actions. When the Remonstrants with whom Locke corresponded offered an alternative explanation of human free will that made God—who, in their scheme, still foreordains all that comes to pass—seem less responsible for evil and damnation, they were still left with conceptual problems.[75] The theological background and context of "Of Power" would seem to demand some discussion of divine sovereignty. Locke, however, offers none.

The Locke–Molyneux correspondence holds still more that supports an intentional evasion of the metaphysical question. In an April 1693 letter to Locke, Molyneux characterizes Locke as one who avoids controversies when feasible, writing, "I know 'tis none of your Business to ingage in Controversy, or remove Objections; save only such as seem immediately to strike at your Own Positions."[76] Molyneux is not the last to frame Locke as such.[77] Even Locke's letters to Molyneux noting some changes Locke planned on making to "Of Power" for the second edition of the *Essay* and the summary of his argument for the revised chapter do not show any evidence of Locke changing it to answer more clearly the metaphysical question.[78] In Molyneux's first letter to Locke after having obtained the second edition, his comments and compliments seem to be focused on the latter portion of his oft cited critique (again, there he notes that Locke seems to be saying that "Man shall be Damn'd, because he understands no better than he does" and not because of the depravity of our wills). In the 1694 letter, Molyneux writes:

---

[74] Turretin, *Institutes of Elenctic Theology*, VI.vi.1.
[75] Cf. Richard A. Muller, *God, Creation, and Providence in the Thought of Jacob Arminius* (Grand Rapids: Baker, 1991).
[76] Molyneux, "L1622. William Molyneux to Locke," 668.
[77] For example, John C. Higgins-Biddle, Introduction, cxiv; Alan P. F. Sell, *John Locke and the Eighteenth-Century Divines* (Cardif: University of Wales Press, 1997), 186–88. Cf. Marko, *Measuring the Distance*, 246.
[78] Locke, "L1643. Locke to William Molyneux," 700–1; Locke, "L1655. Locke to William Molyneux," 722.

I have yet only looked over those Parts which are newly added, particularly that of *Liberty*, the alterations wherein I take to be most Judiciously made; and now I think that the whole Chapter stands so wel put together, and the Argumentation is so legitimate, that nothing can shake it. I was mightily pleased to find therein a Rational Account of what I have often wonderd at, viz, Why Men should content themselves to stay in this Life for ever, tho at the same time they will grant, that in the next Life they expect to be infinitely Happy? of this you give so clear an account in the 44th section of your 21 Chapter. Book. 2d. that my Wonder no Longer Remains. That Candid recession from your former Hypothesis which you shew in this Chapter, where Truth required it, raises in me a Greater Opinion (if possible) of your Worth than ever.[79]

There is nothing here to suggest that Locke changed his approach and finally turned to the metaphysical question, the first point of Molyneux's initial critique. Instead Molyneux simply commends Locke for the "Rational Account" of a soteriologically focused epistemological question, to which I now turn.

The Theological Message of "Of Power" that Eludes Sectarian Categorization

Covering Some Familiar Ground before Culling the Theological Message

For John Locke, power is the ability to change or the ability to be changed (§1). We tend to make a distinction between active powers and passive powers, although what is an example of a merely active power or merely passive power is hard to determine. Locke muses whether matter is wholly passive as God is wholly active and whether we will be both active and passive in the intermediate state (heaven). But he abruptly cuts himself off, asserting, "my present Business being not to search into the original of Power, but how we come by the *Idea* of it" (§2).[80] Clearly, this is intended to be an epistemological project, not a metaphysical one.

---

[79] Molyneux, "L1763. William Molyneux to Locke," 92–93.
[80] It is perhaps worth mentioning that when Locke gives an example of where we get an idea of active power, as he does in §4, that does not necessarily mean he is advocating one of the conceivably inferable positions. That is, we should be hesitant to conclude that Locke is promoting libertarian

In §5, Locke offers a few very important definitions. He defines the will as the power the mind has "thus to order the consideration of any *Idea*, or the forbearing to consider it; or to prefer the motion of any part of the body to its rest, and *vice versâ* in any particular instance." Volition or willing is the "actual exercise of that power, by directing any particular action, or its forbearance." Such a forbearance or performance due to the command of the mind is called voluntary while an action performed without such a direction is called involuntary.

It is in §8 where Locke shifts the topic to human freedom, with a surprising (and, to many, an unsatisfying) twist. He asserts that a human is free only where she may do or forbear any particular action that she prefers. Furthermore, he takes the terms "liberty" and "necessity"—terms that had come to have metaphysical import—and redefines them:

> So that the *Idea* of *Liberty*, is the *Idea* of a Power in any Agent to do or forbear any particular Action, according to the determination or thought of the mind, whereby either of them is preferr'd to the other; where either of them is not in the Power of the Agent to be produced by him according to his *Volition*, there he is not at *Liberty*, that Agent is under *Necessity*. So that *Liberty* cannot be, where there is no Thought, no Volition, no Will; but there may be Thought, there may be Will, there may be Volition, where there is no *Liberty*.

In other words, the idea of liberty is the idea of an agent's ability (again, this is more about our perception and experience: primarily a descriptive project) to do or not do a particular action; otherwise, the agent is not free. An agent has no liberty where there is no thought or willing, but the presence of those does not equate to the idea of liberty. He spells this out through a series of examples in the next section. A tennis ball is under necessity as is a man falling into the water. An involuntary action is an instance of necessity (§9). A man staying willingly in a secret prison, although voluntarily done, does not have liberty for he does not have the alternative choice as an option (§10). And the same assertions applied to human motions are to be applied to thoughts, the other type of human action (§12; cf. §4). While humans have no liberty that they think—thinking being a ceaseless operation—they

---

self-determination or agent causation in his pointing to our minds moving our bodies as the source of the idea of the beginning of motion.

often have the liberty to contemplate or not contemplate according to their preferences. But when pains or passions are so intense that we cannot stop our ideas presenting themselves in the mind, we are not free agents with respect to our thoughts (§12). He writes, "Where-ever Thought is wholly wanting, or the power to act or forbear according to the direction of Thought, there *Necessity* takes place" (§13).

Having so far defined and expounded upon the doctrine now commonly known as freedom of action—an agent is free or has liberty if she can do or forbear an action according to her preference of either of them—he explains why the discussion of liberty and necessity has been fruitless. He writes, "I leave it to be considered, whether it [his definition of liberty] may not help put an end to that long agitated, and, I think, unreasonable, because unintelligible, Question, *viz. Whether Man's Will be free, or no*." He continues on: "For if I mistake not, it follows, from what I have said, that the Question it self is altogether improper; and it is as insignificant to ask, whether Man's *Will* be free, as to ask, whether his Sleep be Swift, or his Vertue square: *Liberty* being as little applicable to the *Will*, as swiftness of Motion is to Sleep, or squareness to Vertue" (§14). He explains that powers belong to agents and not to other powers. The will and liberty are two powers that belong to agents, so the power of the will cannot have the power of liberty (§14–16). Besides, it is not reasonable to frame various faculties as personal agents; in fact, this prevalent way of speaking has bred confusion. It has become common to speak of the will directing the understanding or vice-versa (§17–18). While Locke grants that a thought may be an occasion of a volition, it is not, however, one power working on another: "But it is the Mind that operates, and exerts these Powers; it is the Man that does the Action, it is the Agent that has power, or is able to do" (§19).[81] Moreover, because liberty consists in a power to act or forbear, the human is not free with respect to the will for "That in all proposals of present Action, *a Man is not at liberty to will, or not to will, because he cannot forbear willing.*"[82] The mind cannot avoid a determination on an issue brought to the mind. The agent is constantly willing, even if it is

---

[81] In §20, he is wrestling with what we mean when we speak of different "faculties." At one point he writes, "For *Faculty, Ability,* and *Power,* I think, are but different names of the same things: Which ways of speaking, when put into more intelligible Words, will, I think, amount to thus much . . . ." This is a clear instance of Locke admitting that his intent, at least for the chapter, is a descriptive project. For places where he does this in Book IV: Marko, *Measuring the Distance,* ch. 3. Also, the 1694 second edition reads differently in §19: "But it is the Mind, or the Man, that operates, and exerts these Powers; that does the Action, he has power, or is able to do."

[82] The 1694 second edition (Locke 1694) reads: "*A Man is not at liberty to will, or not to will any thing in his power, that he once considers of.*" Both have the same effect.

simply the will to do nothing about the situation at hand and to say "yes" or "no" later. In short, we are free when we have the ability to act or forbear according to our will, but the mind is not free in its constant application of the will (§24).

The next question Locke turns to is: If the mind determines the will, what determines the mind? Locke's answer is that it is uneasiness, which is a desire of an absent good: "This *Uneasiness* we may call, as it is, *Desire*; which is an *uneasiness* of the Mind for want of some absent good." For instance, when there is pain there is desire of ease from said pain, an absent good (§31). He subtly interjects that the will is not immediately determined by the uneasiness of desire: "But that which immediately determines the *Will*, from time to time, to every voluntary Action, is the *uneasiness* of *desire*, fixed on some absent good" (§33). Locke admits that in the first edition he had thought the greatest good as apprehended by the agent was what determined the will, "But yet upon a stricter enquiry, I am forced to conclude, that *good*, the *greater good*, though apprehended and acknowledged to be so, does not determine the *will*, until our desire, raised proportionably to it, makes us *uneasy* in the want of it."[83] In other words, in order not to be determined by our most pressing and immediate desires for a good that is not the greatest good, we would need to be able to cultivate our desires for the greater good to make it supersede the uneasiness produced by the absence of a lesser good. To illustrate his point, he notes that all who have great goals in this world, or hopes in the next, know the advantages of virtues, "yet till he *hungers and thirsts after righteousness*; till he feels an *uneasiness* in the want of it, his *will* will not be determin'd to any action in pursuit of this confessed greater good" (§35). He remarks that if we were merely determined by views of the good, the prospects of the joys of heaven would constantly guide and direct us. Unfortunately, that is not our experience: "The infinitely greatest confessed good being often neglected, to satisfy the successive *uneasiness* of our desires pursuing trifles" (§38; cf. §37).

Locke subsequently turns to the question: With all the uneasiness that we have, what determines the will? His answer, in brief, is: "that ordinarily, which is the most pressing of those, that are judged capable of being then removed" (§40). Our happiness or the reduction of our misery alone moves desire and as soon as any good is perceived to be necessary for one's happiness

---

[83] These sentiments push against his regular connection of actual belief and action observable in his critiques of innatists in the *Essay* and those who seem to make faith solely an intellectual affair in *ROC*.

one desires it. But the greatest perceivable good does not necessarily move us (§41–43). This might strike us as unfortunate, but, Locke writes, "All present pain, whatever it be, makes a part of our present *misery*: But all absent good does not at any time make a necessary part of our present *happiness*, nor the absence of it make a part of our *misery*. If it did, we should be constantly and infinitely miserable; there being infinite degrees of happiness, which are not in our possession." He subsequently shifts his focus back to the precariousness of the current determination of so many people: they are so often determined by, what on the grand scheme of things, are trifling desires. If readers doubt that this is so, he suggests that they simply reflect on the last time that they traveled far from home and their responses to the slightest discomfort. And although no one can deny the possibilities of an afterlife with unending joys so far surpassing any found here on earth, and even more no one can deny that this afterlife is much more likely than an everlasting continuation of the pittance of pleasures they seek here on earth (and which may very well keep them from the aforementioned eternal joys), still the desires of many are not changed, "nor their *wills* determin'd to any action, or endeavor for its attainment" (§44). The situation is compounded by the fact that we are constantly bombarded by returning desires such as hunger, thirst, sleepiness, etc., and uneasiness of desires acquired by social pressures, example, and education, such as riches and honor, all of which leaves little room to concentrate on absent goods. And even when we do focus on the joys of eternal life, there are other desires ready to push them out of line (§45).

Locke then attempts to answer the question: Is there anything that we can do to help ourselves out of this precarious situation? He asserts that "by a due consideration and examining any good proposed, it is in our power, to raise our desires, in a due proportion to the value of that good, whereby in its turn, and place, it may come to work upon the *will*, and be pursued." Because of the "multitude of wants, and desires, we are beset with in this imperfect State, we are not like to be ever freed from in this World" (§46). But, while the most pressing and removable uneasiness most often determines the will, it does not always. "For the mind having in most cases, as is evident in Experience, a power to *suspend* the execution and satisfaction of any of its desires, and so all, one after another, is at liberty to consider the objects of them; examine them on all sides, and weigh them with others. In this lies the liberty Man has."[84] It is with this ability that we can, in modern day parlance, stop and

---

[84] Notice that Locke is asking the reader to reflect on their "experience" to confirm his assertion.

think about what we are doing. Not using our power of suspense is the source of mistakes, errors, and the like. They come from engaging our wills before a proper examination can be had. Locke adds, "This seems to me the source of all liberty; in this seems to consist that, which is (as I think improperly) call'd *Free will*." The moments of suspension are our opportunities to examine and judge whether we are going to do good or evil (§47).

It is this doctrine of suspense that has been one of the main foci of discussion in scholarship interpreting "Of Power." Many ask themselves the questions: Is this an indication that "Of Power" was libertarian all along? Or, is this an indication that Locke switched views in the second edition, or an indication that he admits of instances of libertarian freedom? Or, can "Of Power" still be necessitarian in light of this doctrine of suspension? It would seem that Locke has attempted to change the focus of the discussion from freedom of the will to freedom of action, despite whether one thinks he is additionally answering metaphysical questions or not. His definition of necessity does not comport with those of the then-recent necessitarians, and his definition of liberty is far from those described by libertarians in his day. Locke, however, is discussing the powers of liberty and the will from the perspective of one closely reflecting upon the ideas and their connection. As previously indicated, this is a descriptive project without any clear metaphysical pronouncement. It is also prescriptive as Locke describes rightly ordered mental operations. Locke offers no metaphysical conversation regarding the mind or agent.

Beyond this, Locke evidences a significant concern for salvation throughout the chapter. Even the first edition, although notably different from the second, still has a theme of his concern for eternal salvation in it (§29, §30, §35, §37, §38, and §45 in the first edition). Molyneux's original critique had recognized this soteriological aspect of "Of Power."[85]

The Theological Message of "Of Power"

The remainder of the chapter, "Of Power," is a development of the concept of suspension and its utility. The first aspect of suspension that Locke focuses

---

[85] Molyneux, "L1579. William Molyneux to Locke," 600 fn 4; Harris, *Of Liberty and Necessity*, 26; cf. Locke, *Essay*, II.xxi.71.

upon is its connection to reason. Suspension, again, is so important because it is that which allows the mind to employ the faculty of reason in examining and judging the situation at hand and carefully decide what one should do.[86] For Locke, "This is so far from being a restraint or diminution of *Freedom*, that it is the very improvement and benefit of it; 'tis not an Abridgement, 'tis the end and use of our *Liberty*; and the farther we are removed from such a determination, the nearer we are to Misery and Slavery." He further notes that we would be in a much worse state if the will were so indifferent that the mind was not determinable by the mind's last judgment of a reasonable examination (§48). Locke thinks asserting that the will directs the understanding or vice-versa is an improper and unhelpful way of discussing our freedom.[87] Anticipating objections to his claim that we can be determined by our reason and that this is a good thing, he writes, "Is it worth the Name of *Freedom* to be at liberty to play the Fool, and draw Shame and Misery upon a Man's self? If to break loose from the conduct of Reason, and to want that restraint of Examination and Judgment, which keeps us from chusing or doing the worse, be *Liberty*, true Liberty, mad Men and Fools are the only Freemen" (§50).

He has much more to say about this "true liberty" throughout the chapter. A few of the most important quotations are as follows. In §51 he writes that "the highest perfection of intellectual nature, lies in a careful and constant pursuit of true and solid happiness; so the care of our selves, that we mistake not imaginary for real happiness, is the foundation of our *liberty*." In other words, our inclination and drive for true happiness combined with our ability to be determined by foresight and not near-sightedness is a vital aspect of a liberty worth having (§51; cf. §52). And in §67, Locke asserts, "Without Liberty the Understanding would be to no purpose: And without Understanding, Liberty (if it could be) would signify nothing." He adds, "The first therefore and great use of Liberty, is to hinder blind Precipitancy; the principle exercise of Freedom is to stand still, open the eyes, look about, and

---

[86] If Locke's treatment of free will is not a metaphysical pronouncement, then neither is his treatment of suspension.

[87] It is difficult for Locke to completely avoid any hint of hypostatization as he is doing here but he does a fair job of doing so. He is clear that the voluntarist-intellectualist debate and its framing is unhelpful in §17 and §18 (cf. §6, §14, §15, §16, §20, §29). He writes, "This way of talking, nevertheless, has prevailed, and, as I guess, produced great confusion. For these [willing, understanding, etc.] being all different Powers in the Mind, or in the Man, to do several Actions, he exerts them as he thinks fit: But the power to do one Action, is not operated on by the power of doing another Action..." (§18).

take a view of the consequence of what we are going to do, as much as the weight of the matter requires."[88]

Whereas our most pressing and removable desires determine our minds most of the time, we do have the ability to have reason determine our minds.[89] Locke argues, however, that we do not always have the ability to suspend our wills and make a definitive decision. He asserts that extreme disturbances like the pain of torture or uneasiness such as "Love, Anger, or any other violent Passion running away with us, allows us not the liberty of thought, and we are not Masters enough of our own Minds to consider thoroughly, and examine fairly." Now it is important to point out that he does not completely rule out the application of our reason in these situations: he frames our ability to deliberate as either not occurring or not being sufficiently applied. Moreover, in the context of our minds being overrun by these occasional desires, with a mind to the coming judgment he writes, "God, who knows our frailty, pities our weakness, and requires of us no more than we are able to do, and sees what was, and what was not in our power, will judge as a kind and merciful Father" (§53).

In short, liberty worth having is that which involves human reason. Liberty, in the earlier sections of "Of Power," was viewed as the power an agent has to do or forbear doing any particular action, according to the actual preference of the mind for its doing or forbearance. Once suspension is emphasized, however, Locke's definition of liberty is qualified. Now it appears that the liberty of intellectual beings consists in the power not to be always determined immediately by the greatest and present uneasiness that has not been deliberated upon by human reason, but to be determined instead by an uneasiness or desire for better things that tend more truly to our innate drive for true happiness by the interposition of an appropriate deliberation or reasoning.[90]

But this definition can be further qualified. Within the context of the latter half of the chapter, where he works out the idea of suspension, it is constantly

---

[88] This quotation is found in the fourth and fifth editions, but not in the second edition. It lends clarity to the section and not new ideas. Cf. Harris, 2005, 31–35.

[89] Locke considers how good our application of reason is in, "Of Wrong Assent, or Errour." Just because our reason is employed does not mean that our decisions will be good. The said chapter is IV.xix in the 1690, 1694, and 1695 editions and IV.xx in later editions, including the critical edition. This adds some additional complexities to the conversation of suspension and reason. Because "Of Power" has enough concerns of its own, nettling over the interconnections with "Of Wrong Assent, or Errour" will be avoided. For a discussion of suspense, freedom of the will, and reason in light of the chapter, see: Marko, *Measuring the Distance*, ch. 3.

[90] Cf. Locke, "L1655. Locke to William Molyneux," 722.

with an eye toward the importance of it for our prospects of salvation and the afterlife. He also discusses our abilities to habituate ourselves and thus make our responses to situations better in an automatic sort of way. Given Locke's focus on salvation and the afterlife and on our ability to give ourselves habits, there is yet another qualification that the doctrine of suspense adds to Locke's definition of liberty: Liberty of intellectual beings in its most important aspect is the power not to be determined by desires of the flesh but to habituate ourselves and otherwise decide for that which tends to our salvation and eternal rewards. A corollary to this is that the pursuit of salvation or eternal life with God is the pursuit of true happiness. Such statements are fundamental to Locke's response to Molyneux's critique that the first edition of the *Essay*'s chapter "Of Power" frames humans as being damned not for the depravity of their wills but because of their understanding.

Regarding our habituation, Locke has much to say. In a few places he explains that we can change the relishes of our mind similarly to the way we change the relishes of the body. He asserts that we should go to lengths to "suit the relish of our Minds to the true intrinsick good or ill, that is in things." Thus, we should "not permit an allow'd or supposed possible great and weighty good to slip out of our thoughts, without leaving any relish, any desire of it self there, till, by a due consideration of its true worth, we have formed appetites in our Minds suitable to it, and made our selves uneasie in the want of it, or in the fear of losing it." That is, we need to cultivate desires—strong desires—for that which we understand is truly most worthy. This, in fact, is a way to govern our passions. People who claim that they cannot control their passions, with the exclusion of some of the situations already noted above, are not trying hard enough. Locke writes, "Nor let anyone say, he cannot govern his Passions, nor hinder them from breaking out, and carrying him into action; for what he can do before a Prince, or a great Man, he can do alone, or in the presence of God, if he will" (§53).

Subsequently, Locke asks whether we change the pleasantness or unpleasantness that accompanies any sort of action. He answers that just as we can acquire a taste for tobacco, we can acquire desires for virtues. He notes that the prospects of the healthful effects of an acrid potion will determine someone's mind to drink the brew. He writes, "any action is rendred more or less pleasing, only by the contemplation of the end, and the being more or less perswaded of its tendency to it, or necessary connexion with it: But the pleasure of the action it self is best acquir'd, or increased, by use and practice." In other words, we can get ourselves to do something that we do not enjoy doing because we are able to exercise restraint and foresight—a result of an application of reason amidst the suspense of our wills—and we can even start to enjoy the action itself through trials and practice. "Habits have powerful charms, and put so strong attractions of easiness and pleasure into what we accustom our selves to, that we cannot forbear to do, or at least be easy in the omission of actions, which habitual practice has suited, and thereby recommends to us." That is, we are able to better our own inclinations toward good actions. In fact, "Pains should be taken to rectify these; and contrary habits change our pleasures, and give a relish to that, which is necessary, or conducive to our Happiness" (§69). And if one were to object, thinking this made us less free, Locke says that the superior beings above us "who enjoy perfect Happiness" are "more steadily *determined in their choice of Good*," but that it would be wrong to think of them as less happy or free than ourselves. Even, "the Freedom of the Almighty hinders not his being determined by what is best" (§49).

Just as Locke worked out his initial unqualified definition of liberty with a serious concern for salvation, so also is it in his working out of suspension, the application of our reason, and habituation. Locke discusses our necessity or inclination and tendency to happiness that "establishes *suspense, deliberation*, and scrutiny of each successive desire" (§52). In the surrounding passages, he makes mention of "true happiness" (§51), "true felicity," and "real Bliss" (§52). He soon thereafter treats two related questions: (1) How do our wills carry us to what is evil and not to happiness? and (2) How do things come to be represented under deceitful appearances and how does the judgment pronounce wrongly concerning them? Therein he demonstrates his concern, again, with salvation and the afterlife. For instance, he notes that unfortunately we are often content and happy with a lesser present good that detracts from a better, attainable future good: "For whilst such thoughts possess them, the Joys of a future State move them not; they have little concern or uneasiness about them; and the *will*, free from determination of such desires, is left to the pursuit of nearer satisfactions." What one can do to help such a person is, "Change but a Man's view of these things; let him see, that Virtue and Religion are necessary to his Happiness; let him look into the future State of Bliss or Misery, and see there God the righteous Judge, ready to *render to every Man according to his Deeds*." One needs also to realize that the joys or miseries in this life are nothing in comparison to the joys or miseries in the afterlife. And if they grasp this they will (hopefully) change their behavior upon which their prospects of the afterlife depend (§60).

In discussing our wrong judgments, he asserts "*The cause of our judging amiss*, when we compare our present Pleasure and Pain with future, seems to me to be *the weak and narrow Constitution of our Minds*" (§64). We find ourselves often consumed with a present pleasure that detracts from our future, better pleasures. It is in some cases difficult to counterbalance the present desire with the prospect of a pleasure with which we are unacquainted. We may say to ourselves the future pleasure may not be as good as we think. Locke indicates that there is some merit in this objection in general but not with respect to the future pleasures: that would equate to the claim, "God cannot make those happy he designs to be so" (§65). In his final section prior to §71, his summary statement of the chapter, Locke claims that while a book could be written on the way we mislead ourselves, "Morality, established upon its true Foundations, cannot but determine the Choice in any one" who seriously reflects upon the "infinite Happiness and Misery." If one does this and does not change, one "must needs condemn himself, as not making that use of his Understanding he should"; and, it would be hard to call such a person a rational creature. "The Rewards and Punishments of another Life, which the Almighty has established, as the Enforcements of his Law, are of weight enough to determine the Choice, against whatever Pleasure or Pain this Life can shew, when the eternal State is considered but in its bare possibility, when no Body can make any doubt of." In other words, even if one were not convinced of the afterlife, but rightly admitted its possibility, the bare possibility would determine the decisions and intellectual pursuits of the truly rational creature. If people live virtuous lives in light of their belief in the afterlife, the worst that can befall them is that they are wrong and they feel and regret nothing in the end. If wicked people who hope for immediate annihilation are wrong, they will experience infinite miseries (§70). Any truly rational creature would understand that the former is the better, safer, and the only truly reasonable path.

There is, thus, an important theological message in Locke's chapter "Of Power." This message is undergirded by Locke's initial definition of liberty and his qualified understanding of it with a substantial emphasis on suspense and reason all fleshed out throughout the chapter with a concern for salvation in mind. Thus, the free agent has the power to do or forbear according to her will. The truly free agent is reasonable, and the truly reasonable agent will have her eyes fixed on the afterlife, thus aiming for herself to be a slave, and determined, therefore, by her ever-cultivated desire for righteousness and not by her fleshly desires. In other words, our true human liberty is the power to free ourselves from damning (or rewards-reducing) desires and thus to cultivate good ones and otherwise decide for, and be determined by, the good. It is descriptive of the rightly used will, and, thus, in that sense prescriptive. And it seems to be Locke's reply to his "very Judicious friend," William Molyneux (§71).

Eluding Theological Categorization Points to Avoiding Metaphysical Categorization

Once one has given an initial response to the metaphysical question of human free agency in light of God's sovereignty, there are still other questions that need attention. Does one need the Holy Spirit and grace to turn to God? If so, is that assistance irresistible or resistible? If it is resistible, do we actively work alongside of it, or do we simply have the ability to resist it? Further, to what degree and in what sense, if any, are we deprived and/or depraved? How is the human race affected by Adam's original transgression? It is the answers to these questions that determine whether one's soteriology is labeled as Pelagian, Socinian, Semi-pelagian, Arminian, Lutheran, or Calvinist.[91]

From a late seventeenth-century perspective, it was hardly worthwhile to determine if humans have some variety of libertarian or necessitarian free will until one answers the above questions. One could deny necessitarianism but believe that human beings are so broken that without the supernatural assistance from God they are incapable of desiring to follow God and thus not free in the most important respect. By way of example, Calvin commented, "All this being admitted, it will be beyond dispute, that free will does not enable man to perform good works, unless he is assisted by grace; indeed, the special grace which the elect alone receive through regeneration."[92] Similarly,

---

[91] These labels are commonly discussed in systematic theology texts, especially in those of the Reformed: for example, Turretin, *Institutes of Elenctic Theology*; Herman Bavinck, *Reformed Dogmatics*, vol. 3, ed. John Bolt and trans. John Vriend (Grand Rapids: Baker Academic, 2006); Louis Berkhof, *Systematic Theology*, new combined ed. (Grand Rapids: William B. Eerdmans, 1996). For an example of Locke's use of these labels, see Locke, *A Second Vindication*, 52, 103; cf. Jonathan S. Marko, "Justification, Ecumenism, and Heretical Red Herrings," *Philosophy and Theology* 26, no. 2 (2014): 245–66.

[92] Calvin, *Institutes*, II.ii.6. In his recent work on freedom, Muller acknowledges that Calvin is difficult to pin down and label despite what so many others have claimed regarding his views on human freedom: "In sum, Calvin's approach to human freedom is untechnical and, consequently, somewhat vague, perhaps even imprecise. He certainly did assume both an overarching divine determination of all things and a human freedom from necessity or coaction, and, as in the case of Adam, indicating that, in some sense, a choice or act could have been otherwise." Muller, *Divine Will and Human Choice*, 192.

"In this way, then, man is said to have free will, not because he has a free choice of good and evil, but because he acts voluntarily, and not by compulsion. This is perfectly true: but why should so small a matter have been dignified with so proud a title? An admirable freedom!"[93] Because of the depravity of human wills, humans do not have the ability, unassisted, to earnestly follow the Christ of the Bible unto salvation; but they are free regarding how they might continue to sin in rebellion to God. For Calvin, such freedom was hardly worth celebrating. Locke, unlike Calvin, although also interested in the salvation of humans is curiously silent on the questions above, except for some acknowledgment of the weakness of our wills, which for many orthodox theologians is not exhaustive of the total depravity of human beings, and a dislike of hypostatization of the faculties.

A professed and well-read Christian like Locke surely knows what needs to be addressed in a conversation involving the question of so-called human free will coupled with the issue of salvation, the primary and secondary topics of "Of Power." Whether or not grace is needed and, if it is, if it is given to all or is limited and whether it is resistible or irresistible are all issues that are more pressing but not unrelated to the question of metaphysical human free agency. Even if Locke denied that grace is needed because humans in the post-fallen state are still sufficiently sound to respond appropriately to God without it,[94] and were simply attempting to answer the metaphysical question of human freedom, there remains the problem of how his position on metaphysical human free agency can still be considered "freedom" in light of God's sovereignty and free agency. Without, at least, an answer to the latter question, the metaphysical question regarding human agency alone is only a partial answer to the larger metaphysical question of human agency vis-à-vis divine agency, and only a partial answer to the question of human salvation.[95]

---

[93] Calvin, *Institutes*, II.ii.7.

[94] Locke does discuss the Holy Spirit's assistance in: Locke, *The Reasonableness of Christianity*, 292–93. Cf. Marko, "Justification, Ecumenism, and Heretical Red Herrings"; Jonathan S. Marko, "The Promulgation of Right Morals: John Locke on the Church and the Christian as the Salvation of Society," *Journal of Markets and Morality* 19, no. 1 (2016): 41–59.

[95] Although beside the point, there are a few observations that are perhaps instructive for the reader. As already noted, in Christian Protestant theology there are not only soteriological Calvinists and Arminians. As noted in Part I, there are Pelagians, Arminians, Lutherans, Calvinists, and more depending on the aspect of soteriology at which one is looking. Also, an incorporation of middle knowledge does not necessitate Molinism or Armininianism: there is also Congruism. What is more, synergism does not require a libertarian providential arrangement. And compatibilism and Calvinism do not necessarily go together. In short, well-trained theologians understand that libertarian-Arminianism and compatabilistic-Calvinism are hardly the only conceivable options in Locke's day or any other period of Christian history.

In sum, Locke's argument could be read as simply lacking in clarity, but a more favorable reading frames him as avoiding the metaphysical question altogether, eschewing metaphysical labeling and, similarly, intentionally leaving out key theological pieces of personal, positional evidence to take a more or less Latitudinarian position and to elude sectarian categorization.

Conclusions

In this chapter, I contended that "Of Power" is not a metaphysical pronouncement but more along the lines of what those like James Harris portray it to be: a description of our experience of freedom of the will. It is also prescriptive, however, because it is descriptive of the right use of the will. All this is due to two key pieces of evidence that are responses to Molyneux's critique. The first is an admission from Locke in his correspondence with Molyneux that he is attempting to avoid metaphysical pronouncements, at least partly, because trying to reconcile divine and human agency is too difficult. This comports with what he says elsewhere in the *Essay*. The second is that the theological message of "Of Power"—the truly free agent is reasonable, and the truly reasonable agent will have her eyes fixed on the afterlife, thus aiming for herself to be a slave and determined, therefore, by her ever-cultivated desire for righteousness and not by her fleshly desires—and his development of it throughout the chapter eludes sectarian categorization by the avoidance of theological issues that are not unrelated to the metaphysical question of human free agency. In fact, when discussing eternal salvation in a Christian context, the metaphysical question of human free agency is simply one piece of the puzzle. To frame his chapter as making metaphysical pronouncements makes him out to be a theological novice or, perhaps, unconcerned with the religious background of his readership.

8
John Locke and the Above Reason Controversy

Histories of philosophy that discuss the religious epistemology of John Locke will routinely juxtapose his categorization of propositions in *An Essay Concerning Human Understanding*—according to reason, contrary to reason, and above reason—with (Lockean) John Toland's categorization of propositions in *Christianity Not Mysterious* (*CNM*)[1]—according to reason and contrary to reason—in an effort to convey the relative orthodoxy of the former and heterodoxy of the latter. Such studies will often mention how the subsequent Lockean deists continue in Toland's path of divergence from Locke. It has become a standard interpretation that Locke accepts divine mysteries or incomprehensible doctrines of the Christian faith and Toland dismisses anything surpassing our natural abilities of discovery, although they share similar epistemological foundations.[2]

---

[1] Locke's *Essay* and *The Reasonableness of Christianity* and his respective defenses of them: John Locke, *An Essay Concerning Human Understanding*, ed. Peter H. Nidditch (Oxford: Clarendon Press, 1979); John Locke, *A Letter to Edward Ld Bishop of Worcester, Concerning Some Passages Relating to Mr. Locke's Essay of Humane Understanding: In a Late Discourse of His Lordships, In Vindication of the Trinity* (London: Printed for A. and J. Churchill, 1697); John Locke, *Mr. Locke's Reply to the Right Reverend the Lord Bishop of Worcester's Answer to His Letter, Concerning Some Passages Relating to Mr. Locke's Essay of Humane Understanding: In a Late Discourse of His Lordships, In Vindication of the Trinity* (London: Printed by H. Clark for A. and J. Churchill, and E. Castle, 1697); John Locke, *Mr. Locke's Reply to the Right Reverend the Lord Bishop of Worcester's Answer to His Second Letter* (Printed by H. C. for A. and J. Churchill and E. Castle, 1699); John Locke, *The Reasonableness of Christianity, as Delivered in the Scriptures*, 2nd ed. (London: Printed for Awnsham and John Churchil, 1696); John Locke, *A Vindication of the Reasonableness of Christianity, etc. From Mr. Edwards's Reflections* (London: Printed for Awnsham and John Churchil, 1695); John Locke, *A Second Vindication of the Reasonableness of Christianity, etc.* (London: Printed for A. and J. Churchil, 1697). John Toland's *CNM* and defenses of it: John Toland, *Christianity Not Mysterious: or, A Treatise Shewing, That There Is Nothing in the Gospel Contrary to Reason, Nor Above It: and That No Christian Doctrine Can Be Properly Call'd a Mystery*, 2nd ed. (London: Printed for Sam Buckley, 1696); John Toland, *A Defence of Mr. Toland in a Letter to Himself* (London: Printed for E. Whitlock, 1697); John Toland, *An Apology for Mr. Toland, In a Letter from Himself to a Member of the House of Commons in Ireland; Written the Day before His Books Was Resolv'd to Be Burnt by the Committee of Religion. To Which Is Prefix'd a Narrative Containing the Occasion of the Said Letter* (London: 1697); John Toland, *Vindicius Liberius: or M. Toland's Defence of Himself, against the Late Lower House of Convocation and Others* (London: Printed for Bernard Lintott, 1702).

[2] A large number of scholars compare Locke's and Toland's categories of propositions: thus, James Livingston, *Modern Christian Thought*, 2 vols., 2nd ed. (Minneapolis: Fortress Press, 2006), namely

Although such a narrative is compelling due to its simplicity, it is rife with problems. First, no study to date actually investigates Locke or Toland in the context of the then-ongoing debate over what the label "above reason" should mean and the resultant categorization of propositions. Such writers as Francis Turretin, Robert Boyle, John Norris, and the Cambridge Platonists offer

1:18–21, offers a brief treatment of Locke and Toland indicating that Locke believes in doctrines that are above but not contrary to reason. He describes the primary difference between Locke and Toland as being that the former accepts doctrinal mysteries and the latter rejects them. Claude Welch, *Protestant Christian Thought in the Nineteenth Century*, 2 vols. (New Haven: Yale University Press, 1972), namely 1:35–36, notes that Locke could be grouped with those who believe that Christianity transcends so-called natural religion and this involves some "mystery." He does not describe what he thinks Locke considers mysteries. He also notes that Toland dismisses mystery and above reason things from the gospel, in a manner similar to Matthew Tindal. Robert E. Sullivan, *John Toland and the Deist Controversy: A Study in Adaptations* (Cambridge: Harvard University Press, 1982), 79. Sullivan does not explore what Toland means by reason, but he notes that Locke believes in ideas that are above but not contrary to reason—a not uncommon label for the times—"for retention of the articles of faith." Gerald R. Cragg, *Church and the Age of Reason, 1648–1789*, rev. ed. (1967, reprint: New York: Penguin Groups, Ltd, 1990), 13, assumes that Locke did not explicitly reject the need of revelation in religion, but his denial could be inferred. Frederick Copleston, *History of Philosophy*, 9 vols (Westminster, UK: The Newman Press, 1964), namely 5:69–70. Copleston does not say much about doctrines or propositions above reason other than that they "may" include revealed things that are not fully comprehensible. James O'Higgins, *Anthony Collins: The Man and His Works* (The Hague: Martinus Nijhoff, 1970), 52, seems to indicate that Locke's epistemology advocated assent to some incomprehensible truths. He seems doubtful that Lock actually did himself accept such doctrines. William Uzgalis, "Anthony Collins," in *Stanford Encyclopedia of Philosophy* (first published on August 25, 2002 with substantive revisions February 23, 2009; accessed on March 13, 2009) http://plato.stanford.edu/entries/collins, 13–14, appears to be uncertain what Locke and others intend to convey by "above reason." He is in good company with those like Boyle and Norris who were also uncertain about the meaning of these categories in others. Manfred Kuehn, "Reason and Understanding," in *The Routledge Companion to Eighteenth Century Philosophy*, ed. Aaron Garret, 167–87 (New York: Routledge, 2014), especially 169–170, notes the categories but does not attempt to hazard a guess regarding what they mean.

As to Toland's views, one set of scholars thinks that either Toland rejects the claims of the existence of divine revelation or that *CNM* posits no distinction between the natural religion of morality and Christianity: Daniel C. Fouke, *Philosophy and Theology in a Burlesque Mode: John Toland and "The Way of Paradox"* (Amherst, MA: Humanity Books, 2007), 81–86, 221, 227, 236–37; Cragg, *Church and the Age of Reason*, 78, 160; cf. Gerald R. Cragg, *Reason and Authority in the Eighteenth Century* (Cambridge: Cambridge University Press, 1964) 67, 78, 83; Welch, *Protesant Christian Thought*, 1:36–38; Philip McGuinness, "Christianity Not Mysterious and the Enlightenment," in *John Toland's Christianity Not Mysterious: Text, Associated Works and Critical Essays*, ed. Philip McGuiness, et al. (Dublin: Lilliput Press, Ltd, 1997), 231–42, especially 233–37; Leslie Stephens, *History of English Thought in the Eighteenth Century*, 2 vols., 3rd ed (New York: Peter Smith, 1949), 1:94–118. Stephens, like most, acknowledges that the whole of Toland's philosophy was substantially derived from Locke (1:94). But he does write the following about *CNM*: "The most obvious interpretation of Toland's words would admit of pure Deism" (1:109). Other scholars indicate that *CNM* allows for the acceptation of revelation as long as it offers clarity or confirmation of some known fact or reasoned conclusion but not novelty: James Turner, *Without God, Without Creed: The Origins of Unbelief in America* (Baltimore: John Hopkins University Press, 1985), 51–53; John C. Higgins-Biddle, Introduction to *The Reasonableness of Christianity*, ed. John C. Higgins-Biddle (Oxford: Clarendon Press, 1999), xv–cxv, especially, xxvii–xxxv; John Herman Randall, Jr., *Making of the Modern Mind: A Survey of the Intellectual Background of the Present Age* (1926, reprinted with a forward by Jacques Barzun; New York: Columbia University Press, 1976), 285–89; Diego Lucci, *Scripture and Deism: The Biblical Criticism of the Eighteenth-Century British Deists* (New York: Peter Lang, 2008), 72–73, 81–82; Lucci, *John Locke's Christianity*, 24.

differing treatments of these issues.³ Second, an often-unnoticed assumption undergirds the received narrative: Locke and Toland are using the same or a sufficiently close notion of reason in their propositional taxonomies. No Toland scholar or commentator has done a rigorous examination of his understanding of reason[4] and Locke scholars do not agree on Locke's definition of reason.[5] Some Locke scholars have noticed that Locke is using multiple senses of the term reason in his *Essay*, although without noticing the potential implications this has for the above narrative.[6] Thus, the major problem

---

[3] Francis Turretin, *Institutes of Elentic Theology*, 3 vols, trans. George Musgrave Giger, ed. James T. Dennison, Jr. (Phillipsburg: P & R Publishing); George Rust, *A Discourse of the Use of Reason in Matters of Religions: Shewing, That Christianity Contains Nothing Repugnant to Right Reason; Against Enthusiasts and Deists*, trans. and annot. Hen. Hallywell (London: Printed by Hen. Hills, Jun for Walter Kettilby, 1683); Robert Boyle, *Reflections upon a Theological Distinction. According to Which, 'tis Said, That Some Articles of Faith Are Above Reason, but Not Against Reason. In a Letter to a Friend* (London: Printed by Edw. Jones, for John Taylor, 1690); Jan W. Wojcik, *Robert Boyle and the Limits of Reason* (Cambridge: Cambridge University Press, 1997); John Norris, *An Account of Reason and Faith: In Relation to the Mysteries of Christianity* (London: Printed for S. Manship, 1697); Jonathan S. Marko, "Above Reason Propositions and Contradiction in the Religious Thought of Robert Boyle," *Forum Philosophicum* 19, no. 2 (2014): 227–39; Jonathan S. Marko, "Supplementing Contemporary Treatments of Doctrinal Mysteries with Largely Forgotten Voices from the Past," *Trinity Journal* 39, no. 1 (2018): 23–42; W. J. Mander, *The Philosophy of John Norris* (Oxford: Oxford University Press, 2008); Peter Browne, *The Procedure, Extent, and Limits of Human Understanding*, 2nd ed. with corrections and amendments (London: Printed for William Innys, 1729); Peter Browne, *A Letter in Answer to a Book Entitled Christianity Not Mysterious etc.* (Dublin: 1697). Cf. Paul C. H. Lim, *Mystery Unveiled: The Crisis of the Trinity in Early Modern England* (Oxford: Oxford University Press, 2012).

[4] Sullivan, *John Toland*; Frederick C. Beiser, *The Sovereignty of Reason: The Defense of Rationality in the Early English Enlightenment* (Princeton: Princeton University Press, 1996); Justin Champion, *Republican Learning: John Toland and the Crisis of Culture, 1696–1722* (Manchester: Manchester University Press, 2003); Ian Leask, "Personation and Immanent Undermining: On Toland's Appearing Lockean," *British Journal for the History of Philosophy* 18, no. 2 (2010): 231–56.

[5] There are numerous scholars who have wrestled with Locke's teachings on reason, revelation, faith, and their relationships. One set of these scholars wrestle with the seeming incongruities they find in Locke: Richard Ashcraft, "Faith and Knowledge in Locke's Philosophy," in *John Locke: Problems and Perspectives*, ed. John W. Yolton (Cambridge: Cambridge University Press, 1969), 194–223; Alan P. F. Sell, *John Locke and the Eighteenth-Century Divines* (Cardif: University of Wales Press, 1997), 97; Wioletta Polinska, "Faith and Reason in John Locke," *Philosophy and Theology* 11, no. 2 (1999): 287–309. Ashcraft and Sell are perplexed by noticing that faith regarding divinely revealed propositions can overturn reasonable probability but, in other instances, Locke appears to make faith regarding divine revelation subordinate to reason. Polinska observes the same conundrums and attempts to reconcile them, rightly acknowledging that divine revelation can overturn reasonable probability but not knowledge. Lucci, *John Locke's Christianity*, 24, 87. Lucci acknowledges that Locke accepts some theological truths that are beyond reason but does not comment further. Another set of Locke scholars believes that Locke's position on the relationship between reason and revelation is such that if reason and revelation are ever in conflict, revelation must submit: Paul Helm, "Locke on Faith and Knowledge, *The Philosophical Quarterly* 23, no. 90 (January 1973): 52–66; David C. Snyder, "Faith and Reason in Locke's Essay," *Journal of the History of Ideas* 47, no. 2 (April–June 1986): 197–213; R. S. Woolhouse, *Locke: A Bibliography* (Cambridge: Cambridge University Press, 2007); Michael Ayers, *Locke: Epistemology and Ontology*, 2 vols (New York: Routledge, 1991). Oddly, this is the very similar to the position that Stillingfleet accuses Locke of holding and which the latter denounces.

[6] Greg Forster, *John Locke's Politics of Moral Consensus* (Cambridge: Cambridge University Press, 2005), 141, 181, 188–91; Nicholas Jolley, "Locke on Faith and Reason," in *The Cambridge Companion to Locke's 'Essay Concerning Human Understanding,'* ed. Lex Newman (Cambridge: Cambridge University Press), 436–55; Antonio LoLordo, *Locke's Moral Man* (Oxford: Oxford University Press,

is that until one understands Locke's and Toland's respective uses of the term reason in their categorization of propositions, one cannot know what Locke's acceptance of propositions above reason and John Toland's rejection of propositions above reason actually mean.

In this chapter, I will argue that, for Locke, propositions "above reason" simply refer to what Scripture tells the individual that is beyond the discovery of his or her faculty of reason, although Locke is unclear to what extent this encompasses incomprehensible doctrines. I will further argue that this position is closer than traditionally thought to that of John Toland, who does not deny biblical revelation that surpasses our natural abilities of discovery, but only incomprehensible doctrines of a particular sort derived from revelation. In short, John Locke's orthodoxy is more open to question than is often framed and John Toland's heterodoxy is less drastic than it is consistently presented.

Historical Context: The Debate over Things Above Reason

Introduction

The debate concerning things above reason, or debates, depending on how one delineates the literature, is closely related to the Trinitarian debates that took place in the 1690s through early 1700s. The main reason that they were so intertwined is because something above reason often referred to something that was incomprehensible, necessarily revealed, or perhaps both, as in the case of the doctrine of the Trinity. A few scholars have noted how some in the Trinitarian debates decided that instead of focusing on defending the doctrine of the Trinity, they would concentrate their efforts on the defense of

---

2012), 105. Although Jolley does not try to reconcile many of the logical conundrums in Locke's religious epistemology, he does convincingly argue that Locke is using two different senses of the term reason. LoLordo speaks of a narrow and broad sense of reason somewhat similar to Jolley's (105). Forster, whose work predates Jolley's and LoLordo's, clearly works with the notion that reason and natural reason are different in Locke. There is a related conversation on the scope of the reasoning faculty. Ayers, *Locke: Epistemology and Ontology*, 1:121; Jolley, "Locke on Faith and Reason," 442; Nicolas Wolterstorff, *John Locke and the Ethics of Belief* (Cambridge: Cambridge University Press), 87–89. Ayers thinks that reason is all the natural faculties. Jolley thinks the broader sense of reason is the natural faculties in general but the narrow or discovery sense deals with discovering the probability or certainty of propositions. Wolterstorff thinks that reason is a very narrow faculty and deals with the perception of the logical force of an argument.

assent to the incomprehensible.[7] Also, whereas the debate over things above reason has close ties with its Trinitarian counterpart and was definitely fueled by it, it dealt more directly with the religious epistemological relationships of revelation, faith, reason, and other human faculties.[8]

Locke identifies three categories of propositions that are employed in the debate: "above reason" (sometimes "above but not contrary to reason" in other thinkers), "according to reason," and "contrary to reason." These three labels were not new to the era, nor was disagreement regarding the proper use of the terms. Along with a thinker's categories of propositions, the term reason would have to be defined, often with multiples senses. The capacity or power of faith would inevitably be discussed as these often corresponded with the things above reason. And the relationship of revelation and reason would also be common fare in the defense or explanation of a taxonomy of propositions.

Precursors to the 1690s Debate Concerning Things Above Reason

Cambridge Platonists

Two Cambridge Platonists that took an interest in the categorization of propositions and the concomitant relationships of faith, reason, and revelation were Bishop George Rust and Henry Hallywell, sometimes editor of and commentator on the works of the former. Their works predated those of Locke and John Norris, the latter who is often associated with the Cambridge Platonists and is the central touchpoint for the above reason debate. Furthermore, John Locke appropriated (or at least shared) a number of important sentiments and larger themes found in these Platonists. Locke thinks, like these Cambridge Platonists, that Christianity is eminently reasonable in its parts and the whole.[9] And on a related point, assent is reasonable assent. Reason and faith are not to be understood as opposed. What is more, the Platonists and Locke are in one accord that salvation is closely associated with doing one's epistemic best.[10] They also believe that soteriologically

---

[7] Wojcik, *Robert Boyle*, 74–75; Lim, *Mystery Unveiled*, 208; cf. Marko, "Supplementing Contemporary Treatments," 25–28.
[8] Mander, *John Norris*; cf. Marko, "Supplementing Contemporary Treatments," 25–28.
[9] [Hallywell], *Discourse*, 50.
[10] [Hallywell], *Discourse*, 77–79.

necessary truths must be expressly revealed. One notable difference, however, is the importance placed on the theological conclusions of the primitive and Protestant church by Rust and Hallywell in contrast with Locke's wariness of any notion that might lead us to implicit faith in important matters (Rust and Hallywell will use the term "implicit faith" in a different and positive way as shown below).[11] Hallywell is explicit that the church is required for determining together what is according to right reason,[12] while Locke seems to make this more emphatically an individual affair (although not at the expense of dialoguing with others). Rust and Locke are in agreement, however, that religion is of the highest and gravest concern.[13]

Rust crafted a small work on 1 Peter 3:15 that was written to combat the deists and enthusiasts; Hallywell wrote the preface and greatly enlarged the work with his many annotations. The full title of the work is *A Discourse of the Use of Reason in Matters of Religion: Shewing, That Christianity Contains Nothing Repugnant to Right Reason* (*Discourse*). In other words, its main contention is that nothing in Christianity is contrary to *right* reason. He offers two congruent definitions of right reason, asserting in the first, "By Right Reason therefore I understand that innate Faculty of the Soul of Man, by which it discerns the Reasons and Mutual Affections of things, and argues, and concludes one thing from another, And now I say that Christian Religion is not contrary to Reason thus understood."[14] Then, later, he simply says by "right reason" he means "incorrupted Reason, freed from all evil Affections and inlighted by the Spirit of God."[15] He believes and argues that Christianity is not opposed to that understanding of reason. Hallywell adds, "Right Reason is a Participation of the Divine Understanding."[16] Christianity will be contrary to corrupt reason, however (and therefore we will struggle with seeing the rightness in certain revealed things).[17] He argues, as will be echoed later by Locke, that "anything contrary to the dictates of right reason" has no credibility. (Later, he writes, "the Mind cannot assent to any thing where Right Reason, or at least some shadow of it does not give a preceding light;

---

[11] [Hallywell], *Discourse*, preface. One could see the same sentiment implicitly in Rust that is explicit in Hallywell, but perhaps not as strong: cf. Rust, *Discourse*, 41.
[12] [Hallywell], *Discourse*, preface.
[13] Rust, *Discourse*, 39.
[14] Rust, *Discourse*, 25.
[15] Rust, *Discourse*, 29, cf. 33–37. His discussion of the Holy Spirit and His assistance is illuminating, yielding a better understanding of his soteriology, pneumatology, and epistemology. On pp. 42–43 he discusses even more about our corruption that came from the fall.
[16] [Hallywell], *Discourse*, 68–69; cf. Rust, *Discourse*, 18.
[17] Rust, *Discourse*, 24.

And then, That Christian Religion requiring Faith, cannot force or compel assent against the Dictates of Right Reason."[18]) He asserts that we cannot yield assent to anything without the application of reason. Thus, we must be careful of opposing faith and reason, as we cannot assent to that which opposes our reason.[19] In fact, in one place he writes: "And it is a thing abhorrent from all Reason, that that which is most Natural, and the sole Propriety of Man [that is, religion], should yet be contradictory to his own faculties."[20]

In discussing reasonable assent, Rust treats the above reason category. He writes, "whatever is propounded to us as matter of belief ought not to be taken so much as above Reason, unless these words be taken in this Acception, namely, That a thing is so high and remote from common sense, that bare Intellect could not light upon it."[21] He appears to be saying two important things. First, he does not exactly approve of the use of above reason as a category. He acknowledges that, at least with the help of others, even the most complex doctrines, like the hypostatic union of Christ, is highly reasonable in the context of the doctrinal narrative of the Christian religion. Maybe the doctrine is not easy to fathom when focused upon in an isolated manner but its assertion makes so much sense according to our needs.[22] Hallywell adds in his annotations his caution in describing things that we can discuss and think about as being above reason because, technically speaking, something above reason could not be discussed: "Now that which is wholly and absolutely above Reason is likewise unintelligible" and, therefore, could not be argued or debated or even considered.[23] He states, "And that which dazles our Eyes with such an amazing lustre in Christianity, that is the Doctrine of the Trinity, was not thought either unintelligible or irrational by the wisest and most learned Pagans, though such is the Profoundness of the Mystery, that Human Understanding could never have fall'n upon any such Thing without a Divine Revelation."[24] Second, Rust is giving a limit to what he will concede to call above reason. It is possible that he is allowing anything that is necessarily revealed as being above reason because his stated exception

---

[18] Rust, *Discourse*, 30.
[19] Rust, *Discourse*, 31, 32.
[20] Rust, *Discourse*, 38.
[21] Rust, *Discourse*, 26.
[22] Rust, *Discourse*, 42. This is not unlike C. S. Lewis's reasoning laid out in Ch. 14 of *Miracles*. There he acknowledges that some things might be so abstruse when considered alone but that they make sense of so many other issues. Clive Staples Lewis, *Miracles: A Preliminary Study* (San Francisco: Harper Collins, 1996).
[23] Rust [Hallywell], *Discourse*, 49.
[24] Rust [Hallywell], *Discourse*, 50.

standing alone could be read that way. But the very next line he notes "*some* Articles of the Faith which may be said to be above Reason" [emphasis mine] but not all. And then he makes a distinction between those things for which there is an express revelation and require explicit belief and those things "not clearly revealed" that require only an implicit faith:

> it exceeds the strength of Reason to give an Exact Account of the manner of our Resurrection & Glorification, or to make a perfect Description of the Joys and Pleasures of the Future life, or to shew how the three *Hypostasess* are one God, or the Divine and Humane Nature one Christ: But of these things as there is no express Revelation, so neither is there an explicit Faith required[25]

So, while the Bible expressly declares a resurrection, we need not know how that will be effected, but simply believe it is so—God knows. (There is a further implicit sub-dividing of incomprehensible things here that will be echoed somewhat by Robert Boyle in his taxonomy of propositions and doctrines: singular, not fully conceivable things; the manner how things are done; and two or more true propositions that are not reconcilable.[26]) In short, something might be denominated as being above reason in a concessionary fashion if it is difficult or impossible to imagine and is not expressly stated in Scripture: "But there is nothing to which an Explicit Faith is required, which so far exceeds Reason, as that it is not able to form any Conception of it."[27] But more is to be said on the distinction between explicit and implicit belief and their respective objects.

Later in the work, Rust tells his readers how they ought to proceed when confronted by something that might be contrary to reason or, differently, above reason:

> Therefore if any thing propounded under the Plausible Name of Divine Revelation shall seem to contradict Reason, I ought to suspect that I do not fully comprehend the meaning of it, and therefore must insist upon a further search, and resolve that God intended that to be believed, which should be most consonant to the Principles of Nature. Nevertheless I would not have Humane Understanding arrogate too much to it self, nor rashly

---

[25] Rust, *Discourse*, 26.
[26] Rust, *Discourse*, 26. It is unfortunate that genre, among other details, are not discussed here.
[27] Rust, *Discourse*, 26.

attempt to condemn presently that which exceeds its Capacity. For if the chiefest Part of those things which are delivered and consigned by Divine Testimony, be worthy of God, and Consonant to our Faculties, as to other things we ought to yield an implicit Faith to Divine Revelations, though they seem otherwise to clash with Reason, yet to give our Assent to them, at least according to the sense of the Spirit of God, although what that is, we cannot yet so fully understand.[28]

So, Scripture is to be trusted, but our interpretations need not be. If something seems to be contrary to reason, we ought to first check our interpretations. If we have no other reasonable and biblical conclusion, then we must admit that we do not have the ability to fully understand that which God has truly revealed and ought to accept it. Moreover, clearly not all things delivered in Scripture clash with reason, thus lending a second instance of distinguishing between reasonable revealed things and revealed things above reason.

Rust also offers three scenarios where some alleged revelation is being considered as such. Regarding the objects of explicit faith, one must have a clear conception of the things proposed and they are conformable to our God-given faculties.[29] "For whatever is proposed as a matter of Explicit Belief, there must in the first place be a Conception formed of it; but now whatever we can frame a Conception of, there Reason either discovers the Harmony of the Terms of which it consists, and its Agreement with some common Notion, and so pronounces the Thing to be true." Otherwise, if the terms are contrary and repugnant or opposed to some innate principle, we know the thing to be false. But if the terms are partly in agreement, we allow that the thing might be possible or probable, which if accompanied by a miracle will be accepted as true. He uses the example of the story of Christ being subject to doubt from the standpoint of the people in his day as an example of this third category; but the description seems to fit for things that are frequently denominated above reason that can be received only by implicit faith. Perhaps he meant that Christ and the Old Testament accounts of the coming Messiah appeared to clash at places in their minds—but he does not expressly say that.[30] Moreover, Hallywell's definition of implicit faith—"to believe that the sense of all those Things that are delivered and consigned by

---

[28] Rust, *Discourse*, 41.
[29] Rust, *Discourse*, 27, 28.
[30] Rust, *Discourse*, 29–30.

Divine Testimony, though they transcend my Capacity, whatever it is which was intended by God"—agrees with Rust's. And similar to others of the era, Hallywell asserts that there is no necessity to go beyond implicit faith in obscurely revealed doctrines for salvation. In other words, assent to particular explanations or positions regarding obscurely revealed doctrines is not salvific. [31]

Hallywell expands a bit on the traditional incomprehensible doctrines of Christianity. Again, he notes that it is not as if we do not have any idea of those doctrines. We just do not have full, clear, and distinct ideas of them. He thinks that the Trinity and other incomprehensible doctrines, "being revealed, they bear a pleasing and agreeable Harmony with our Reasons, and do intimately correspond with something in our own Minds."[32] While this statement might be a bit too far for Locke, the notion that Christianity is reasonable and harmonious undergirds his theology.

In sum, the category of things above reason is significantly concessionary. On a related point, Rust is clear in the relative nature of his above reason category. For him, at least, some things that strike one as being above reason early on, will not be so, or will become less so, as one starts to see the coherent whole of the Christian religion and how things fit. Besides, objectively he would say that all aspects of Christianity are really according to reason, although subjectively and focusing on particular doctrines that is often not the case. Unfortunately, we are not all operating with uncorrupted reasoning faculties. He would acknowledge that even the seemingly troubling things are accepted due to their reasonably assessed divine provenance. All things considered, Rust has many reasons to reject the opposition of faith and reason. Finally, the emphasis or focus of the discussion on isolated ideas or doctrines that we will see in later thinkers is not shared by Rust, who viewed Christianity as generally reasonable.

Francis Turretin's Protestant Scholasticism

There are a number of reasons to treat Turretin here. He is perhaps the paradigmatic example of a Protestant scholastic who employs the categorization of propositions in a robust treatment of the relationships of reason, revelation, and faith. He is a fine example of Protestant orthodoxy just prior to the publication of Locke's writings. He is also well apprised of the debates in the

---

[31] [Hallywell], *Discourse*, 70.
[32] [Hallywell], *Discourse*, 50.

era and his grasp of them is clear in his writings. And Locke was familiar with his writings. What is more, juxtaposition with Rust's *Discourse* and Locke's *Essay* is highly illuminating. For instance, he, like Rust (and as I will argue, Locke), believes that reason and faith, when properly understood, are not to be opposed. And he, like Rust and Locke, believes Christianity is, in one or more senses, reasonable.[33] He and Rust (and Hallywell) have higher deference to the decisions of the church than do Locke and others of the era. Turretin disagrees with those, like Hallywell (and Rust) and Locke, who affirm that all obligatory doctrines are expressly stated in Scripture: he asserts that "The darkness of the human intellect does not hinder sound reason from judging the truth of connections and so contradictions"[34] and that crucial doctrines of the faith are plainly *proved*.[35] He also argues that while some things are plain and evident to all, something that is not so plain might still be perspicuous: "For often many things are obscure to many persons (which could and would be very plain to them) either because they did not give proper attention or because they were blinded by prejudice."[36]

Turretin, as is common in his day, has numerous senses of the term "reason." Generally speaking, however, "Human reason is taken subjectively for that faculty of the rational soul by which man understands and judges between intelligible things presented to him (natural and supernatural, divine and human); or objectively for the natural light both externally presented and internally impressed upon the mind by which reason is disposed to the forming of certain conceptions and the eliciting of conclusions concerning God and divine things."[37] The most recurrent and specific distinctions beyond the above bifurcation are: right reason (the abstract notion), fallen and unregenerate reason, and the latter's significantly rehabilitated (regenerated) and (ideally) always improving counterpart. Prior to believing and being made a new creation, one has the second or fallen reason; after truly believing one has the third or rehabilitated and assisted reason; and due to its new orientation, the person ought to always aspire to the first. The doctrines of the Christian faith and revelation is contrary only to corrupted reasoning.[38]

---

[33] Turretin, *Institutes of Elenctic Theology*, I.ix.3, 5.
[34] Turretin, *Institutes of Elenctic Theology*, I.x.8; cf. [Hallywell], *Discourse*, 70. Locke and the Cambridge Platonists would have different explanations of the statement that all obligatory doctrines are explicitly stated in Scripture.
[35] Cf. Turretin, *Institutes of Elenctic Theology*, I.xii.
[36] Turretin, *Institutes of Elenctic Theology*, I.xii.34.
[37] Turretin, *Institutes of Elenctic Theology*, I.viii.1.
[38] Turretin, *Institutes of Elenctic Theology*, I.viii.18

While natural truths and revealed truths should not disagree, they may appear to do so because "natural truth itself is often not what human reason dictates." Human reasoning faculties are fallen and apt not to see the truth in some true, natural propositions or to make wrong conclusions in that sphere and thus liable to see a conflict between what is taken to be a natural truth and a revealed truth.[39]

In the First Topic of his *Institutes*, Turretin asserts that reason is not the rule or principle of theology but it is nonetheless an instrument.[40] For instance, while the reasoning faculties enlightened or illuminated by the Holy Spirit cannot overturn the propositions delivered to us in divine revelation, "it does not follow from this that it cannot judge of the contradiction of the expositions, opinions and interpretations which men give of these mysteries."[41] He asserts, "Reason can judge not only of a direct and formal contradiction (containing in the same terms both an express affirmation and negation), but also of an indirect and implied (deduced by necessary consequence)."[42] Accordingly, our assent to express and inferred doctrines is never to be understood as having nothing to do with reason or being unreasonable.

Turretin also discusses the interrelationships of three ways of knowing: faith, reason, and the senses. Thus, he asserts that there are three kinds of things to be known: things known by faith, those known by the senses, and things known by the intellect. Each faculty—sense, reason, and faith—is concerned with its own objects but the faculties ought not be opposed. As already intimated, even faith may not oppose a properly functioning faculty operating wholly in its own sphere. But just as faith sometimes relies on reason for judgment of contradictions, for instance, sometimes faith relies on the senses. Some mysteries like the doctrine of the Trinity and the incarnation are "entirely spiritual and placed beyond our

---

[39] Turretin, *Institutes of Elenctic Theology*, I.viii.21.
[40] Cf. Turretin, *Institutes of Elenctic Theology*, I.viii.
[41] Turretin, *Institutes of Elenctic Theology*, I.x.8.
[42] Turretin, *Institutes of Elenctic Theology*, I.x.9; cf. III.xxi.10, 11. In the latter section he writes: "Hence we gather what must be judged concerning contradictories; for that is said to be contradictory which is logically impossible, i.e., which has a repugnancy and includes contradictory predicates (for example, a corporeal God, an irrational man). Now a repugnance may be immediate and explicit when the terms are explicitly contradictory (for example, a deed undone, a man not man). Or it may be mediate and implicit when the repugnant terms only virtually and implicitly include a contradiction (for example, when inseparable properties are denied or contrary predicates are affirmed of the subject—as God corporeal and mortal, man not risible, the body not extended, accident not inherent). For such things involve contradictory predicates which strike against the first principle of indubitable truth (i.e., 'it is impossible for the same thing to be and not to be at the same time')."

comprehension" but others are "placed in sensible and corporeal things." The spiritual aspect is still an object of faith, but the corporeal aspect is an object of the senses. So, for instance, while the Roman Catholics may claim that the body and blood of Christ has substantially taken the place of the bread and the wine in the Eucharist, accepting that has many detrimental implications and insurmountable opposition: Christ has the disciples use the senses to prove He had risen and if we could not trust our senses then how could we trust what we read and hear in Scripture, just to name a few points of opposition.[43] Moreover, for the faith, intellect, and senses he notes three corresponding categories of doctrines or propositions: above reason, according to reason, and below reason. At one place he writes of three of his categories and conveys their relationships: "nor can one truth be destroyed by another (although one may transcend and surpass the other) because whatever the one may be—whether below, according to or above reason, and apprehended by the senses, the intellect or faith—it has come from no other source than God, the parent of truth."[44]

In sum, then, Turretin sees three ways of knowing with corresponding categorizations of propositions. There are the spheres of the senses, the intellect, and faith and the corresponding categorizations of below, according to, and above reason. But, partly because we are not operating with right reason, the boundaries are necessarily blurred in our subjective apprehension. Because we aspire to right reason and are operating with a corrupted reason, faith has the ability to correct reason. And reason can infer consequences of theological truths and judge contradictions.[45] And we all know that due to memory, bias, interpretations, etc. we occasionally realize that we did not sense exactly what we thought we sensed.

Although Turretin is more interested in explaining the relationship of faith, revelation, and reason than in outlining the concomitant categories of propositions and doctrines, he does note the issue. In his division of natural theology and supernatural theology, the distinction between according to reason and above reason is clearly stated, and the problem of knowing is complicated by the corruption of human beings.[46] While some revealed truths will frequently contradict and correct the corrupted reason and even the regenerated reason, they will surpass and supplement right reason:[47]

---

[43] Turretin, *Institutes of Elenctic Theology*, I.xi.
[44] Turretin, *Institutes of Elenctic Theology*, I.xiii.3.
[45] Turretin, *Institutes of Elenctic Theology*, I.viii.12.
[46] Turretin, *Institutes of Elenctic Theology*, I.ii.7.
[47] Cf. Turretin, *Institutes of Elenctic Theology*, I.i.9; I.ii.6–7; I.ix.4.

"Although light is not contrary to light, and natural and revealed truths are not at variance with each other, yet natural truth itself is often not what human reason dictates, which is often mistaken by an abuse of natural and revealed light." Thus a revealed thing can oppose "ratiocination and human conceptions, although it may agree with natural truth which reason often does not see or apprehend."[48] On a related note, he writes, "It is not repugnant that one and the same thing in a different relation should both be known by the light of nature and believed by the light of faith; as what is gathered from one only obscurely, may be held more certainly from the other."[49] In sum, the according to reason categorization is connected with what we might be *expected* to discover on our own that is true and the above reason categorization is what is true but not discoverable by right reason.

Having juxtaposed propositions from theology and philosophy, Turretin writes, "Reason is taken either materially for the kind of doctrine derived from the light of reason, or formally for the manner of delivering it which is commonly called the mode of instruction."[50] He then goes on to make the following distinction between contrary and above reason things: "For a thing to be contrary to reason is different from its being above and beyond it; to be overthrown by reason and to be unknown to it." Something that is contrary to reason is false; something above reason is not discoverable by reason. Turretin makes a further qualification: "The mysteries of faith are indeed contrary to corrupt reason and are assailed by it, but they are only above and beyond right reason and are not taught by it."[51] In other words, things above reason are above right reason and not contrary to it, but they are frequently contrary to the conclusions of corrupt reason. Further, "Although things of faith agree with reason and doctrine can be at variance with sound enlightened reason, it does not follow that they agree with corrupted and blind reason, or that even sound reason is its principle."[52] Among other things that might be inferred, it seems he is asserting that above reason things, although outside the pale of what we could attain by right reason, still might appear to be at odds or potentially so with our regenerated reasoning faculties but it will make sense or fit into the overall orthodox theology scheme. He makes similar distinctions and assertions later in his work. "Reason as corrupt and

---

[48] Turretin, *Institutes of Elenctic Theology*, I.viii.21.
[49] Turretin, *Institutes of Elenctic Theology*, I.iii.10.
[50] Turretin, *Institutes of Elenctic Theology*, I.viii.17.
[51] Turretin, *Institutes of Elenctic Theology*, I.viii.18.
[52] Turretin, *Institutes of Elenctic Theology*, I.viii.19.

in the concrete may be at variance with theology, but not reason as sound and in the abstract (which possibly may be ignorant of mysteries and may not teach them, but must not therefore be considered as denying them)."[53] On a related note, he asserts that due in part to the relationships of revelation and reason, "Reason is perfected by faith and faith supposes reason."[54] They work together to make a more cohesive and coherent understanding of God and His world.[55]

A bit more might be said about things above reason. There are truths and knowledge not discoverable by reason in any of its senses:

> For we readily grant that there are things which far surpass the comprehension not only of men, but even of angels the disclosure of which was a work of supernatural revelation. We also grant that reason is not only incapable of discovering them without a revelation; not only weak in comprehending after being revealed; but also slippery and fallible (readily pursuing falsehood for truth and truth for falsehood), and never believing the word of God and its mysteries unless enlightened by the grace of the Spirit[56]

Thus, Turretin makes distinctions between what angels and humans would discover and what the unregenerate and regenerate are liable to believe. And despite the fact that he does not clearly delineate levels of abstruseness among the things above reason, he seems to consider some revealed truths as being more clearly justified in being denominated above reason than others. For instance, he seems to have more particular doctrines in mind than just simply revealed ones when he labors over making the distinction between "incomprehensible" and "incompossible" things: "An incomprehensible thing (which cannot be grasped) is different from an incompossible (which cannot be conceived)." The examples that he uses as incomprehensible mysteries are the Trinity, the incarnation, and predestination doctrines that are considered incomprehensible in Christianity regardless of the time and tradition: we have only "an obscure and imperfect knowledge" of these truths.[57] These "mysteries are entirely spiritual and placed far beyond our comprehension; such as the mysteries of the Trinity, of the incarnation, etc. But others

---

[53] Turretin, *Institutes of Elenctic Theology*, I.ix.10.
[54] Turretin, *Institutes of Elenctic Theology*, I.ix.5.
[55] Turretin, *Institutes of Elenctic Theology*, I.xiii.3.
[56] Turretin, *Institutes of Elenctic Theology*, I.ix.4; cf. I.ii.2-3; I.viii.3-4; I.viii.17-19; III.xxi.14.
[57] Turretin, *Institutes of Elenctic Theology*, I.ix.9.

are placed in sensible and corporeal things ... such as the miracles of Christ, the types and figures of the Old Testament," etc. The former are the proper objects of the faith. In the other areas, such as the Eucharist, the senses must judge as well.[58] By contrast, claims of the ubiquity of Christ's human nature—not held by Turretin—yield a contradiction, and so are neither reasonable nor above reason.

Turretin gives significant attention to things contrary to or overturned by reason. Things contrary to reason always involve a contradiction or are simply false. There are things contrary to the universal principles of reason and, therefore, also contrary to revelation,[59] such as "inconceivable things" like ubiquity and transubstantiation.[60] While he does not offer a full-blown treatment of "things contrary to reason" in his First Topic, Turretin does have much to say about "things contrary to reason," "repugnant to reason," or "impossible with reason" in his Third Topic, where he explains possibility and impossibility.[61] Turretin points out that some have claimed that absolute power means "that God can do whatever can be imagined by us whether good or evil, contradictory or not: for instance, that he could lie and sin; that he could do what would be repugnant to the nature of things."[62] By contrast, Turretin asserts that the possible is "whatever is not repugnant to be done" and that "the impossible falls not under the omnipotence of God, not from a defect in his power, but from a defect in the possibility of the thing because it involves in its conception contradictory predicates."[63] Muller notes that for Turretin "the limit of the divine power is not merely logical" and thus "there are things that are logically possible, as not involving a [explicit] contradiction, that God also cannot do because he is just and good."[64] It is not a defect in God for Him to be unable to sin or produce absurdities and the like, all of which entail contradictions.[65] Such things are impossible "by nature."[66]

---

[58] Turretin, *Institutes of Elenctic Theology*, I.xi.4–5.
[59] Turretin, *Institutes of Elenctic Theology*, I.x.15–16.
[60] Turretin, *Institutes of Elenctic Theology*, I.ix.9; cf. I.x.15–16.
[61] Turretin, *Institutes of Elenctic Theology*, III.xxi.
[62] Turretin, *Institutes of Elenctic Theology*, III.xxi.5.
[63] Turretin, *Institutes of Elenctic Theology*, III.xxi.6.
[64] Richard A. Muller, *Divine Will and Human Choice: Freedom, Contingency, and Necessity in Early Reformed Thought* (Grand Rapids: Baker Academic, 2017), 272. There Muller also notes the following: "there are two ways in which something is understood to be possible: first, the possible is something that 'can be done' or is 'not repugnant' *a parte rei*—which is to say, something that can be done without a contradiction; and second, something that God can do or is 'not repugnant' *a parte Dei*, not a violation of God's 'most perfect nature.'" Cf. Turretin, *Institutes of Elenctic Theology*, III.xxi.3, 10.
[65] Turretin, *Institutes of Elenctic Theology*, III.xxi.6.
[66] Turretin, *Institutes of Elenctic Theology*, III.xxi.8.

If God could do contradictory things then nothing would be impossible.[67] In addition to things that are either explicitly or implicitly contradictory, Turretin adds yet another categorization of impossibilities: (1) supernaturally impossible, (2) naturally impossible, and (3) morally impossible. The first refers to that which God cannot even do like the creation of a sensitive stone or irrational man. The second, "The naturally impossible is what cannot be done by the powers of nature and second causes, but yet can be done by supernatural power (as the creation of a world, the conception of a virgin, etc.)." The third refers to "what cannot be done [by God] according to the laws of holiness."[68]

Turretin also notes how various theological adversaries violate his categorization of doctrines. He accuses the Socinians of using reason as their rule of faith and not simply an instrument. This is why they reject doctrines like the Trinity, incarnation, and satisfaction as traditionally understood.[69] While not rejecting the divinity of revelation per se, they will not accept any teachings that are above reason in the incomprehensible sense of the term. He accuses Lutherans and Roman Catholics of going too far in the opposite direction, "attributing little or nothing to it [reason]." He asserts, "These hold that the testimony of reason is not to be heard when it judges of certain mysteries of the faith." Some Lutheran doctrines said to be above right reason are actually contrary to it.[70]

The Formal Above Reason Debate

Robert Boyle's *Reflections upon a Theological Distinction*

Robert Boyle is the primary thinker involved in the debate concerning things above reason in the 1690s of whose thoughts on incomprehensible doctrines Locke was most likely aware prior to the publication of the first edition of the *Essay*. And he has more writings on the topic than the others directly involved in the debate.

Boyle published *Reflections Upon a Theological Distinction. According to Which 'tis Said That Some Articles of Faith Are Above Reason but Not against*

---

[67] Turretin, *Institutes of Elenctic Theology*, III.xxi.12.
[68] Turretin, *Institutes of Elenctic Theology*, III.xxi.7. One could sub-divide the second category by being and state—angels, Christ, pre-fall humans, post-fall humans, pilgrims, glorified saints.
[69] Turretin, *Institutes of Elenctic Theology*, I.viii.2–3; cf. I.ix.1.
[70] Turretin, *Institutes of Elenctic Theology*, I.viii.24–I.ix.1 [quotations, I.ix.1]; cf. I.viii.2.

Reason (*RTD*) in 1690 and appended it to the first part of *The Christian Virtuoso* in lieu of his completion of the second part. This is the final writing on his categorization of propositions and defense of revealed and incomprehensible things. This is also the writing with which John Norris directly interacts (and critiques). Boyle's primary intent in the short work is to define and argue for the legitimacy of the use of the label of "above but not against reason." He thinks that how the term has been used and the recent lackluster defenses of it by the learned, have made the term open to abuse and to become nearly a byword for ridiculousness. He asserts, that "there are *divers* that employ this Distinction, *few* that have attempted to explain it, (and that I fear, not sufficiently) and *none* that has taken care to justifie it."[71]

His definition of things above reason and contrary to reason is worth unpacking:

> By such things then in Theology, as may be said to be *above Reason*, I conceive such Notions and Propositions, as mere Reason, that is, Reason unassisted by supernatural Revelation, would never have discover'd to us: Whether those things be to our finite Capacities, clearly incomprehensible or not. And by things *contrary to Reason*, I understand such Conceptions and Propositions, as are not only undiscoverable by mere Reason, but also, when we understand them, do evidently and truly appear to be repugnant to some Principle, or to some Conclusion, of Right Reason.[72]

There is right reason and mere reason or "Reason unassisted by supernatural Revelation" and, by implication, reason in a broader scope: that is reason assisted by supernatural revelation (If we were to only use the latter, inferable sense—reason in the broader scope—then his categorization of propositions could arguably be according to reason things and contrary to reason things). He does not discuss the fallen nature of reason nor the Holy Spirit's influence and work upon the faculty as Turretin and Rust do. He could therefore by mere reason mean fallen reason or one's individual reason. But his contrary to reason category is technically contrary to right reason, so it follows that the reason in his other categories have right reason in mind as well, and thus mere reason and right reason, are, for our purposes at least, identical. The

---

[71] Boyle, *RTD*, 1–2.
[72] Boyle, *RTD*, 3.

according to reason category would simply involve anything that agrees with right reason and the above reason category, as will be discussed, is that which our faculties at their best would not discover or that which is necessarily revealed by God.

His above reason category is a generalized one and is unpacked later in *RTD*. Things above reason are first and foremost above reason in the sense that our unassisted reason would not have arrived at or discovered these notions or propositions. A little later he also explicitly notes that there are "Two kinds" of things above reason: "For it seems to me, that there are some Things, that Reason by its own Light cannot *Discover*; and others, that, when propos'd, it cannot *Comprehend*." In other words, there are things that we cannot discover but are comprehensible and things that we cannot discover that are incomprehensible. For the first kind he gives the following examples: six-day creation, the virgin birth, the hypostatic union, and the resurrection. These are truths that "depend upon the Free Will and Ordination of God" [and thus not discoverable from the principles imbedded in the created order].[73] In his discussion of incomprehensible things above reason he delineates subcategories, that comport with Rust's list of incomprehensible things given above: (1) things "not clearly *conceivable* by our Understanding, such as the Infiniteness and Perfections of the Divine Nature;" (2) things that are "*inexplicable* by us, such as the Manner, how God can create a rational Soul; or how, this being an immaterial Substance, it can act upon a Human Body, and be acted on by it"; and (3) things that are "*asysmmetrical*, or unsociable; that is, such as we see not how to reconcile with other Things, which also manifestly are, or are by us acknowledged to be, true." He offers human metaphysical liberty and God's unlimited foreknowledge as an example of two such things that are acknowledged to be true but cannot be reconciled.[74]

Boyle adds several clarifications concerning things above reason. For one, there are singular things in the natural world that are difficult to conceive,

---

[73] Boyle, *RTD*, 5–6.

[74] Boyle, *RTD*, 8–9. This is arguably not an above reason conundrum. One might argue that while this might be functionally above reason for some, it is not technically above right reason. The doctrine of the Holy Trinity would be a much better example. According to his definition of asymmetrical or unsociable things, it appears that the thing that is labeled as such is something revealed that is not seemingly reconcilable with an already established truth (naturally discoverable or no, he does not say). But then he gives two notions that seem to go hand-in-hand: free will and divine prescience. Does Boyle think that one is revealed and unsociable with the other that is better and/or earlier established, or does he think of both *together* as unsociable? He does not say. It matters little in the end, however. That is, whatever the case one still is left with the inability to perceptually reconcile multiple propositions that are each sufficiently clear from an insular or individualized consideration.

like place, time, and motion.[75] Even so, there are truths revealed in Scripture that are undiscoverable, yet are compelling to the rational mind "because they do not only Agree with the doubtful or imperfect Notions we already had of things, but Improve them, if not Compleat them." In fact, they are so helpful that it is unreasonable to call them contrary to or against reason in any meaningful sense. And in the instances when certain revealed things seem to be unreasonable at first blush, reason is often helped by such truths, a tacit admittance that reason has broader and narrower senses.[76] Thus, like Turretin and the Cambridge Platonists, Boyle views Christianity as a fairly reasonable religion. Like them, he also recognizes the species-relative nature of above reason: "For to be *above our Reason*, is not an Absolute thing, but a Respective one, importing a Relation to the Measure of Knowledge, that belongs to the Human Understanding, such as 'tis said to transcend: And therefore it may not be *above Reason*, in reference to a more enlightned [sic] Intellect" such as an angel.[77]

His definition of contrary to reason is, again, as follows: "And by things *contrary to Reason*, I understand such Conceptions and Propositions, as are not only undiscoverable by mere Reason, but also, when we understand them, do evidently and truly appear to be repugnant to some Principle, or some Conclusion, of Right Reason." To make this clearer he employs an analogy that will be repeated by others after him: the diver who searches for oysters and pearls.[78] If a diver told you that there were oysters or muscles beyond your sight, there would be nothing incredible about that. Analogously, that reportage is above reason. But if the diver were to tell one that the oysters' pearls were bigger than the shell that enclosed them or upon showing one these whitish round treasures that they were actually cubical and black, these would be analogous to reportages contrary to reason: one is simply compossible, and the latter is simply false. Right reason would not, if it were truly reasoning rightly, make these assertions. All of that is easy enough, but what of his strange wording of "do evidently and truly appear to be repugnant"? At the very least he is saying that things contrary to reason are those that are given via a testimony—human reportage or an allegedly divine revelation—and are or appear to offend some logical principle or some sure

---

[75] Boyle, *RTD*, 10; cf. 11–13.
[76] Boyle, *RTD*, 19.
[77] Boyle, *RTD*, 24. Rust is careful to mention right reason having associations with human faculties. My guess is that he would rightly acknowledge a difference in capacities between angels and humans.
[78] Boyle, *RTD*, 3–5.

conclusion derived from right reason. Also, perhaps the tentativeness points to his experience with the difficulty of ruling certain assertions out definitively and a tentativeness to dogmatism in theology and natural philosophy and/or simply an acknowledgment that we ought to simply strive to do our epistemic best. He could have been trying to convey that the distinction between above reason and contrary to reason is that the former is revealed (or at least it can be plausibly argued from revelation) and the latter is not, and it is or appears to be in some way antithetical to our overall reasonable view of God and the world. Norris will pounce upon this definition and show its difficulties.

John Norris's Response to Boyle
The publication of John Toland's *Christianity Not Mysterious* was the circumstance that eventually led to the publication of John Norris's *An Account of Reason and Faith*. He maintains that it is not worthwhile to make a direct response to Toland. Instead, Norris thinks that after reading his own book, readers could easily overturn Toland's positions themselves.[79] In the book's third chapter, "The Distinction of Things Contrary to Reason, and Above Reason, Consider'd," he takes aim primarily at Boyle's taxonomy as delivered in *RTD*, addressed above. He agrees with Boyle that "none have taken care to justifie" the distinction above but not against reason. He claims that Boyle is the only one who has. While appreciative, he does think Boyle could have treated the question of the taxonomy of propositions with more depth and clarity. What is more, despite the discussions of things above reason and contrary to reason in the era, Norris considers the taxonomy of propositions an almost "*Virgin* Subject."[80]

Norris's first issue with Boyle's work is the latter's assertion that undiscoverability, first and foremost, makes something above reason. Norris claims that no divines use above reason in that sense. They always intend the incomprehensible sense with the term in defending the Christian mysteries against the attacks of the Socinians, who call such things contrary to reason. And even the Socinians own that there are things in Scripture that are otherwise above reason (or above reason in the undiscoverable sense). That is, when they reject things "above reason" as being contrary to reason they are rejecting the incomprehensible things. In other words, discoverability or the

---

[79] Norris, *An Account*, 1–7.
[80] Norris, *An Account*, 101–2.

necessity of being revealed is not what is at issue in the era: incomprehensibility is. What is more, for Norris, being otherwise undiscoverable unless revealed is too small a point to call something a mystery.[81]

There is more that can be said about the problematic nature of Boyle's treatment of the categories of propositions. Norris pounces upon Boyle's indefinite and awkward definition of contrary to reason, first citing Boyle's definition in brackets:

> [By such things then in Theology, as may be said to be *above Reason*, I conceive such Notions and Propositions, as mere Reason, that is, Reason unassisted by supernatural Revelation, would never have discover'd to us: Whether those things be to our finite Capacities, clearly comprehensible or not. And by *contrary to Reason*, I understand such Conceptions and Propositions, as are not only undiscoverable by mere Reason, but also, when we understand them, do evidently and truly appear to be repugnant to some Principle, or to some Conclusion of Right Reason]
>
> Instead therefore of saying *undiscoverable*, he should have said *incomprehensible* by Reason. Into which he slips unawares in the account of the other part of the Distinction, *things Contrary to Reason*, by saying that they are such as when we *do* understand them do appear repugnant, etc. which plainly implies that the former things that were said to be above Reason are such as we do *not* understand, even when discover'd, and not such as we are not able only to Discover, since otherwise there will be no Antithesis in the Second part, in which there is nothing amiss except those words *as are not only undiscoverable*, which in my judgment ought to be expung'd as the Production of the first Mistake.[82]

Norris acknowledges that Boyle's intent was to show the appropriateness of using the above but not contrary to reason label. He thinks he should have limited above reason to the incomprehensible. Then one could mean by "above but not contrary to reason" that although the thing is incomprehensible it is not repugnant to reason. He thinks that saying that an above reason thing in the comprehensible sense is also not contrary to reason goes without saying. Whereas Boyle may prefer to call things above reason somewhat

---

[81] Norris, *An Account*, 103–5.
[82] Norris, *An Account*, 105–6.

similar to the way that Turretin does—it is not something we could have discovered but once revealed and given due consideration, seems rather reasonable—but when theological debaters in the era use the phrase above but not contrary to reason, they intend to focus upon the incomprehensible but not incompossible distinction posited by Turretin. Moreover, Norris does also take issue with Boyle's use of "appear." He makes the interesting point that his use of "appear" obliterates the distinction Boyle was trying to make. That is, saying that a contrary to reason thing were only to "appear" to be repugnant is precisely the defense some will use to distinguish an above reason thing from the contrary to reason thing: the above reason thing only appears to be impossible, but it is not definitively so.[83]

Norris's categorization of propositions is more interesting yet than his critiques of Boyle. Norris reduces "reason" in its most important aspect to understanding or, more precisely, perception.[84] This is vital to his taxonomy of propositions. According to reason would be anything true that one can comprehend. He defines above reason and contrary to reason as follows:

> By things above Reason then (as the Expression is used in this Distinction) I conceive to be Meant, Not such as Reason of it self cannot Discover, but such as when proposed it cannot Comprehend. And by things Contrary to Reason I conceive such as it can and does actually comprehend, and that to be absolutely Impossible. Or in other words, a thing is above Reason when we do not comprehend how it can be, and then Contrary to Reason when we do positively comprehend that it cannot be. Thus in the General.[85]

Norris quickly asserts that above reason does not mean "perfectly unintelligible" but not perceiving the truth of the proposition. And this not comprehending the truth of the proposition does not mean being unable to comprehend the truth of the thing in its whole latitude and extent. If that were the case almost all things would be above reason. Something is therefore above reason "not because the simple and direct Meaning of its Terms is unintelligible, or because the Truth of it is not comprehensible in its remotest and utmost Extent, but purely because the Connexion of its Ideas, or the manner of it, is not discernible." The "Connexion" is not discernible because

---

[83] Norris, *An Acccount*, 115.
[84] Norris, *An Account*, 22–25.
[85] Norris, *An Account*, 116–17.

the ideas are not sufficiently clear to immediately see their connections and we lack "a due and proper Medium whereby to compare them."[86]

Moreover, there are two situations that give rise to an impossibility: (1) there is an immediate opposition or mutual exclusivity between two ideas "as in a Contradiction," or (2) because the union of both is inconsistent with either a principle or conclusion of right reason.[87] Therefore, "for a thing to be Contrary to Reason, is, in short, for the Understanding to perceive the Absolute Impossibility of it, or that its Ideas cannot stand together, which it does either Immediately by perceiving the direct inconsistency of those Ideas, or Mediately by perceiving their inconsistency with some evident and incontestable Truth or other, whether Principle or Conclusion."[88] In sum, there are certain notions that immediately reveal contradictions like one plus one is three or the notion of a square circle. But there also other truths that might be pictured but we know cannot be true (e.g., an angel locked into its righteous standing by God's power who sins). I can picture it, but it at base is a contradiction.

Further, "A thing is then above Reason when we do not Perceive or Comprehend how it can be. And then Contrary to Reason when we do Perceive it Cannot be, or Impossible."[89] In other words, we know what it is not to comprehend an idea, doctrine, or proposition and to comprehend that the idea, doctrine, or proposition is impossible. "For a thing to be above Reason implies only a *Negation*, the Not Comprehending how a thing can be, but for a thing to be Contrary to Reason implies the *Position* of an Intellectual act, the Comprehending that it cannot be." He follows that assertion with: "Again, in things above Reason the Proposition is supposed not to be understood, whereas in things Contrary to Reason, it is supposed to be well understood, and that to be false and impossible."[90] With respect to things above reason, the mind is in suspense. With respect to contrary things the mind is not in suspense. There is a difference between non-perception and knowing a thing to be false.[91] Norris also notes that above reason is relative: "For to be Above Reason is not to be Above Reason in general or all Reason, so as to be absolutely incomprehensible, but only Human Reason." An angel, for instance, might find certain above human reason things not to be above angelic reason.

---

[86] Norris, *An Account*, 117–19 [quotation, pp. 118–19].
[87] Norris, *An Account*, 119–20 [quotation, p. 119].
[88] Norris, *An Account*, 120–21.
[89] Norris, *An Account*, 122.
[90] Norris, *An Account*, 124.
[91] Norris, *An Account*, 125–26.

Contrary to reason, however, is absolute: "whatever is Contrary to Reason, is contrary to all Reason, and so consequently to Truth."[92]

Whether a thing is discoverable or undiscoverable, revealed or not, does not factor into Norris's taxonomy. This means that (according to) reason's proper scope encompasses many revealed truths in Scripture and the above reason category encompasses even many natural or non-revealed truths. Both are objects of assent. Moreover, regardless of what one thinks the proper definition of the term reason is or how prevalent certain definitions were, Norris's explanation of his taxonomy is very clear. And his analysis and critique of Boyle seemed to be charitable and appreciative, which is not always the case in the era.

Locke's Treatment of Reason, Faith, and Categorization of Propositions

Locke's Treatment of Reason and Assent

Like other thinkers of his era, Locke has different senses of reason. In his chapter on reason in book IV of the *Essay*, he puts forth a very lengthy definition. There reason is the faculty that is used "both for the enlargement of our Knowledge, and regulating our Assent: For it hath to do, both in Knowledge and Opinion, and is necessary, and assisting to all our other intellectual Faculties, and indeed contains two of them, *viz. Sagacity and Illation*." It discovers certainty and probability: "For as Reason perceives the necessary, and indubitable connexion of all the *Ideas* or Proofs one to another, in each step of any Demonstration that produces Knowledge: so it likewise perceives the probable connexion of all the *Ideas* or Proofs one to another, in every step of a Discourse, to which it will think Assent due." It keeps us from being governed by randomness, arbitrary choices, and no direction.[93]

Whereas he describes reason as one larger human faculty among others, he at other times identifies reason as all the natural (mental) faculties. In a passage where he is discussing the fact that no simple ideas come from traditional revelation—although God could give us a faculty beyond our five senses to receive such ideas in an immediate, original revelation—he asserts

---

[92] Norris, *An Account*, 128–29.
[93] Locke, *Essay*, IV.xvii.2.

the following: "For our simple *Ideas* then, which are the Foundation, and sole Matter of all our Notions, and Knowledge, we must depend wholly on our Reason, I mean, our natural Faculties; and can by no means receive them, or any of them, from *Traditional Revelation*."[94] At another place, when asserting that there are things delivered to us that are beyond the "Discovery of *Reason*," he notes that these same things are "beyond the Discovery of our natural Faculties" and then later implies the same when mentioning "the natural Use of our Faculties."[95] Later still, he asserts that propositions that the mind can determine and judge with its natural faculties are matters of reason.[96]

These differing claims can be reconciled if all the natural faculties are understood as reason when the mind or agent acts reasonably. Because this is not always the case, Locke ends his *Essay* with a chapter on enthusiasm (a later addition) and another on wrong assent or error. In the chapter on enthusiasm, he discusses how some assent wrongly. But more importantly, in the other chapter, he delineates the sources of error or wrong assent. Sometimes it is lack of mental power in an individual or time or lack of education. At other times, people are lazy or given into their passions and do not want to investigate a matter further for fear of what he or she will find out. In fact, when the latter does occur, but the person later applies his or her reason to investigate, Locke says, "there, I think, *a Man*, who has weighed them [evidence on both sides], *can scarce refuse his Assent* to the side, on which the greater Probability appears."[97] But, much of the time, in the chapter on enthusiasm and in the chapter on wrong assent, we assent wrongly because we do not apply reason as we should. More importantly, however, when the rest of book IV is compared to these chapters, it appears that Locke has been largely describing reason working at its best in humans. It is not an abstract description of right reason, but more how an individual can position him or herself to reason rightly and do so, despite variances in education and mental quickness. What is more, he thinks Christianity is generally reasonable and that individuals can be convinced of this when they assiduously apply the reasoning faculty to the evidence, arguments, and Scripture.

Not only does Locke have different senses of reason as a faculty, but he also writes of two different senses of the operation of reason. The preferred sense

---

[94] Locke, *Essay*, IV.xviii.3.
[95] Locke, *Essay*, IV.xviii.7.
[96] Locke, *Essay*, IV.xviii.9.
[97] Locke, *Essay*, IV.xx.15.

that he employs clearly in the chapters prior to IV.xviii, is one where our assent to revealed propositions is governed by reason. The second sense opposes reason to faith (assent to revealed propositions). This is concessionary and is done because it is infeasible to root out such erroneous ways of speaking. But after offering the concessionary view, he deconstructs it, showing that it is ridiculous. Locke, then is in good company of those who dislike the opposition of faith and reason.

This conclusion becomes clear in his chapters on probability, assent, and reason (chapters xv–xvii of book IV), where Locke expressly calls assent in general faith, asserts that all assent ought to be reasonable, and exclaims that it is ludicrous to think of faith (in revealed things) and reason in opposition, similar to the express sentiments of Turretin and Rust. In his chapter on probability he identifies "faith" as simply assent in general: "I shall come now, (having, as I think, found the bounds of humane Knowledge and Certainty,) in the next place to consider *the several degrees and grounds of Probability, and Assent or Faith*" and "herein lies the *difference between Probability* and *Certainty, Faith* and *Knowledge*, that in all the parts of Knowledge, there is intuition."[98] Assent ought to be reasonable: when we do not have knowledge, Locke asserts probability ought to direct assent.[99] And although revelation must have precedence over probable conjectures, it cannot contradict the "dictates" of reason.[100] Thus, revelation cannot overturn things that are certain or where we have knowledge, but few would disagree with Locke, certainly not Turretin.[101] Locke bolsters the notion that we should not consider assent in revealed matters, or what some call faith, as being outside of the pale of reason in his chapter on assent. After discussing miracles as an external mark of divine revelation and how many call assent to revelation "faith," he writes, "But of Faith, and the Precedency it ought to have before other Arguments of Perswasion, I shall speak more hereafter, where I treat of it, as it is ordinarily placed, in contradistinction to Reason; though in Truth, it be nothing else but an Assent founded on the highest Reason."[102] Regardless of what he means precisely by "highest Reason," he is writing disparagingly of

---

[98] Locke, *Essay*, IV.xv.2–3.
[99] Locke, *Essay*, IV.xviii.1.
[100] Locke, *Essay*, IV.xviii.6.
[101] Locke does not think, however, that probable arguments can add or detract from sure interpretations of Scripture. He accuses Edward Stillingfleet of maintaining this position. Marko, *Measuring the Distance*, 57–59.
[102] Locke, *Essay*, IV.xvi.14.

the contradistinction. And later, in his chapter on reason, he makes the following statement:

> There is another use of the Word *Reason*, wherein it is *opposed to Faith*; which though it be in it self a very improper way of speaking, yet common Use has authorized it, that it would be folly either to oppose or hope to remedy it: Only I think it may not be amiss to take notice, that however *Faith* be opposed to Reason, *Faith* is nothing but a firm Assent of the Mind: which if it be regulated, as is our Duty, cannot be afforded to any thing, but upon good Reason; and so cannot be opposite it . . . For he governs his Assent right, and places it as he should, who in any Case or Matter whatsoever, believes or disbelieves, according as Reason directs him. He that does otherwise, transgresses against his own Light, and misuses those Faculties, which were given him to no other end, but to search and follow the clearer Evidence, and greater Probability.[103]

Clearly, he thinks our reasoning faculties ought to guide our assent, even in religious matters. There are very few theologians in the era—in fact, none that I have explored—who actually separate faith and reason. He even finishes the chapter on reason with the following: "But since Reason and Faith are by some Men opposed, we will so consider them in the following Chapter." It is in that following chapter where he gives alternative definitions to faith and reason. Moreover, as I have shown in *Measuring the Distance*, not recognizing that the definitions in IV.xviii are concessionary and are not his preferred definitions wreaks havoc in trying to determine the religious implications of book IV.

Before making his concessionary definitions in chapter xviii, "Of Faith and Reason, and Their Distinct Provinces," Locke offers a brief apology: "For till it be resolved, how far we are to be guided by Reason, and how far by Faith, we shall in vain dispute, and endeavor to convince one another in Matters of Religion."[104] His definitions follow:

> *Reason* therefore here, as contradistinguished to *Faith*, I take to be the discovery of the Certainty or Probability of such Propositions or Truths, which

---

[103] Locke, *Essay*, IV.xvii.24.
[104] Locke, *Essay*, IV.xviii.1.

the Mind arrives at by Deductions made from such *Ideas*, which it has got by the use of its natural Faculties, *viz.* by Sensation or Reflection.

Faith, on the other side, is the Assent to any Proposition, not thus made out by the Deductions of Reason; but upon the Credit of the Proposer, as coming from GOD, in some extraordinary way of Communication. This way of discovering Truths to Men we call *Revelation*."[105]

Reason is here limited in scope to only that which we can determine unassisted by divine revelation. This notion of unassisted reason is understood and distinguished by others in Locke's era. Locke has a few different names for it in his other works: "natural reason," "unassisted reason," and "human reason."[106] This is also the notion of reason in its limited scope used in his chapter on enthusiasm. There he writes: "*Revelation* is natural *Reason* enlarged by a new set of Discoveries communicated by GOD immediately, which *Reason* vouches the Truth of, by the Testimony and Proofs it gives, that they come from GOD."[107] Later in that same chapter he makes mention of the "Principles of Reason or Word of GOD."[108] Moreover, the definition of faith given above is assent limited to revelatory issues, ones that surpass reason's discoveries. Locke even answers the question what if they were to somehow overlap; that is, what if reason had an answer that was opposed to revelation? He writes: "And therefore, *Nothing that is contrary to, and inconsistent with the clear and self-evident Dictates of Reason, has a Right to be urged, or attested to, as a Matter of Faith, wherein Reason hath nothing to do.*"[109] This echoes a sentiment and corresponding wording shared with Rust that we cannot assent contrary to the dictates of right reason. But he makes clear in the previous section and right after this excerpt that, "I say, an evident *Revelation* ought to determine our Assent even against Probability."[110] In other words, right faith does not assent to contradictions or things against knowledge, but it very well may contradict our assent based on natural probability.

---

[105] Locke, *Essay*, IV.xviii.2.
[106] Examples of Locke's "natural reason" usage: Locke, *ROC*, 268, 278; Locke, *Mr. Locke's Reply . . . Answer to his Second Letter*, 418, 421, 423, 426, 427, 428, 429, 439. Examples of "unassisted reason": Locke, *ROC*, 268, 270. Examples of Locke using "human reason": Locke, *Mr. Locke's Reply . . . Answer to his Second Letter*, 418–19; Locke, *Second Vindication*, xvi. Cf. Marko, *Measuring the Distance*, 63 fn 2.
[107] Locke, *Essay*, IV.xix.4.
[108] Locke, *Essay*, IV.xix.15.
[109] Locke, *Essay*, IV.xviii.10.
[110] Locke, *Essay*, IV.xvii.9.

That he finds this contradistinction between faith and reason an untenable separation is made clear in what follows in the rest of chapter IV.xviii and beyond. In chapter xviii and in his chapter on assent, he is clear that it is the faculty of reason that must decide whether or not some alleged revelation is such.[111] In fact, it is in his next chapter on enthusiasm where he takes back up the topic of miracles and his rules for the human agent identifying a true revelation. We need our reason to interpret, and even sift through potential interpretations, of sure and alleged revelations: "it still belongs to *Reason*, to judge of the Truth of its being a Revelation, and of the signification of the Words, wherein it is delivered."[112] Thus, try as we might, the *actual* separation of reason and faith leads to enthusiasm: "whatever groundless Opinion comes to settle it self strongly upon their Fancies, is [taken as] an Illumination from the Spirit of GOD." One is left to act upon their impulses and desires and claim their doing so is a matter of faith![113]

Locke's Categorization of Propositions from IV.XVII.23

The question that is of interest here is which sense of reason—natural, unassisted reason or reason taken in its full scope—is the one undergirding Locke's category of propositions in section 23 of his chapter on reason. There he acknowledges and seems to accept "above reason" things, which as indicated above, in some means incomprehensible things for which we cannot form a proper conception. Recall that Norris claimed that all divines mean incomprehensible doctrines when mentioning the category, with the exception of Robert Boyle, who emphasizes the novelty of revelation that makes if first and foremost above right reason (Turretin, too, acknowledges that revealed things beyond the discovery of unassisted reason can be said to be above reason).

Numerous scholars have defended Locke's relative orthodoxy by pointing out that he creates room for the incomprehensible with the above reason category. But few have noted that Locke employs multiple senses of reason. The issue is not resolved by referring to the taxonomy in Locke's formal treatment of reason, or by noting either that it is prior to chapter xviii where the concessionary definitions of faith and reason are given, or that right after his

---

[111] Locke, *Essay*, IV.xviii.6, 8.
[112] Locke, *Essay*, IV.xviii.8.
[113] Locke, *Essay*, IV.xix.6.

mention of the categorization of propositions he chides people for making an incorrect separation between faith and reason. There are, then, three reasons that could be presented as evidence that "reason" in the categories of propositions is reason in its broadest scope, but given both Locke's wording and his reference to the category of things above reason in the *Essay*, such a reading is untenable. That is to say, "reason" is natural reason in his taxonomy and not reason considered in its full scope.

Here is the section including the taxonomy in full:

> By what has been before said of *Reason*, we may be able to make some guess at the distinction of Things, into those that are according to, above, and contrary to Reason. 1. *According to Reason* are such Propositions, whose Truth we can discover, by examining and tracing those *Ideas* we have from *Sensation* and *Reflexion*; and by natural deduction, find to be true, or probable. 2. *Above Reason* are such Propositions, whose Truth or Probability we cannot by Reason derive from those Principles. 3. *Contrary to Reason* are such Propositions, as are inconsistent with, or irreconcilable to our clear and distinct *Ideas*. Thus the existence of one GOD is according to Reason; the Existence of more than one GOD, contrary to Reason; the Resurrection of the Dead, above Reason. Farther, as *Above Reason* may be taken in a double Sense, *viz.* either as signifying above Probability, or above Certainty: so in that large Sense also, Contrary to Reason, is, I suppose, sometimes taken.

Locke casts this taxonomy with a wary tone, by writing "we may be able to make some guess." The very last line seems to indicate some uncertainty. It could be the case that Locke, like Boyle and Norris, is exasperated by how imprecisely these labels have been applied and thus he is guessing what everyone might be saying. Or he might be making a guess regarding how he thinks that they should be delineating categories of propositions. Both interpretations are possible, but the former would be peculiar. It would be unusual for Locke to be so incautious and promulgate something he did not maintain himself. It is more in line with Locke's character to take this as an honest attempt to offer his own categorization scheme incorporating the common usage of faith and reason.

There is support in Locke's description of propositions according to reason and above reason to maintain that "reason" is simply natural reason or unassisted reason, or, equally, his concessionary definition of reason, and that things above reason correspond to his concessionary definition of faith. In his description of propositions according to reason he notes that these are propositions "by natural deduction, [we] find to be true, or probable." These are propositions we could come to be certain of or to which we could rightly assent under our own mental powers in a "natural" way and thus without divine revelation. After promulgating his concessionary definitions of faith and reason in IV.xviii, he defines the "Matter of Faith" as being "only Divine Revelation, and nothing else, *Faith*, as we use the Word, (called commonly, *Divine Faith*) has to do with no Propositions, but those which are supposed to be divinely revealed."[114] In the very next sections of the same chapter he identifies matters of faith and "above reason things" among other assertions:

> There being many Things, wherein we have very imperfect Notions, or none at all; and other Things, of whose past, present, or future Existence, by the natural Use of our Faculties, we can have no Knowledge at all; these, as being beyond the Discovery of our natural Faculties, and above *Reason*, are, when revealed, *the proper Matter of Faith*. Thus that part of the Angels rebelled against GOD, and thereby lost their first happy state: And that the dead shall rise, and live again: These, and the like, being beyond the Discovery of *Reason*, are purely Matters of Faith; with which *Reason* has, directly, nothing to do.[115]

In other words, things above reason conclusively corresponds to matters of the faith, faith understood in its chapter xviii or concessionary sense. Those things cannot be discovered by unassisted reason. He repeats all this later:

> *First*, Whatever Proposition is revealed, of whose Truth our Mind, by its natural Faculties and Notions, cannot judge, that is purely *Matter of Faith*, and above Reason.
>
> *Secondly*, All Propositions, whereof the Mind, by the use of its natural Faculties, can come to determine and judge, from naturally acquired *Ideas*, are *Matter of Reason*; with this difference still [that is uncertain deductions ought to be overturned by an evident Revelation].[116]

---

[114] Locke, *Essay*, IV.xviii.6.
[115] Locke, *Essay*, IV.xviii.7.
[116] Locke, *Essay*, IV.xviii.9.

Locke, then, repeatedly identifies above reason propositions as pure or proper matters of faith and identifies according to reason propositions as matters of reason.

There are a few issues that warrant immediate clarification. First, when Locke makes the distinction between matters of the faith and "proper matters of the faith" he could be intending one of two different distinctions. This might be an acknowledgement that many revealed things might be naturally discovered and rightly assented to by some people or groups but that there are other things in revelation, a subset of revealed things—the pure or proper matters of the faith—that would not be discovered and rightly assented to by natural reason. Or Locke could simply mean that there are some religious things that people believe, but they also could know, had they the opportunity, like the existence of God.[117] The existence of God is knowable and thus not necessarily a matter of faith in any sense.[118] Based on his connection of above reason things and proper matters of the faith, it is most likely the former. Second, the last portion of the taxonomy of propositions—"Farther, as *Above Reason* may be taken in a double Sense, *viz.* either as signifying above Probability, or above Certainty: so in that large Sense also, Contrary to Reason, is, I suppose, sometimes taken"—might be explained as the following. Things above reason are labeled as such because they are supplementary to our knowledge and right assent in natural probability: thus, they are above certainty and above probability. Further, because things above reason have the ability to trump natural probability, they are also sometimes called contrary to reason. Third, why Locke did not put the taxonomy of propositions after he had made his concessionary definitions, is not completely clear. What is clear is that the taxonomy of propositions corresponds to the concessionary definitions. Sections 23 and 24, which conclude the chapter on reason (IV.xvii) and section 1 that begins the chapter on faith and reason (IV.xviii) create a bridge from one set of definitions to another.

Much of this is rather straightforward, but there are two important issues that are unclear in his taxonomy of propositions: what are the precise bounds of things above reason and contrary to reason. Locke repeatedly notes that matters of the faith or things above reason are beyond the discovery of our reason, but it is not clear what kinds of incomprehensible propositions, if any,

---

[117] For example, Locke, *ROC*, 282.
[118] Locke, *Essay*, IV.x.

this entails. The only examples he gives of doctrines above reason are ones for which we can create mental representations in our minds: the resurrection and the fall of one third of the angels. He appears to accept what Boyle would indicate as being above reason but comprehensible (Locke's understanding of reason is, however, more focused on the individual working at his or her best as opposed to right reason). Also, he does not refer to difficult to comprehend claims from the natural world as being above reason like Norris does. Locke, like Boyle and many in the era, acknowledges that God effects miracles despite his not knowing how, which corresponds to Boyle's second sub-type of incomprehensible above reason things. We can imagine and observe a miracle so miracles per se are not incomprehensible, but just how God does them is such.

There is no evidence that Locke considers God's attributes to be considered as other than sufficiently comprehensible things that produce some difficulties (like Boyle) (Locke would undoubtedly consider many attributes to be naturally discoverable). The main question is whether his taxonomy is generous enough to include what would fit within Boyle's unsociable or asymmetrical propositions or Norris's above reason propositions (although, recall, for Norris they need not be revealed to count as such) like the doctrine of the Holy Trinity. Locke evidently accepts free choice, as does Boyle, but that could be a special case given that Locke's short description of things contrary to reason—"Propositions, as are inconsistent with, or irreconcilable to our clear and distinct *Ideas*"—sounds like a rejection of Boyle's unsociable category—"*asymmetrical* or unsociable; that is, such as we see not how to reconcile with other Things, which also manifestly are, or are by us acknowledged to be, true." That is, Locke's category of contrary to reason seems to assert that inconsistent or contradictory claims and even that which cannot be mentally reconciled (Boyle's unsociable sub-category) will be counted as being contrary to reason. How we have potencies to multiple effects regarding our will and moral responsibility in light of God's providence could be admitted as unsociable or asymmetrical. Of the five writers examined, only Locke fails to explain how incomprehensible doctrines like the Trinity might fit into his taxonomy of propositions.

At this point, we can conclude that Locke appropriates Boyle's otherwise undiscoverable sense of "above reason," but it is unclear if his epistemology makes room for Boyle's unsociable sub-category, or perhaps Norris's revealed above reason propositions.

Further Comments on Locke and the Incomprehensible

Locke admits a relativity or superiority of intellect in angels and "just Men made perfect" in reasoning.[119] This is a loose connection to the sentiments of those treated above who directly state that "above reason" seems to be a relative term. Locke also acknowledges that there are things beyond our notice. These are things that Hallywell would identify as above reason. Locke suggests that Paul is unable to convey what he saw when in the third heaven (1 Corinthians 2:9) because he was given faculties that we do not have.[120] It is not as if Locke denies that there are incomprehensible things. The question is whether Locke thinks we are obligated or even can assent in any meaningful sense to incomprehensible things.

Furthermore, there is a potentially important difference between Locke's and Rust's views of explicit and implicit faith. Rust acknowledges that even though we cannot explicitly assent to certain doctrines that "seem otherwise to clash with Reason" that we ought to "yield an implicit Faith to Divine Revelations."[121] He puts the doctrine of the Holy Trinity as an example of those things that require only an implicit faith.[122] Locke uses the term implicit faith in *A Second Vindication* (of *ROC*): "the Obedience of assent must be implicitly to all that is deliver'd there; That is true. But for as much as the particular acts of explicit assent cannot go farther than his understanding."[123] This resembles Hallywell's definition of implicit faith, taken in isolation from the rest of his annotations: "to believe that the sense of all those Things that are delivered and consigned by Divine Testimony, though they transcend my Capacity, whatever it is which was intended by God, is true."[124] Locke's sense of implicit faith and Hallywell's definition (without context) of it seem to be a disposition that Scripture is true even when one cannot understand it. On a related point, Locke's instructions in *ROC* for one that "cannot put several [assuredly revealed or Scriptural] Texts, and make them *consist* together" (emphasis mine) is: "He must either interpret one by the other, or suspend his Opinion."[125] Now, he does not reject the revealed texts and he does not, like Rust, suggest an implicit faith that amounts to an affirmation

---

[119] Locke, *Essay*, IV.xvii.14.
[120] Locke, *Essay*, IV.xviii.3.
[121] Rust, *Discourse*, 41.
[122] Rust, *Discourse*, 26.
[123] Locke, *A Second Vindication*, 83; cf. Locke, *ROC*, 300–1.
[124] [Hallywell], *Discourse*, 70.
[125] Locke, *ROC*, 304.

of, in some cases, traditional doctrines like the Trinity. As intimated above, Rust discusses implicit faith in the context of traditionally held doctrines derived over long debates over proper exegesis, while Locke, again, seems to make this more of an individual affair of the reading or hearing of biblical texts (likely in a gathered body or service if one is illiterate). Rust, however, would say that one should affirm the traditional doctrine of the Trinity or the Athanasian rendering of it, while Locke simply says to suspend one's judgment regarding the proper reconciliation of seemingly inconsistent passages. One could use this to argue that this is evidence that Locke thinks that it is really impermissible to affirm such incomprehensible doctrines. That is, such an instruction is a tacit rejection of the doctrines because the doctrine of the Trinity, as traditionally taught, is conceptually irreconcilable. One could respond that, based on the immediate context of his suspense instructions, the instructions should not cast a pall of doubt on Locke's advocating a "Rustian" implicit assent to incomprehensible doctrines to those who are educated. Because he is discussing suspension while defending the simplicity of the Christian religion for the poor and uneducated, he is perhaps instructing his readers not to press overly complex doctrines upon those without the proper time and education to understand them correctly.

Toland's Treatment of Reason, Faith, and Categorization of Propositions

Toland's Treatment of Reason and Assent

John Toland is a thinker who is often mentioned, especially in the context of John Locke and/or the rise of deism, but whose works have often been under-analyzed. He is best known as the thinker who appropriated and altered the fundamentals of Locke's theology and rejected above reason things in his first major work, *Christianity Not Mysterious*. He most often is mentioned in the narratives of the rise of deism to show how the Lockean deists deviated from Locke: Locke accepts above reason things and Toland rejects above reason things and the other Lockean deists follow in Toland's footsteps. It is an unfortunate assumption that Toland and Locke mean the same by "reason" in their categorizations of propositions. On the basis of this and other assumptions, Stillingfleet accused Locke of unwittingly paving the way for the heresy of John Toland.

Toland, however, is not an outlier in his outlining various senses of the term reason. At one point he identifies reason and "demonstration" and defines it as *"That Faculty of the Soul which discovers the Certainty of any thing dubious or obscure, by comparing it with something evidently known."*[126] Still, he also offers a broader sense of the term:

> Everyone experiences in himself a Power or Faculty of forming various Ideas or Perceptions of Things: Of affirming or denying, according as he sees them to agree or disagree: and so of loving and desiring what seems good unto him; and of hating and avoiding what he thinks evil. The right Use of all these Faculties is what we call Common Sense, or *Reason* in general.[127]

This is similar to Locke's broader sense of reason. Toland might have intended to allude to all the faculties in the above excerpt. Also, like Locke, Toland notices that there will be many times when the faculties will not be used so well: "The right Use of all these Faculties" is called reason. In a later chapter he acknowledges at length that these faculties are often not used well: "But if by *Reason* be understood a constant right Use of these Faculties, *viz. If a Man never judges but according to clear Perceptions, desires nothing but what is truly good for him, nor avoids but what is certainly evil*: Then, I confess, it is extreamly *corrupt*."[128] What is more, both Locke and Toland are focused on the individual reasoning rightly as opposed to the corporate and abstract notion of right reason used by Rust, Turretin, and Boyle in their categorization of propositions.

Toland's treatment of faith is similar to Locke's, too. Even though Toland dislikes relying on probability,[129] he realizes that we must often rely on probability in "Matters of common Practice"—as opposed to speculative matters—where strict demonstration fails us: "for these must of necessity sometimes admit *Probability* to supply the Defect of *Demonstration*."[130] He also does acknowledge that some distinguish faith in a limited sense to revealed matters even though, in the end, it is all assent grounded in reasoning. In one place he writes:

---

[126] Toland, *CNM*, 14.
[127] Toland, *CNM*, 9.
[128] Toland, *CNM*, 57.
[129] Toland, *CNM*, 15.
[130] Toland, *CNM*, 21.

> The word [Faith as used by many in various senses] imports *Belief* or *Perswasion*, as when we give Credit to any thing which is told us by God or Man; whence *Faith* is properly divided into *Human* and *Divine*. Again, *Divine Faith* is either when God speaks to us immediately himself, or when we acquiesce in the Words or Writings of those to whom we believe he has spoken. All *Faith* now in the World is of this last sort, and by consequence entirely built upon *Ratiocination*.[131]

Toland emphasizes the need to reasonably assess claims of revelation as being such, while noting that "The Author of the Epistle to the *Hebrews* do's not define *FAITH* a Prejudice, Opinion, or Conjecture, but Conviction or Demonstration . . . Besides, there can be properly no *Faith* of things seen or present, for then 'tis Self-evidence, and not Ratiocination."[132] Toland is clear throughout *CNM* that reason is required for interpretation.[133]

It is commonly said that Toland would reject any alleged revelation that necessarily introduces novelty. In his response to the questions, "whether we could discover all the Objects of our *Faith* by Ratiocination," he answers: "I have prov'd on the contrary, that no Matter of Fact can be known without *Revelation*. But I assert, that what is once reveal'd we must as well understand as any other Matter in the World, *Revelation* being only of use to inform us whilst the Evidence of its Subject perswades us."[134] In other words, there are many things given by revelation that we would never have determined on our own, but we must still understand them to accept them. The entire third section of *CNM* is based on the assertion that the Bible revealed to us what once were mysteries that technically should no longer be called such. Within that section, Toland asserts: "The most perspicacious *Philosophers* were not able to foretel the Coming of *Christ*, to discover the *Resurrection* of the Body, nor any other Matter of Fact that is deliver'd in the Gospel: And if they happen'd now and then to say something like the Truth, they did but divine at best, and could never be certain of their Opinion."[135] In other words, the most brilliant minds could not anticipate some of the truths given by the New Testament; but if a person were to invent one of the revealed doctrines in his or her mind without having Scripture's attestation, he or she would have no reason to

---

[131] Toland, *CNM*, 127.
[132] Toland, *CNM*, 129–30.
[133] For example, Toland, *CNM*, 46–56 (chapter 3 of section II).
[134] Toland, *CNM*, 140.
[135] Toland, *CNM*, 90.

assent to that contrived doctrine. What is more, Toland echoes the orthodox of the era in his description of reason as an "instrument" as opposed to it being the rule of faith.[136] And also within the preface of *CNM*, he explains that he takes the divinity of the New Testament for granted in the first section.[137] He does later in the book, like Locke, employ miracles, among other things, to index that divinity. In short, Toland's *CNM* clearly allows revelation to deliver novelty.

Toland's Categorization of Propositions

The very title of Toland's chief work indicates a rejection of doctrines "above reason": *Christianity Not Mysterious: or, A Treatise Shewing, That There Is Nothing in the Gospel Contrary to Reason, Nor Above It: And That No Christian Doctrine Can Be Properly Call'd a Mystery*. Appropriating Boylean terms, Toland does not reject that which is above reason in the discovery sense as long as it is comprehensible. He just would not call it above reason. Likewise, he would not call such things mysteries. He states that in the New Testament the term mystery always is used "for *things naturally very intelligible, but so cover'd by figurative Words or Rites, that Reason could not discover them without special Revelation*; and that the Vail is actually taken away; then it will manifestly follow that the Doctrines so reveal'd cannot now be properly call'd *Mysteries*."[138]

Toland does not reject all that Boyle would have categorized as above reason in the incomprehensible sense. He resists giving the above reason or mystery label to what Boyle considers his first sub-category of incomprehensible things above reason: things "not clearly *conceivable* by our Understanding, such as the Infiniteness and Perfections of the Divine Nature." Toland denies that God's attributes are mysteries: "As for GOD, we comprehend nothing better than his Attributes." He explains that it is not mysterious that we do not know God's true essence because we do not know the essence of any of the creatures. God has so arranged us that we know only that about Him which is necessary and useful.[139]

---

[136] Toland, *CNM*, vii, viii–ix.
[137] Toland, *CNM*, xxiv.
[138] Toland, *CNM*, 73.
[139] Toland, *CNM*, 86. Toland's entire chapter should be read to unpack what he is saying in the excerpt above.

Furthermore, Toland accepts miracles but refuses to label them as Boyle would: "*inexplicable by us, such as the Manner.*" Boyle would call miracles or how the soul moves the body above reason in the incomprehensible sense. Toland defines a miracle as follows: "*is some Action exceeding all humane Power, and which the Laws of NATURE cannot perform by their ordinary Operations.*"[140] But, Toland argues, miracles are always intelligible, "tho the manner of doing it be extraordinary." He offers a number of so-called miracles that result in contradictions and would thus not be credible. For one he says that a severed human head without a tongue speaking would be impossible and incredible. No one can speak without a tongue. Another example is Jesus not being born through an opening in the virgin. Being "born" implies more than simply appearing outside of a woman's body. By contrast, a man not being consumed by the fire in which he is immersed is conceivable and thus credible.[141] In response to someone who says that this latter is above reason according to the manner (as Boyle would), Toland can say that it is still a phenomenon that we can observe and imagine. It is not only the manner of miracles that eludes us in all the phenomena we observe. The manner of many other natural things elude us as well.[142]

What Toland does dismiss, however, are the unsociable or asymmetric propositions that Boyle promulgates. He identifies such things as being contrary to reason, which he defines as: "*what is evidently repugnant to clear and distinct Ideas, or to our common Notions.*"[143] He says that he is going to show that nothing in the gospel is such. He knows most will never say that reason and the gospel are contrary to one another, but he still plans to disabuse those who:

> affirm, that tho the Doctrines of the latter [Gospel] cannot in themselves be contradictory to the Principles of the former [reason], as proceeding both from God; yet, that according to our Conceptions of them, *they may seem directly to clash*: And that tho we cannot reconcile them by reason of our corrupt and limited Understandings; yet that from the Authority of *Divine Revelation*, we are bound to believe and acquiesce in them; or, as the *Fathers* taught 'em to speak, *to adore what we cannot comprehend.*[144]

---

[140] Toland, *CNM*, 144.
[141] Toland, *CNM*, 145–46 [quotation, p. 145].
[142] Toland, *CNM*, 149–50; cf. 6.
[143] Toland, *CNM*, 25.
[144] Toland, *CNM*, 26.

The title of the very next chapter is "The Absurdity and Effects of Admitting Any Real or Seeming Contradictions in Religion." Toland does not deal with any traditionally incomprehensible doctrines such as the Trinity. Unfortunately, he provides only the most obvious of examples, such as a ball being at once white and black and the idea—limbus infantum—that one can be damned without pain, an explicit and implicit contradiction, respectively. He at least explains his epistemology in its context. He asserts that "Now if we have no Ideas of a thing, it is certainly but lost Labour for us to trouble our selves about it: For what I don't conceive, can no more give me right Notions of God, or influence my Actions, than a Prayer delivered in an unknown Tongue can excite my Devotion." In other words, if one cannot conceive the idea of a doctrine then it is not a proper thought and cannot have an effect on us:[145]

> A *seeming* Contradiction is to us as much as a *real* one; and our Respect for the *Scripture* does not require us to grant any such in it, but rather to conclude, that we are ignorant of the right Meaning when a Difficulty occurs; and so *to suspend our Judgment concerning it, till with sutable Helps and Industry we discover the Truth*. As for acquiescing in what a Man understands not, or cannot reconcile to his Reason, they know best the fruits of it that practice it ... A Man may give his verbal Assent to he knows not what ... but as long as he conceives not what he believes, he cannot sincerely acquiesce in it, and remains depriv'd of all solid Satisfaction.[146]

A person ought to suspend judgment when one fails to understand a doctrine or proposition. And one cannot assent to such a doctrine or a proposition because we assent to ideas. Toland reasserts this principle about assent later as well: "for the conceiv'd Ideas of things are the only Subjects of Believing, Denying, Approving, and every other Act of the Understanding."[147]

Toland, thus indicates two categories of propositions: according to reason and contrary to reason. According to reason, however, includes most of which Boyle would admit as above reason: (1) things that are undiscoverable yet comprehensible, (2) things that are undiscoverable but are singular things that are not satisfactorily clear like certain of God's attributes (Boyle would

---

[145] Toland, *CNM*, 28–30 [quotation, pp. 29–30].
[146] Toland, *CNM*, 35–36.
[147] Toland, *CNM*, 42.

call them incomprehensible); and (3) things that are undiscoverable and incomprehensible in terms of the manner in which they are performed. These three are, arguably, included in Locke's concessionary category of above reason. Toland, then, does not reject revelation because he denies doctrines and propositions above reason. There is nothing in the New Testament or any other acceptable revelation that actually conveys something inconceivable. Interpreters are the ones that make it appear to yield such things. In Toland's thinking, alleged doctrines and propositions that we cannot reconcile are considered contrary to reason, along with all varieties of logical contradictions.

Conclusions

In this chapter, I have endeavored to point out problems with the received narrative regarding the religious epistemologies of John Locke and John Toland and to offer a solution. In much of the literature, a comparison of John Locke's taxonomy of propositions with John Toland's taxonomy has been used to argue the relative orthodoxy of the former and the heterodoxy of the latter, despite their similar epistemological foundations. Locke accepts things above reason and Toland rejects them.

For Locke, propositions "above reason" simply refer to what Scripture reveals that is beyond the discovery of the faculty of reason. Unfortunately, he is unclear to what extent this encompasses incomprehensible doctrines. (I will explore this question more thoroughly in the next chapter.) Locke's primary difference with Toland is that whereas the latter rejects things above reason, that category only pertains to the things that Locke may or may not accept. Toland does not deny biblical revelations that surpasses our natural abilities of discovery; they are reasonable in one or more senses as far as he is concerned. He only rejects incomprehensible doctrines for which we cannot create a summative mental representation. They are not a legitimate construal from Scripture for Toland and may not be a legitimate construal from Scripture for Locke.

9
Can One Assent to The Doctrine of the Trinity According to Lockean Epistemological Principles?

John Locke never published anything explicitly accepting or denying the Christian doctrine of the Holy Trinity; yet the question of whether he was a Trinitarian or antitrinitarian has frequently drawn the attention of scholars from his day to the present. There are many reasons why Locke has been viewed as antitrinitarian. After Locke published his theological treatise, *The Reasonableness of Christianity* (*ROC*), John Edwards charged Locke with being, at the very least, a sympathizer of Socinians for not clearly promulgating positions decried by the sect.[1] What is more, after being charged by Edward Stillingfleet with having unwittingly paved the way for the Socinianism of a younger thinker (John Toland) with his *An Essay Concerning Human Understanding* (*Essay*), Locke entered into a protracted

---

[1] In order of dissemination: John Locke, *The Reasonableness of Christianity, as Delivered in the Scriptures*, 2nd ed. (London: Printed for Awnsham and John Churchil, 1696); John Edwards, *Some Thoughts Concerning the Several Causes and Occasions of Atheism, Especially in the Present Age: With Some Brief Reflections on Socinianism; and on a Late Book Entitled "The Reasonableness of Christianity as Deliver'd in the Scriptures"* (London: Printed for J. Robinson, 1695); John Locke, *A Vindication of the Reasonableness of Christianity, etc. From Mr. Edwards's Reflections* (London: Printed for Awnsham and John Churchil, 1695); John Edwards, *Socinianism Unmask'd. A Discourse Shewing the Unreasonableness of a Late Writer's Opinion Concerning the Necessity of Only One Article of Christian Faith; and of His Other Assertions in His Late Book, Entituled, The Reasonableness of Christianity as Deliver'd in the Scriptures, and in His Vindication of It. With a Brief Reply to Another (Professed) Socinian Writer* (London: Printed for J. Robinson, 1696); John Locke, *A Second Vindication of the Reasonableness of Christianity, etc.* (London: Printed for A. and J. Churchil, 1697); John Edwards, *The Socinian Creed: or, A Brief Account of the Professed Tenents and Doctrines of the Foreign and English Socinians. Wherein Is Shew'd the Tendency of Them to Irreligion and Atheism. With Proper Antidotes Against Them* (London: Printed for J. Robinson, 1697).

The Grand Jury of Middlesex determined that *ROC*, among other books, should be suppressed and its author, publishers, and printers punished. The charges are vague. A close reader of *ROC* would likely see Locke's clear dismissal of the Trinity as a fundamental article of belief for justification as a probable basis for the charges. Note, Jean Gailhard, *The Epistle and Preface to the Book against the Blasphemous Socinian Heresie Vindicated, and the Charge Therein against Socinianism, Made Good in Answer to Two Letters* (London: Printed for J. Hartley, 1698), 82–83; cf. John Yolton, *John Locke and the Way of Ideas* (London: Oxford University Press, 1956), 11.

debate with him on some finer points of theology and philosophy. During the course of the controversy, Locke charged the bishop with delivering a treatment of the doctrine of the Holy Trinity, including his discussions of person, substance, and their distinction (concepts considered crucial for the acceptance of the foundational Christian doctrine), that was unintelligible. And when offered the opportunity by the good bishop to end their debate by publicly accepting the doctrine of the Trinity, Locke, perhaps wryly, or just smartly—considering the disagreement and stir the Trinitarian controversy was causing in England—responded by asking, "Whose version?"[2]

Several issues have been raised in the scholarship concerning Locke's trinitarianism. Some think that his exclusion of the doctrine of the holy Trinity as an essential or fundamental doctrine in *ROC*, points to antitrinitarianism. Some have also noted that Locke's *Paraphrases* on Paul's Epistles is also not overtly trinitarian in places one would expect Trinitarian arguments. But, if Locke's theological project in *ROC* was truly ecumenical and irenic, then those omissions do not necessarily point to a personal antitrinitarianism. Perhaps all they point to is Locke's thoroughgoing caution. Something similar could be said regarding the charge made by some that the antitrinitarian positions held by some of his friends and associates point to Locke's own antitrinitarian leanings.[3] Some explorations into Locke's involvement in the

---

[2] In order of dissemination: John Locke, *An Essay Concerning Human Understanding*, ed. Peter H. Nidditch (Oxford: Clarendon Press, 1979); Edward Stillingfleet, *A Discourse In Vindication of the Trinity with An Answer To the Late Socinian Objections against It from Scripture, Antiquity and Reason*, 2nd ed. (London: Printed by J. H. for Henry Mortlock, 1697); John Locke, *A Letter to Edward Ld Bishop of Worcester, Concerning Some Passages Relating to Mr. Locke's Essay of Humane Understanding: In a Late Discourse of His Lordships, In Vindication of the Trinity* (London: Printed for A. and J. Churchill, 1697); Edward Stillingfleet, *The Bishop of Worcester's Answer to Mr. Locke's Letter, Concerning Some Passages Relating to His Essay of Humane Understanding, Mention'd in the Late Discourse in Vindication of the Trinity* (London: Printed by J. H. for Henry Mortlock, 1697); John Locke, *Mr. Locke's Reply to the Right Reverend the Lord Bishop of Worcester's Answer to His Letter, Concerning Some Passages Relating to Mr. Locke's Essay of Humane Understanding: In a Late Discourse of His Lordships, In Vindication of the Trinity* (London: Printed by H. Clark for A. and J. Churchill, and E. Castle, 1697); Edward Stillingfleet, *The Bishop of Worcester's Answer to Mr. Locke's Second Letter; Wherein His Notion of Ideas Is Prov'd to Be Inconsistent with It Self, and with the Articles of the Christian Faith* (London: Printed by J. H. for Henry Mortlock, 1698); John Locke, *Mr. Locke's Reply to the Right Reverend the Lord Bishop of Worcester's Answer to His Second Letter* (London: Printed by H. C. for A. and J. Churchill and E. Castle, 1699). G. A. J. Rogers, Introduction to *The Philosophy of Edward Stillingfleet*, vol. 1, ed. G. A. J. Rogers (Bristol: Thoemmes Press, 2000), vii–x. According to G. A. J. Rogers, Stillingfleet only owned the 1694 second edition of the *Essay*.

[3] Herbert McLachlan, *The Religious Opinions of Milton, Locke and Newton* (Manchester: University of Manchester Press, 1941), 71–113; John Redwood, *Reason, Ridicule, and Religion: The Age of Enlightenment in England 1660–1750*, corrected ed. (London: Thames and Hudson, 1996), 170–71; G. A. J. Rogers, "John Locke: Conservative Radical," in *The Margins of Orthodoxy: Heterodox Writing and Cultural Response, 1660–1750*, ed. Roger D. Lund (Cambridge: University of Cambridge Press, 1995), 97–118. Rogers suggests Locke became a Unitarian but held that the Trinity was too complex and sensitive an issue to discuss. John Marshall, "Locke, Socinianism, 'Socinianism,' and Unitarianism," in *English Philosophy in the Age of Locke* (Oxford: Clarendon Press, 2000), 111–182.

Trinitarian debates describe his distaste for Aristotelianism, the philosophical framework of the older orthodox doctrine of the Trinity, and his ardent adherence to Scripture as the *sole* rule of faith, at the expense of all other religious authorities—both characteristic of antitrinitarianism in the late seventeenth century.[4] Be that as it may, no one has shown that these positions and decisions necessarily lead to antitrinitarianism.

Some are not convinced labeling Locke as antitrinitarian is appropriate. Indeed, Vickers, working with evidence just noted, maintains that Locke was an "irenic trinitarian" in the fashion of his colleague Philip Van Limborch: that is, he believed in the doctrine of the Holy Trinity but, because it was unessential and not easily proven from Scripture, it should not be discussed. The key to Vickers's argument is that he puts more weight on the closeness and respect Locke had for Limborch.[5] Others note that Locke's acceptance of things above reason is an indication that Locke accepted

---

Marshall, like McLachlan, emphasizes the importance of distinguishing all the different groups called "Socinians" in the era. And they both approach the question of Locke's position on the doctrine of the Trinity through an exploration of Locke's letters, journals, works, and colleagues. Marshall's work is much more painstaking, and his cataloguing is unmatched. This is a revision of sorts to one of his conclusions in: *John Locke: Resistance, Religion and Responsibility* (Cambridge: Cambridge University Press, 1994). Diego Lucci, *John Locke's Christianity* (Cambridge: Cambridge University Press, 2022), 150, 171–73. Lucci finds Marshall's conclusions to be accurate. Robert Todd Carroll, *The Common-Sense Philosophy of Bishop Edward Stillingfleet 1635–1699* (The Hague: Martinus Nijhoff, 1975). Carroll apparently holds an uncommon position. It seems that he thinks that Locke was unaware of the effects his teaching on ideas had on substance and that this caused Locke to change his epistemology. As a result, Locke affirmed the mysteries of religion to be true, but he claimed that he (still) could not understand what they meant (96–99). Cf. Jonathan S. Marko, "Justification, Ecumenism, and Heretical Red Herrings in John Locke's *The Reasonableness of Christianity*," *Philosophy and Theology* 26, no. 2 (2014): 245–66.

[4] William S. Babcock, "A Changing of the Christian God," *Interpretation* 45 (1991): 133–46. Babcock believes that Locke's account of ideas was intended to de-normative-ize Aristotelian discourse even further. McLachlan and Marshall above and Vickers below emphasize the way that the so-called "rule of faith" came into play in Locke's rejection of the doctrine of the Trinity and/or the rejection of the necessity of it. The unmatched treatment of these theological issues and more in the Trinitarian debates (although not discussing Locke): Richard A. Muller, *Post-Reformation Reformed Dogmatic: The Rise and Development of Reformed Orthodoxy, ca. 1520–1725*, 4 vols. (Grand Rapids: Baker Academic, 2006), especially *Volume 4: The Triunity of God*. Moreover, while Muller gives considerable space to the so-called Trinitarian debates that took place in the late 1600s and early 1700s, Paul Lim treats the English context at greater length and, among other things, intends to "challenge the notion that *the* Trinitarian controversy occurred in the 1690s" (13). Paul C. H. Lim, *Mystery Unveiled: The Crisis of the Trinity in Early Modern England* (Oxford: Oxford University Press, 2012). His excellent work builds upon another commendable work: Philip Dixon, *Nice and Hot Disputes: The Doctrine of the Trinity in the Seventeenth Century* (London: T&T Clark, 2003).

[5] Jason E. Vickers, *Invocation and Assent: The Making and Remaking of Trinitarian Theology* (Grand Rapids: Eerdmans, 2008), 135–68. He borrows the term "irenic Trinitarian" from John Marshall (see above). There is also a whole host of scholars that label Locke "Socinian," "Arminian," more vaguely "anti-Calvinist," and the like. But those labels are applied in part or wholly in relation to Locke's soteriology and not theology proper. Cf. Marko, "Justification, Ecumenism, and Heretical Red Herrings."

Christian mysteries, like the Trinity. They traditionally label Locke as "orthodox." These scholars typically juxtapose Locke with the deists, framed as mystery-rejecters, and not with more traditionally "orthodox" thinkers like Edwards and Stillingfleet.[6] Moreover, there is a line of scholarship that shows that his thought was appropriated by orthodox *and* heterodox theologians alike in the next generations.[7] (There is also scholarship that recognizes the backdrop of Trinitarian debates, but does not assess Locke's orthodoxy).[8]

A sizeable body of scholars has examined Locke's treatment of ideas without much comment on his doctrine of the Trinity. They recognize the relevance of ideas to determining Locke's position on the Trinity, but they typically focus on the idea of substance, at issue in the Locke–Stillingfleet debate. While the discussion of substance in the debate is important, these treatments have potential application to the questions of whether Locke

---

[6] James Livingston, *Modern Christian Thought*, 2nd ed. (Minneapolis: Fortress Press, 2006), 1:18–21. Livingston vaguely refers to "mystery" in noting what is salvaged by Locke's acceptance of above reason things, but also notes that Locke rejects much of traditional Christianity. Claude Welch, *Protestant Christian Thought in the Nineteenth Century* (New Haven: Yale University Press, 1972), 1:35–36. He likewise mentions vaguely that Locke accepts revelation supplied "mysteries." Frederick Copleston, *A History of Philosophy*, vol. V (Westminster: The Newman Press, 1964), 69–70. Copleston claims that propositions above reason "may" include revelations not fully understandable. James O'Higgins, *Anthony Collins: The Man and His Works* (The Hague: Martinus Nijhoff, 1970), 52. O'Higgins apparently believes that Locke accepts that there are irreconcilable truths capable of being believed. William Uzgalis, "Anthony Collins," *Stanford Encyclopedia of Philosophy*, first published August 25, 2003 with substantive revisions February 23, 2009 (accessed on March 13, 2009), http://plato.stanford.edu/entries/collins, 13–14. Uzgalis admits that he is not sure what Locke and others are intending by the term "above reason." Cf. Jonathan S. Marko, *Measuring the Distance between Locke and Toland: Reason, Revelation, and Rejection during the Locke–Stillingfleet Debate* (Eugene, OR: Wipf & Stock, 2017), 66 n 6.

[7] John Yolton, *John Locke and the Way of Ideas* (London: Oxford University Press, 1956). Yolton is to be commended for reading Locke and Stillingfleet in context as best he can. There are numerous, important thinkers involved in the Trinitarian debates or the tangential debates regarding incomprehensible doctrines that are infrequently mentioned in scholarship. Yolton identifies three groups in the era with respect to the Trinitarian debates: Athanasians, less guarded traditionalists, and deists. Both the middle group and the deists appropriated Locke's thinking, but the middle group in a more serious fashion (204–08). Alan P. F. Sell, *John Locke and the Eighteenth-Century Divines: Prolegomena to Christian Apologetics* (Cardiff: University of Wales Press, 1997). This work, like Marshall's mentioned above, is also painstaking in detail and cataloguing of thinkers.

[8] Udo Thiel, "The Trinity and Human Personal Identity," in *English Philosophy in the Age of Locke* (Oxford: Clarendon Press, 2000), 217–43. Thiel's very interesting chapter distinguishes the problem of the principle of individuation from the problem of identity, two live issues during the time of the English Trinitarian debates. He puts forth an argument that Locke's theory of identity in the *Essay* has striking similarities to a theory of the individuation of persons that shows up during the debates, namely in the thought of William Sherlock. In the end, he maintains that Locke was trying to avoid touching upon the doctrine of the Trinity in his chapter on identity. Victor Nuovo, "Locke's Theology, 1694–1704," in *English Philosophy in the Age of Locke* (Oxford: Clarendon Press, 2000), 183–215. Oddly, Nuovo says nothing about Locke's position on the doctrine of the Trinity. Nuovo is elsewhere silent on the issue: Victor Nuovo, Introduction to *John Locke and Christianity: Contemporary Responses to The Reasonableness of Christianity*, ed. Victor Nuovo (Bristol: Thoemmes Press, 1997), ix–xli; Victor Nuovo, *Christianity, Antiquity, and Enlightenment: Interpretations of Locke* (New York: Springer, 2011), 25–29.

was a Trinitarian and whether his religious epistemology had room for the doctrine.[9]

So, most scholars hold that Locke was antitrinitarian although he did not find it helpful, or at least wise, to publicize his position. Some think Locke was a trinitarian, but also view him as unwilling to express his personal opinion. Still others focus on Locke's involvement in the trinitarian debates but hold back from making any adjudications regarding his orthodoxy. And some, while not expressly indicating that Locke is a trinitarian, note that his acceptance of doctrines above reason make it possible (or even likely) that he was orthodox. Then there is the large group of works on Locke's ideas that evidently unbeknownst to their authors have varying degrees of relevance to whether or not Locke's epistemological principles could support orthodox Trinitarianism. There has been surprisingly little interaction between these groups of scholars. It is with works of the latter two groups that I engage here.

In this chapter I am not so much concerned with Locke's personal position on the doctrine of the Holy Trinity and other incomprehensible doctrines but

---

[9] Works placing Locke's treatment of ideas in a historical narrative of the topic: Yolton, *John Locke and the Way of Ideas*; Alan P. F. Sell, *John Locke and the Eighteenth-Century Divines*; Keith Allen, "Ideas," in *the Oxford Handbook of British Philosophy in the Seventeenth-Century*, ed. Peter R. Antsey (Oxford: Oxford University Press, 2013), 329–48; Kenneth P. Winkler, "Perception and Ideas, Judgment" in *Cambridge History of Eighteenth-Century Philosophy*, vol. 1, ed. Knud Haakonssen (Cambridge: Cambridge University Press, 2006), 234–85; Paul Schuurman, "Locke's Logic of Ideas in Context: Content and Structure," *British Journal for the History of Philosophy* 9, no. 3 (2001): 439–65; Paul Schuurman, *Ideas, Mental Faculties and Method: The Logic of Ideas of Descartes and Locke and Its Reception in the Dutch Republic, 1630–1750* (Leiden: Brill, 2004). This latter work by Schuurman is very helpful for comparing Descartes's and Locke's clear and distinct ideas and their places in the thinkers' methods. Yolton, Allen, and Sell discuss Locke's innate ideas as do the following works: Margaret Atherton, "Locke and the Issue over Innateness," in *Locke*, ed. Vere Chappell (Oxford: Oxford University Press, 1998), 48–59; Samuel C. Rickless, "Locke's Polemic against Nativism," in *The Cambridge Companion to Locke's "Essay Concerning Human Understanding,"* ed. Lex Newman (Cambridge: Cambridge University Press, 2007), 33–66; cf. John E. Platt, "The Denial of the Innate Idea of God in Dutch Remonstrant Theology: From Episcopius to Van Limborch," in *Protestant Scholasticism in Essays in Reassessment*, ed. Carl R. Trueman and R. Scott Clark (Glasgow: Pater Noster Press, 1999), 213–26. There are numerous other works, but one in particular that is worthy of mention for its deft treatment of issues pertinent to this chapter: Jonathan Walmsley, "The Development of Lockean Abstraction," *British Journal for the History of Philosophy* 8, no. 2 (2000): 395–418. He shows how partial consideration (of complex ideas) and abstraction, though not evidently related in the *Essay*, were so early on in Lockean thought. Locke's thought on abstraction is important here as it points to the issues of Locke's apparent dismissal of the Cartesian distinction between the pure intellect and the imagination and thus the potential to assent or know something inconceivable or unimaginable. His view goes against the grain of a very able Lockean commentator: Michael Ayers, *Locke: Epistemology and Ontology*, 2 vols. (New York: Routledge, 1992), especially vol. 1, chs. 5 and 27. Many of the others above touch upon the questions of abstraction and the differences between Descartes and Locke on the pure intellect. Cf. Peter Remnant and Jonathan Bennett, Introduction to *New Essays on Human Understanding* by G. W. Leibniz, ed. and trans. Peter Remnant and Jonathan Bennett (Cambridge: Cambridge University Press, 1997), vii–xxx; Rene Descartes, *The Philosophical Writings*, 2 vols., trans. John Cottingham, Robert Stoothof, and Dugald Murdoch (Cambridge: Cambridge University Press, 1984).

rather whether or not his religious epistemology provides room for belief in them. I already gave an argument in the last chapter that Locke accepts above reason things at least in the sense that we are obligated to assent to revealed doctrines that are otherwise undiscoverable but the events or the doctrines are comprehensible. Here I will argue that while there are comments Locke makes, positions he takes, and qualifications made by critics that could be added to his published thought to make his epistemology accepting of assent to incomprehensible doctrines, including the doctrine of the Trinity, there are other positions Locke takes and appropriators' interpretations and adaptations of his thought that are incompatible with assenting to incomprehensible doctrines.[10] He could have clarified his position if he were

---

[10] The contours of this argument in its nascent stages can be found in: Marko, *Measuring the Distance*. The appropriators of Locke that I will investigate are: John Toland, *Christianity Not Mysterious: or, A Treatise Shewing, That There Is Nothing in the Gospel Contrary to Reason, Nor Above It: and That No Christian Doctrine Can Be Properly Call'd a Mystery*, 2nd ed. (London: Printed for Sam Buckley, 1696); William Stephens, *An Account of the Growth of Deism in England* (London: 1696); Richard Burthogge, *Organum Vetus and Novum: or, A Discourse of Reason and Truth. Wherein the Natural Logick Common to Mankinde Is Briefly and Plainly Described* (London: Printed for Sam. Crouch, 1678); Richard Burthogge, *An Essay upon Reason, and the Nature of Spirits* (London: Printed for John Dunton, 1694); M. R. Ayers, "Richard Burthogge and the Origins of Modern Conceptualism," in *Analytic Philosophy and the History of Philosophy*, ed. G. A. J. Rogers and Tom Sorrell (Oxford: Oxford University Press, 2005), 179–200; Margaret W. Landes, Introduction to *The Philosophical Writings of Richard Burthogge*, ed. Margaret W. Landes (Chicago: The Open Court Publishing Company, 1921), ix–xxiv. Cf. Stephen Nye, *Considerations on the Explications of the Doctrine of the Trinity, Occasioned by Four Sermons Preached by His Grace the Lord Archbishop of Canterbury, etc.* in *A Third Collection of Tracts, Proving the God and Father of Our Lord Jesus Christ, the Only True God, etc.* (1695); Stephen Nye, *A Brief History of the Unitarians, Called also Socinians. In Four Letters, Written to a Friend*, 2nd ed., corrected; with some additions (1691). Stephen Nye, *Considerations on the Explications of the Doctrine of the Trinity by Dr. Wallis, Dr. Sherlock, Dr. South, Dr. Cudworth, and Mr. Hooker as Also on the Account Given by Those That Say the Trinity Is an Unconceivable and Inexplicable Mystery: Written to a Person of Quality* (London: 1693); Stephen Nye, *The Exceptions of Mr. Edwards, in His Causes of Atheism, against the Reasonableness of Christianity, as Delivered in the Scriptures, Examin'd; and Found Unreasonable, Unscriptural, and Injurious. Also It's Clearly Proved by Many Testimonies of Holy Scripture, That the God and Father of Our Lord Jesus Christ Is the Only God and Father of Christians* (London: 1695).

Contemporaries who pointed out problems of rejecting incomprehensible things: John Tillotson, *A Sermon Concerning the Unity of the Divine Nature, and the Blessed Trinity, etc.* (London: Printed for B. Aylmer and W. Rogers, 1693); Robert Boyle, *Reflections upon a Theological Distinction. According to Which, 'tis Said, That Some Articles of Faith Are Above Reason, but Not Against Reason. In a Letter to a Friend* (London: Printed by Edw. Jones, for John Taylor, 1690); John Norris, *An Account of Reason and Faith: In Relation to the Mysteries of Christianity* (London: Printed for S. Manship, 1697); cf. Jonathan S. Marko, "Above Reason Propositions and Contradiction in the Religious Thought of Robert Boyle," *Forum Philosophicum* 19, no. 2 (2014): 227–39; Jonathan S. Marko, "Supplementing Contemporary Treatments of Doctrinal Mysteries with Largely Forgotten Voices from the Enlightenment," *Trinity Journal* 39, no. 1 (2018): 23–42. I have compressed much of what I have said about Norris and Boyle in the preceding two works and have put their thinking in a broader theological context in: Jonathan S. Marko, "Reason and Revelation in Early Modern Protestantism," *Encyclopedia of Early Modern Philosophy and Sciences*, ed. Dana Jalobeanu & Charles T. Wolfe (Cham: Springer, 2022), 1774–84; Jonathan S. Marko, "Why Locke's 'Of Power' Is Not a Metaphysical Pronouncement: Locke's Response to Molyneux's Critique," *Philosophy and Theology* 29 no. 1 (2017): 41–68; W. J. Mander, *The Philosophy of John Norris* (Oxford: Oxford University

reading his appropriators and their critics, but he did not give clarity. He knew there were issues with rejecting all incomprehensible conclusions and propositions, but none were soteriologically necessary or had enough practical importance to require his attention further.

Historical Context: Two Intertwined Controversies

English Trinitarian Debates in the Time of Locke

The Mature Doctrine
The doctrine of the Holy Trinity is one of the foundational doctrines of Christianity. It is the subject of two ecumenical creeds: the Niceno-Constantinopolitan Creed and the Athanasian Creed. The Athanasian Creed even concludes with a declaration that belief in the Trinity is necessary for eternal salvation. The doctrine was not a major subject of debate in the Reformation and was considered by many to be a fundamental doctrine. By Locke's era, there were differing opinions over in what sense, if any, the Trinity should be considered a fundamental doctrine and whether the doctrine was even tenable.

The orthodox doctrine, in Locke's era, held that God is one eternal and simple incorporeal substance. Yet, God is three persons that are consubstantial or coessential or *homoousios*. All three persons share the same substance not in a generic sense but in numeric sense. That is, the divine substance is not a secondary substance shared by three primary substances but one individual God-substance. Because all three—Father, Son, and Holy Spirit— have the same individual substance, what distinguishes them is their manner

---

Press, 2008); Peter Browne, *The Procedure, Extent, and Limits of Human Understanding*, 2nd ed. with corrections and amendments (London: Printed for William Innys, 1729); Peter Browne, *A Letter in Answer to a Book Entitled Christianity Not Mysterious, etc.* (Dublin: 1697); George Rust, *A Discourse of the Use of Reason in Matters of Religion: Shewing, That Christianity Contains Nothing Repugnant to Right Reason; Against Enthusiasts and Deists*, trans. and ann. Hen. Hallywell (London: Printed by Hen. Hills, Jun for Walter Kettilby, 1683). There are also developments in mathematics during this time that have some relevance to this conversation: Jason Socrates Bardi, *The Calculus Wars: Newton, Leibniz, and the Greatest Mathematical Clash of All Time* (New York: Thunder's Mouth Press, 2006); Carl B. Boyer, *The History of the Calculus and Its Conceptual Development: The Concepts of the Calculus* (New York: Dover Publications, Inc., 1959); Charles Henry Edwards, Jr., *The Historical Development of the Calculus* (New York: Springer Verlag, 1979); A. Rupert Hall, *Philosophers at War: The Quarrel between Newton and Leibniz* (New York: Cambridge University Press, 1980); Paul J. Nahin, *An Imaginary Tale: The Story of [the Square Root of Minus One]* (Princeton: Princeton University Press, 1998).

of subsistence or properties. The Father is eternally unbegotten, but he eternally begets or generates the Son and eternally spirates the Spirit. The Son is eternally begotten (not made) and (according to the Western Churches) also, along with the Father, spirates the Holy Spirit. The Holy Spirit, therefore, eternally proceeds from or is eternally spirated by the Father and (according to the Western Churches) the Son. What is generated and spirated are not substances but persons. What is more, the generation and spiration are eternal in that these operations are without beginning and without end. God is necessarily one in substance, and three with respect to persons. All of this is an incomprehensible mystery.[11]

Incomprehensibility of the Doctrine of the Holy Trinity
The doctrine of the Holy Trinity may be explained, as above, but it remains incomprehensible. While there were various disputes over varying examples of "Trinitarian" precursors in Greek philosophy or nature, the doctrine was acknowledged to be above reason in the sense that it was beyond our discovery and in the sense that even after revealed it was beyond our conceptualization. Whereas various analogies were used to attempt to understand or conceive of certain aspects of the doctrine there was no possibility of arriving at a single mental representation that simultaneously and appropriately maintains all the necessary propositions. There is no single, clear representation of even the following reduced formulation of the Trinity: there is one God; God is three distinct persons: Father, Son, and Holy Spirit; and each of the persons is individually and unqualifiedly the individual God-substance. These are what Robert Boyle would have most likely identified as asymmetrical or unsociable propositions or doctrines: true statements that cannot be mentally reconciled.[12]

The church has long denied that the incomprehensibility of this doctrine was rooted in a contradiction. As John Norris was quick to point out,

---

[11] This, admittedly, is a difficult doctrine to summarize. I have done my best to follow the Athanasian Creed. Cf. Richard A. Muller, s.v. "Trinitas," *Dictionary of Latin and Greek Theological Terms: Drawn Principally from Protestant Scholastic Theology*, 2nd ed. (Grand Rapids: Baker Academic, 2017); Jonathan S. Marko, "Locke–Stillingfleet Controversy," *Encyclopedia of Early Modern Philosophy and Sciences*, ed. Dana Jalobeanu and Charles T. Wolfe (Cham: Springer, 2022), 1138–44.

[12] I might have appropriated Boyle's categories not precisely in the same way that Boyle employed them, namely in the case of asymmetric or unsociable propositions and doctrines. Regarding Locke, I am calling doctrines that are comprised of irreconcilable propositions as being asymmetric or unsociable while Boyle might have been identifying each revealed proposition or doctrine as being such that is irreconcilable with another established truth (necessarily revealed or not, he does not say). The result—a perceptual irreconcilability—is still the same in both ways of looking at that which is labeled as asymmetric or unsociable.

there is a difference between something that is above reason in the merely incomprehensible sense and a contradiction: while neither can be affirmed via conceptualization, the contradiction can be proven to be wrong through conceptualization. Moreover, there was generally little expectation that all assertions regarding God would be comprehensible. We know God and discourse about God via analogy and thus cataphatically but also apophatically. We are finite creatures and He alone is infinite. In short, theologians and philosophers have historically accepted our inabilities to comprehend all the doctrines God has revealed; it is expected.

British Trinitarian Debates of the 1690s

Socinianism entered Britain in the mid-seventeenth century through the works of John Biddle, among others.[13] The Socinians maintained that the doctrine of the Holy Trinity was contrary to reason. Nor were the Socinians alone: Stephen Nye writes of the kinship of the Socinians and Arians. While they both acknowledged that God is only one person, they differed over their interpretations of the Son and the Holy Spirit. "This difference notwithstanding, because they agree in the principle Article, that there is *but one God,* or *but one who is God*; both Parties (*Socinians* and *Arians*) are called *Unitarians,* and esteem of one another as Christians and true Believers."[14] In 1652, Parliament ordered all copies of the Racovian Catechism (the catechism of the Socinians) to be burned.

There were also a variety of developments in philosophy that negatively affected the steadiness of the doctrine:

> The new philosophies of the seventeenth century tended to detach themselves from traditional conceptions of essence, substance, and individuality and, in so doing, critiqued not only the older philosophy but also the theology that had grown attached to it and had reached, during the course of centuries, a linguistic concordat with traditional philosophical vocabulary.[15]

---

[13] For example, John Biddle, *The Apostolic and True Opinion Concerning the Holy Trinity* (London: 1691). A series of Biddle's works were republished in the late 1600s. This work was originally from 1653. John Biddle, *XII Arguments Drawn Out of Scripture: Wherein the Commonly-Received Opinion Touching the Deity of the Holy Spirit Is Clearly and Fully Refuted: To Which Is Prefixed a Letter Tending to the Same Purpose, Written to a Member of Parliament* (London: 1647).

[14] Stephen Nye, *A Brief History*, 12.

[15] Muller, *PRRD*, vol. 4, 99.

The theological vocabulary that had long been attached to Aristotelian categories had become outmoded and associated with significantly different concepts. Muller cites the new developments in philosophy and "altered patterns and models of exegesis" as transforming Christian doctrine, and he asserts that this transformation "is nowhere more apparent than in the doctrine of the Trinity."[16] What is more, movement away from or discomfort with tradition—and thus the ecumenical creeds—was well underway by the time of the start of the British Trinitarian debates of the 1690s. The Trinitarian creeds were no longer so quickly taken for granted as being correct; there was a clearer demarcation between the authoritative text and the tradition of the church in some Protestant quarters.[17]

The common narrative of the British debates typically starts with the Socinians, although there were numerous other issues fueling it. One thinker who is often inserted into the narrative is the Cambridge Platonist Ralph Cudworth (d. 1688), who fashioned the doctrine of the Holy Trinity after the Platonic One and its emanations, resulting in a tritheistic or Arian-esque view of God. Stephen Nye's publishing career and attack on the doctrine of the Trinity was well underway by 1690. In the same year disputations were held at Exeter College over Arthur Bury's 1690 publication of *The Naked Gospel*, which was condemned by many as a heretical tract. The main contributors to the ensuing Trinitarian debates beyond Nye are William Sherlock, Robert South, and John Wallis.[18] To combat the Socinian charge that the doctrine of the Holy Trinity was not contrary to reason, Sherlock attempted to show that the doctrine was possible. He conceived of each person of the Trinity as consisting of three distinct minds who are mutually and exhaustively conscious of one another's minds, wherein lays their unity. Robert South, who upheld the traditional the doctrine of the Trinity with traditional Aristotelian terminology, responded to Sherlock, which resulted in a back-and-forth between the two thinkers.[19] The Cambridge mathematician John Wallis, who

---

[16] Muller, *PRRD*, vol. 4, 120.

[17] Vickers, *Invocation and Assent*; Muller *PRRD*, vol. 4; Paul C. H. Lim, *Mystery Unveiled*, 11–12. Lim writes: "The antitrinitarian critique of the unbiblical nature of the Trinity was couched in its desire to complete the Reformation" (11). "Thus a crucial component of completing the work of the Reformation was to completely dismantle the Babylonian ziggurat. Their battle cry can be summarized as the three Ts: Tradition, Transubstantiation, and Trinity" (12).

[18] For example, Nye, *Considerations on . . . Dr. Wallis, etc.*; Vickers, *Invocation and Assent*; Muller, *PRRD*, vol. 4; Redwood, *Reason, Ridicule, and Religion*, ch. 7; Dixon, *Nice and Hot Disputes*, ch. 4.

[19] In order of dissemination: William Sherlock, *A Vindication of the Holy and Ever Blessed Trinity, and the Incarnation of the Son of God. Occasioned by the Brief Notes on the Creed of St. Athanasius, and the Brief History of the Unitarians, or Socinians, and Containing an Answer to Both* (London: W. Rogers, 1690); Robert South, *Animadversions upon Dr. Sherlock's Book, Entituled A Vindication of the Holy and Blessed Trinity, etc. Together with a More Necessary Vindication of that Sacred, and Prime*

had published writings focused on explaining the doctrine earlier, also responded to Sherlock. His explanation, however, strikes of modalism and not the Athanasian Creed.[20]

There were numerous other disputants entering the lists. By 1693, Nye identified several different explanations of the doctrine of the Holy Trinity coming from the so-called Trinitarians. In his taxonomy, he notes first "*the Trinity according to Tully*, or the *Ciceronian Trinity*; which maketh the three Divine Persons, to be nothing but three *Conceptions* of God." This corresponds to Wallis's explanation and amounts to modalism. He then describes Sherlock's explanation as "the *Cartesian* Trinity, or *the Trinity according to Des Cartes*: which maketh three Divine Persons, and three Infinite *Minds*, *Spirits* and *Beings*, to be but one God; because they are mutually, and internally, and universally *conscious to each others Thoughts*." The third indexed version of the doctrine of the Trinity by Nye is connected with Cudworth's explanation: "The Third is *the Trinity of Plato*, or the *Platonick* Trinity; maintained by Dr. *Cudworth*;" "This Trinity is of the three Divine Co-eternal Persons, whereof the second and third are subordinate or inferior to the first; in Dignity, Power, and all other Qualities, except only Duration." They are but one God only in the sense that they are rooted in the Father. Their oneness is a generic oneness. The fourth explanation or version of the Trinity is what Nye calls "*the Trinity according to Aristotle*, or the *Aristotelian* or *Peripatetick* Trinity" or the "*Reformed* Trinity, and the Trinity of *the Schools*." This he identifies with South's explanation. Here, "the Divine Persons are one God, because they have the same *Numerical* Substance . . . and tho each of the

---

Article of the Christian Faith from His New Notions, and False Explications of It. Humbly Offered to His Admirers, and to Himself the Chief of Them. (London: Printed for Randall Taylor, 1693); William Sherlock, *A Defence of Dr. Sherlock's Notion of a Trinity in Unity, in Answer to the Animadversions upon His Vindication of the Doctrine of the Holy and Ever Blessed Trinity. With a Post-Script Relating to the Calm Discourse of a Trinity in the Godhead. In a Letter to a Friend.* (London: Printed for W. Rogers, 1694); Robert South, *Tritheism Charged upon Dr. Sherlock's New Notion of the Trinity and the Charge Made Good, In Answer to the Defense of the Said Notion against the Animadversions upon Dr. Sherlock's Book, Entituled, A Vindication of the Doctrine of the Holy and Ever Blessed Trinity, etc.* (London: Printed for John Whitlock, 1695); cf. Nye, *Considerations on . . . Dr. Wallis, etc*, 10–13; Thiel, "The Trinity and Human Personal Identity," 221–24; Muller, *PRRD*, vol. 4, 123–29.

[20] John Wallis, *The Doctrine of the Blessed Trinity Briefly Explained, in a Letter to a Friend* (London: Printed for Tho. Parkhurst, 1690); John Wallis, *Three Sermons Concerning the Sacred Trinity* (London: Printed for Tho. Parkhurst, 1691); John Wallis, *An Answer to Dr. Sherlock's Examination of the Oxford Decree: In a Letter from a Member of that University, to His Friend in London* (London: Printed, by M. Whitlock, 1696); John Wallis, *Eight Letters Concerning the Blessed Trinity*, new ed., ed. Thomas Flintoff (London: Printed for J. G. & F. Rivington, J. H. Parker, and T. Sowler, 1840); cf. Nye, *Considerations on . . . Dr. Wallis, etc*, 7–10; Thiel, "The Trinity and Human Personal Identity," 221; Muller, *PRRD*, vol. 4, 128–29.

three Persons is Almighty, All-knowing, and most Good; yet 'tis *by one individual and self-same Power, Knowledge and Goodness, in Number.*" Although noting other variations within these versions, the other major version of the Trinity that he describes is "*the Trinity of the Mobile*; or the Trinity held by the common People, and by those ignorant or lazy Doctors, who . . . tell you in short, that the Trinity is an unconceivable, and therefore an inexplicable *Mystery*; and that those are as much in fault, who presume to explain it, as those who oppose it."[21]

Brief Remarks upon the Locke–Stillingfleet Debate
The debate[22] between Stillingfleet, Locke, and Toland stands in significant relation to the main Trinitarian controversy. Their debate began when Stillingfleet accused Locke of unwittingly paving the way for the heresy found in the pages of John Toland's *Christianity Not Mysterious*. Stillingfleet thought that Toland was more consistent with Locke's fundamental epistemological principles found in the *Essay* than was Locke. Stillingfleet's reading of the *Essay*, furthered by his misreading of Toland, was that one could only reason about clear and distinct ideas; and that ruled out reasoning about substance; and that ruled out the doctrine of the Holy Trinity. Stillingfleet groups Toland and Locke among the thinkers of a new way of thinking or the new way by ideas. He thinks that Locke had no ill-intent, however, based on his inconsistency in his seeming approval of the immaterial human soul and likely Locke's seeming acceptance of so-called above reason propositions and doctrines. Locke was nettled by the censure and thus brought the controversy with the good bishop from smolder to flame. Ultimately, Locke would produce three more books out of this controversy. Stillingfleet would produce only two additional responses to Locke, prior to the former's death in 1698. Toland excused himself from this battle most likely because he was satisfactorily defended by Locke, was under attack by numerous scholarly assailants, and sustained legal problems due to his book.

There are a few reasons that the Locke–Stillingfleet debate has not received sufficient attention in accounts of the Trinitarian debates. For one, the debate is prolix and the doctrine of the Holy Trinity is only one of the many philosophical and theological notions discussed. What is more, not much can be gleaned from Locke beyond clarifications of his epistemology in the *Essay*,

---

[21] Nye, *Considerations on . . . Dr. Wallis, etc*, 10–12.
[22] For longer treatments of this brief narrative: Marko, *Measuring the Distance*, ch. 2; Marko, "Locke–Stillingfleet Controversy."

much of which can be inferred there, and his critiques of Stillingfleet's own writings. He is eminently cautious, not giving more than beyond that. Locke and Toland, forever associated in histories of philosophy due to Stillingfleet, are often juxtaposed in studies of the rise of deism or natural religion in England. In these narratives, it is Stillingfleet who fades into the background. Toland, who was originally labeled a Socinian by Stillingfleet, gets labeled by others as a deist and is known for being the first of a notable group of deists who adapted Lockean epistemology. This epistemological issue connects with the Trinitarian debate and the related debate concerning things above reason.

Ideas and Incomprehensibility

Introduction to the So-Called Way of Ideas

The term "idea" drew much attention in the seventeenth and eighteenth centuries as philosophers continued to move away from Aristotelianism. A precise and agreed upon definition or conception of ideas, however, eluded philosophers for generations. The term consistently implied mental images. While some of the major philosophers could not agree upon the details, they were generally united in their determination that the newer, idea-based philosophies of the relationship of the mind to the world, in which these varied definitions of ideas were ensconced, were preferable to Aristotelian scholastic philosophical teachings on the same relationship.[23] They denied that the human intellect "can penetrate to the simple core or essence of the substance," as the Aristotelians supposed.[24] Also, the thinkers of the way of ideas frequently faulted Aristotelianism for a peculiar indirectness of reasoning, such as the syllogism, that was not natural to humans. Richard Burthogge characterized scholasticism as being too heavily reliant on Aristotle and limited to artificial logic.[25] In response, Burthogge promulgated a "Natural Logick, that of plain and illiterate men, of which I designe to discourse, is the natural method of Reasoning."[26] Locke carries this same sentiment about his own works. When Stillingfleet styled Locke's *Essay* as Locke's

---

[23] Cf. Yolton, *John Locke and the Way of Ideas*; Allen, "Ideas"; Winkler, "Perception and Ideas." Winkler gives the most detailed perusal of the scholastic position that the so-called way of ideas opposed.
[24] Ayers, *Locke: Epistemology and Ontology*, 1:29–30.
[25] Cf. Muller, *PRRD*, vol. 1. He cautions the wary of identifying scholasticism and Aristotelianism.
[26] Burthogge, *Organum Vetus*, 43–44.

"new way by ideas," Locke responded by saying there is nothing new about it, "For I think it will not be doubted, that Men always perform'd the Actions of Thinking, Reasoning, Believing, and Knowing, just after the same manner that they do now."[27]

The philosopher most credited with having given the way of ideas its impetus was René Descartes, whose views on ideas would be debated by Hobbes, Malebranche, Arnauld, and Locke. According to Descartes, "Some of my thoughts are as it were the images of things, and it is only in these cases that the term 'idea' is strictly appropriate—for example when I think of a man, or a chimera, or the sky, or an angel, or God." There are other "thoughts" that are called ideas, but not in the strict sense. These include such forms as volitions and emotions that occur when a particular idea is the object of our thoughts.[28] Moreover, he defends his assertion that we can legitimately have ideas of immaterial beings like God and angels:

> [I]t is easy for him [a critic] to prove that there can be no proper idea of an angel or of God. But I make it quite clear in several places throughout the book [*Meditations on First Philosophy*], and in this passage in particular, that I am taking the word 'idea' to refer to whatever is immediately perceived by the mind. For example, when I want something, or am afraid of something, I simultaneously perceive that I want, or am afraid; and this is why I count volition and fear among my ideas. I used the word 'idea' because it was the standard philosophical term used to refer to the forms of perception belonging to the divine mind, even though we recognize that God does not possess any corporeal imagination.[29]

Whereas we may have no "proper" idea of God, it still is the idea of that which we cannot perceive directly with our faculties.

Locke's *Essay* offers a pertinent example of the so-called way of ideas. For him, ideas are the objects of our mind. We always have ideas in our mind. If we are thinking, we are thinking about ideas.[30] All of our ideas are derived from sensation of the outer world and reflections of the operations of ourselves that register in the mind. We have the ability to create new ideas, but

---

[27] Locke, *Mr. Locke's Reply . . . Answer to His Letter*, 72–73; cf. Marko, *Measuring the Distance*, 51.
[28] Descartes, *Philosophical Writings*, 2:25–26.
[29] Descartes, *Philosophical Writings*, 2:127.
[30] Ayers rightly notes that "Aristotle himself asserted roundly that there is no thought without images." Ayers, *Locke: Epistemology and Ontology*, 1:27.

they are always combinations and abstractions from what we have perceived. Locke's way of ideas has been identified as being a two-stage way of ideas. First, our faculties are understood as aids in obtaining ideas and constructing further ideas, ideas being the building blocks of the second stage. There is an emphasis on clear and distinct ideas and the understanding faculty has an elevated importance. The second stage involves applying the reasoning faculties in pursuit of knowledge. The process is akin to geometrical proofs, creating any number of mental links, as opposed to a reliance on syllogisms.[31]

The Way of Ideas and Incomprehensibility

There are two points of disagreement among proponents of the way of ideas that bear upon the question of whether or not we can accept incomprehensible propositions and doctrines. One is whether we ought to posit something like the distinction between the imagination and pure understanding or intellect as Descartes had done. The other is in what ways or to what degree must a proposition (or revealed doctrine) or idea under consideration be clear to be the object of legitimate and reasonable assent.[32]

In *Meditations on First Philosophy*, Descartes discusses the difference between the "imagination" and "pure understanding." He notes that with his "mind's eye" he can imagine a triangle perfectly or even a pentagon. And while he cannot so imagine the thousand sides of a chiliagon, he understands what a chiliagon is just like he understands what a triangle is.[33] He thus makes the following statement to posit the difference between the imagination and pure understanding:

> So the difference between this mode of thinking [imagination] and pure understanding may simply be this: when the mind understands, it in some way turns toward itself and inspects one of the ideas which are within it; but when it imagines, it turns toward the body and looks at something in the body which conforms to an idea understood by the mind or perceived by the senses.[34]

---

[31] Schuurman, "Locke's Logic of Ideas." Cf. Schuurman, *Ideas, Mental Faculties*, 2.4: "Locke's point that syllogisms are based merely on words and that Aristotelian philosophers fail to check the correspondence between words and things, had already been made by the latter [Bacon and Descartes]."

[32] Schuurman, *Ideas, Mental Faculties*, 25. Here Schuurman discusses how ideas, and not just propositions, can be true and false in Descartes and Locke. I am a bit puzzled by his statement that clarity and distinctness do not concern propositions as a requirement of truth but only the constituent ideas. The problem with the distinction is that propositions are envisioned, whether they are mental or verbal. They are the instructions of creating further specific ideas.

[33] Descartes, *Philosophical Writings*, 2:50–51.

[34] Descartes, *Philosophical Writings*, 2:51.

Descartes here makes an assertion that gave many philosophers pause. He appears to be saying that there are ideas that we understand but cannot conjure in our imagination. In other words, there is a hidden structure to thought.[35] Kenneth Winkler expresses the typical rejection of this distinction in what follows: "Some philosophers, many of them materialists, denied the existence of the pure intellect; all our ideas, they contended, are ideas of sense, or ideas concocted by sense-based memory and imagination with the power to recall ideas of sense and combine them in new ways."[36] Locke is frequently numbered among those who deny the pure intellect or pure understanding of Descartes. He is often referred to as a type of "imagist." Michael Ayers asserts that "it is easy to find passages in which Locke was at least implicitly engaging in the dispute as to the need to postulate pure intellect over and above sense and imagination."[37] Not all are convinced that Locke is a thorough-going imagist.[38]

The other issue for which Descartes is well known is the precise meaning of "clear and distinct perceptions" and its appropriate employment as a criterion of assent. John Norris, a Platonist of sorts, self-professed Cartesian, and one-time opponent of John Locke, catalogues how Descartes's application of clear and distinct perceptions is differently interpreted and argues for what he thinks is Descartes' intended application.[39] Norris writes, "It must therefore be admitted by all what the Philosophers of the *Cartesian way* so earnestly stand and Contend for, that Clearness of Perception is the great Rule and *Criterion* of Truth, so far that whatever we do clearly and distinctly perceive to be true is really in it self True." He notes that some use this criterion to argue that human understanding or reason is to be the measure of truth. In other words, if one cannot conceive of something or some proposition or

---

[35] Cf. Atherton, "Locke and the Issue over Innateness," 58.
[36] Winkler, "Perception and Ideas," 237–38.
[37] Ayers, *Locke: Epistemology and Ontology*, 1:47.
[38] Allen, "Ideas," 342.
[39] Schuurman, *Ideas, Mental Faculties*, 2.4. He rightly notes that all ideas are perceptions but not all perceptions are ideas. Perceptions can correspond to ideas or propositions. Descartes, *Philosophical Writings*, 2:207–08. Here is Descartes's definition of clear and distinct perceptions: "*What is meant by a clear perception, and by a distinct perception.* Indeed that there are very many people who in their entire lives never perceive anything with sufficient accuracy to enable them to make a judgment about it with certainty. A perception which can serve as the basis for a certain and indubitable judgment needs to be not merely clear but also distinct. I call a perception 'clear' when it is present and accessible to the attentive mind—just as we say that we see something clearly when it is present to the eye's gaze and stimulates it with a sufficient degree of strength and accessibility. I call a perception 'distinct' if, as well as being clear, it is so sharply separated from all other perceptions that it contains within itself only what is clear."

doctrine one cannot believe it. Norris hastens to add that none of the great authors had this intent.[40]

Norris devotes an entire chapter to the defense of a closely related "Cartesian maxim"—"we are to assent only to what is clear [and distinct] and evident"—circulating in the era, from the abuse of mis-interpreters and mis-appliers of it.[41] He notes that many accuse Descartes of being a Socinian or his philosophy being an introduction to Socinianism because some understand that maxim to indicate that we are not or cannot assent to propositions that are incomprehensible as the Socinians maintain.[42] He argues that Descartes's maxim's true intent is to help us avoid error in the application of our mental faculties. Incomprehensibility of a claim, assertion, or doctrine is an indication that we should be cautious and suspend our assent until there appears a motive from reason or authority to assent.[43] More to the point, a doctrine may have obscure or unclear internal evidence or manifest difficulties in creating a clear idea of the thing proposed and its truth, but it may have clear external evidence.[44] In Norris's words:

> But if by Evidence here be Meant Evidence at large, abstracting from Internal or External, and the Sense be that we are to assent to nothing but what has some Evidence or other, either Internal or External, or what is some way or other evident to us, and what we see plainly to be true by a Light shining from within or from without, in short, what we have one way or other sufficient ground or Reason to assent to, then the Maxim is undoubtedly true, and will hold Universally, not only in Matters of Reason, but also in Matters of Faith too.[45]

In short, we will find ourselves obligated to assent to some incomprehensible natural assertions or revealed assertions and doctrines because of external evidence. The statement or assertion under consideration may be very difficult to fathom, but the evidence and arguments pointing to that conclusion are clearly perceivable.[46] The true Cartesians do not reject the

---

[40] Norris, *An Account*, 143–44 [quotation, p. 143].
[41] Cf. Ayers, *Locke: Epistemology and Ontology*, 1:34. He indicates that this is a deviation from Descartes, founding knowledge upon the senses alone.
[42] Norris, *An Account*, 252–56, 277–81.
[43] Norris, *An Account*, 256.
[44] Norris, *An Account*, 271–72.
[45] Norris, *An Account*, 272.
[46] Norris, *An Account*, "Chapter 1: Of Reason."

incomprehensible propositions simply because they are incomprehensible. They want to ascertain as much internal clarity or clarity of the perception and concomitant ideas proposed, but after that, they must also be attentive to the external evidence. Norris lays out a number of examples of the incomprehensible propositions that we are compelled to believe in the natural and supernatural realm based on natural reasoning or reasoning with divine revelation.

It is difficult to envision Norris's opponents, who reject incomprehensible perceptions, defeating him through Descartes's own words. For instance, in the "Third Meditation," Descartes asserts that his idea of God "is the truest and most clear and distinct of all my ideas." Considering our inability to properly conceive or ideate an immaterial being and infinitude, one will best infer that there is something else other than the utter clarity of the contrived image that makes it the truest and clearest and most distinct of all his ideas.[47]

Epistemological Limitations and Ideas

There are other thinkers in the era, who intersect with the way of ideas tradition, who wrestled over the issue of whether or not God gave us epistemological limits. Robert Boyle is one. Through his scientific and theological explorations, he readily points out the need to assent to incomprehensible propositions. A thinker of the era who is adverse to the reality of such things is the noted Socinian thinker Stephen Nye.

Robert Boyle, who could be considered part of the "way of ideas" tradition, has some views on ideas (or notions or conceptions) and propositions that generally comport with those of Norris. The two thinkers largely agree on the ridiculousness of dismissing anything natural or revealed simply on the basis that it is incomprehensible, although they do disagree on how one should label different sorts of propositions and ideas. Boyle thinks that notions and propositions that we could not discover and were delivered by divine revelation are "above reason." It does not matter if they are comprehensible or not. The necessity of their divine revelation to come to our attention and assent is the key characteristic that earns them the label "above reason." In other words, they are such that it would be highly unlikely to

---

[47] Descartes, *The Philosophical Writings*, 2:32. The translators and editors give a footnote indicating that for him, "one can know or understand something without fully grasping it. They record an excerpt from one of his letters to Mersenne: "just as we can touch a mountain but not put our arms around it. To grasp something is to embrace it in one's thought; to know something, it suffices to touch it with one's thought."

arrive at these propositions through our own natural reasoning, but if, hypothetically, we did, we would have no reason to assent to them through natural considerations. Whereas Norris thinks the key factor that determines if something should be labeled "above reason" is its incomprehensibility, Boyle not only divides above reason ideas and propositions into comprehensible and incomprehensible sub-groupings, but goes further, dividing up the incomprehensible sort into three non-mutually exclusive types: (1) not clearly conceivable by our understanding (such as the infiniteness and perfections of the divine nature); (2) inexplicable by us (such as the manner how God creates a rational soul or how the immaterial soul acts on the material body); or (3) asymmetrical or unsociable things where we see not how to reconcile them like Divine prescience and human free choice.[48] Moreover, for Boyle ideas and propositions should be considered contrary to reason if they yield a logical contradiction or oppose some surer conclusion arrived at based on right reason or revelation.

Boyle has some helpful discussions regarding the absurdity of rejecting incomprehensible revealed propositions and ideas. Incomprehensible is a relative and not an absolute description. That is, there are beings, like angels and God, with higher intellects that comprehend what our minds can only touch upon. Of God and His relationship to the so-called incomprehensible ideas and propositions, he writes: "we must ascribe to him a perfect Understanding, and boundless Knowledge. This being supposed, it ought not to be denied, that a Superior Intellect may both comprehend several Things that we cannot; and discern such of them to be congruous to the fixt and eternal *Idea's* of Truth ... as dim-sighted Mortals are apt to suspect, or to think, to be separately False."[49] What is more, Boyle points out that thinkers have run into queries whose answers go beyond our conceptual abilities. For instance, he notes that there is an on-going debate whether quantity is endlessly divisible.[50] And he notes a number of assertions made in natural theology. All of these elude the comprehension of our minds (even when discussed by Scripture).[51]

---

[48] Again, it is unclear how Boyle intended the reader to understand asymmetric things. That is, it is unclear if he intended individual, revealed notions to be labeled as such or the grouping of irreconcilable propositions to be labeled as such. Either way, the result is the same: one is unable to envision the multiple truths in one coherent picture.
[49] Boyle, *Reflections upon*, 25.
[50] Boyle, *Reflections upon*, 26.
[51] Boyle, *Reflections upon*, 28.

On the other end of the spectrum of the way of ideas are those who only assent to that which they can comprehend. Peter Browne, Bishop of Cork and Ross, makes the following claims about some of these heterodox thinkers in his era:

> The whole sum and substance of the Deist's and Freethinker's reasoning may be resolved into this. You must grant, say they, that we neither know nor believe any thing but what we have some kind of Idea or Conception of; and you must grant likewise, that the Christian mysteries are incomprehensible, that is, that we have no Idea at all of them; therefore we can neither know nor believe them. And pursuant to this, they every where oppose the Certainty and Evidence of Sense and Reason, and the clear and distinct knowledge we have of *Their* proper Objects; to the Uncertainty, and Obscurity, and Unconceivableness of Revelation and Mystery.[52]

In other words, the deists and free thinkers reject anything as incomprehensible for which they are unable to frame a singular, but complex, idea as representation. If there is no summative idea that can be mentally envisioned, there can be no assent. In theory, while they acknowledge one cannot assent to the incomprehensible doctrine or proposition because there can be no assent without a summative idea or mental representation, there is a difference of opinion regarding whether or not there are some things beyond our ken.

Nye's writings involving assent and ideas appear to be as far from Boyle's as one can fathom. Nye thinks that it is acceptable to say that we are able to conceive of God's attributes and thus our minds are infinite, at least in this respect.[53] What is more, in reply to Tillotson's sermons in defense of the Trinity, he writes, "[Tillotson] utterly mistakes, in Thinking, that we deny the Articles of the *New Christianity*, or *Athanasian Religion*, because there are *Mysteries*, or because we do not comprehend them; we deny 'em, *because we do comprehend them*; we have a *clear and distinct Perception*, that they are not *Mysteries*, but Contradictions, Impossibilities, and pure Non-sense." Mysteries, in Nye's economy are intelligible secrets that had been secret, but

---

[52] Browne, *The Procedure, Extent, and Limits*, 29; cf. 39 "They rigorously confine the Understanding within the narrow bounds of *direct* and *immediate* objects of Sense and Reason; and will not suffer the Mind of Man in any one Instance to reach about the strictly literal and immediate acceptation of Words." Browne's attacks on Toland are perhaps two of the foremost reasons that the latter is so often identified as a deist as opposed to Socinian.

[53] Nye, *Considerations . . . Occasioned by Four Sermons*, 7–8.

that were revealed in the "*Gospel-Times*."[54] Notions like God's attributes, again, are not mysteries because we have a clear, distinct, and adequate conception of them, i.e., we can comprehend them.[55] But, the so-called incomprehensible mysteries are incomprehensible because they are contradictions or impossibilities.[56] He persistently resists, however, the claims that he and his brethren disregard anything that cannot be understood. In a response to John Edwards, Nye claims that Edwards's teaching of the Trinity boils down to the following contradiction: "That one God is three Gods, that the Unity of God is a *Trinity* of Gods."[57] Despite his protests, the description of his religious epistemology by Browne and Tillotson seems to be correct.

Important Qualification to Incomprehensibility and Ideas
There is an important difference between calling both the chiliagon, with all the difficulties of envisioning one, and the doctrine of the Trinity incomprehensible, other than the overarching idea of the former is naturally conjured and the latter is divinely revealed. It is true we are unable to form a clear and distinct imagined idea, or image or picture, of either of them, but that is for different reasons. The chiliagon's incomprehensibility is rooted in a particular natural complexity. Our minds have the inability to picture a figure that we are certain has one thousand sides. We could conjure an image of one in our minds but after a certain number of sides the same obscure idea could stand for a polygon with one hundred sides, 101 sides, two hundred sides, etc. If, however, someone drew a chiliagon, we could count the sides. Locke points all this out. So, there could be a person who could immediately distinguish the difference between a polygon with 999 sides and a chiliagon just like the typical person can immediately distinguish a triangle and a square. By contrast the incomprehensibility of doctrine of the Trinity is rooted in God's transcendence. No one with human faculties, even the chimerical brilliant human above, could imagine the Trinity. Two contemporary theologians, Boyer and Hall, to distinguish between these two types of incomprehensibility would call the former an extensive mystery—"quantitative inexhaustibility, a magnitude or an internal complexity that puts some proposed objects of knowledge out of reach"—and the latter a dimensional

---

[54] Nye, *Considerations . . . Occasioned by Four Sermons*, 4.
[55] Nye, *Considerations . . . Occasioned by Four Sermons*, 7.
[56] Admittedly, he shrewdly picks out aspects of Tillotson's sermons that are problematic and not carefully written.
[57] Nye, *Exceptions of Mr. Edwards*, 19; cf. Edwards, *Causes of Atheism*, 68.

mystery—"*an unclassifiable superabundance* that transcends but does not invalidate rational exploration."[58]

To draw on a modern analogy, if we were Flatlanders,[59] who could only perceive two-dimensional objects, we would know the difference between a circle and a rectangle. We could even observe a chiliagon and identify it as such once we counted its sides. Turning away from it, we could not hold its true shape in our minds. But there exist three-dimensional objects beyond our comprehension but which can "reveal" themselves. If a cylinder were to pass lengthwise through Flatland we would see a circle appear that would last for the amount of time it took for the cylinder to pass through the plane. If it were to pass through again but with a 90-degree turn before doing so, we would see a line that expands widthwise until a certain point and then contracts widthwise. We know that circle and rectangle are different shapes, but when a prophet were to tell us that those shapes were produced by a singular higher dimensional "object," we are perplexed. But we are perplexed in a different way than when we encounter a chiliagon with its one thousand sides, which we cannot certainly picture all together and in their actual arrangement with accuracy; we can at least count them.[60]

So, even if one were to posit something like the pure intellect, it does not necessarily mean that one would understand or in some unconscious way grasp incomprehensible doctrines of the dimensional variety, for which there is clear evidence (according to Norris). The pure intellect and assent to incomprehensible dimensional doctrines need not be related in a thinker's epistemology. One might posit a pure intellect that has only to do with mysteries of extension. One might claim that we can assent to that which is potentially and in theory imaginable but not to that which, based on our current faculties, will never be imagined. While this is just one distinction, many more could be propounded.[61]

The primary concern of what follows is the issue of whether or not Locke's epistemology allowed for assent to incomprehensible, "dimensional" claims

---

[58] Steven D. Boyer and Christopher A. Hall, *The Mystery of God: Theology for Knowing the Unknowable* (Grand Rapids: Baker Academic, 2012), 8–13.
[59] Edwin Abbott, *Flatland: A Romance of Many Dimensions* (London: 1884).
[60] Cf. Boyer and Hall, *The Mystery of God*, 11.
[61] For instance, while some issues in mathematics and physics are inconceivable, it is not clear to me that they should all be considered extensive mysteries. For instance, there is a big difference between a chiliagon that could potentially be envisioned and i (the square root of negative one). Even more so, the idea of dimensions beyond the ones that we experience on a daily basis are incomprehensible. For instance, I know what five is, but I cannot possibly (no human even could potentially with present-day faculties) envision the speculated fifth dimension of some theoretical physicists.

rather than whether there was something like the pure intellect by which we might claim to understand something that is in some way incomprehensible, which *may* only have to do with naturally reasoned assertions. Locke's dislike of claiming knowledge of a moral principle when one has never consciously held the idea makes exploring that route highly doubtful.

Drawing on the above distinction between an extensive mystery and a dimensional mystery and its corresponding analogy, there are those in the era who accept dimensional mysteries, and those who reject dimensional mysteries, either because there is nothing beyond this dimension or because perception is the main rule of the epistemological game. Spinoza arguably thinks, and sometimes even Nye gives the impression that he thinks, God and humans are in the same dimensional space, while others like Toland and Locke, both of whom will be treated below, clearly indicate that there are dimensional issues beyond our comprehension. For instance, both acknowledge that how miracles are performed is incomprehensible, but they say the fact or phenomena of the miracle is comprehensible—it is observable after all![62]

Knowledge of and Assent to the Incomprehensible in Locke?

Knowledge and Ideas

Foundational to Locke's epistemology is his notion of ideas. This topic occupies numerous chapters in the *Essay* either directly or indirectly. Ideas are the subject matter or the objects of knowledge and reasoning. According to Locke, they are all from experience of external, sensible objects or from reflection on the internal operations of our minds.[63] The primary categories of ideas are simple and complex. Simple ideas pertain to sensible qualities of external objects like hard, bitter, sweet, red, and yellow and internal operations of the mind like thinking, doubting, and willing.[64] The mind is wholly

---

[62] Benedict de Spinoza, "Miracles," in *Theological-Political Treatise*, ed. Jonathan Israel, trans. Michael Silverthorne and Jonathan Israel (New York: Cambridge University Press, 2007), 81–96. Locke, even if he did reject assent to the incomprehensible, mentions Paul's epistemological assent to the third heaven and that the Apostle could not communicate anything of it to us. Locke, *Essay*, IV.xviii.3. Locke and Toland clearly maintain that miracles had happened.
[63] Locke, *Essay*, II.i.1–4.
[64] Locke, *Essay*, II.ii.

passive in the reception of simple ideas.[65] Complex ideas are combinations of simple ideas of objects in front of us, complex internal operations (e.g., vacillating), or abstract ideas (e.g., justice). The mind must often apply its will regarding complex ideas. As a case in point, a trained investigator on the scene of a crime will see more detail than would a person looking at the exact same scene.[66]

Locke also offers a detailed description of ways to categorize ideas beyond the simple and complex distinction: clear versus obscure, distinct versus confused, real versus fantastical, adequate versus inadequate, and true versus false. Only the first two need explanation here. These two couplets' antipodes often go hand-in-hand: clear and distinct ideas versus confused and obscure. Locke writes, "As a *clear Idea* is that whereof the Mind has a full and evident perception . . . so a *distinct Idea* is that wherein the Mind perceives a difference from all other; and a *confused Idea* is such an one, as is not sufficiently distinguishable from another, from which it ought to be different."[67] So, clarity, obscurity, distinctness, and confusedness are relative labels. An idea's clarity—the relative vividness, number, and order of its simple ingredients[68]—will typically make it distinct from other ideas, most importantly ones that are similar; but, when that is not the case, the idea is then considered, relative to another idea, confused due to the obscurity of the idea, or, in other words, its relative lack of clarity in comparison with a similar idea from which it ought to be different. In the case of confusion of multiple ideas in relation to each other, the reality is that the same idea in the mind has two or more different labels or names attached to it or the mind knows that there ought to be differences between multiple ideas but cannot identify them, due to a certain vacillation of the mind as to what is being considered.

Understanding what Locke intends to convey through the above labels is important for understanding the various senses of the term "knowledge" that he uses in the *Essay*. His often-referenced definition of knowledge is: "*Knowledge* then seems to me to be nothing but the *perception of the connexion and agreement, or disagreement and repugnancy of any of our Ideas.*"[69] Knowledge often comes about through a juxtaposing of ideas (and

---

[65] Locke, *Essay*, II.xxx.3.
[66] Cf. Locke, *Essay*, II.i.1–3; II.xxx.3.
[67] Locke, *Essay*, II.xxix.4.
[68] Locke, *Essay*, II.xxix.2.
[69] Locke, *Essay*, IV.i.2.

these ideas do not have to be ideas of things that exist). The clearer and more distinct two ideas are when juxtaposing them, the more specific points of knowledge one can glean in the comparison. But there is an even more fundamental sense of knowledge with which Locke works:

> 'Tis the first Act of the Mind, when it has any Sentiments or *Ideas* at all, to perceive its *Ideas*, and so far as it perceives them, to know each what it is, and thereby also to perceive their difference, and that one is not another. This is so absolutely necessary, that without it there could be no Knowledge, no Reasoning, no Imagination, no distinct Thoughts at all. By this the Mind clearly and infallibly perceives each *Idea* to agree with it self, and to be what it is; and all distinct Ideas to disagree, *i.e.*, the one not to be the other.[70]

In other words, we cannot have knowledge, as defined above, unless we have knowledge or know something in a more fundamental sense: we perceive it and can hold it in our minds. To perceive an idea is to know that idea in a qualified sense. If the idea is rather complex and too cumbersome to take in all at once, we can compare and contrast particular aspects of that idea, as long as we perceive those aspects, and arrive at knowledge in different respects.

Margaret Atherton somewhat recently argued that Locke rejected the employment of "innate ideas" in philosophical discourse because that meant that we have innate knowledge or unconscious knowledge. She thinks that Locke, in addition to attacking the variety of innatists that are commonly named in his day, was *also* attacking the Cartesians by arguing that "innate" is opposed to the nature of mentality. That is, "His position is that the explanations in terms of innate ideas or principles can be rejected out of hand on grounds of incoherence. This is because he believes there is no way to have such mental states as ideas or principles except through being aware of them, so that the mark of the mental is that the mental states are conscious states." In other words, by virtue of the way Locke conceives of the nature of mentality, speaking of innate ideas (or knowledge) is akin to discussing unconscious awareness, an inherently contradictory label. This did create a problem of coherence in Locke's *Essay*. Whereas Descartes and some of his followers maintain a hidden or unconscious structure to thought, Locke has no interest in such speculation: "For Locke has no commitment at all to

---

[70] Locke, *Essay*, IV.i.4.

showing that his account of how we construct our ideas describes a system that is just as powerful as that of the nativist, and he feels no need to say that he can explain whatever the nativist seeks to explain."[71]

Propositions and Doctrines

Propositions are closely related to perceptions and ideas. Locke embarks into a discussion on propositions in Book IV of the *Essay*. In remarking that the proper import of the word truth signifies "nothing but *the joining or separating of Signs, as the Things signified by them, do agree or disagree with another*," he identifies a proposition as: "The *joining or separating* of signs." Thus, while he does speak of ideas as being true and false, truth properly belongs to propositions. Moreover, there are two types of propositions. Verbal propositions are ones that use words as the signs and mental propositions use ideas as the signs.[72] Locke acknowledges, however, the difficulty of treating them separately: it is unavoidable to use words in speaking of mental propositions, which thus, become verbal: "For a *mental Proposition* being nothing but a bare consideration of the *Ideas*, as they are in our Minds stripp'd of Names, they lose the Nature of purely *mental Propositions*, as soon as they are put into Words."[73] He gives more formal definitions of each later on in the chapter: "*Mental* [Propositions], *wherein the Ideas* in our Understandings *are* without the use of Words *put together, or separated* by the Mind, perceiving, or judging of their Agreement, or Disagreement," whereas, "*Verbal Propositions*, which *are Words* the signs of our *Ideas put together or separated in affirmative or negative Sentences.*"[74] He eventually has a summary statement connecting truth, falsehood, ideas, words, and knowledge as they relate to propositions:

> *Truth* is the marking down in Words, the agreement or disagreement of *Ideas* as it is. *Falshood* is the marking down in Words, the agreement or disagreement of *Ideas* otherwise than it is. And so far as these *Ideas*, thus marked by Sounds, agree to their Archetypes, so far only is the *Truth real*. The knowledge of this Truth, consists in knowing what *Ideas* the Words

---

[71] Atherton, "Locke and the Issues over Innateness," 58.
[72] Locke, *Essay*, IV.v.2.
[73] Locke, *Essay*, IV.v.3.
[74] Locke, *Essay*, IV.v.5.

stand for, and the perception of the agreement or disagreement of those *Ideas*, according as it is marked by those Words.[75]

Thus, propositions use ideas and thus perceptual knowledge of the ideas to create knowledge.[76] In our mind, they clearly create further ideas, too, although Locke does not make this express. To convey these propositions and ideas to others requires words. But the words *and* propositions not undergirded by ideas are just sounds.

These observations are reinforced by Burthogge's assumption that propositions do create further ideas and count as such. Burthogge's logic texts both predate and postdate the *Essay*'s first edition and they are known for their many affinities to Lockean epistemology. Burthogge does not use the term "ideas" and his distinctions are finer than are Locke's. For Burthogge, sense or meaning is the immediate object of the mind in apprehension (i.e., perception).[77] "Sense or Meaning is that Conception or Notion that is formed in the Minde, on a proposal to it of an Object, a Word or Proposition."[78] He is clearer later, where he remarks:

> Those Words or Propositions any one hath a sence of, those things to which the Words or Propositions relate, he hath a Notion of. Sence is Notion; onely it is called *Sence* as it relates to the Words or Propositions, and *Notion* as it relates to the Things; but *indeed* Sence is Notion, and to have the sence of a Word or Proposition, is to frame a Notion of it, or of the thing signified by it.[79]

In other words, while one does put ideas into propositions, one must understand or conceive of the over-arching idea of the proposition.

These considerations create difficulty for the doctrine of the Trinity. Even the most basic set of propositions—(1) God is three persons, (2) each person is God, and (3) there is one God—does not allow a summative representation that simultaneously incorporates the three propositions. Appropriating Boylean categories, these could perhaps be called asymmetrical or unsociable ideas. But there is no one complex idea (or proposition), whose truth

---

[75] Locke, *Essay*, IV.v.9.
[76] Cf. Locke, *Essay*, IV.vi.3.
[77] Burthogge, *Organum Vetus*, §7.
[78] Burthogge, *Organum Vetus*, §8.
[79] Burthogge, *Organum Vetus*, §14.

we can affirm and of which we are capable of forming with respect to the Trinity, that does not inherently contradict one of its propositions in the way that we envision each proposition in isolation from the others.

This raises the question of what kind of knowledge we may actually claim regarding the doctrine of the Holy Trinity when applying the principles of the *Essay* to it. In the *Essay*'s economy, can one claim to know something or affirm or deny without a summative idea or representation? Would it be legitimate to claim true knowledge of each of the propositions all the while realizing that the several ideas are ultimately irreconcilable in the way in which we envision them?

Must We Have Knowledge for Assent?

Concerning eternity, by which Locke ostensibly means endless duration, as opposed to referring to God's timelessness, he says, "we are apt to think, we have a positive comprehensive *Idea* of it, which is as much to say, that there is no part of that Duration, which is not clearly contained in our *Idea*." One cannot envision, however, endlessness: "that part of his *Idea*, which is still beyond the Bounds of that large Duration, he represents to his own Thoughts, is very obscure and undetermined." This is not to say that we have no idea of eternity, but rather the idea is problematic when the mind tries to explore it further. "And hence it is, that in Disputes and Reasonings concerning Eternity, or any other *Infinite*, we are very apt to blunder, and involve our selves in manifest Absurdities" (II.xxix.15).

It is in Locke's *ROC* and his defenses of it where he offers more detailed comment on incomprehensible doctrines and the harm that they can wreak. In *ROC*, Locke teaches that we should consider someone to be a Christian who meets the following three conditions: believes there is one God, believes Jesus is the Messiah foretold of in the Old Testament, and actively takes Christ as their King.[80] That is the simple message of salvation that Christ revealed to the poor and illiterate masses. But, if one were to realize that a certain proposition was taught in Scripture, beyond the above, one must necessarily assent to it; not to do so would be a rejection of Christ as King. To this end, he writes, "As far as the rest of the Divine Truths, there is nothing more required of him, but that he receive all parts of Divine Revelation, with a

---

[80] Marko, "Justification, Ecumenism."

docility and disposition prepared to imbrace, and assent to all Truths coming from God." And, when one has a difficulty in rightly interpreting a text and understanding it, and no other text can be found that helps with the interpretation, the student must suspend his or her opinion. The same applies to a person trying to make a number of texts "consist together": "He must either interpret one by the other, or suspend his Opinion." Locke concludes, "He that thinks that more is, or can be required, of poor frail Man in matters of Faith, will do well to consider what absurdities he will run into. God out of the infiniteness of his Mercy, has dealt with Man as a compassionate and tender Father."[81] He continues in the same vein until the close of the book, proclaiming how the message of salvation is crafted for the simple and those without time or ability for complex reasoning.

Most scholars have realized that the Trinity and other complicated doctrines are not to be deemed fundamental in Locke's mind. In none of his works does he explicitly accept or deny the Trinity. Thus, he is sometimes labeled as an "irenic trinitarian." The scholarship is in accord in acknowledging that Locke does not think it prudent to advance his opinion on the matter. What remains to be addressed is whether Locke's comments on incomprehensible doctrines and the "impossibility" of believing in them relate directly to the problem of fundamentals: because the poor and uneducated do not have the ability to understand difficult doctrines is it reasonable for God only to require a simple understanding?

There is a potential problem, however, with interpreting Locke's comments as simply advancing his teaching of two fundamental articles, that there is one God and Jesus is the Messiah. First, Locke uses the word "impossible" and not "infeasible." In the preface to the *A Second Vindication of The Reasonableness of Christianity*, Locke notes that he wrote *ROC* in part for "those who thought . . . that the Revelation of our Saviour required the Belief of such Articles for Salvation, which the settled Notions and their way of reasoning in some, and want of Understanding in others, made impossible to them."[82] This technically inaccurate or hyperbolic use of the term impossible, as understood by some interpreters, would be easy to gloss over if it were an isolated instance, but it is not. For example, Locke writes, in response to Edwards:

---

[81] Locke, *ROC*, 303–4; cf. Locke, *A Second Vindication*, 392–449.
[82] Locke, *A Second Vindication*, xvii.

> If his [Edwards's] Articles, some of which contain Mysteries, are necessary to be believed to make a Man a Christian, because they are in the Bible; than according to this rule it is necessary for many Men to believe, what is not *intelligible* to them; what their *Noddles* cannot apprehend . . . *i.e.* it is necessary for them to do, what is impossible for them to do . . .[83]

We have here another instance of him noting that it is impossible to assent to that which is not intelligible or apprehensible. Similarly, in his *A Second Vindication* he writes:

> All that is contain'd therein [in Scripture], as coming from the God of Truth, they are to receive as Truth, and imbrace as such. But since it is impossible explicitly to believe any Proposition of the Christian Doctrine but what men understand, or in any other sense that we understand it to have been deliver'd in; An explicit belief is, or can be required in no Man, of more than what he understands of that Doctrine.[84]

While still couched broadly in the context of defending the common human, this above quote is much more overt regarding our inability to assent to that which we cannot comprehend. Add to this his rejection of having "knowledge" of things of which we are unaware, namely innate ideas and principles. Furthermore, some scholars have pointed out Locke's responses to Descartes's chiliagon example as a rejection of the pure intellect or understanding by which Descartes said we can claim to understand something for which we cannot create a clear image.[85] In other words, Locke's *Essay* may not allow a claim to understand something for which one cannot form a summative mental representation.

All of what has been said would appear to contradict Locke's approach in the *Essay*, where he purportedly admits, or at least opens a pathway, for

---

[83] Locke, *A Second, Vindication*, 95.
[84] Locke, *A Second Vindication*, 337.
[85] Locke, *Essay*, II.xxix.13–14 (Locke calls the shape a "*Chiliaëdron*"); cf. 15–16; cf. for example, Ayers, *Locke: Epistemology and Ontology*, 1:47–48. Ayers writes, "Descartes had tried to prove the difference between conceiving and imagining by arguing that a chiliagon may be clearly conceived, but cannot be imagined . . . Locke's response was to deny that we can form a clear and distinct idea of the *shape* of (in his case) a chiliagon. We can reason about it accurately because we have a precise idea of the *number* of its sides. Such an idea is possible, as Locke had gone to some pains to show in the chapter on number, because of the technique of counting, which breaks the apprehension of large numbers into easy and recorded steps. This explanation is very like Hobbes's, and the whole argument is evidently a rebuttal of the Cartesian distinction between imagination and intellect from an imagist point of view."

assent to above reason things. In turn, this has been taken as evidence that Locke accepts incomprehensible doctrines. Arguably, this conclusion is incorrect. In IV.xvii.23 of the *Essay*, Locke writes:

> By what has been before said of *Reason*, we may be able to make some guess at the distinction of Things, into those that are according to, above, and contrary to Reason. 1. *According to Reason* are such Propositions, whose Truth we can discover, by the examining and tracing those *Ideas* we have from *Sensation* and *Reflexion*; and by natural deduction, finds to be true, or probable. 2. *Above Reason* are such Propositions, whose Truth or Probability we cannot by Reason derive from those Principles. 3. *Contrary to Reason* are such Propositions, as are inconsistent with, or irreconcilable to our clear and distinct *Ideas*. Thus the existence of one GOD is according to Reason; the Existence of more than one GOD, contrary to Reason; the Resurrection of the Dead, above Reason. Farther, as *Above Reason* may be taken in a double sense, *viz*. either as signifying above Probability, or above Certainty; and in that large Sense also, Contrary to Reason, is, I suppose, sometimes taken.

The first category, propositions according to reason, are ones that are discovered or discoverable by natural means, such as "the existence of one God." Special revelation, in principle, at least, is not required to determine them. Reason here, as argued in the last chapter, is reason working at its best and without revelation. Propositions above reason are those that we only discover and believe because of special revelation. It is important to note that in the few places where he gives examples of things above reason, here, and in IV.xviii.7, he only gives two examples: one third of the angels rebelled and the resurrection of the body will occur. Neither are doctrines considered significantly incomprehensible—I cannot picture immaterial beings as immaterial, but I can sufficiently represent a picture of both assertions in my mind. Thus, the position that Locke accepts incomprehensible doctrines due to his delineation of propositions is a bit hasty. He is at least matching Boyle's labeling of comprehensible and necessarily revealed things as being "above reason." In fact, the only sub-category of Boylean incomprehensible doctrines above reason that Locke does not clearly accept are the asymmetric or unsociable doctrines and propositions. In addition, it appears that he considers to be contrary to reason propositions that are not only contradictory or inconsistent but are also "irreconcilable to clear and distinct ideas." This last phrase could very well mean things for which we cannot form a representative idea. These descriptions of what is above reason and what is contrary to reason, if accurate, gives a little more weight to the idea that candidates for assent are summatively representable. Thus, that the aforementioned propositions of the Trinity cannot be mentally reconciled appears to put the doctrine in the contrary to reason category. If not that, then it could be that there is no category in which to put the doctrine and the propositions are suspended until an intelligible representation can be conceived—which will not happen with the Athanasian (or orthodox) explanation of the doctrine of the Trinity.

Contexual Support for Denominating Locke's Epistemology as Antitrinitarian

Richard Burthogge

Richard Burthogge, whose name is occasionally together with Locke's and Immanuel Kant's for his similarities to both, wrote prior to and alongside of Locke. In fact, he dedicated his *An Essay upon Reason, and the Nature of Spirits* to Locke. Yolton finds their epistemology to be similar and speculates why Locke's *Essay* would gain so much notoriety and Burthogge's *Organum Vetus & Novum*, which "was in many ways an anticipation of Locke's *Essay*," did not. One reviewer of Burthogge's 1694 *An Essay upon Reason*, however, pointed out his debt to Locke.[86] It is therefore difficult to say to what degree that he is predecessor or an appropriator and adaptor of Locke, but there are numerous affinities between the two, as evidenced by a brief perusal of Burthogge's *Organum Vetus* and *An Essay upon Reason*.

Burthogge appears to deny the legitimacy of assent to the incomprehensible. In *Organum Vetus* he uses sense and notion for what Locke would generally call idea. That said, in *An Essay upon Reason*, when discussing falsity, he cautions the reader from identifying falsity and non-sense. "Sense" for Burthogge in the *Essay*, "is *compossibility*, not actuality." Many false things were or are possible and not actual. The impossible is nonsense.[87] "But though all Falsity is not Nonsense; all *impossible* Falsity is." In other words,

---

[86] Yolton, *John Locke and the Way of Ideas*, 19–20.
[87] Burthogge, *An Essay upon Reason*, 38–39. It appears as though Burthogge is limiting his use of the word "non-sense." Burthogge would unlikely call a speech delivered in an unknown language non-sense. If he did, it would be in a relative sense.

the impossible or nonsensical things are a subset of false things. But he gives the following description of the identification of the impossible:

> I mean, every proposition is Nonsense, that is false to that degree, that it is impossible (absolutely impossible) it should be true; for no proposition is absolutely impossible to be true but that which implies a contradiction, and that which implies a contradiction must needs be Nonsense; since the Understanding cannot frame any Notion or Idea of it, and so cannot make any real sense of it, and so cannot make any real sense of the words, that compose it.[88]

If one cannot conceive of or form an idea of a proposition, it is, or at least counts as, a "contradiction." Burthogge makes statements along similar lines in *Organum Vetus*. There he writes, "Sence, Meaning, or Notion arises from a Congruity in the Object to the Faculty; so that to enquire *why* one cannot understand or apprehend a *Non-sensical* Proposition or Word, is to enquire why he cannot see or hear Tastes."[89] And he is clear that to understand and apprehend a proposition one must not only have a sense and meaning of the words in the proposition but a notion of the total proposition.[90] Moreover, in discussing transubstantiation, he says to believe against the faculties is to believe a "contradiction."[91] In short, truth cannot exist as incongruity and inconsistency with our faculties.[92]

For Burthogge, propositions to which we can honestly assent must be ones that comport with our God-given faculties. If it does not agree with our faculties, it goes against this rule. To assent to something inconsistent or incongruous gives us pain just as when we affirm a clear and explicit contradiction, like "love is hatred." An incongruity counts as contradiction because it is "Affirmation and Negation of the same thing, and consequently an Assent and Dissent at the same time, and Assent and Dissent being contrary motions." He finishes by asserting, "it follows, that to say, or go about to Assent unto, a Contradiction, is to *distract* and distort the mind, and put it to pain, because it is to draw it contrary ways at the same time."[93]

---

[88] Burthogge, *An Essay upon Reason*, 39.
[89] Burthogge, *Organum Vetus*, §16.
[90] Burthogge, *Organum Vetus*, §17.
[91] Also, if we need to envision in the proper sense all that we believe, one does not have the ability to negate the accidents of one thing and replace them with another. All we have in our notices are the accidents. So, one cannot make sense of the image of bread really being Christ's bodily flesh. Burthogge, *Organum Vetus*, §32.
[92] Burthogge, *Organum Vetus*, §32.
[93] Burthogge, *An Essay upon Reason*, 40.

Burthogge demurs when it comes to making a clear pronouncement on the doctrine of the Holy Trinity. He critiques some of those involved in the then-raging English trinitarian debates. But he does not try to enter the fray and argue for a particular rendering of the doctrine. He states, "For my own part, I believe as the Scriptures instruct me, that there is but *one God*, tho' *Three Persons*; each of which is *God*; which I say only to prevent Mistakes."[94] Other than the last clause, all seems rather orthodox. In a footnote or excursus at the bottom of the book's final page, he notes that he had no intention of entering into a discourse on the Trinity. He only brought it up "as an inquiry after the Idea and notion of a *Suppositum*, and that of a *Person*, obliged me." He goes on to say, "The *Doctrine* of the *Trinity* is a point of pure *Revelation*, not of *Philosophy* or Science; all Discourses and explications of it, not derived from the Holy Scriptures, and grounded upon them, but on Analogies and Resemblances in *nature*, or on Principles of Human *Discourse* and meer Reason, are as Foreign unto it, as Earth is to Heaven." It is a fundamental one and the chief of those doctrines of which the Apostle says "*neither Eye saw, nor Ear heard of, not entred into the heart of man to conceive*, before they were brought to light in the Gospel" (1 Corinthians 2:9, the verse he references, however, is not necessarily pointing out incomprehensible doctrines). He then notes that Scripture is the only place where we are obliged to seek the truth of this doctrine, a practice that, if devoid of the guidance of the theologians that had gone on before, ends in heresy.[95] So, Burthogge might be orthodox and give certain incomprehensible doctrines a pass because our faculties were not so constructed to adjudicate theological truths as they are philosophical ones.

Burthogge's treatment of contradiction or impossibility is instructive. What he says about it appears to be along the lines of Locke's description of contrary to reason propositions: "3. *Contrary to Reason* are such Propositions, as are inconsistent with, or irreconcilable to our clear and distinct *Ideas*." Burthogge counts clear impossibilities and inconceivable propositions as "contradictions" (although perhaps not revealed ones). Locke seems to accept the rejection of propositions, or denominating them contrary to reason, when they are inconsistent with clear and distinct ideas or simply irreconcilable. A proposition being irreconcilable could mean that one cannot create

---

[94] Burthogge, *An Essay upon Reason*, 275.
[95] Burthogge, *An Essay upon Reason*, 280.

an idea of it, meaning that it is incongruous with our God-given faculties, consistent with Burthogge's assertions.

John Toland

One of the earliest known Lockean appropriators, noted for his heterodoxy, was John Toland. Stillingfleet thought he ended up in heresy by adhering more closely to the *Essay*'s principles than did Locke himself. As I argued in *Measuring the Distance between Locke and Toland*, while Stillingfleet significantly misunderstood the principles of Locke's *Essay* and Toland's *Christianity Not Mysterious* (*CNM*), he was correct in connecting the two. Toland, although much briefer in his treatment of religious epistemology, appropriates much of the *Essay* without conceptual modification.

Toland, at least as he portrays his positions in *CNM*, is not the incautious heretic he is sometimes framed as being. When it comes to the Trinity, he never explicitly affirms or denies it. He does mention the Trinity in his chapter, "The Absurdity and Effects of Admitting Any Real or Seeming Contradictions in Religion." In the space of a few lines he attacks Roman Catholics, Eastern Orthodox, Lutherans, Socianians, Arians, and Trinitarians:

> THIS famous and admirable doctrine [to adore what we cannot comprehend] is the undoubted Source of all the *Absurdities* that ever were seriously vented among the *Christians*. Without the Pretence of it, we should never hear of the *Transubstantiation,* and other ridiculous Fables of the Church of *Rome*; nor of any of the *Eastern Ordures*, almost all receiv'd into this *Western Sink*: Nor should we be ever banter'd with the *Lutheran Impanation*, or the Ubiquity it has produc'd, as one Monster ordinarily begets another. And tho the *Socinians* disown this Practice, I am mistaken if either they or the *Arians* can make their notions of a *dignifi'd and Creature-God capable of Divine Worship*, appear more reasonable than the Extravagancies of other *Sects* touching the Article of the *Trinity*.[96]

At no point does he expressly reject the doctrine of the Trinity. He is trying to lay censure to all professed biblical monotheists.

---

[96] Toland, *CNM*, 26–27.

Accordingly, it is Toland's treatment of knowledge that is of interest here. First, Toland's definition of knowledge is conceptually identical to Locke's, both of which are given, respectively, as follows: "nothing else but *the Perception of the Agreement or Disagreement of our Ideas in a greater or lesser Number, whereinsoever this Agreement or Disagreement may consist*"[97] and "*Knowledge* then seems to me to be nothing but the *perception of the connexion and agreement, or disagreement and repugnancy of any of our Ideas.*"[98] Second, Toland uses knowledge in the sense of perception of an idea, as does Locke. To this effect, Toland writes:

> From all these Observations, and what went before, it evidently follows that *Faith* is so far from being an implicite Assent to any thing above Reason, that this Notion directly contradicts the Ends of Religion, the Nature of Man, and the Goodness and Wisdom of God. But at this rate, some will be apt to say, *Faith* is no longer *Faith* but *Knowledg*. I answer, that if *Knowledg* be taken for a present and immediate View of things, I have no where affirm'd any thing like it, but the contrary in many Places. But if by *Knowledg* be meant understanding what is believ'd, then I stand by it that *Faith* is *Knowledg*: I have all along maintain'd it, and the very Words are promiscuously us'd for one another in the *Gospel*.[99]

Like Locke, Toland calls "understanding what is believed" knowledge. For Toland, that is a way in which one might say that doctrines of faith are knowledge: when one understands them. He is even clearer elsewhere: "for *to comprehend* in all correct Authors is nothing else but *to know*; and *as of what is not knowable we can have no Idea, so it is nothing to us.*"[100] Moreover, a similar correspondence of belief and knowledge is also seen in the Cambridge Platonist George Rust, discussed in the previous chapter of this text. Although he appears to accept well-attested incomprehensible doctrines, Rust does write the following: "For Faith consists in Assent; the Assent follows the Judgment, but no Judgment can be made of a thing that is not at all known or understood; therefore whatever exceeds all Knowledge, must needs likewise exceed all Belief."[101]

---

[97] Toland, *CNM*, 12.
[98] Locke, *Essay*, IV.i.2.
[99] Toland, *CNM*, 139.
[100] Toland, *CNM*, 76–77.
[101] Rust, *Discourse*, 26.

Toland is also explicit in his dismissal of incomprehensible assertions and contradictions. Toland places both contradictions and incomprehensible assertions into his category of ideas and propositions contrary to reason. In the preface he admits that part of his desire to write *CNM* is to "*vindicate his [God's] reveal'd Will from the most unjust Imputations of Contradiction and Obscurity.*"[102] And his last excerpt from his introduction to the book is: "*there is nothing in the Gospel contrary to Reason, nor above it; and that no Christian Doctrine can be properly called a Mystery.*"[103] A little later he asserts: "*what is evidently repugnant to clear and distinct Ideas, or to our common Notions, is contrary to Reason.*"[104] In other words, "without *Evidence* in the things themselves," it is incomprehensible.[105] He rejects those who claim that certain religious principles only seem to clash "[a]nd that tho we cannot reconcile them by reason of our corrupt and limited Understandings; yet that from the Authority of *Divine Revelation*, we are bound to believe and acquiesce in them; or, as the Fathers taught 'em to speak, *to adore what we cannot comprehend.*"[106] Again commenting on so-called seeming contradictions, he writes, "A *seeming* Contradiction is to us as much as a *real* one; and our Respect for the *Scripture* does not require us to grant any such in it, but rather to conclude, that we are ignorant of the right Meaning when the Difficulty occurs; and so *to suspend our Judgment concerning it, till with sutable Helps and Industry we discover the Truth.*"[107] He later expressly groups mysteries and contradictions together: "*Contradiction* expresses Nothing by a couple of Ideas that destroy one another, and *Mystery* expresses Nothing by Words that have no Ideas at all."[108] In one passage he associates the incomprehensible, contradictory, and "non-sense" (the term used by Burthogge for contradictions).[109] He later asserts, "*Contradiction* is only another word for *Impossible* or *Nothing*."[110] While Burthogge makes impossibility a subset of false things, Toland does not discuss false things per se. Maybe it is because false things are inconceivable: for any assertion made that is false would be irreconcilable juxtaposed with the true statement. Caesar cannot cross and not cross the Rubicon at the same time.

---

[102] Toland, *CNM*, xiv.
[103] Toland, *CNM*, 6.
[104] Toland, *CNM*, 25.
[105] Toland, *CNM*, 39. This sounds like Norris's discussion of internal evidence.
[106] Toland, *CNM*, 26.
[107] Toland, *CNM*, 35–36.
[108] Toland, *CNM*, 134–35.
[109] Toland, *CNM*, 49; cf. 55–56.
[110] Toland, *CNM*, 145.

Toland is adamant throughout the work that the New Testament cannot have any incomprehensible doctrines in it and be God's word.[111] His reasoning is that one assents only to ideas or propositions and if there is no proposition or idea there is no possibility of faith: "*the Subject of Faith must be intelligible to all, since the Belief thereof is commanded under no less a Penalty than Damnation*: He that believeth not, shall be damn'd" (Mark 16:16). No one will be damned for impossibilities. Obligation supposes an ability to understand.[112] In another passage, he asserts that it is not worthwhile bothering about something for which we cannot form an idea: "For what I don't conceive can no more give me right Notions of God, or influence my Actions, than a Prayer deliver'd in an unknown Tongue can excite my Devotion."[113] God has made it such that we are unable to conceive of impossibilities and contradictions. They are simply ideas that "destroy one another, and cannot subsist together in the same Subject."[114] What is more, he spends much time arguing that "mystery" in Scripture never refers to anything incomprehensible:

> *Mystery in the whole New Testament is never put for any thing inconceivable in it self, or not to be judg'd of by our ordinary Notions and Faculties, however clearly reveal'd*: And whether, on the contrary, it do's not always signify *some things naturally intelligible enough; but either so vail'd by figurative Words and Rites, or so lodg'd in God's sole Knowledge and Decree, that they could not be discover'd without special Revelation.*[115]

Once the veil is removed, all the things in Scripture are fully intelligible. Intelligibility is a hermeneutical principle to employ when confronted with competing interpretations of a passage. Finally, miracles are intelligible and can be mentally envisioned. But how God effects those, as well as many other things, is beyond our ken.[116]

The seeming difference between Toland and Locke on the use of the term knowledge appears to be that the former admits one must be capable of forming an idea of something to assent to it, while the latter is less clear. That is, Locke makes statements to the same effect but not to the degree and

---

[111] For example, Toland, *CNM*, 55–56; 97–98; 170.
[112] Toland, *CNM*, 134.
[113] Toland, *CNM*, 29–30.
[114] Toland, *CNM*, 40.
[115] Toland, *CNM*, 108.
[116] Toland, *CNM*, 145.

consistency of Toland. It should be noted that this was the entire theme of *CNM*. And again, Toland never goes so far as to deny the doctrine of the Trinity in express terms. Considering the times, it was probably prudent that he did not, especially if he did not find himself a part of a particular sect. Also, in *CNM*, for a doctrine to be "reconcilable" is for it to be possible. This is at least evidence of the way in which one other thinker from the era uses the term that Locke uses in his definition of things contrary to reason. Whatever Locke truly intended, Toland is an example of an early appropriation of the *Essay*.[117]

William Stephens, Anthony Collins, and Other Deists and Free-Thinkers

There are others in the era that promulgate the same epistemological rule as do Toland and Burthogge. Bishop Browne, who attacked Toland's *CNM*, refers to deists and freethinkers, in his state of the question in his 1729 magnum opus, as being those who claim, "that we can neither know nor believe any thing but what we have some kind of Idea or Conception of; And you must grant likewise, that the Christian Mysteries are incomprehensible, that is, that we have no Idea at all of them; therefore we can neither know nor believe them."[118]

William Stephens is an example of someone more than aware of Locke who holds the same epistemological principle as Toland and Burthogge: one cannot assent to that for which one cannot form an idea. Stephens writes a pamphlet close on the heels of Locke's *ROC*, entitled *An Account of the Growth of Deism in England*. In it, he critiques the church and its theologians couched in the words of deists he has interviewed, most likely a maneuver to avoid personal attacks. In his work, Locke's *ROC* receives praise for its convincing argument and John Edwards, Locke's assailant, receives a parting blow on the last page.[119] Stephens presents Lockean assumptions in the form a quotation from a deist: "But what greater slavery than to force on Men a Belief of such things as necessary to Salvation, of which 'tis not possible

---

[117] Toland is heavily reliant on Locke: see Marko, *Measuring the Distance*.
[118] Browne, *Procedure, Extent, and Limits*, 29.
[119] Stephens, *An Account*, 25, 32.

to form any Idea?" Stephens's deist goes on to give an example of what he considers an absurd doctrine with no idea:

> Though I am satisfied there is no such thing as a change of Bread into Flesh of Christ, yet I can form an Idea, that such a thing may be, that the same Power which changed Earth into a Man, may change Bread into Flesh: But I can frame to my self no Idea of what your Church Teacheth in the Sacrament, that the Body and Blood of Christ are *verily and indeed taken and received of the faithful*: And when I ask how can this be understood by a Protestant, who believeth that there is no other Body but that of the Bread? I am told that the Church meaneth it in a Spiritual Sense. Now I have try'd, and find it impossible for me to form my self an Idea of a Body verily and indeed in a Spiritual Sense.[120]

The deist's point is that one is incapable of forming an idea of a material thing existing in an immaterial sense. Although he does frame the doctrines in unqualified ways that no theologian would accept, recalling Nye, he does not call them contradictions as does Nye. Nevertheless, the deist (or Stephens) continues on to chide the church for imposing "absurd or unintelligible Notions (especially such Speculations, which tend to make no body the better) as necessary to Salvation."[121] This last statement, again, is very similar to what Locke says in *ROC*.

Anthony Collins's *An Essay Concerning the Use of Reason in Propositions*, also articulates a rule of intelligibility for assent. Collins was well-associated with Locke, his epistemology is clearly influenced by the great thinker, and he wades into the Trinitarian controversy. The short pamphlet is the best example of Collins's logic and epistemology. He does not, however, follow Locke precisely. There are clearly matters upon which they disagree, and Collins is far more willing to make pronouncements on controversial issues than is Locke.

In discussing the "credibility of things" he offers various rules about testimonies (divine or human). The first rule is: "That the words made use of in the *Relation* stand for known Ideas, or Ideas that we are capable of forming; for if they stand for Ideas that we know not, or want Faculties to perceive, there are then no objects for the Mind to exert it self upon."[122] A little later

---

[120] Stephens, *An Account*, 27–28.
[121] Stephens, *An Account*, 28; cf. 32.
[122] Collins, *Essay*, 7.

in the pamphlet he identifies perception as the rule of credibility. He knows of no other criterion than "*Perception*: for tho Truth abstractly consider'd consists in the relations of agreements between Ideas; yet being here consider'd relatively to human Understanding, it is not my Truth till I perceive it, nor can I know it to be true but by my own Perception. *Perception* therefore must be every Man's *Criterion* to distinguish Truth from Falshood." And although he admits that there is a difference between real and seeming contradictions, nevertheless, "if Perception be our *Criterion*, we cannot assent to two Propositions, which we perceive, or think that we perceive to be repugnant to each other."[123] Ultimately there may be no contradiction, but according to Collins, one cannot assent to those propositions as long as there is a perception of repugnance. He reasserts this very same sentiment later in the work, writing, "for while things appear repugnant, we must judg them to be repugnant, if we will ever make any judgment at all" and "[I] affirm, that wherever we have capacity enough to perceive the truth of a Proposition, we have capacity enough to perceive that there is no repugnancy between that and another true Proposition."[124]

Implications

There are some pertinent things that can be said of the excerpts above. The careful phrasing of the statements are much akin to the ones given earlier from Locke's *A Second Vindication*. Both Locke and the deist (or Stephens) both note that the church should not force doctrines that are impossible to be believed for salvation. The same sentiment is arguably inferable from Burthogge.[125] Collins is abundantly clear that perception is the main criterion of credibility: one cannot assent to nothing. Locke's questionable use of the word "impossible," as discussed above, is employed in 1697, while Stephens's work is 1696 and affirmative of Locke's *ROC*. All of this makes it more likely that Locke's employment of the word "impossible" was not indicative of a hastily inked (and repetitious) hyperbole but rather indexes a careful selection, one that is not unique to Locke. In addition, what Burthogge, Toland, Stephens, and Collins reject does appear to be consistent with a plausible

---

[123] Collins, *Essay*, 10.
[124] Collins, *Essay*, 33.
[125] Burthogge, *Organum Vetus*, §41.

interpretation of Locke's contrary to reason description. Even though it is not beyond doubt that he approves of the taxonomy (it could be what he thinks others are saying) Locke's rejection of the incomprehensible would seem to comport with his teachings on ideas and assent.

Way-Of-Ideas-Trinitarians and Contexual Support for Arguing that Locke's Epistemology Was Not Antitrinitarian

John Norris and Potential Implications

Locke's adversary, John Norris, was an able defender of incomprehensible propositions and doctrines. The doctrine of the Trinity was one of many doctrines he intended to defend with his *An Account of Reason and Faith*. He argued that the true Cartesian position, to which he adhered, is that we may find ourselves obligated to assent to incomprehensible natural assertions or revealed assertions: the perception under consideration may be very difficult to fathom, but the external evidence and arguments pointing to that conclusion might be clearly perceivable.[126]

In the third chapter of *An Account of Reason and Faith*, Norris explains his preferred taxonomy of propositions. Responding to Boyle's categorization of propositions, he thinks that something being beyond our discovery is too small a point to call it above reason, as Boyle does. What is more, when Socinians, their opponents, reject things above reason, they mean incomprehensible things.[127] Furthermore, reason and understanding are synonymous for Norris.[128] He offers his distinction of what above reason and contrary to reason things are:

> By things above Reason then (as the Expression is used in this Distinction) I conceive to be Meant, Not such as Reason of it self cannot Discover, but such as when proposed it cannot Comprehend. And by things Contrary to Reason I conceive such as it can and does actually comprehend, and that to be absolutely Impossible. Or in other words, a thing is then above Reason

---

[126] Norris, *An Account*, "Chapter 1: Of Reason."
[127] Norris, *An Account*, 104–5; cf. 110.
[128] Norris, *An Account*, "Chapter 1: Of Reason."

when we do not comprehend how it can be, and then Contrary to Reason when we do positively comprehend that it cannot be.[129]

He explains that to understand something is to comprehend or perceive it. And something being above reason does not mean that the thing is perfectly unintelligible, we are just unable to comprehend the connection between the ideas that the propositions propose.[130] He explains impossible as well. Impossibility occurs when two or more ideas cannot consist with one another, "Which may be either because of the immediate Opposition and Inconsistency of the Ideas themselves with themselves so as to Mutually to Exclude each other (as in a Contradiction) or because of their inconsistency with some other Truth, with which it cannot comport."[131] Put another way, he asserts "So that for a thing to be Contrary to Reason, is, in short, for the Understanding to perceive the Absolute Impossibility of it, or that its Ideas cannot stand together, which it does either immediately by perceiving the direct inconsistency of those Ideas, or Mediately by perceiving their inconsistency with some evident and incontestable Truth or other, whether Principle or Conclusion."[132] So, impossibilities can be detected immediately, like the assertions of the existence of a round square, or mediately, like claiming that all angels have and always have had physical bodies. This latter statement would contradict the consensus view that angels are immaterial and would be an impossibility for anyone that held the consensus view.

The aspect of his exposition that is the most illuminating is his further description of above reason versus contrary to reason doctrines. There he describes more incisively the epistemological experiences we have when pondering above reason and contrary to reason things. He writes, "For a thing to be above Reason implies only a *Negation*, the Not Comprehending how a thing can be, but for a thing to be Contrary to Reason implies the *Position* of an Intellectual act, the Comprehending that it cannot be." In other words, he asserts, "in things above Reason the Proposition is supposed not to be understood, whereas in things Contrary to Reason, it is supposed to be well understood, and that to be false and impossible."[133] In short, the unwary

---

[129] Norris, *An Account*, 116–17.
[130] Norris, *An Account*, 117–19.
[131] Norris, *An Account*, 119.
[132] Norris, *An Account*, 120–21.
[133] Norris, *An Account*, 124.

mind might be perplexed by both, but the wary mind should be able to separate out the things contrary to reason, noting that they can perceive the falsity of them.[134]

Whether or not Locke's taxonomy of propositions allows for Norris's distinction is not completely clear. At times Norris uses the words "inconsistent" and "incompatible" in reference to the relationship between the ideas in contrary to reason propositions.[135] Locke uses the words "inconsistent" and "irreconcilable," but there is too little context to determine with the precision characteristic of Norris and Burthogge to determine what is intended or, again, if Locke even cared to claim absolute legitimacy for the definitions of propositions that are according to, above, and contrary to reason.

Norris does not address Locke in his work and Locke gives no evidence of reacting to Norris's *An Account of Reason and Faith*. Mander expresses a little perplexity on the former count in his work on Norris. Among other things, he notes that Locke's category of things above reason emphasized undiscoverability and not incomprehensibility and that Locke was under suspicion of maintaining "precisely the sort of Socinianism that Norris was trying to fight against."[136] Moreover, Norris critiques Boyle primarily on the basis of his taxonomy of propositions, namely how he labels propositions, and not his acceptance of the incomprehensible or his more substantive treatment of it. He clearly goes after Toland and other rejectors of mysteries, especially those who would point to Descartes's works as being influential to them on that count. It would be surprising if Locke was not aware of Norris's arguments, given their history, but Locke does not seem to have changed anything in the *Essay* to make acceptance of incomprehensible things more overt.

---

[134] Cf. Mander, *The Philosophy of John Norris*, 109. Mander says the following about Norris's explanation of the distinction between above reason and contrary to reason things: "Overall, Norris's conception of propositions above reason does not withstand well the scrutiny of modern philosophy of language. We cannot determine whether they are true, we do not understand how they could be true, we do not even know if their truth is possible; in view of these three defects for Norris to continue to talk about the 'plain and simple meaning' of such propositions shows an uncritical attitude to meaning, not less unfortunate than it was typical of his age." While the era may have been lax in their attitude toward meaning, nonetheless I think his critique is uncharitable. The clear and evident perceptions upon which the truth of the above reason assertions lie, at least in the case of revealed things, is of the "external" variety. See the discussion at the beginning of this chapter.

[135] Norris, *An Account*, 120–21, 126.

[136] Mander, *Philosophy of John Norris*, 121–23.

Peter Browne and Potential Implications

Another thinker who is both Trinitarian and one of the new philosophers of ideas is Peter Browne. Like Norris and Boyle, he is interested in defending the legitimate assent to incomprehensible doctrines in his *A Letter in Answer to a Book Entitled Christianity Not Mysterious, etc.* and his lengthier and later *The Procedure, Extent, and Limits of Human Understanding*. All three thinkers are indicative of a trend noted by Lim of those who became more focused on addressing the limits of reason than defending the incomprehensible doctrine of the Trinity.[137] And, Browne, like Norris, was an opponent of Toland, although his *Procedure* goes far beyond his earlier response, the *Letter*, to Toland in content and pages. And also like Norris, he is a critic of Locke. One of the main motivating factors of his *Procedure* was that he was convinced that the defenders of traditionally incomprehensible doctrines have not relied enough upon the proper employment and understanding of analogy in their defense against the antitrinitarians.[138]

The foundational epistemology that undergirds Browne's teachings on analogy is fairly straightforward and is given most expressly in the *Procedure*. His thought is more incisive in the *Procedure* than it is in the *Letter* but the most salient aspects, especially his use of analogies, are prominent in both. Although he is occasionally loose with his terminology in *Procedure*, "idea" "ought to be confined intirely to our simple and compound Ideas of *Sensation*;" "consciousness" refers to the operations and affections of the mind "without the Intervention of any Idea;" and, "complex *Notions* or *Conceptions*" are what is "form'd by the Mind out of its own Operations and the Ideas of Sensation." Thus, "we have an *Idea* of an House, a *Consciousness* of Thinking or Grief, and a *Complex Notion* of Justice, Mercy, and Charity."[139] He acknowledges that we have nothing other than our senses and reason for these mental objects. He finds it ridiculous that some will claim that we have purely intellectual ideas that are independent of the ones rooted in our sensations.[140] Even in abstraction, we cannot have ideas of divine things entirely independent of sensations and the operations of our minds about those ideas.[141] In short, all our rational materials are rooted in our senses. Browne thinks we must make another

---

[137] Lim, *Mystery Unveiled*, 208.
[138] Browne, *Procedure, Extent*, 6–8.
[139] Browne, *Procedure, Extent*, 133; cf. Browne, *Letter*, 37–39.
[140] Browne, *Procedure, Extent*, 51–57; cf. for example, Browne, *Letter*, 39, 48.
[141] Browne, *Procedure, Extent*, 198–99; cf. for example, Browne, *Letter*, 39, 48.

important distinction: we have proper and immediate ideas or conceptions of things from this world, "which are the proper and immediate Objects of our Senses and our Reason" and mediate and improper ideas, "such as we necessarily form of the things of another world."[142]

These definitions and distinctions undergird Browne's teaching on the employment of analogy as the way to claim the legitimate belief in incomprehensible things. He judges that the antitrinitarians wrongly limit the import of the understanding regarding other-worldly things:

> They rigorously confine the Understanding within the narrow bounds of *direct* and *immediate* objects of Sense and Reason; and will not suffer the Mind of Man in any one Instance to reach above the strictly literal and immediate acceptation of Words; so as to transfer them and their Ideas Analogically with the least Truth and Reality to things incorporeal, and otherwise inconceivable and ineffable.[143]

Because we do not directly observe the insensible creation or God, to set the bounds of reason to those things as one should to observable things is an ill-fated move and unreasonable: this is what the Socinians, Free-Thinkers, Deists, and Arians do in one way or another. Browne asserts that because we were created in some way after the image of God, especially spiritually, "this serves to render all the Analogy rationaly built on such Conceptions and Notions, *Real* and *Just* with respect to him and his Attributes; as well as to other purely spiritual Beings who are created in a yet *Nearer* Likeness to him."[144] Therefore, according to Browne, "in Divine Analogy the Resemblance, or at least the *Correspondency* and *Proportion* is *Real*, and built on the very *Nature* of Things on both sides of the Comparison." He immediately adds the following: "There is something realy correspondent and answerable and proportionable in heavenly and spiritual Beings, to those Conceptions which are justly substituted to represent them."[145] In other words, because all our ideas and conceptions ultimately are rooted in the sensible world, the wholly

---

[142] Browne, *Procedure, Extent*, 2; cf. for example, Browne, *Letter*, 39–42, 48.
[143] Browne, *Procedure, Extent*, 39.
[144] Browne, *Procedure, Extent*, 139–40.
[145] Browne, *Procedure, Extent*, 137. At one place, Browne writes, "That the Scripture terms expressive of those Mysteries, first understood and apprehended literaly, and then transfer'd by Analogy to things Divine and Incomprehensible, do contain as much solid and substantial *Truth* and *Reality* for an Object of our *Knowledge* and *Faith*, as when they are applied to things Natural and Human" (Browne, *Procedure, Extent*, 30).

spiritual things are technically inconceivable. But God made us so that our notions do say something about God, but according to our finite capacities. So, we are able to affirm and deny important truths about God, although not literally, in the sense that our terms and descriptions are bounded by our finite notions rooted in the material order.

He expressed the same sentiments against Toland's *CNM*, about three decades earlier. In the *Letter*, he makes explicit the notion that we have proper and improper ideas of things depending upon their nature: "As to the first by a *proper and immediate Idea* I mean, *a conception or notion of the thing as it is in it self*, By a *mediate or improper Idea* I mean, *a notion we form of any thing in our Minds by Analogy or Similitude*.[146] He argues that this is not implicit assent, however. Rather, he argues:

> God never requires our *Assent* to any Proposition, but upon such testimonies and proof as shall cause this Evidence. But as to the thing it self which is signified by this analogy, as the *real state* and condition of the blest in Heaven is in this Mystery, it is wholly exempted from the enquiry of *Reason*. And herein is my *Faith* that I give my assent to a proposition which is sufficiently prov'd to come from God, thô I have no notion at all of that divine truth which is represented to me under the *similitude* of some worldly Object.[147]

While the analogous idea is not proper and immediate, it is intelligible. One must be cautious in trying to rationalize these analogies together, however, as if they were proper and immediate. Like Norris, Browne critiques Toland for positing that the crucial evidence of the credibility of a proposition or notion is internal: "And for the *Divine Revelation* of which, they had sufficient proofs (if they did but consider them) to raise up in their minds an *Evidence* as clear and distinct as they can have of any thing in this World."[148] In other words, the fact that Scripture plainly tells us certain things is proof or evidence enough of what it says is true. Of course, when speaking of God, angels, and the like, it must employ, at best, analogical language.

Before moving away from the Browne it is worthwhile to index the distinctions he makes pertaining to analogy. It is one of the motifs of his work

---

[146] Browne, *Letter*, 37–38; cf. 55, 58.
[147] Browne, *Letter*, 154.
[148] Browne, *Letter*, 155.

that has earned him a place in ongoing conversations.[149] He makes the following distinctions: between analogies and metaphors, human and divine analogies, and human and divine metaphors. Although he makes his general point regarding analogy clear in the *Letter*, his teaching about it, like other epistemological details, is more precise in the *Procedure*.[150] Browne asserts that human and divine metaphors are "figurative Words, and Ideas, and Conception" that are "us'd without any *Real Similitude or Proportion, or Correspondent Resmemblance* in the things compared." That is, the "Comparison is not founded in the *Real Nature* of the Things, but is a pure Invention of the Mind and intirely *Arbitrary*."[151] In the analogy, there is real proportion and correspondence. Human metaphors associate two observable things, while divine metaphors associate an observable thing to something supernatural: "in Human Metaphor, the Ideas or Conceptions *Designed* to be express'd, are or may be as *Directly* known and as *Immediate*, as the Ideas and Conceptions placed in their *Stead*," whereas, "in Divine Metaphor the *Substituted* Ideas are *Immediately* and *Directly* known, but what is designed to be express'd and convey'd to us thus, is no way conveivable by any *Direct* and *Immediate* Idea, Conception, or Notion." And they are not necessary for a true and real knowledge of the things to which the metaphor alludes.[152] The distinction between human and divine analogies is similar to the same metaphorical distinctions: a human analogy is used to conceive of things in this world, like the instincts of brutes via the analogue of reason in humans, while divine analogies help us conceive of things in the other (supernatural) world. And, as alluded to above, analogies are necessary to conceive of certain things, while metaphors are not.

Browne attempts to show the utility of his doctrine of analogy for the doctrine of the Holy Trinity. Again, we have no purely intellectual ideas in the sense that they are independent of the basic ideas we receive from the material order in our interaction with it. So, we are not to try to attempt to achieve "any *Abstract* intellectual Ideas of that incomprehensible Unity and Distinction in the Divine Nature" because it simply "can never be obtained." The employment of the terms father, son, and spirit are to be understood analogically but still "expressive of what is *Answerable*, tho' *Still inconceivable* in the Divine Nature." He notes, "Now in proceeding thus we must

---

[149] Cf. Yolton, *John Locke*.
[150] Browne, *Letter*, 48. Note that here he says that God's "hands and feet" are analogies.
[151] Browne, *Procedure, Extent*, 106.
[152] Browne, *Procedure, Extent*, 106–7.

necessarily infer, that if the Mystery is revealed to us under such Analogical Resemblances as evidently imply a *Real* and even *Personal* Distinction; we are to think and speak of it as such or not think or speak of it at all."[153] In other words, God has revealed himself as Father, Son, and Spirit and we are advised to think of Him as such but without falling into the logical conundrums from restraining "person" in our limited and experiential scope while concurrently asserting that God is only one being; the literal resemblances are not congruous when taken as such; and there is no expectation that they should be congruous.

Locke does make mention of analogy in *Essay* IV.xvi.12. In that section he is discussing things that are not capable of observation. There are those things that cannot be sensed, namely "The Existence, Nature, and Operation of finite immaterial beings without us" and material beings that are too small or too far away—like inhabitants of other planets. There are also the operations in most parts of nature where we see the effects but not the causes. In both situations, thinkers rely on the apparent characteristic in God's creation that we typically find as an aid to our reasoning: "a gradual connexion of one with another, without any great or discernible gaps between, in all that great variety of Things we see in the World." Locke believes that it is likely the case for the supernatural as well as the material world: just as we see a gradual descent from humans to lower life forms, this rule or principle of analogy that we see so often, "may make it probable, that it is so also in Things above us, and our Observation . . . ascending towards the infinite Perfection of the Creator, by gentle steps and differences." These probabilities wrought from the principle of analogy help us with hypotheses and "a wary Reasoning from Analogy leads us often into the discovery of Truths, and useful Productions, which would otherwise lie concealed."

Both Locke and Browne, then, discuss analogies and find them eminently useful. But one of the main presuppositions of modern natural sciences is unobservable processes and artifacts are often analogous to that which is observable. Locke's above comments are not novel. And at no point does he employ analogy to the same ends as does Browne or is there evidence that anything changed in the *Essay* based on a knowledge of Browne's writings. Given minor modifications, there is no reason that the fundamentals of Locke's epistemology are adverse to employing analogy as did Browne. If Locke accepts incomprehensible doctrines and, as argued, rejects a Cartesian

---

[153] Browne, *Procedure, Extent*, 198–201 [quotations, pp. 199–200].

notion of pure intellect, it is likely that his thoughts on analogy parallel those of Norris and Browne.

Problems with Rejecting the Incomprehensible

Summary

So far, I have laid out two major threads of evidence that point to Locke's epistemological principles excluding affirmation of incomprehensible doctrines, namely asymmetrical or unsociable ones. First, Locke's articulations of certain of his own positions, at first blush at least, give the appearance that his epistemology does not accommodate for doctrines without a summative idea. Second, there are Lockeans, in varying degrees, who use the same principles found in Locke to argue against our ability to affirm incomprehensible doctrines. There were those, however, who were part of the loose tradition of the way of ideas whose epistemologies were an adaptation of Locke's, or at least "Locke-ish," who assiduously defended assent to the incomprehensible. Although Locke does not modify his *Essay* or other works based on these writings, there are a few reasons to think that Locke at least found an all-out rejection of incomprehensible doctrines untenable.

Human Free Choice and God's Attributes

There is one major problem with a Lockean rejection of incomprehensible doctrines: Locke's occasional comments on human liberty vis-à-vis divine sovereignty. In a letter to Molyneux, where he admits that his *Essay*'s chapter "Of Power," decidedly avoids any metaphysical conclusions, he writes:

> But if you will argue for or against liberty, from consequences, I will not undertake to answer you. For I own freely to you the weakness of my understanding, that though it be unquestionable that there is omnipotence and omniscience in God our maker, and I cannot have a clearer perception of any thing than that I am free, yet I cannot make freedom in man consistent with omnipotence and omniscience in God, though I am as fully perswaded of both as of any truth I most firmly assent to. And therefore I have long since given off the consideration of that question, resolving all

into this short conclusion, That if it be possible for God to make a free agent, then man is free, though I see not the way of it.[154]

Thus, Locke explicitly admits that he accepts two ideas or propositions that he cannot reconcile. In the *Essay*, Locke, in discussing the imperfection of our ideas and the fact that they bring about difficulties and contradictions in some instances, writes the following: "Thus, we having but imperfect *Ideas* of the Operations of our Minds, and of the Beginning of Motion or Thought how the Mind produces either of them in us, and much imperfecter yet, of the Operation of GOD, run into great Difficulties about free created Agents, which Reason cannot well extricate it self out of."[155] Similarly, in his debate with Stillingfleet, he says the following: "Omnipotency, I know, can do any thing that contains in it no Contradiction; so that I readily believe whatever God has declared, though my Reason finds Difficulties in it, which it cannot master." He follows with an example: "God having revealed, that there shall be a day of Judgment, I think that *Foundation* enough to conclude Men are *free* enough to be made answerable for their Actions, and to receive according to what they have done, though how Man is *a free* Agent, surpass my Explication or Comprehension."[156] Thus, Locke admits in a number of places that he accepts two seemingly contradictory propositions or ideas: humans are metaphysically free and God is sovereign.

This very fact would appear to overturn all the evidence that Locke's thought does not allow for incomprehensible doctrines. It appears he assents to something for which there is no summative idea, and two things together which are beyond envisioning, perhaps even "irreconcilable." Locke does not simply suspend his judgment: he claims to believe these. And while these may not be foundational to the *Essay*, they are odd examples to include if Locke were negating unsociable or asymmetrical propositions.

Locke's acceptance of human metaphysical freedom is in line with two of his close associates, John Tillotson and Robert Boyle, who use the fact of human free will together with the attributes of God to defend acceptance of the incomprehensible. In one of his published sermons, Tillotson gives biblical proof that amounts to the three propositions on the Trinity named above: there is one God, each person is God, and God is three persons.[157] He

---

[154] John Locke, "L1592. Locke to William Molyneux," 625–26; cf. Marko, "Why Locke's 'Of Power.'"
[155] Locke, *Essay*, IV.xvii.10; cf. IV.xvii.4.
[156] Locke, *Mr. Locke's Reply ... Answer to His Second Letter*, 444.
[157] Tillotson, *A Sermon Concerning*, 28–36.

points out that we have better evidence for the Trinity than we do for other incomprehensible things; and, what is more, should we give up on incomprehensible things we would have to throw out so many things in the realms of philosophy and theology on which we do not have a satisfactory mental grasp,[158] not the least of which is the simultaneous acceptance of human free will and divine foreknowledge. "The same may be said of God's certain knowledge of future Contingencies which depend upon the uncertain Wills of free Agents: It being utterly inconceivable how any Understanding, how large and perfect soever, can certainly know beforehand that which depends upon the *free Will* of another, which is an arbitrary and uncertain Cause."[159] Boyle similarly decries the ridiculousness of trying to expunge incomprehensible doctrines derived from nature or special revelation in a number of works. In his taxonomy of above reason doctrines, described earlier, he gives the following definition of the incomprehensible above reason doctrines that he calls asymmetrical or unsociable doctrines: "that is, such as we see not how to reconcile with other Things, which also manifestly are, or are by us acknowledged to be, true; such as the Divine Prescience of future Contingents, and the Liberty that belongs to Man's Will."[160] So, human freedom in light of the idea of God, is chosen by Boyle, too, as an important representative of incomprehensible things that we must accept.

Anthony Collins, who is a definite appropriator of Lockean thought, rejects contingency in free choice due to his perception criterion, the very criterion that he seems to have appropriated from Locke. Collins notes that if liberty stands "for a Power in Man to determin himself, and consequently that there are several Actions of Man absolutely contingent, since they depend as to their Existence from himself, without regard to any extrinsecal Causes" is inconsistent with the idea of God's (exhaustive) prescience, which would make human actions certain.[161] He is unable to "put together certain and contingent, or certain and incertain at the same time."[162] Collins goes on to use very Lockean sounding assertions to claim that humans are free only via "Freedom from Compulsion," or being free to follow one's determination.[163] Collins soon after would become one of the most noted proponents of necessitarianism in opposition to metaphysical liberty.

---

[158] Tillotson, *A Sermon Concerning*, 37–39.
[159] Tillotson, *A Sermon Concerning*, 40.
[160] Boyle, *Reflections upon*, 8–9.
[161] Collins, *Essay*, 34.
[162] Collins, *Essay*, 35.
[163] Collins, *Essay*, 36.

Locke, apparently, stood with Tillotson and Boyle rather than with Collins in accepting incomprehensible doctrines. Other than this reading of Locke there are several ways to explain this seeming hypocrisy or blunder on Locke's part. One could posit that Locke accepted the one incomprehensible couplet because it is derivable, arguably, from general revelation, but did not grant the same privilege to mysteries of special revelation. While one could see that being the case in other thinkers, it would be a significant stretch in the case of Locke. Many scholars have noted Locke's high view of Scripture. Furthermore, in one of the excerpts above, Locke admits he is convinced of human free will because of divine revelation. That admission seems to rule out another alternative explanation that, because Scripture was written for the uneducated, there is nothing in it that is incomprehensible.

Perhaps a more plausible explanation why he would accept metaphysical free will while not making room for other incomprehensible doctrines is based on the nature of the former. Perhaps Locke believes that God's sovereignty, although revealed in Scripture, can be made logically certain. And human free will, although not certain in the same sense, is something that we experience on a daily basis and to claim that we are perpetually mistaken is tantamount to saying God lies, leaving us with a worse conundrum. That could go along with a general principle that the mysteries revealed in the Bible can be verified in other ways; but that little addition would appear to undercut the Bible's authority in some way, something Locke was keen on avoiding. In fact, he attacks Stillingfleet for maintaining that something revealed is made surer or less sure based on how naturally reasonable it was.[164]

It could also be that the Trinity or other incomprehensible doctrines were not on Locke's radar when writing large portions of the *Essay*. In one of his replies to Stillingfleet, he says that, "my Book is no more concerned in the Controversie about the Trinity, than any other Controversie extant; nor any more opposite to that side of the Question, that your Lordship has *endeavoured to defend*, than to the contrary."[165] And in numerous places in debate with Stillingfleet, Locke claims that his *Essay* was putting forth nothing new but simply recounts how we think.[166] But he, again, does not recalibrate the *Essay* in any obvious pro-Trinitarian ways.

---

[164] Marko, *Measuring the Distance*, 58–59.
[165] Locke, *Mr. Locke's Reply... Answer to His Letter*, 106–7.
[166] Locke, *Mr. Locke's Reply... Answer to His Letter*, 72ff; Locke, *Mr. Locke's Reply... Answer to His Second Letter*, 239ff, 284, 292–93, 314, 353.

Problems of Ideas and Images

There are a few additional instances in Locke's writings where limiting ideas to contrivable images (save ideas from reflection) appears problematic in understanding Locke. For instance, as already pointed out, it is generally thought that Locke's treatment of the chiliagon was a reaction against Descartes's incorporation of the same in positing the existence of the pure intellect. Locke claims that the chiliagon is obscure and confused in its figure (relatively speaking) but clear and distinct in the number of its sides. In this case the idea goes beyond the image and our knowledge or idea of the number one thousand accompanies the relatively obscure and confused idea.[167] In other words, the idea of a chiliagon is a vague shape accompanied by a rule (which is itself understandable or conceivable).

Moreover, in Locke's discussion of ideas, he discusses adequate and inadequate ideas. Adequate ideas "perfectly represent those Archetypes, which the Mind supposes them taken from; which it intends them to stand for, and to which it refers them." Inadequate ideas are those that "are but a partial, or incomplete representation of those Archetypes to which they are referred."[168] A complex idea is adequate and is the real essence of any substance when "the Properties we discover in that Body, would depend on that complex *Idea*, and be deducible from it, and their necessary connexion with it be known." The idea of properties of iron are not inferable from the complex idea of iron. But the properties of a triangle are: "all Properties of a Triangle depend on, and as far as they are discoverable, are deducible from the complex *Idea* of three Lines, including a Space."[169] If the geometric principles of the triangle are known, the rules of a symmetric chiliagon are discoverable as well (whether Locke knew them or not). So, it is a little odd that we have ideas that are in part relatively obscure and confused but overall adequate.

More importantly, however, is the example that Allen offers in support of Walmsley's argument that Locke eventually moved away from Hobbes and separated partial consideration from abstraction. In the *Essay*, Locke asserts that we have general ideas (again using the idea of the triangle):

> For abstract *Ideas* are not so obvious or easie to Children, or the yet unexercised Mind, as particular ones. If they seem so to grown Men, 'tis

---

[167] Locke, *Essay*, II.xxix.13.
[168] Locke, *Essay*, II.xxxi.1.
[169] Locke, *Essay*, II.xxxi.6.

only because by constant and familiar use they are made so. For when we nicely reflect upon them, we shall find, that general *Ideas* are Fictions and Contrivances of the Mind, that carry difficulty with them, and do not easily offer themselves, as we are apt to imagine. For example, Does it not require some pains and skill to form the *general Idea* of a *Triangle*, (which is yet none of the most abstract, comprehensive, and difficult,) for it must be neither Oblique, nor Rectangle, neither Equilateral, Equicrural, nor Scalenon; but all and none of these at once. In effect, it is something imperfect, that cannot exist; an *Idea* wherein some parts of several different and inconsistent *Ideas* are put together.[170]

This is an instance where Locke appears to indicate that we have ideas that cannot be imagined. Or, in other words, we know the general idea of a triangle. We have this idea only after experience with various triangles. But this is knowing without an image. Perhaps there can be belief without one, then, too.

Conclusions

The answer to whether Locke's epistemology excluded incomprehensible things is much more complicated than a simple yes or no. Various positions he takes and statements he makes seem to point toward the theoretical rejection of the Trinity and other incomprehensible notions. There are some who understand his epistemology as accepting only of the comprehensible. Others show how readily Locke's own teachings that appear to rid us of the incomprehensible can be clarified, qualified, or slightly modified to accept the incomprehensible. What is more, Boyle, who greatly influenced Locke, thought it ridiculous to reject the incomprehensible outright. Locke seems to agree, at least on one issue. He expressly admits of free will in light of God's sovereignty, as an indication of sorts that his *Essay* was far from perfect. And there are other problems with the identification of non-reflective ideas and images as well.

Locke's *Essay* may have served, in part, as a project for himself to work out his own thinking. It may never have been his intention to rule out the Trinity per se, but the tracing out of his own thinking at least, during the course of

---

[170] Locke, *Essay*, IV.vii.9.

decades, gave the impression that incomprehensible things could not be affirmed, or at least not without significant toil (but if this last qualification is true, he did not do well at conveying it). Perhaps he had suspended his judgment on the Trinity and was still working it out and/or he simply did not want to reveal his true thoughts about it as doing so would ruin his ecumenical project: thus, he continuously dodges Stillingfleet on crucial matters of doctrinal acceptance, as he did with Edwards, never letting the aged bishop in close enough for a knockout punch, while he, himself, was not willing to attempt one either. He knew there were issues with rejecting all incomprehensible conclusions and propositions, even if none were soteriologically necessary or had enough practical weight to require his attention further. Besides, worse things would come about through giving people license to believe all sorts of incomprehensible and poorly thought-out claims without forcing them to think through the issues.

Epilogue

The Coherence of John Locke and his Theological Project

Overall Argument Briefly Stated

John Locke's intent for *ROC* was to describe and defend "mere Christianity" during a very theologically and philosophically controversial time and not to convey his own personal views. In the book and its vindications, he expressed his great concern for salvation (as he had in other works) and explained the content of and the reasonableness of a simple gospel—Part I with support from Chapter 7 of Part III—and the manner and the reasonableness of its conveyance—Part II with support from Chapters 8 and 9 from Part III. He thought if everyone could just see God's wisdom in these basics, the church and all that it touches would have a better likelihood of flourishing. And it was not only in *ROC* where evidence of this theological and philosophical approach were witnessed. There are adumbrations of his method within his other works. His attempts to avoid the theological and philosophical fray that had inundated the English book printers were thwarted by a few missteps and he was drawn into the debates. Even in the midst of attacks he did not deviate from his earlier course much to the consternation of his interlocutors. It was not his general practice to present new ideas in the course of debate but to instead lend clarity to what he had already asserted.

The Pervasive Theme of Salvation and Its Impact on His Corpus

Some Restatements

Eternal salvation is clearly one of Locke's fundamental concerns within his corpus of major works. In Locke's mind it is the height of irrationality not to give ample time—or the time one can muster—to determine the way of salvation. Even though Locke personally reasons from Scripture that the non-Christian will be immediately annihilated, he still goes on to caution those who think and act as if physical death is one's ontological demise. Eternity is not something one leaves to chance or questionable interpretations of Scripture. Applying one's God-given reason to the question of salvation is the call of every individual.

Freedom of Religion

Locke's call for freedom of religion works in two distinct realms. First there is the call to the church for freedom of assent. Intramurally, Locke decries the positing of theology texts, catechisms, etc. into the hands of congregants as opposed to Scripture. Arguments from authority, especially in areas of maximal concernment, are illegitimate and thus dangerous. Of course, one is free to reason biblically with another, but the goal is to have each person convinced of that to which they are claiming assent. Elders, pastors, priests, and bishops must be careful how much they exercise their authority. As Locke indicates at the end of *ROC*, some of the teachers in the congregations on different sides of the justification debates were not completely clear what each side maintained. Intermurally, Locke thinks that if a monotheist takes Christ as King and believes He is the Messiah, one should consider that person justified. This was rather generous stance in his day. But he thought that this would make for a more peaceful Kingdom where those who submitted themselves to Christ and the Scriptures could see their common ground and work together.

Second, Locke calls for freedom of religion to be respected and protected by the government. While it would be illegitimate and infinitely damaging for the government to choose the people's religion for them, one of its main goals should be to create space for people to have freedom of assent. It is dangerous, therefore, for the government to do any number of things such as: censor religious materials, promote particular sects, or oppress particular lawful sects. It is an unreasonable thing to think that a civil government that puts the eternal salvation of its people in peril could be a good or even acceptable one. All of this said, Locke does desire for Christians to keep the Bible front and center as the common touch point for ethics in the church and society. He realizes true morals are too difficult for cultures to come up with on their own with any degree of completeness; thus, Scripture is needed to correct its citizens over and over again and produce a Christianized ethical milieu.

This ecclesiastical and civil freedom coheres with a non-metaphysically focused treatment of freedom of the will. This explains why Locke was very interested in pointing to the importance of freedom from external restraint in his *Essay* as opposed to questions over various sectarian and metaphysical questions. According to his epistemology, if we lose ecclesiastical and civil freedoms as so outlined, we lose even the opportunity to discuss the other aspects of freedom of the will pertinent to salvation. Freedom of thought is the most important freedom.

Review of His Personal and Programmatic Doctrine

Personally Held Doctrine, Namely the Fall

The most obvious personal doctrine that created problems for Locke was the fall of mankind. Although he seems to accept the historical Adam and Eve from *ROC*, he appears rather Pelagian in his thoughts on the result of the fall. He rejects the traditional notion of total depravity, corruption, and the like (again, just peruse the opening pages of *ROC*). He does admit that human beings are affected by the fall—they are now mortal—but their ontological and epistemological functions are not affected to the degree most sects have claimed.[1]

Programmatic Doctrine

Locke's soteriology was rather simple and unqualified. We should consider one justified who is a monotheist, believes Jesus is the Messiah foretold of in the Old Testament, and actively takes Christ as King. Doing the last points not only to attempts to do what He and His Scriptures command but also to trying to understand what the Scriptures say. A fair attempt is what should characterize a true believer: the person is not believing from authority but

---

[1] Francis Turretin, *Institutes of Elenctic Theology*, 3 vols., ed. James T. Dennison, Jr. and trans. George Musgrave Giger (Phillipsburg: P & R Publishing, 1992), IX.vi–xii; Philip Van Limborch, *A Compleat System, or Body of Divinity, Both Speculative and Practical, Founded on Scripture and Reason*, trans. William Jones (London: 1702), 191–98.

from their own reasoned conviction and culling from Scripture. Ideally, the person also interacted with others in the course of their determination.

The other doctrinal issue that Locke clearly could not avoid was the doctrine of revelation. He was clear about the necessity of it: functionally, for issues like morality, and absolutely, for facts we could not possibly discover and accept. He thus had to defend the reasonableness of revelation as a means of conveyance of such information. He did not completely answer, as Toland did, whether God would give doctrines in His revelation of which one could not create a summary representation. But that, in Locke's mind, is perhaps intertwined with the doctrine of the Trinity.

Locke, apparently, studiously avoided making pronouncements on a number of doctrines, notably the Trinity. For this he perpetually sustained attacks from the theologically minded. Still, to make such a pronouncement, based on the combative context, would have been an undercutting of his program. The same goes for issues like the atonement, the necessity and working of grace, and the like.

Locke attempted to show that the entrance to the Kingdom of God is much broader than many thought. One's position on the doctrine of the Trinity or the person of Christ, other than the belief in one, all-powerful God and that Jesus was the Messiah was what a true follower believed. If a follower was convinced that Jesus was ontologically subordinate to the Father through their study of Scripture, one must believe that is the case or he or she is not taking Christ as King and thus not a follower. But if a different follower thought that Scripture pointed to Christ being fully God, then that person is obliged to believe that. Locke, however, did not think that antinomians were true believers as they did not actually take seriously what Scripture tells us to do. Enthusiasts could find themselves in a position to be guilty of the same. A self-professed deist who might take the dictates of Scripture seriously, but not think that Jesus was the foretold of Messiah was not a follower and not part of the Kingdom.

Locke's Prescribed Approach to Scripture: Personal and Programmatic

Locke's approach to Scripture in his own personal and programmatic views is to approach Scripture being prepared to have whatever is uncertain to be overturned. Or with some qualification, one might say his approach to Scripture was his preparedness to have whatever seems "reasonable" (probable) to be overturned. One might think a particular action is permissible, impermissible, or obligatory but one might find Scripture to say something different. The same applies to speculative claims or historical events, etc. This principle of approach is simple, but there are plenty of questions unanswered, such as: are we obligated or even able to assent to that for which we cannot form a summative idea? At times he seems to be approving of it and other times he does not. But, again, those are hardly the only questions that he does not address or clearly address in *ROC* and its vindications.

Pastoral Issues Not (Sufficiently) Addressed by Locke

There are some pastoral issues that I want to address briefly where Locke gives no express guidance. In some cases, what he would say can be inferred. One, to which he gives no guidance, is the question of an expected level of orthodoxy regarding speculative doctrines that accompanies one indwelt by the Holy Spirit. That he does not address this is not at all surprising if one were to consider his theological program. In fact, having done so would have undercut much of what he was trying to do in *ROC* and elsewhere. He did, at least, give guidance in terms of practical orthodoxy. Locke would admit that it and practical orthopraxy have a mutually reinforcing relationship and that one would expect both to progress if one were to take Christ as King, especially as we expect some help from the Holy Spirit. Major digressions or a lackadaisical attitude toward such matters (and perhaps even speculative doctrines) over time would be an indication that the person was not taking Christ as king and should not be considered a kingdom member.

Another issue that would have been instructive is some express guidance how preachers might avoid having their people rely too much on their "say-so" and to cultivate a more reasoned approach to preaching. Of course, plenty could be inferred from his epistemology and some very helpful guidance was given in terms of what the general Christian's approach to Scripture might look like in *ROC*. This is an issue that could have fit nicely within *ROC* that would not have a detrimental effect on his program.

Who Locke Is: Narratives and Labels

Locke was a thinker of many parts. He was an epistemologist, natural philosopher, political scientist, pedagogue, a past practitioner of medicine, and a theologian. The limits of his personal orthodoxy are difficult to pin down. He is a thinker and writer who can be labeled as a defender of the Christian faith in one narrative and then framed as being overly critical or dangerously broad in another. He would defend the authority and necessity of Scripture— a worthwhile task in the minds of many in his day—but would undercut nativism in doing it—a reason for alarm for many in his day. When juxtaposed with Edwards or Stillingfleet, noted theologians of their day, Locke is often framed as heterodox or too liberal. When pitted against the deists in his generation or the next he is often a defender of orthodoxy.

Locke thought of himself as follower of Jesus Christ. Right or wrong, he did his best to produce unity and peace amongst the various sects. He was amazingly reserved and controlled in debate. He has, however, demonstrated moments of indiscretion: again, the first pages of *ROC* and elsewhere make that clear. Despite those places, he would have still likely been attacked. And while he demurred from candidly speaking his theological mind, he was resolved that this could not be the case for the need for revelation and the gospel. They must be robustly explained and defended. They were to Locke the common-ground and basis for unity within the Kingdom.

Bibliography

Primary Sources

Abbott, Edwin. *Flatland: A Romance of Many Dimensions*. London: 1884.

Baxter, Richard. *The Judgment and Advice of the Assembly of the Associated Ministers of Worcester-shire, Held at Worcester Aug. 6th 1658. Concerning the Endeavours of Ecclesiasticall Peace, and the Waies and Meanes of Christian Unity, which Mr. John Durey Doth Present; Sent unto Him in the Name, and by the Appointment of the Aforesaid Assembly*. London: Printed for T. Underhill, 1658.

Biddle, John. *XII Arguments Drawn Out of Scripture: Wherein the Commonly-Received Opinion Touching the Deity of the Holy Spirit Is Clearly and Fully Refuted: To Which Is Prefixed a Letter Tending to the Same Purpose, Written to a Member of Parliament*. London: 1647.

Biddle, John. *The Apostolic and True Opinion Concerning the Holy Trinity*. London: 1691.

Blount, Charles. *Miracles, No Violations of the Laws of Nature*. London: Printed for Robert Sollers, 1683.

Blount, Charles. *Summary Account of the Deists Religion: In a Letter to that Excellent Physician, the Late Dr. Thomas Sydenham*. In *A Summary Account of the Deists Religion: In a Letter to that Excellent Physician, the Late Dr. Thomas Sydenham. To Which Are Annex'd, Some Curious Remarks on the Immortality of the Soul; and An Essay by the Celebrated Poet, John Dryden, Esq; to Prove that Natural Religion Is Alone Necessary to Salvation, in Opposition to All Divine Revelation*. London: 1745.

Bold, Samuel. *A Reply to Mr. Edwards's Brief Reflections on A Short Discourse of the True Knowledge of Christ Jesus, etc. To Which is Prefixed a Preface, Wherein Something Is Said Concerning Reason and Antiquity, in the Chief Controversies with the Sociniansm*. In *A Collection of Tracts, Publish'd in Vindication of Mr. Lock's Reasonableness of Christianity, as Deliver'd in the Scriptures, etc.* London: Printed for A. and J. Churchil, 1706.

Bold, Samuel. *A Short Discourse of the True Knowledge of Christ Jesus*. In *A Collection of Tracts, Publish'd in Vindication of Mr. Lock's Reaosnableness of Christianity, as Deliver'd in the Scriptures, etc.* London: Printed for A. and J. Churchil, 1706.

Bold, Samuel. *Some Passages in The Reasonableness of Christianity, etc. and Its Vindication. With Some Animadversions on Mr. Edwards's Reflections on the Reasonableness of Christianity, and on His Book, Entituled, Socinianism Unmask'd*. In *A Collection of Tracts, Publish'd in Vindication of Mr. Lock's Reasonableness of Christianity, as Deliver'd in the Scriptures, etc.* London: Printed for A. and J. Churchil, 1706.

Boyle, Robert. *Reflections upon a Theological Distinction. According to Which, 'tis Said, That Some Articles of Faith Are Above Reason, but Not Against Reason. In a Letter to a Friend*. London: Printed by Edw. Jones, for John Taylor, 1690.

Bramhall, John. "Bramhall's Discourse of Liberty and Necessity." In *Hobbes and Bramhall on Liberty and Necessity*, edited by Vere Chappell, 15–42. Cambridge: Cambridge University Press, 1999.

Bramhall, John. *Castigations of Mr. Hobbes: His Last Animadversions, in The Case Concerning Liberty, and Universal Necessity. With an Appendix concerning The Catching of Leviathan, or the Great Whale*. London: Printed by E. T. for J. Crook, 1658.

Bramhall, John. *A Defence of True Liberty from Ante-cedent and Extrinsicall Necessity, Being an Answer to a Late Book of Mr. Thomas Hobbs of Malmsbury, Intituled, A Treatise of Liberty and Necessity*. London: Printed for John Crook, 1655.

Browne, Peter. *A Letter in Answer to a Book Entitled Christianity Not Mysterious, etc.* Dublin: 1697.

Browne, Peter. *The Procedure, Extent, and Limits of Human Understanding*. 2nd ed., with corrections and amendments. London: Printed for William Innys, 1729.

Burnet, Gilbert. *Some Passages of the Life and Death of the Right Honourable John Earl of Rochester*. London: 1680.

Burnet, Gilbert. *A Treatise Concerning the Truth of the Christian Religion. To Which Is Added, A Discourse on Miracles, by John Locke Esq*. Glasgow: Printed by Robert Foulis, 1743.

Burnet, Thomas. *Remarks upon An Essay Concerning Humane Understanding: In a Letter Address'd to the Author*. London: Printed for M. Wotton, 1697.

Burnet, Thomas. *Second Remarks upon An Essay Concerning Humane Understanding in a Letter Address'd to the Author. Being a Vindication of the First Remarks, Against the Answer of Mr. Lock, At the End of His Reply to the Lord Bishop of Worcester*. London: Printed for M. Wotton, 1697.

Burnet, Thomas. *Third Remarks upon An Essay Concerning Humane Understanding: In a Letter Address'd to the Author*. London: Printed for M. Wotton, 1699.

Burthogge, Richard. *An Essay upon Reason, and the Nature of Spirits*. London: Printed for John Dunton, 1694.

Burthogge, Richard. *Organum Vetus and Novum: or, A Discourse of Reason and Truth. Wherein the Natural Logick Common to Mankinde Is Briefly and Plainly Described*. London: Printed for Sam. Crouch, 1678.

Calvin, John. *Institutes of the Christian Religion*. Translated by Henry Beveridge. Grand Rapids: Eerdmans, 1989.

Clarke, Samuel. *Remarks upon a Book Entituled, A Philosophical Enquiry Concerning Human Liberty*. London: 1717.

Collins, Anthony. *A Philosophical Inquiry Concerning Human Liberty*. 2nd ed., cor. London: 1717.

Dryden, John. *An Essay on Natural Religion as Opposed to Divine Revelation*. In *A Summary Account of the Deists Religion: In a Letter to that Excellent Physician, the Late Dr. Thomas Sydenham. To Which Are Annex'd, Some Curious Remarks on the Immortality of the Soul; and An Essay by the Celebrated Poet, John Dryden, Esq; to Prove that Natural Religion Is Alone Necessary to Salvation, in Opposition to All Divine Revelation*. London: 1745.

Dryden, John. *The Works of John Dryden, Volume II: Poems, 1681–1684*. Berkeley: The University of California Press, 1972.

Edward, Lord Herbert of Cherbury. *De Veritate*. Translated by Merick H. Carré. Bristol: J. W. Arrowsmith, Ltd., 1937.

Edwards, John. *The Socinian Creed: or, A Brief Account of the Professed Tenents and Doctrines of the Foreign and English Socinians. Wherein Is Shew'd the Tendency of Them* to *Irreligion and Atheism. With Proper Antidotes Against Them*. London: Printed for J. Robinson, 1697.

Edwards, John. *Socinianism Unmask'd. A Discourse Shewing the Unreasonableness of a Late Writer's Opinion Concerning the Necessity of Only One Article of Faith; and of His Other Assertions in His Late Book, Entituled, The Reasonableness of Christianity as Deliver'd in the Scriptures, and in His Vindication of It. With a Brief Reply to Another (Professed) Socinian Writer*. London: Printed for J. Robinson, 1696.

Edwards, John. *Some Thoughts Concerning the Several Causes and Occasions of Atheism, Especially in the Present Age. With Some Brief Reflections on Socinianism: And on a Late Book Entituled The Reasonableness of Christianity as Deliver'd in the Scriptures*. London: Printed for J. Robinson, 1695.

Filmer, Robert. *Patriarcha; or The Natural Power of Kings*. London: Printed for Ric. Chiswell, 1680.

Hobbes, Thomas. *Of Libertie and Necessitie: A Treatise, Whererin All Controversie Concerning Predestination, Election, Free-will, Grace, Merits, Reprobation, etc. Is Fully Decided and Cleared, in Answer to a Treatise Written by the Bishop of London-derry, on the Same Subject*. London: Printed by W. B. for F. Eaglesfield, 1654.

Hobbes, Thomas. *The Questions Concerning Liberty, Necessity, and Chance. Clearly Stated and Debated between Dr. Bramhall Bishop of Derry, and Thomas Hobbes of Malmsbury*. London: Printed for Andrew Cook, 1656.

Gailhard, Jean. *The Epistle and Preface to the Book against the Blasphemous Socinian Heresie Vindicated, and the Charge Therein against Socinianism, Made Good in Answer to Two Letters*. London: Printed for J. Hartley, 1698.

Limborch, Philip Van. *A Compleat System, or Body of Divinity, Both Speculative and Practical, Founded on Scripture and Reason*. Translated by William Jones. London: 1702.

Limborch, Philip Van. "L1101. Philippus Van Limborch to Locke, 27 January/6 February 1689." In *The Correspondence of John Locke*, vol. 3, edited by E. S. de Beer, 542–44. Oxford: Oxford University Press, 1978.

Limborch, Philip Van. "L1112. Philippus Van Limborch to Locke, [2/12 April?] 1689." In *The Correspondence of John Locke*, vol. 3, edited by E. S. de Beer, 586–89. Oxford: Oxford University Press, 1978.

Limborch, Philip Van. "L1158. Phillipus Van Limborch to Locke, 8/18 July 168." In *The Correspondence of John Locke*, vol. 3, edited by E. S. de Beer, 646–50. Oxford: Oxford University Press, 1978.

Limborch, Philip Van. "L1283. Philippus Van Limborch to Locke, 15/25 April 1690." In *The Correspondence of John Locke*, vol. 4, edited by E. S. de Beer, 55–60. Oxford: Oxford University Press, 1979.

Limborch, Philip Van. "L2110. Philipppus Van Limborch to Locke 14/24 July, 1696." In *The Correspondence of John Locke*, vol. 5, edited by E. S. de Beer, 665–71. Oxford: Clarendon Press, 1979.

Limborch, Philip Van. "L2222. Philippus Van Limborch to John Locke, 16 March 1697." In *The Correspondence of John Locke*, vol. 6, edited by E. S. de Beer, 42–53. Oxford: Clarendon Press, 1981.

Limborch, Philip Van. "L2318. Philippus Van Limborch to John Locke, 28 September 1697." In *The Correspondence of John Locke*, vol. 6, E. S. de Beer, 206–10. Oxford: Clarendon Press, 1976.

Locke, John. *An Answer to Remarks Upon an Essay Concerning Humane Understanding*. Appended to *Mr. Locke's Reply to the Right Reverend the Lord Bishop of Worcester's*

Answer to His Letter, Concerning Some Passages Relating to Mr. Locke's Essay of Humane Understanding: In Late Discourse of His Lordships, In Vindication of the Trinity. London: Printed by H. Clark, for A. and J. Churchill, 1697.

Locke, John. "A Discourse of Miracles." In *Posthumous Works of Mr. John Locke, etc.*, 217–31. London: Printed by W. B. for A. and J. Churchill, 1706.

Locke, John. *An Essay Concerning Humane Understanding*. 1st ed. London: Printed for Tho. Basset, 1690.

Locke, John. *An Essay Concerning Humane Understanding*. 2nd ed. London: Printed for A. and J. Churchil and Samuel Manship, 1694.

Locke, John. *An Essay Concerning Humane Understanding*, 3rd ed. London: A. and J. Churchil, 1695.

Locke, John. *An Essay Concerning Humane Understanding*. 4th ed. London: Printed for A. and J. Churchil and Samuel Manship, 1700.

Locke, John. *An Essay Concerning Humane Understanding*. 5th ed. London: Printed for A. and J. Churchil and Samuel Manship, 1706.

Locke, John. *An Essay Concerning Human Understanding*. Crit. ed. Edited by Peter H. Nidditch. Oxford: Clarendon Press, 1979.

Locke, John. "L868. Locke to Philippus Van Limborch, 1/11 October [1686]." In *The Correspondence of John Locke*, vol. 3, edited by E. S. de Beer, 43–45. Oxford: Oxford University Press, 1978.

Locke, John. "L964. Locke to Philippus Van Limborch, 13/23 September 1687." In *The Correspondence of John Locke*, vol. 3, edited by E. S. de Beer, 270–72. Oxford: Oxford University Press, 1978.

Locke, John. "L1127. Locke to Philippus Van Limborch, 12 April 1689." In *The Correspondence of John Locke*, vol. 3, edited by E. S. de Beer, 596–601. Oxford: Oxford University Press, 1978.

Locke, John. "L1473. Locke to Philippus Van Limborch, 29 February 1692." In *The Correspondence of John Locke*, vol. 4, edited by E. S. de Beer, 399–403. Oxford: Oxford University Press, 1979.

Locke, John. "L1592. Locke to William Molyneux, 20 January 1693." In *The Correspondence of John Locke*, vol. 4, edited by E. S. de Beer, 623–28. Oxford: Clarendon Press, 1979.

Locke, John. "L1643. Locke to William Molyneux, 15 July 1693." In *The Correspondence of John Locke*, vol. 4, edited by E. S. de Beer, 700–1. Oxford: Clarendon Press, 1979.

Locke, John. "L1655. Locke to William Molyneux, 23 August 1693." In *The Correspondence of John Locke*, vol. 4, edited by E. S. de Beer, 719–23. Oxford: Clarendon Press, 1979.

Locke, John. "L1804. Locke to Philippus Van Limborch, 26 October 1694." In *The Correspondence of John Locke*, vol. 5, edited by E. S. de Beer, 169–75. Oxford: Oxford University Press, 1979.

Locke, John "L1901. Locke to Philippus Van Limborch, 10 May 1695." In *The Correspondence of John Locke*, vol. 5, edited by E. S. de Beer, 368–72. Oxford: Clarendon Press, 1979.

Locke, John. "L2059: Locke to William Molyneux, March 30 [c. April 5] 1696." In *The Correspondence of John Locke*, vol. 5, edited by E. S. de Beer, 593–96. Oxford: Clarendon Press, 1979.

Locke, John. "L2126. Locke to Philippus Van Limborch, 3 September 1696." In *The Correspondence of John Locke*, vol. 5, edited by E. S. de Beer, 694–97. Oxford: Oxford University Press, 1979.

Locke, John. *A Letter Concerning Toleration*. 2nd ed., corrected. London: Printed for Awnsham Churchill, 1690.

Locke, John. *A Letter to Edward Ld Bishop of Worcester, Concerning Some Passages Relating to Mr. Locke's Essay of Humane Understanding: In a Late Discourse of His Lordships, In Vindication of the Trinity*. London: Printed for A. and J. Churchill, 1697.

Locke, John. *Mr. Locke's Reply to the Right Reverend the Lord Bishop of Worcester's Answer to His Letter, Concerning Some Passages Relating to Mr. Locke's Essay of Humane Understanding: In Late Discourse of His Lordships, In Vindication of the Trinity*. London: Printed by H. Clark, for A. and J. Churchill, 1697.

Locke, John. *Mr. Locke's Reply to the Right Reverend the Lord Bishop of Worcester's Answer to His Second Letter*. London: Printed by H. C. for A. and J. Churchill and E. Castle, 1699.

Locke, John. *A Paraphrase and Notes on the Epistles of Paul to the Galatians, I and II Corinthians, Romans, and Ephesians. To Which Is Prefixed, An Essay for the Understanding of St. Paul's Epistles, by Consulting St. Paul Himself*. London: Printed for Thomas Tegg, W. Sharpe and Son, etc., 1823.

Locke, John. "Part of a Fourth Letter for Toleration." In *Posthumous Works of Mr. John Locke*, 235-77. London: Printed by W. B. for A. and J. Churchill, 1706.

Locke, John. *The Reasonableness of Christianity, as Delivered in the Scriptures*. 2nd ed. London: Printed for A. and J. Churchil, 1696.

Locke, John. *The Reasonableness of Christianity: As Delivered in the Scriptures*. Edited by John C. Higgins-Biddle. Oxford: Clarendon Press, 1999.

Locke, John. *A Second Letter Concerning Toleration*. London: Printed for A. and J. Churchill, 1690.

Locke, John. *A Second Vindication of the Reasonableness of Christianity, etc*. London: A. and J. Churchil, 1697.

Locke, John. *Some Thoughts Concerning Education*. London: Printed for A. and J. Churchill, 1693.

Locke, John. *A Third Letter for Toleration, to the Author of the Third Letter Concerning Toleration*. London: Printed for Awhsham and John Churchill, 1692.

Locke, John. *Two Treatises on Government: In the Former, The False Principles and Foundation of Robert Filmer, and His Followers Are Detected and Overthrown. The Latter Is an Essay Concerning the True Original, Extent, and End of Civil Government*. London: Printed for A. and J. Churchil, 1698.

Locke, John. *A Vindication of the Reasonableness of Christianity, etc, From Mr. Edwards's Reflections*. London: A. and J. Churchil, 1695.

Malebranche, Nicolas. *Nature and Grace*. In *Father Malebranche: His Treatise Concerning Search after Truth. The Whole Work Complete. To Which Is Added the Author's Treatise of Nature and Grace: Being a Consequence of the Principles Contained in the Search*. 2nd ed., corrected and translated by T. Taylor, 1–40. London: Printed by W. Bowyer for Thomas Bennet, 1700.

Milner, John. *An Account of Mr. Lock's Religion*. London: Printed by J. Nutt, 1700.

Molyneux, William. "L1579. William Molyneux to Locke, 22 December 1692." In *The Correspondence of John Locke*, vol. 4, edited by E. S. de Beer, 599-602. Oxford: Clarendon Press, 1979.

Molynuex, William. "L1622. William Molyneux to Locke, 18 April 1693." In *The Correspondence of John Locke*, vol. 4, edited by E. S. de Beer, 667-69. Oxford: Clarendon Press, 1979.

Molyneux, William. "L1763. William Molyneux to Locke, 28 July 1694, July 1693." In *The Correspondence of John Locke*, vol. 5, edited by E. S. de Beer, 92-93. Oxford: Clarendon Press, 1979.

Norris, John. *An Account of Reason and Faith: In Relation to the Mysteries of Christianity*. London: Printed for S. Manship, 1697.

Nye, Stephen. *A Brief History of the Unitarians, Called also Socinians. In Four Letters, Written to a Friend*. 2nd ed. London: 1691.

Nye, Stephen. *Considerations on the Explications of the Doctrine of the Trinity by Dr. Wallis, Dr. Sherlock, Dr. South, Dr. Cudworth, and Mr. Hooker as also on the Account Given by Those That Say the Trinity Is an Unconceivable and Inexplicable Mystery: Written to a Person of Quality*. London: 1693.

Nye, Stephen. *Considerations on the Explications of the Doctrine of the Trinity, Occasioned by Four Sermons Preached by His Grace the Lord Archbishop of Canterbury, etc*. In *A Third Collection of Tracts, Proving the God and Father of Our Lord Jesus Christ, the Only True God, etc*. London: 1695.

Nye, Stephen. *The Exceptions of Mr. Edwards, in His Causes of Atheism, against the Reasonableness of Christianity, as Delivered in the Scriptures, Examin'd; and Found Unreasonable, Unscriptural, and Injurious. Also It's Clearly Proved by Many Testimonies of Holy Scripture, That the God and Father of Our Lord Jesus Christ Is the Only God and Father of Christians*. London: 1695.

Owen, John. *The Works of John Owen*. 16 vols. Edited by William H. Goold. Carlisle, PA: Banner of Truth Trust, 1966.

Patrick, Symon. *The Witnesses to Christianity; or, The Certainty of Our Faith and Hope: in a Discourse upon 1 S. John v. 7, 8*. London: Printed for R. Royston, 1675.

Proast, Jonas. *The Argument of the Letter Concerning Toleration Briefly Consider'd and Answer'd*. Oxford: Printed for H. West and A. Clements, 1690.

Proast, Jonas. *A Third Letter Concerning Toleration: In Defence of the Argument of the Letter Concerning Toleration Briefly Consider'd and Answer'd*. Oxford: Printed by H. Lichfield for G. West and H. Clements, 1691.

Przypkowski, Samuel. *The Life of that Incomparable Man, Faustus Socinus Senensis*. London: Printed for Richard Moone, 1653.

The Racovian Catechism, with Notes and Illustrations. Translated by Thomas Rees. London: Printed for Longman, et al., 1818.

Rust, George. *A Discourse of the Use of Reason in Matters of Religions: Shewing, That Christianity Contains Nothing Repugnant to Right Reason; Against Enthusiasts and Deists*. Translated and annotated by Hen. Hallywell. London: Printed by Hen. Hills, Jun for Walter Kettilby, 1683.

Sherlock, William. *A Defence of Dr. Sherlock's Notion of a Trinity in Unity, in Answer to the Animadversions upon His Vindication of the Doctrine of the Holy and Ever Blessed Trinity. With a Post-Script Relating to the Calm Discourse of a Trinity in the Godhead. In a Letter to a Friend*. London: Printed for W. Rogers, 1694.

Sherlock, William. *A Vindication of the Holy and Ever Blessed Trinity, and the Incarnation of the Son of God. Occasioned by the Brief Notes on the Creed of St. Athanasius, and the Brief History of the Unitarians, or Socinians, and Containing an Answer to Both*. London: W. Rogers, 1690.

Socini, Fausti. *De Jesu Christo Servatore, Hoc Est, Cur & Qua Ratione Jesus Christus Noster Servator Sit* in *Fausti Socini Senensis Operum Tomus Alter Continens ejusdem Scripta Polemica*. Irenopoli, 1656.

South, Robert. *Animadversions upon Dr. Sherlock's Book, Entituled A Vindication of the Holy and Blessed Trinity, etc. Together with a More Necessary Vindication of that Sacred, and Prime Article of the Christian Faith from His New Notions, and False Explications of It. Humbly Offered to His Admirers, and to Himself the Chief of Them*. London: Printed for Randall Taylor, 1693.

South, Robert. *Tritheism Charged upon Dr. Sherlock's New Notion of the Trinity and the Charge Made Good, in Answer to the Defense of the Said Notion against the Animadversions upon Dr. Sherlock's Book, Entituled, A Vindication of the Doctrine of the Holy and Ever Blessed Trinity, etc*. London: Printed for John Whitlock, 1695.

Spinoza, Benedict de. "On Miracles." In *Theological-Political Treatise*, edited by Jonathan Israel, translated by Michael Silverstone and Jonathan Israel, 81-96. New York: Cambridge University Press, 2007.

Stephens, William. *An Account of the Growth of Deism in England*. London: 1696.

Stillingfleet, Edward. *The Bishop of Worcester's Answer to Mr. Locke's Letter, Concerning Some Passages Relating to His Essay of Humane Understanding, Mention'd in the Late Discourse in Vindication of the Trinity*. London: Printed by J. H. for Henry Mortlock, 1697.

Stillingfleet, Edward. *The Bishop of Worcester's Answer to Mr. Locke's Second Letter; Wherein His Notion of Ideas is Prov'd to Be Inconsistent with It Self, and with the Articles of the Christian Faith*. London: Printed by J. H. for Henry Mortlock, 1698.

Stillingfleet, Edward. *A Discourse in Vindication of the Trinity with an Answer to the Late Socinian Objections against It from Scripture, Antiquity and Reason*. 2nd ed. London: Printed by J. H. for Henry Mortlock, 1697.

Tillotson, John. "Sermon XI: Of the Miracles Wrought in Confirmation of Christianity." In *Fifteen Sermons on Various Subjects*, edited by Ralph Barker, 301-42. London: Ri. Chiswell, 1703.

Tillotson, John. "Sermon XII: Of the Miracles Wrought in Confirmation of Christianity." In *Fifteen Sermons on Various Subjects*, edited by Ralph Barker, 343-70. London: Ri. Chiswell, 1703.

Tillotson, John. "Sermon XIII: Of the Miracles Wrought in Confirmation of Christianity." In *Fifteen Sermons on Various Subjects*, edited by Ralph Barker, 371-96. London: Ri. Chiswell, 1703.

Tillotson, John. *A Sermon Concerning the Unity of the Divine Nature, and the Blessed Trinity, etc*. London: Printed for B. Aylmer and W. Rogers, 1693.

Tindal, Matthew. *Christianity as Old as the Creation: or, The Gospel, a Republication of the Religion of Nature*. London: 1730.

Toland, John. *An Apology for Mr. Toland, In a Letter from Himself to a Member of the House of Commons in Ireland; Written the Day before His Books Was Resolv'd to Be Burnt by the Committee of Religion. To Which Is Prefix'd a Narrative Containing the Occasion of the Said Letter*. London: 1697.

Toland, John. *Christianity Not Mysterious: or, A Treatise Shewing, That There Is Nothing in the Gospel Contrary to Reason, Nor Above It: And That No Christian Doctrine Can Be Properly Call'd a Mystery*. 2nd ed., enlarged. London: Printed for Sam. Buckley, 1696.

Toland, John. *A Defence of Mr. Toland in a Letter to Himself*. London: Printed for E. Whitlock, 1697.

Toland, John. *Vindicius Liberius: or M. Toland's Defence of Himself, against the Late Lower House of Convocation and Others*. London: Printed for Bernard Lintott, 1702.

Turretin, Francis. *Institutes of Elenctic Theology*. 3 vols. Translated by George Musgrave Giger and edited by James T. Dennison, Jr. Phillipsburg: P&R Publishing, 1997.

Wallis, John. *An Answer to Dr. Sherlock's Examination of the Oxford Decree: In a Letter from a Member of that University, to His Friend in London.* London: Printed by M. Whitlock, 1696.

Wallis, John. *The Doctrine of the Blessed Trinity Briefly Explained, in a Letter to a Friend.* London: Printed for Tho. Parkhurst, 1690.

Wallis, John. *Eight Letters Concerning the Blessed Trinity.* New ed. Edited by Thomas Flintoff. London: Printed for J. G. & F. Rivington, J. H. Parker, and T. Sowler, 1840.

Wallis, John. *Three Sermons Concerning the Sacred Trinity.* London: Printed for Tho. Parkhurst, 1691.

Waterland, Daniel. *An End to Discord: Wherein Is Demonstrated, That No Doctrinal Controversy Remains between the Presbyterian and Congregational Ministers, Fit to Justify Long Divisions. With a True Account of Socinianism as to the Satisfaction of Christ.* London: 1699.

Westminster Confession. Glasgow: Free Presbyterian Publications, 1994.

Votes of Parliament Touching the Book Commonly Called The Racovian Catechism. London: Printed by John Field, Printer to the Parliament of England, 1652.

Secondary Sources

Allen, Keith "Idea." In *The Oxford Handbook of British Philosophy in the Seventeenth-Century*, edited by Peter R. Antsey, 329–48. Oxford: Oxford University Press, 2013.

Ashcraft, Richard. "Faith and Knowledge in Locke's Philosophy." In *John Locke: Problems and Perspectives*, edited by John W. Yolton, 194–223. Cambridge: Cambridge University Press, 1969.

Asselt, William J., J. Martin Bac, and Roelf T. te Velde, translators, editors, and commentators. *Reformed Thought on Freedom: The Concept of Free Choice in Early Modern Reformed Theology.* Grand Rapids: Baker Academic, 2010.

Atherton, Margaret. "Locke and the Issue over Innateness." In *Locke*, edited by Vere Chappell, 48–59. Oxford: Oxford University Press, 1998.

Ayers, M. R. "Richard Burthogge and the Origins of Modern Conceptualism." In *Analytic Philosophy and the History of Philosophy*, edited by G. A. J. Rogers and Tom Sorrell, 179–200. Oxford: Oxford University Press, 2005.

Ayers, Michael. *Locke: Epistemology and Ontology.* 2 vols. New York: Routledge, 1991.

Babcock, William S. "A Changing of the Christian God." *Interpretation* 45 (1991): 133–46.

Bardi, Jason Socrates. *The Calculus Wars: Newton, Leibniz, and the Greatest Mathematical Clash of All Time.* New York: Thunder's Mouth Press, 2006.

Bavinck, Herman. *Reformed Dogmatics.* Vol. 3. Edited by John Bolt and translated by John Vriend. Grand Rapids: Baker Academic, 2006.

Beach, J. Mark. "The Hobbes–Bramhall Debate on the Nature of Freedom and Necessity." In *Biblical Interpretation and Doctrinal Formulation in the Reformed Tradition*, edited by Arie C. Leder and Richard A. Muller, 231–61. Grand Rapids: Reformed Heritage Books, 2014.

Beiser, Frederick C. *The Sovereignty of Reason: The Defense of Rationality in the Early English Enlightenment.* Princeton: Princeton University Press, 1996.

Berkhof, Louis. *Systematic Theology*. New combined ed. Grand Rapids: William B. Eerdmans, 1996.

Boersma, Hans. *A Hot Pepper Corn: Richard Baxter's Doctrine of Justification in Its Seventeenth-Century Context of Controversy*. Vancouver: Regent College Publishing, 2004.

Boyer, Carl B. *The History of the Calculus and Its Conceptual Development: The Concepts of the Calculus*. New York: Dover Publications, Inc., 1959.

Boyer, Steven D., and Christopher A. Hall. *The Mystery of God: Theology for Knowing the Unknowable*. Grand Rapids: Baker Academic, 2012.

Broadie, Alexander. "Philosophy, Revealed Religion, and the Enlightenment." In *The Oxford Handbook of British Philosophy in the Eighteenth Century*, edited by James A. Harris, 621-37. Oxford: Oxford University Press, 2013.

Brown, Stuart. "Locke as Secret 'Spinozist': The Perspective of William Carroll." In *Disguised and Overt Spinozism Around 1700: Papers Presented at the International Colloquium Held at Rotterdam, 5-8 October 1994*, edited by Wiep Van Bunge and Wim Klever, 213-34. New York: E. J. Brill, 1996.

Burns, R. M. *The Great Debate on Miracles: From Joseph Glanvill to David Hume*. Lewisburg: Bucknell University Press, 1981.

Carroll, Robert Todd. *The Common-Sense Philosophy of Bishop Edward Stillingfleet 1635-1699*. The Hague: Martinus Nijhoff, 1975.

Champion, Justin. "'Directions for the Profitable Reading of the Holy Scriptures': Biblical Criticism, Clerical Learning and Lay Readers, c. 1650-1720." In *Scripture and Scholarship in Early Modern England*, edited by Ariel Hessayon and Nicholas Keene, 208-30. Burlington: Ashgate Publishing Company, 2006.

Champion, Justin. "'A law of continuity in the progress of theology': Assessing the Legacy of John Locke's *Reasonableness of Christianity*, 1695-2004." *Eighteenth-Century Thought* 3 (2007): 111-42.

Champion, Justin. *Republican Learning: John Toland and the Crisis of Culture, 1696-1722*. Manchester: Manchester University Press, 2003.

Chappell, Vere, ed. Introduction to *Hobbes and Bramhall on Liberty and Necessity*, ix-xxiii. Cambridge: Cambridge University Press, 1999.

Chappell, Vere. "Locke on the Suspension of Desire." In *John Locke: An Essay Concerning Human Understanding in Focus*, edited by Gary Fuller, Robert Stecker, and John P. Wright, 236-48. London: Routledge, 2000.

Craig, William Lane. "Middle Knowledge: A Calvinist-Arminian Rapprochement?" In *The Grace of God and the Will of Man*, edited by Clark H. Pinnock, 141-64. Grand Rapids: Zondervan, 1989.

Coleman, Dorothy. "Baconian Probability and Hume's Theory of Testimony." *Hume Studies* 27, no. 2 (November 2001): 195-226.

Conrad, Jonathan Donald. "Locke's Use of the Bible in: *The Two Treatises*, *The Reasonableness of Christianity*, and *A Letter Concerning Toleration*." PhD diss., Northern Illinois University, 2004.

Copleston, Frederick. *History of Philosophy*. 9 vols. Westminster, UK: The Newman Press, 1964.

Cragg, Gerald R. *Reason and Authority in the Eighteenth Century*. Cambridge: Cambridge University Press, 1964.

Cranston, Maurice. *John Locke: A Biography*. New York: The MacMillan Company, 1957.

Descartes, Rene. *The Philosophical Writings*. 2 vols. Translated by John Cottingham, Robert Stoothof, and Dugald Murdoch. Cambridge: Cambridge University Press, 1984.

Dockrill, D. W. "'No Other Name': the Problem of Salvation of the Pagans in Mid-Seventeenth Century Cambridge." In *The Idea of Salvation: Papers from the Conference on the Idea of Salvation, Sacred and Secular, Held at St. Paul's College, University of Sydney, 22-25 August, 1986*, edited by D. W. Dockrill and R. G. Tanner, 117-51. Auckland: University of Auckland, 1988.

Dixon, Philip. *Nice and Hot Disputes: The Doctrine of the Trinity in the Seventeenth Century*. London: T&T Clark, 2003.

Dumsday, Travis. "Locke on Competing Miracles." *Faith and Philosophy* 25, no. 4 (October 2008): 416-24.

Dunn, John. *The Political Thought of John Locke: An Historical Account of the Argument of the 'Two Treatises of Government.'* Cambridge: Cambridge University Press, 1969.

Dworetz, Steven M. *The Unvarnished Doctrine: Locke, Liberalism, and the American Revolution*. Durham: Duke University Press, 1990.

Edwards, Jr., Charles Henry. *The Historical Development of the Calculus*. New York: Springer Verlag, 1979.

Forde, Steven. "Natural Law, Theology, and Morality in Locke." *American Journal of Political Science* 45, no. 2 (April 2001): 396-409.

Forster, Greg. *John Locke's Politics of Moral Consensus*. Cambridge: Cambridge University Press, 2005.

Foster, David. "The Bible and Natural Freedom in John Locke's Political Thought." In *Piety and Humanity*, edited by Douglas Kries, 181-212. Lanham: Rowman and Littlefield, 1997.

Fouke, Daniel C. *Philosophy and Theology in a Burlesque Mode: John Toland and "The Way of Paradox."* Amherst, MA: Humanity Books, 2007.

Hampton, Stephen. *Anti-Arminians: The Anglican Reformed Tradition from Charles II to George I*. Oxford: Oxford University Press, 2008.

Hall, A. Rupert. *Philosophers at War: The Quarrel between Newton and Leibniz*. New York: Cambridge University Press, 1980.

Harris, James A. *Of Liberty and Necessity: The Free Will Debate in Eighteenth-Century British Philosophy*. Oxford: Oxford University Press, 2005.

Harrison, Peter. "Miracles, Early Modern Science, and Rational Religion." *Church History* 75, no. 3 (September 2006): 493-510.

Helm, Paul. "Locke on Faith and Knowledge." *The Philosophical Quarterly* 23, no. 90 (January 1973): 52-66.

Helm, Paul. "Thomas Halyburton and John Locke on the Grounding of Faith in Scripture." In *Reformed Orthodoxy in Scotland: Essays on Scottish Theology, 1560-1775*, edited by Aaron Clay Denlinger, 213-30. London: Bloomsbury T&T Clark, 2015.

Higgins-Biddle, John C., ed. Introduction to *The Reasonableness of Christianity*, xv-cxv. Oxford: Clarendon Press, 1999.

Houston, Joseph. *Reported Miracles: A Critique of Hume*. New York: Cambridge University Press, 1994.

Grant, Ruth W., and Benjamin R. Hertzberg, "Locke on Education." In *A Companion to Locke*, edited by Matthew Stuart, 448-65. Oxford: Blackwell, 2016.

Green, Michael. *The Second Epistle of Peter and the Epistle of Jude: An Introduction and Commentary*. Rev. ed. Grand Rapids: Eerdmans, 1987.

Griffin, Martin I. J., Jr. *Latitudinarianism in the Seventeenth-Century Church of England*. Annotated by Richard H. Popkin and edited by Lila Freedman. New York: E. J. Brill, 1992.

Gunton, Colin. "Transcendence, Metaphor, and the Knowability of God." *Journal of Theological Studies* 31, no. 2 (Oct. 1980): 501–16.

Joldersma, Clarence W. "Providential Deism, Divine Reason, and Locke's Educational Theory." *The Journal of Educational Thought* 45, no. 2 (Autumn, 2011): 113–25.

Jolley, Nicholas. "Locke on Faith and Reason." In *The Cambridge Companion to Locke's "Essay Concerning Human Understanding,"* edited by Lex Newman, 436–55. Cambridge: Cambridge University Press, 2007.

Klauber, Martin I. "Between Protestant Orthodoxy and Rationalism: Fundamental Articles in the Early Career of Jean LeClerc." *Journal of the History of Ideas* 54, no. 4 (1993): 611–36.

Klauber, Martin I. "The Drive Toward Protestant Union in Early Eighteenth-Century Geneva: Jean-Alphonse Turrettini on the 'Fundamental Articles' of the Faith." *Church History* 61, no. 3 (1992): 334–49.

Knapp, Henry M. "John Owen, on Schism and the Nature of the Church." *Westminster Theological Journal* 72, no. 2 (2010): 333–58.

Keener, Craig. *Miracles: The Credibility of the New Testament Accounts*. 2 vols. Grand Rapids: Baker Academic, 2011.

Elmar Kremer, "Antoine Arnauld." In *Stanford Encyclopedia of Philosophy* (first published on January 27, 2007; accessed on August 10, 2019), edited by Edward N. Zalta. https://plato.stanford.edu/archives/sum2018/entries/arnauld/.

Kremer, Elmer J. "Malebranche on Human Freedom." In *The Cambridge Companion to Malebranche*, edited by Steven Nadler, 190–219. Cambridge: Cambridge University Press, 2000.

Kort, E. D. "Stillingfleet and Locke on Substance, Essence, and Articles of Faith." *Locke Studies* 5 (2005): 149–78.

Kurun, İsmail. *The Theological Origins of Liberalism*. New York: Lexington Books, 2016.

Kuehn, Manfred. "Reason and Understanding." In *The Routledge Companion to Eighteenth Century Philosophy*, edited by Aaron Garret, 167–87. New York: Routledge, 2014.

Landes, Margaret W., ed. Introduction to *The Philosophical Writings of Richard Burthogge*, ix–xxiv. Chicago: The Open Court Publishing Company, 1921.

Leask, Ian. "Personation and Immanent Undermining: On Toland's Appearing Lockean." *British Journal for the History of Philosophy* 18, no. 2 (2010): 231–56.

Lee, Sungho. "All Subjects of the Kingdom of Christ: John Owen's Conceptions of Christian Unity and Schism." PhD diss., Calvin Theological Seminary, 2007.

Lewis, C. S. *Miracles: A Preliminary Study*. San Francisco: Harper Collins, 2000.

Lim, Paul Chang-Ha. *In Pursuit of Purity, Unity, and Liberty: Richard Baxter's Puritan Ecclesiology in Its Seventeenth-Century Context*. Boston: Brill, 2004.

Lim, Paul C. H. *Mystery Unveiled: The Crisis of the Trinity in Early Modern England*. Oxford: Oxford University Press, 2012.

Livingston, James. *Modern Christian Thought*. 2 vols. 2nd ed. Minneapolis: Fortress Press, 2006.

LoLordo, Antonia. *Locke's Moral Man*. Oxford: Oxford University Press, 2012.

LoLordo, Antonia. "Reply to Rickless." *Locke Studies* 13 (2013): 55–64.

Lucci, Diego. *John Locke's Christianity*. Cambridge: Cambridge University Press, 2020.

Lucci, Diego. *Scripture and Deism: The Biblical Criticism of the Eighteenth-Century British Deists*. New York: Peter Lang, 2008.
MacGregor, Kirk R. *Luis de Molina: The Life and Theology of the Founder of Middle Knowledge*. Grand Rapids: Zondervan, 2015.
MacIntosh, J. J. "Locke and Boyle on Miracles and God's Existence." In *Robert Boyle Reconsidered*, edited by Michael Hunter, 193–215. Cambridge: Cambridge University Press, 1994.
Mander, W. J. *The Philosophy of John Norris*. Oxford: Oxford University Press, 2008.
Marko, Jonathan S. "Above Reason Propositions and Contradiction in the Religious Thought of Robert Boyle." *Forum Philosophicum* 19, no. 2 (2014): 227–39.
Marko, Jonathan S. "The Brave New World of Discordant Voices into Which Jonathan Edwards Was Born." In *A Collection of Essays on Jonathan Edwards*, edited by Robert Boss, 85–92. Fortworth: Jonathan Edwards Society Press, 2017.
Marko, Jonathan S. "Early Modern Discussions of Grace." In *Encyclopedia of Early Modern Philosophy and Sciences*, edited by Dana Jalobeanu and Charles T. Wolfe, 770–81. Cham: Springer, 2022.
Marko, Jonathan S. "The Locke-Stillingfleet Controversy." In *Encyclopedia of Early Modern Philosophy and Sciences*, edited by Dana Jalobeanu and Charles T. Wolfe, 1138–44. Cham: Springer, 2022.
Marko, Jonathan S. "Justification, Ecumenism, and Heretical Red Herrings in John Locke's *The Reasonableness of Christianity*." *Philosophy and Theology* 26, no. 2 (2014): 245–66.
Marko, Jonathan S. *Measuring the Distance between Locke and Toland: Reason, Revelation, and Rejection during the Locke-Stillingfleet Debate*. Eugene, OR: Pickwick Publications, 2017.
Marko, Jonathan S. "The Promulgation of Right Morals: John Locke on the Church and the Christian as the Salvation of Society." *Journal of Markets and Morality* 19, no. 1 (2016): 41–59.
Marko, Jonathan S. "Reason and Revelation in Early Modern Protestantism." In *Encyclopedia of Early Modern Philosophy and Sciences*, edited by Dana Jalobeanu and Charles T. Wolfe, 1774–84. Cham: Springer, 2022.
Marko, Jonathan S. "Revisiting the Question: Is Anthony Collins the Author of the 1729 *Dissertation on Liberty and Necessity*?" *Philosophy and Theology* 22, nos. 1 & 2 (2010): 77–104.
Marko, Jonathan S. Review of *The Theological Origins of Liberalism* by İsmail Kurun. *Journal of Markets & Morality* 21, no. 2 (Fall, 2018): 209–12.
Marko, Jonathan S. "Supplementing Contemporary Treatments of Doctrinal Mysteries with Largely Forgotten Voices from the Past." *Trinity Journal* 39, no. 1 (2018): 23–42.
Marko, Jonathan S. "Why Locke's 'Of Power' Is Not a Metaphysical Pronouncement: Locke's Response to Molyneux's Critique." *Philosophy and Theology* 29 no. 1 (2017): 41–68.
Marshall, John. "John Locke and Latitudinarianism." In *Philosophy, Science, and Religion in England 1640-1700*, edited by Richard Kroll, Richard Ashcraft, and Perez Zagorin, 253–82. New York: Cambridge University Press, 1992.
Marshall, John. *John Locke: Resistance, Religion and Responsibility*. Cambridge: Cambridge University Press, 1994.
Marshall, John. *John Locke, Toleration and Early Enlightenment Culture*. Cambridge: Cambridge University Press, 2006.

Marshall, John. "Locke, Socinianism, 'Socinianism', and Unitarianism." In *English Philosophy in the Age of Locke*, edited by M. A. Stewart, 111–82. Oxford: Clarendon Press, 2000.

McCann, Edwin. "Locke's Theory of Substance Under Attack!" *Philosophical Studies* 106 (2001): 87–105.

McGuinness, Philip. "Christianity Not Mysterious and the Enlightenment." In John Toland's *Christianity Not Mysterious: Text, Associated Works and Critical Essays*, edited by Philip McGuinness et al., 231–42. Dublin: Lilliput Press, Ltd., 1997.

McLachlan, Herbert. *The Religious Opinions of Milton, Locke and Newton*. Manchester: University of Manchester Press, 1941.

Mclachlan, Herbert. *Socinianism in Seventeenth Century England*. Oxford: Oxford University Press, 1951.

Mitchell, Joshua. "John Locke and the Theological Foundation of Liberal Toleration: A Christian Dialectic of History." *The Review of Politics* 52, no. 1 (Winter, 1990): 64–83.

Mitchell, Joshua. *Not by Reason Alone: Religion, History, and Identity in Early Modern Political Thought*. Chicago: The University of Chicago Press, 1993.

Moreau, Denis. "The Malebranche–Arnauld Debate." In *The Cambridge Companion to Malebranche*, edited by Steven Nadler, 87–111. Cambridge: Cambridge University Press, 2000.

Moreland, J. P., and William Lane Craig. *Philosophical Foundations for a Christian Worldview*. Downers Grove: IVP Academic, 2003.

Mooney, T. Brian, and Anthony Imbrosciano. "The Curious Case of Mr. Locke's Miracles." *International Journal for Philosophy of Religion* 57, no. 3 (Jun. 2005): 147–68.

Moore, J. T. "Locke on the Moral Need for Christianity." *The Southwestern Journal of Philosophy* 11 (1980): 61–68.

Mortimer, Sarah. *Reason and Religion in the English Revolution: The Challenge of Socinianism*. Cambridge: Cambridge University Press, 2010.

Müller, Patrick. *Latitudinarianism and Didacticism in Eighteenth-Century Literature: Moral Theology in Fielding, Sterne, and Goldsmith*. New York: Peter Lang, 2009.

Muller, Richard A. "Arminius's 'Conference' with Junius and the Protestant Reception of Molina's *Concordia*." In *Beyond Dordt and De Auxiliis: The Dynamics of Protestant and Catholic Soteriology in the Sixteenth and Seventeenth Centuries*, edited by Jordan Ballor, Matthew Gaetano, and David Sytsma, 103–26. Leiden: Brill, 2019.

Muller, Richard A. *Dictionary of Latin and Greek Theological Terms: Drawn Principally from Protestant Scholastic Theology*. 2nd ed. Grand Rapids: Baker Academic, 2017.

Muller, Richard A. *Divine Will and Human Choice: Freedom, Contingency, and Necessity in Early Modern Reformed Thought*. Grand Rapids: Baker Academic, 2017.

Muller, Richard A. *God, Creation, and Providence in the Thought of Jacob Arminius: Sources and Directions of Scholastic Protestantism in the Era of Early Orthodoxy*. Grand Rapids: Baker, 1991.

Muller, Richard A. "Grace, Election, and Contingent Choice: Arminius's Gambit and the Reformed Response." In *The Grace of God, the Bondage of the Will, Vol. 2: Historical and Theological Perspectives on Calvinism*, edited by Thomas R. Schreiner and Bruce A. Ware, 251–78. Grand Rapids: Baker Books, 1995.

Muller, Richard A. *Post-Reformation Reformed Dogmatics: The Rise and Development of Reformed Orthodoxy, ca. 1520 to ca. 1725*. 2nd ed. 4 vols. Grand Rapids: Baker Academic, 2003.

Myers, Peter C. "Locke on Reasonable Christianity and Reasonable Politics." In *Piety and Humanity*, edited by Douglas Kries, 145-80. New York: Rowman and Littlefield Publishers, Inc., 1997.

Nahin, Paul J. *An Imaginary Tale: The Story of the Square Root of Minus One*. Princeton: Princeton University Press, 1998.

Nuovo, Victor. *Christianity, Antiquity, and Enlightenment: Interpretations of Locke*. New York: Springer, 2011.

Nuovo, Victor. *John Locke and Christianity: Contemporary Responses to The Reasonableness of Christianity*. Edited and introduced by Victor Nuovo. Bristol: Thoemmes Press, 1997.

Nuovo, Victor. *John Locke: The Philosopher as Christian Virtuoso*. Oxford: Oxford University Press, 2017.

Nuovo, Victor. "Chapter 3: Locke's Proof of the Divine Authority of Scripture." In *Philosophy and Religion in Enlightenment Britain: New Case Studies*, edited by Ruth Savage, 57-76. Oxford: Oxford University Press, 2012.

Nuovo, Victor. "Locke's Theology, 1694-1704." In *English Philosophy in the Age of Locke*, edited by M. A. Stewart, 183-216. Oxford: Clarendon Press, 2000.

O'Higgins, James. *Anthony Collins: The Man and His Works*. The Hague: Martinus Nijhoff, 1970.

O'Higgins, James. *Determinism and Freewill: Anthony Collins' "A Philosophical Inquiry concerning Human Liberty" Edited and Annotated with a Discussion of the Opinions of Hobbes, Locke, Pierre Bayle, William King and Leibniz*. The Hague: Martinus Nijhoff, 1976.

Pickard, Stephen. "The Purpose of Stating the Faith: An Historical and Systematic Inquiry into the Tradition of Fundamental Articles with Special Reference to Anglicanism." PhD diss., Durham University, 1990.

Platt, John E. "The Denial of the Innate Idea of God in Dutch Remonstrant Theology: From Episcopius to Van Limborch." In *Protestant Scholasticism in Essays in Reassessment*, edited by Carl R. Trueman and R. Scott Clark, 213-26. Glasgow: Pater Noster Press, 1999.

Polinska, Wioletta. "Faith and Reason in John Locke." *Philosophy and Theology* 11, no. 2 (1999): 287-309.

Purpus, Eugene R. "Some Notes on a Deistical Essay Attributed to Dryden." *Philological Quarterly* 29 (January 1950): 342-49.

Rabieh, Michael S. "The Reasonableness of Locke, or the Questionableness of Christianity." *Journal of Politics* 53, no. 4 (November 1991): 933-57.

Randall, Jr., John Herman. *Making of the Modern Mind: A Survey of the Intellectual Background of the Present Age*. 1926, reprinted with a forward by Jacques Barzun. New York: Columbia University Press, 1976.

Redwood, John. *Reason, Ridicule, and Religion: The Age of Enlightenment in England 1660-1750*. Cor. ed. London: Thames and Hudson, 1996.

Remnant, Peter, and Jonathan Bennett, ed. and trans. Introduction to *New Essays on Human Understanding* by G. W. Leibniz, vii-xxx. Cambridge: Cambridge University Press, 1997.

Rickless, Samuel C. "Locke on the Freedom to Will." *The Locke Newsletter* 31 (2000): 43-67.

Rickless, Samuel C. "Locke's Polemic against Nativism." In *The Cambridge Companion to Locke's "Essay Concerning Human Understanding,"* edited by Lex Newman, 33-66. Cambridge: Cambridge University Press, 2007.

Rickless, Samuel C. "Will and Motivation." In *The Oxford Handbook of British Philosophy in the Seventeenth Century*, edited by Peter R. Antsey, 393-414. Oxford: Oxford University Press, 2013.

Rivers, Isabel. *Reason, Grace, and Sentiment: A Study of the Language of Religion and Ethics in England, 1660-1780*, vol. 1. New York: Cambridge University Press, 1991.
Rogers, G. A. J., ed. Introduction to *The Philosophy of Edward Stillingfleet*, vol. 1, vii–x. Bristol: Thoemmes Press, 2000.
Rogers, G. A. J. "John Locke: Conservative Radical." In *The Margins of Orthodoxy: Heterodox Writing and Cultural Response, 1660-1750*, edited by Roger D. Lund, 97-118. Cambridge: University of Cambridge Press, 1995.
Rogers, G. A. J. "Locke and the Latitude-Men: Ignorance as a Ground of Toleration." In *Philosophy, Science, and Religion in England 1640-1700*, edited by Richard Kroll, Richard Ashcraft, and Perez Zagorin, 230-52. New York: Cambridge University Press, 1992.
Rose, Jacqueline. "The Contexts of Locke's Political Thought." In *A Companion to Locke*, edited by Matthew Stuart, 45-63. Oxford: Blackwell, 2016.
Rowe, William L. "Causality and Free Will in the Controversy between Collins and Clarke." *Journal of the History of Philosophy* 25, no. 1 (January 1987): 51-67.
Ryan, Thomas. "Congregatio de auxiliis." In *New Catholic Encyclopedia*, 2nd ed, vol. 4, edited by Thomas Carson and Joann Cerrito, 110-113. Farmington Hills, MI: Gale, 2003.
Schouls, Peter A. *Reasoned Freedom: John Locke and the Enlightenment*. Ithaca: Cornell University Press, 1992.
Schuurman, Paul. *Ideas, Mental Faculties and Method: The Logic of Ideas of Descartes and Locke and Its Reception in the Dutch Republic, 1630-1750*. Leiden: Brill, 2004.
Schuurman, Paul. "Locke's Logic of Ideas in Context: Content and Structure." *British Journal for the History of Philosophy* 9, no. 3 (2001): 439-65.
Schuurman, Paul. "Vision in God and Thinking Matter: Locke's Epistemological Agnosticism Used against Malebranche and Stillingfleet." In *Studies on Locke: Sources, Contemporaries, and Legacy*, edited by Sarah Hutton and Paul Schuurman, 177-93. Dordrecht: Springer, 2008.
Sell, Alan P. F. *John Locke and the Eighteenth-Century Divines: Prolegomena to Christian Apologetics*. Cardiff: University of Wales Press, 1997.
Sellars, John. "Stoic Fate in Justus Lipsius's *De Constantia* and *Physiologica Stoicorum*." *Journal of the History of Philosophy* 52, no. 4 (October 2014): 653-74.
Sheerin, F. L. "Scientia Media." In *New Catholic Encyclopedia*, 2nd ed, vol. 12, edited by Thomas Carson and Joann Cerrito, 821-22. Farmington Hills, MI: Gale, 2003.
Smith, Donald Thomas. "John Locke's Concept of Reasonable Christianity." PhD diss., Southern Methodist Seminary, 1997.
Snobelen, Stephen D. "Socinianism, Heresy and John Locke's *Reasonableness of Christianity*." *Enlightenment and Dissent* 20 (2001): 88-125.
Snyder, David C. "Faith and Reason in Locke's Essay." *Journal of the History of Ideas* 47, no. 2 (April–June 1986): 197-213.
Stanciu, Diana. "Arminian Toleration, Irenicism and Latitudinarianism in Cudworth's Letters to Van Limborch: Text and Context." *Lias* 40, no. 2 (2013): 177-209.
Stanglin, Keith D., and Thomas H. McCall, *Jacob Arminius: Theologian of Grace*. New York: Oxford University Press, 2012.
Stanglin, Keith D. "Scientia Media: The Protestant Reception of a Jesuit Idea." In *Beyond Dordt and De Auxiliis: The Dynamics of Protestant and Catholic Soteriology in the Sixteenth and Seventeenth Centuries*, edited by Jordan Ballor, Matthew Gaetano, and David Sytsma, 148-68. Leiden: Brill, 2019.

Stanton, Timothy. "Locke and His Influence." In *The Oxford Handbook of British Philosophy in the Eighteenth Century*, edited by James A. Harris, 21-40. Oxford: Oxford University Press, 2013.

Stanton, Timothy. "Locke and the Politics and Theology of Toleration." *Political Studies* 54 (2006): 84-102.

Stephens, Leslie. *History of English Though in the Eighteenth Century*. 2 vols. 3rd ed. London: Harbinger, 1962.

Stewart, M. A. "Revealed Religion: The British Debate." In *The Cambridge History of Eighteenth-Century Philosophy*, vol. 2, edited by Knut Haakonssen, 683-709. Cambridge: Cambridge University Press, 2006.

Strauss, Leo. *Natural Right and History*. Chicago: The University of Chicago Press, 1953.

Strauss, Leo. *Persecution and the Art of Writing*. Chicago: The University of Chicago Press, 1952; Reprint, 1988.

Sullivan, Robert E. *John Toland and the Deist Controversy: A Study in Adaptations*. Cambridge: Harvard University Press, 1982.

Svensson, Manfred. "Locke, Toleration, and the Church." *Philosophy of Religion Annual* 15 (2016): 47–66.

Svennson, Manfred. "John Owen and John Locke: Confessionalism, Minimalism, and Toleration." *History of European Ideas* 43, no. 4 (2017): 302-16.

Tetlow, Joanne. "John Locke's Covenant Theology." *Locke Studies* 9 (2009): 167-99.

Thiel, Udo. "The Trinity and Human Personal Identity." In *English Philosophy in the Age of Locke*, edited by M. A. Stewart, 217-43. Oxford: Clarendon Press, 2000.

Toulmin, Joshua. *Memoirs of the Life, Character, Sentiments, and Writings of Faustus Socinus*. London: Printed for the author by J. Brown, 1777.

Tuckness, Alex. "Locke on Toleration." In *A Companion to Locke*, edited by Matthew Stuart, 433-47. Oxford: Blackwell, 2016.

Turner, James. *Without God, Without Creed: The Origins of Unbelief in America*. Baltimore: John Hopkins University Press, 1985.

Tyacke, Nicholas. "From Laudians to Latitudinarians: A Shifting Balance of Theological Forces." In *The Later Stuart Church, 1660-1714*, edited by Grant Tapsell, 46-67. New York: Manchester University Press, 2017.

Uzgalis, William. "Anthony Collins." In *Stanford Encyclopedia of Philosophy* (first published on August 25, 2002 with substantive revisions February 23, 2009; accessed on March 13, 2009). http://plato.stanford.edu/entries/collins.

Vickers, Jason E. *Invocation and Assent: The Making and Remaking of Trinitarian Theology*. Grand Rapids: Eerdmans, 2008.

Wallace, Dewey. "Socinianism, Justification by Faith, and the Sources of John Locke's *The Reasonableness of Christianity*." *Journal of the History of Ideas* 45, no. 1 (January-March 1984): 49–66.

Walmsley, Jonathan. "The Development of Lockean Abstraction." *British Journal for the History of Philosophy* 8, no. 2 (2000): 395-418.

Welch, Claude. *Protestant Christian Thought in the Nineteenth Century*. 2 vols. New Haven: Yale University Press, 1972.

Wilbur, Earl Morse. *History of Unitarianism in Transylvania, England, and America*. Boston: Beacon Press, 1945.

Winkler, Kenneth P. "Perception and Ideas, Judgment." In *Cambridge History of Eighteenth-Century Philosophy*, vol. 1, edited by Knud Haakonssen, 234–85. Cambridge: Cambridge University Press, 2006.

Wolterstorff, Nicholas. *John Locke and the Ethics of Belief*. Cambridge: Cambridge University Press, 1996.

Wolterstorff, Nicholas. "John Locke's Epistemological Piety: Reason is the Candle of the Lord." *Faith and Philosophy* 11, no. 4 (October 1994): 572–91.

Wojcik, Jan W. *Robert Boyle and the Limits of Reason*. Cambridge: Cambridge University Press, 1997.

Woolhouse, R. S. *Locke: A Bibliography*. Cambridge: Cambridge University Press, 2007.

Yaffe, Gideon. *Liberty Worth the Name: Locke on Free Agency*. Princeton: Princeton University Press, 2000.

Yaffe, Gideon. "Locke on Refraining, Suspending, and the Freedom of the Will." *History of Philosophy Quarterly* 18, no. 4 (October 2001): 373–91.

Yolton, John W. "Locke: Education for Virtue." In *Philosophers on Education: New Historical Perspectives*, edited by Amélie Oksenberg Rorty, 173-89. New York: Routledge, 1998.

Yolton, John W. *John Locke and the Way of Ideas*. Oxford: Clarendon Press, 1968.

Index

For the benefit of digital users, indexed terms that span two pages (e.g., 52–53) may, on occasion, appear on only one of those pages.

above reason propositions
  according to reason propositions
    distinguished from, 227–28, 232–33, 245–46, 247
  assent and, 218–20, 221–22, 239, 247, 286–87
  Cambridge Platonists and, 216–18, 219–24, 233–34
  contradictions and, 238, 255
  contrary to reason propositions
    distinguished from, 228–29, 234–37, 238–39, 247–48, 255–56, 299–300
  definitions of, 11, 49, 221–22, 227–28, 232–33, 235–36, 237, 244, 254, 274–75, 287–88, 307–8
  deism and, 250
  Essay and, 112n.5, 134n.84, 215, 244–45, 286–87
  faith and, 219–20, 222–27, 245–47, 249–50
  formal debate on, 231–39
  historical context of, 218–39
  incomprehensibility and, 11, 218–19, 233, 235–38, 244–45, 247–48, 249–50, 253, 255–56, 264–65, 274–75, 287–88, 299, 300, 307–8
  knowledge and, 226–30, 247
  Locke's categorization of propositions and, 7, 37, 215–19, 244–48, 256, 259–60, 268, 300
  mysteries and, 253
  overview of, 215–18
  precursors to debate on, 219–31
  Protestant Reformation and, 219–20, 224–31
  reason's definition in, 216–18, 225–26, 244–46, 250–51
  relative nature of, 233–34, 238–39
  revelation and, 221–29, 274–75, 287–88
  ROC and, 37, 112n.5, 134n.84
  Roman Catholicism and, 231
  scholarship on, 7, 215–19, 215–16n.2, 244–45, 256, 259–60
  scope of, 247–48
  Scripture and, 11, 222–28, 233–34, 239
  Socinianism and, 231, 235–36, 300
  sovereignty of God and, 230–31
  Trinitarian debates and, 218–19, 224, 226–27, 233n.74, 259–60, 261–63, 264–65, 268–69
  types of, 233
  undiscoverability and, 232, 233–36, 239, 248, 255–56, 300
abstraction, 261n.9, 270–71, 301–2, 310
according to reason propositions
  above reason propositions
    distinguished from, 227–28, 232–33, 245–46, 247
  definition of, 287–88
  Essay and, 215
  Locke's categorization of propositions and, 37, 219, 245–46, 247, 287–88
  reason's definition in, 245–46
  revelation and, 239
  ROC and, 37, 112n.5, 134n.84
  Scripture and, 239
Account of Reason and Faith, An (Norris), 235, 298, 300
Account of the Growth of Deism in England, An (Stephens), 122, 295–96
Acts of the Apostles. *See* Scripture

338 INDEX

Allen, Keith, 116, 118nn.23–24, 261n.9, 310
Allison, C. FitzSimons, 51–52
Anabaptists, 4, 56, 72, 78–79, 101
Anglican Church. *See* Church of England
Anti-Arminians (Hampton), 51–52, 79
antinomianism
    Calvinism and, 52–53
    justification and, 9, 49–50, 51–53, 68–69, 72
    Locke's opposition to, 3–4, 9, 49–50, 68–69, 316
    morality and, 61–62
    obedience and, 49–50, 68–69
    ROC and, 9, 49–50, 68–69, 72
    Scripture and, 68–69, 316
    soteriology and, 9, 60–61, 68
Aquinas, Thomas, 184–86, 190–91
Arianism
    Christology and, 51
    historical context of, 51
    incomprehensibility and, 302–3
    Latitudinarianism and, 83
    Socinianism and, 51, 265
    Trinitarian debates and, 50, 266–67
    Unitarianism and, 51
Aristotelianism, 258–59, 266–68, 269–70
Arminianism
    Church of England and, 52, 79, 103–4
    doctrinal minimalism and, 73–75
    free will and, 184–86, 198, 213n.95
    fundamental articles and, 56, 76–77
    Holy Spirit and, 71–72
    ROC charged with, 4–5, 47–49, 65–66, 71–72
    scholarship on, 4–5, 48–49nn.8–9, 71n.100, 73–75, 259n.5
    soteriology and, 5–6n.4, 59–60, 71–72, 212
Arminius, Jacob, 184–86
Arnauld, Antoine, 191–92, 270
articles of faith. *See* fundamental articles
Ashcraft, Richard, 5–6, 112n.5, 138–39, 217n.5
assent
    above reason propositions and, 218–20, 221–22, 239, 247, 286–87
    Cambridge Platonists and, 219–20
    clear and distinct ideas and, 272–73
    contrary to reason propositions and, 243
    error and, 240
    faith and, 62–64, 66–67, 85–86, 243, 251
    freedom of religion and, 314–15
    fundamental articles and, 84–85, 284–85
    ideas and, 272–73, 276–77, 294–96
    incomprehensibility and, 249–50, 252–53, 261–63, 271, 273–76, 278–79, 286, 288–89, 301, 306
    innate ideas and, 116–17, 119, 125–26, 131–32
    intellectual assent, 63–64, 66–67, 79–80, 84–86
    knowledge and, 284–88
    legitimate assent, 10, 30–31, 142–43, 167, 271, 301
    miracles and, 142–43, 156, 157–58, 159–60, 167–70
    overview of, 239–44
    poor and uneducated and, 142–43, 167–70
    reason and, 219–22, 226, 239–42, 271
    revelation and, 244, 245–46, 247
    Scripture and, 167, 252–53, 284–85
    Socinianism and, 273
    toleration and, 107
    Trinitarian debates and, 261–63, 303
Atherton, Margaret, 117–19, 281–82
authority of Scripture
    Essay and, 136, 139–41, 169
    free will and, 309
    Holy Spirit and, 143–44, 145–46, 147–48
    improvement of society and, 134–37
    innate ideas and, 134
    Protestant Reformation and, 143–48
    reason and, 136
    ROC and, 4–6, 135–36
    Roman Catholicism and, 143–44
    scholarship on, 4–5, 139–41
    soteriology and, 134–37
Ayers, Michael, 4–5, 16–17, 139n.3, 217–18n.6, 272, 286n.85

Babcock, William, 259n.4

Bacon, Francis, 141n.10
Barlow, Thomas, 51–52, 64
Baxter, Richard
　ecumenism and, 61–62, 103
　faith and, 61–62
　fundamental articles and, 102–3
　Holy Spirit and, 67–68
　irenicism and, 61–62
　justification and, 52–53, 61–62, 65–66
　Locke interpreted through ideas of, 61–62, 65–66
　scholarship on, 61–62, 71, 75–76n.4, 102–3
　Socinianism and, 52–53, 61–62, 71
　soteriology and, 52–53
　sufficiency of Scripture and, 102–3
the Bible. *See* Scripture
Blount, Charles, 121–22, 148–49, 154
Bold, Samuel
　assent and, 63
　doctrinal minimalism and, 94, 96
　ecumenism and, 7–8, 54, 55
　faith and, 63
　fundamental articles and, 73–75, 84–85
　Holy Spirit and, 67–68
　innate ideas and, 116
　irenicism and, 7–8, 19–20, 54, 55
　justification and, 55, 66, 84–85
　knowledge and, 66
　Locke defended by, 7–8, 19–20, 21, 46–47, 49, 54, 55, 63, 73–75, 84, 116
　soteriology and, 66
　works-righteousness and, 66
Boyle, Robert
　above reason propositions and, 216–18, 222, 231–39, 244, 247–48, 253–54, 255–56, 274–75, 287–88, 298, 307–8
　according to reason propositions and, 232–33, 255–56, 287–88
　contrary to reason propositions and, 232, 234–35, 236, 274–75, 287–88
　epistemological limits and, 274–75
　free will and, 248, 307–8
　ideas and, 274–75
　incomprehensibility and, 235–36, 247–48, 253, 255–56, 274–75, 307–8, 309, 311

　Locke influenced by, 231, 248, 311
　miracles and, 141–42, 254
　moral probability arguments and, 146–47
　reasonableness of Christianity and, 233–34
　revelation and, 244, 307–8
　scholarship on, 141–42
　Trinitarian debates and, 264
　unsociable propositions and, 248, 254, 264, 287–88, 307–8
Bramhall, John
　definition of free will for, 188–89
　faculties and, 190–91
　free will and, 179–81, 183, 185–90, 195–96
　Hobbes-Bramhall debate, 183, 185–90
　libertarianism and, 180n.2
Broadie, Alexander, 139–41
Browne, Peter, 276–77, 295, 301–6
Bull, George, 51–52, 64–65
Burnet, Gilbert, 52, 64, 95–96
Burnet, Thomas, 25
Burns, R. M., 141–42, 146–49, 153–54, 166
Burthogge, Richard
　assent and, 289
　contradiction and, 289–91
　ideas and, 283
　incomprehensibility and, 288–89
　Locke's influence on, 269–70, 288
　nonsense and, 288–89
　scholarship on, 288
　scholasticism and, 269–70
　Trinitarian debates and, 288–91, 297–98

Calvinism
　antinomianism and, 52–53
　Church of England and, 52, 103–4
　ecumenism and, 71–72
　free will and, 183, 212–13
　innate ideas and, 117
　Locke's relation to, 4, 47–49, 56, 71–72
　necessitarianism and, 183, 212–13
　scholarship on, 4, 49n.9, 64, 259n.5
　soteriology and, 64
Cambridge Platonists
　above reason propositions and, 216–18, 219–24, 233–34

Cambridge Platonists (*cont.*)
   assent and, 219–20
   doctrinal minimalism and, 73–75
   faith and, 219–20
   freedom of conscience and, 83
   fundamental articles and, 83
   innate ideas and, 117–19
   Latitudinarianism and, 75–76n.4, 83
   Locke's relation to, 6–7, 73–75, 83, 219–20
   scholarship on, 6–7
   soteriology and, 219–20
Carroll, Robert Todd, 258–59n.3
categorization of propositions, 7, 37, 215–19, 245–46, 256, 259–60, 268, 287–88, 290–91, 294–95, 297–98, 300
Catholicism. *See* Roman Catholicism
Champion, Justin, 49n.10, 90–91
Chappell, Vere, 181–82n.6, 188
Chillingworth, William, 102
Christ as King, 22, 63, 68, 79–80, 81, 87, 101–2, 167, 284–85, 314, 315–16, 317
Christianity as Old as the Creation (Tindal), 120–21
Christianity Not Mysterious (Toland). *See also* Toland, John
   above reason propositions in, 250, 252, 253
   Arianism and, 291
   critiques of, 268, 295, 303
   deism in, 120–21
   incomprehensibility rejected in, 293–95
   Locke's influence on, 2, 120–21, 250, 268, 291
   motivation for, 293
   revelation in, 252–53
   scholarship on, 215–16n.2
   Trinitarian debates in, 291, 294–95
Christian Virtuoso, The (Boyle), 231–32
Christ is Messiah fundamental article, 21–22, 46–47, 57, 58–59, 60, 79–80, 82–83, 93–94, 98–99, 128–29, 167, 284–85, 315–16
Christology
   Arianism and, 51
   church and state relationship and, 32
   deism and, 22–23

   ecumenism and, 9, 49–50
   historical context of, 50–51
   Letter and, 17–19
   ROC and, 9, 21–23, 44–45, 49–50, 57–59
   scholarship on, 17–19
   toleration and, 17–19, 32
church and state relationship, 24, 30–33, 36, 136–37, 314–15
Church of England
   Arminianism and, 52, 79, 103–4
   Calvinism and, 52, 103–4
   fallibility of authority and, 89
   free will and, 194–95
   fundamental articles and, 79
   irenicism and, 52
   justification and, 51–52
   scholarship on, 75–76n.4
   soteriology and, 52, 75–76n.4
   theological debates within, 51–52
   toleration and, 24, 83, 103–4, 194–95
   Unitarianism and, 103–4
civil freedom, 36, 314–15
clarity of Scripture, 58–59, 92, 93
Clarke, Edward, 26
Clarke, Samuel, 181n.4
clear and distinct ideas, 224, 245, 248, 254, 268, 270–71, 272–73, 274, 276–78, 287–88, 290–91
CNM. *See Christianity Not Mysterious* (Toland)
Collins, Anthony, 120–21, 181n.4, 296–98, 308
commentary on Locke. *See* scholarship on Locke
compatibilism, 183, 188
Compleat Body of Divinity, A (Limborch), 154
confessionalism, 48n.7, 79
Conrad, Jonathan Donald, 5n.3, 17n.4, 139n.3
contradictions, 226–27, 230–31, 238, 243, 255, 276–77, 290–91, 293–94, 296, 300, 307
contrary to reason propositions
   above reason propositions distinguished from, 228–29, 234–37, 238–39, 247–48, 255–56, 299–300

assent and, 243
definitions of, 232, 234–35, 237, 254, 290–91, 294–95
Essay and, 215
Locke's categorization of propositions and, 37, 219, 247–48, 290–91, 294–95, 297–98
ROC and, 37
Scripture and, 223
Socinianism and, 235–36, 265, 266–67
Trinitarian debates and, 265, 266–67
Copleston, Frederick, 215–16n.2
Cranston, Maurice, 48–49n.8
Cudworth, Ralph, 191, 266–68

Davenant, John, 102
deism
 above reason propositions and, 250
 Christology and, 22–23
 common religious notions and, 120–22, 127–29
 divinity of Scripture and, 68–69
 ecumenism and, 111–12
 Essay and, 120–23
 ideas and, 276
 incomprehensibility and, 276
 innate ideas and, 9–10, 119–24, 127–28
 justification and, 22–23, 68–69, 130
 Locke's relation to, 2, 6–7, 22–23, 46–49, 53–54, 68–69, 72, 112–13, 119–23, 129, 131–32, 170–71
 major works of, 120–22
 miracles and, 10, 142–43, 174
 morality and, 68–69, 121–23, 170–71, 173
 necessity of Scripture and, 9–10
 obedience and, 121–22
 origins of, 120
 Protestant Reformation and, 122–23
 revelation and, 53–54, 111–12, 119–20
 ROC and, 22–23, 46–49, 53–54, 68–69, 72, 112–13, 129, 131–32, 170–71
 Roman Catholicism and, 122–23
 scholarship on, 6–7, 112–13, 123
 sincerity of, 122
 soteriology and, 119–20, 297–98
 STCE and, 43–44
 Trinitarian debates and, 295–96

Descartes, René
 assent and, 272–73
 clear and distinct ideas and, 272–73
 deism and, 120
 incomprehensibility and, 271, 272–74, 310
 miracles and, 146–47
 pure understanding/pure intellect distinguished from imagination and, 117–19, 271–72, 281–82, 310
 scholarship on, 286
 Socinian charge against, 273
 way of ideas and, 270, 271
determinism. *See* necessitarianism
De Veritate (Edward, Lord Herbert of Cherbury), 117n.22, 123–25, 127–28, 134n.83
"Discourse on Miracles, A" (Locke), 141–42, 150n.44, 164–67
discoverability, 232, 233–36, 239, 248, 255–56, 300
divinity of Scripture
 deism and, 68–69
 enthusiasm and, 139–42
 Essay and, 163
 Holy Spirit and, 147–48
 miracles and, 10, 37, 138–45, 146–47, 149–53, 154–57, 163, 166–67, 169, 173–75
 morality and, 173
 Protestant Reformation and, 143–46
 ROC and, 10, 163, 174
 scholarship on, 141–42, 143–44, 173
doctrinal minimalism, 9, 73–75, 92–94, 96, 98–99, 102–3, 113n.7
Dumsday, Travis, 140n.6, 141–42
Dunn, John, 5–6, 17–19, 112n.6, 138–39
Dworetz, Steven M., 17–19, 138–39

ecumenism
 Calvinism and, 71–72
 Christology and, 9, 49–50
 deism and, 111–12
 Holy Spirit and, 174
 justification and, 49–50, 65–66
 original sin and, 69–70
 preliminary evidence of, 53–56
 ROC and, 3–6, 9, 21, 46–50, 53–56, 65–66, 69–72, 103, 111–12, 258–59

ecumenism (*cont.*)
  scholarship on, 4–6, 17n.4, 61–62, 112–13
  soteriology and, 9, 49–50, 71–72
  Trinitarian debates and, 258–59, 263, 266, 311–12
Edward, Lord Herbert of Cherbury
  common religious notions and, 120–22, 124–25, 127–29
  deism and, 120, 123, 124, 125
  innate ideas and, 25, 111–12, 114, 117–19, 123–25
  Locke's critiques of, 25, 111–12, 114, 117–19, 123–24, 127–29
  revelation and, 120, 125
  scholarship on, 124–25
Edwards, John
  atonement and, 55
  Calvinist identity of, 19–20
  doctrinal minimalism and, 93–94, 98–99
  Epistles and, 98
  faith and, 62
  fundamental articles and, 73–75, 81–82, 93–94, 98–99
  Locke critiqued by, 1, 19–20, 46–47, 54, 55, 62, 73–75, 81, 257–58
  Locke's responses to critiques by, 1, 62, 81–82, 88, 93–94, 98–99, 285–86
  Socinianism and, 1, 4–5, 19–20, 46–47, 71, 257–58
  soteriology and, 71
empiricists, 116, 117, 120–21, 141–42, 146–49, 154–55
enthusiasm, 3–4, 37, 90, 107, 119, 139–42, 143–44, 157–58, 159–60, 240, 243–44
epistemology. *See* knowledge
Epistles. *See* Scripture
error, 68–69, 205–6, 208n.89, 211, 240, 273
Essay Concerning Human Understanding, An (Locke)
  above reason propositions in, 112n.5, 134n.84, 215, 244–45, 286–87
  according to reason propositions in, 215
  analogy in, 305–6
  authority of Scripture in, 136, 139–41, 169
  contrary to reason propositions in, 215
  deism and, 120–23
  divinity of Scripture in, 163
  ecumenical intent of, 10–11
  editions of, 38
  enthusiasm in, 37, 107, 143–44, 157–58, 159–60, 240, 243–44
  epistemology in, 86–87, 111–14
  error in, 240
  faith in, 86–87, 157–59
  free will in, 11, 37–41, 179–82, 199, 201–14, 307
  ideas in, 269–71, 279–80, 286–87, 307, 310–11
  illumination in, 159–60
  incomprehensibility in, 286–87, 307, 309
  innate ideas critiqued in, 9–10, 17–19, 24–25, 111–14, 117–19, 128–29, 130–31
  inspiration for, 90–91, 124
  irenic intent of, 10–11
  knowledge in, 280–82, 284
  as Locke's magnum opus, 24
  miracles in, 37, 155–60
  morality in, 9–10, 44–45, 133–34
  "Of Power" in, 10–11, 37–41, 179–81, 182, 191–92, 195–96, 198–99, 201–14, 306–7
  reason in, 40–41, 107, 157–59, 216–18, 239
  revelation in, 37, 132–34, 155–60, 163
  ROC's relation to, 4–5, 9–10, 17–19, 41, 55–56, 111–14, 112n.5, 128–29, 133–34
  scholarship on, 4–5, 16–19, 36–37, 111–13, 179–81, 181–82n.6
  Scripture in, 44–45
  soteriology in, 37–41, 44
  theological aspects of, 16–17, 36–41, 201–14
  toleration in, 86–87, 107–8, 136–37
  Trinitarian debates and, 36–37, 268–69, 309, 311–12
Essay Concerning the Use of Reason in Propositions (Collins), 296
Essay on Natural Religion, An (Blount), 121–22
Essay upon Reason, An (Burthogge), 288–89

faith. *See also* fundamental articles
  above reason propositions and, 219–20, 222–27, 245–47, 249–50
  assent and, 62–64, 66–67, 85–86, 243, 251
  Cambridge Platonists and, 219–20
  definitions of, 62–63, 66–67, 85–90, 242–43
  Essay and, 86–87, 157–59
  explicit faith, 223–24, 249–50
  grace and, 60, 145–46
  implicit faith, 9, 36, 75–76, 85–90, 119, 169, 219–20
  innate ideas and, 119
  justification and, 47–49, 64
  knowledge and, 292
  Law of Faith, 59–60, 64–65, 93
  Letter and, 17–19, 30–33
  obedience and, 66–67, 249–50
  poor and uneducated and, 36
  probability and, 251
  reason and, 103–4, 157, 220–21, 224–25, 228–29, 240–46, 247–48
  ROC and, 41, 62–63, 249–50
  Roman Catholicism and, 87, 88, 119
  scholarship on, 17–19, 217n.5
  soteriology and, 59–60, 64, 223–24
  Trinitarian debates and, 249–50
Filmer, Robert, 23–24, 26
Forde, Steven, 4–5
Forster, Greg, 17–19, 29–30, 141–42
Foster, David, 5n.3, 16–17, 113n.7
freedom of religion, 24, 30–33, 36, 136–37, 314–15
free will
  Arminianism and, 184–86, 198, 213n.95
  authority of Scripture and, 309
  avoidance of Locke in taking sides on, 8, 41, 179–82, 188, 195–201, 212–14
  Calvinism and, 183, 212–13
  Church of England and, 194–95
  compatibilism and, 183, 188
  definitions of, 187–90, 202–4, 211–12
  error and, 205–6, 211
  Essay and, 11, 37–41, 179–82, 199, 201–14, 307
  faculties and, 190–91, 203n.81
  foreknowledge and, 184
  freedom of religion and, 315
  God's sovereignty and, 184, 198–200, 213, 306–9
  grace and, 183, 212–13
  habituation and, 209–10
  happiness and, 206–10
  historical context of, 183–95
  Hobbes-Bramhall debate on, 185–90
  incomprehensibility and, 306–9
  intellectualism and, 190–91
  knowledge and, 184–86
  Letter and, 41
  libertarianism and, 179–81, 183, 195–97, 198–99, 200, 206, 212–13
  middle knowledge and, 184–86, 213n.95
  Molyneux's critique of Locke on, 181–82, 191, 196, 197–201, 206, 208–9, 211–12, 214
  morality and, 211
  necessitarianism and, 179–81, 183, 187–91, 195–96, 197, 198–99, 206, 212–13, 308
  overview of, 179–82
  pleasure and, 192–94
  Protestant Reformation and, 184–86, 189–90, 200
  providence and, 184
  reason and, 39–41, 207–12
  Roman Catholicism and, 184–86
  scholarship on, 41, 179–81, 183, 186–87, 191–92, 195–97, 206
  scholastic understanding of, 188–89, 194–95
  soteriology and, 37–40, 184, 194–95, 206, 208–13, 214
  state of nature and, 29
  suspension of the will and, 180n.2, 181n.4, 191–94, 196, 205–12
  toleration and, 194–95
  traditional theological elements relevant to, 184–86, 212–13
  Treatises and, 29, 41
  true liberty and, 189, 206–8
  uneasiness and, 204–5
  voluntarism and, 190–91
  weakness of will and, 191, 193–94
fundamental articles. *See also* justification; soteriology
  Arminianism and, 56, 76–77
  assent and, 84–85, 284–85

fundamental articles (*cont.*)
  Cambridge Platonists and, 83
  Christ as King and, 22, 63, 68, 79–80, 81, 87, 101–2, 167, 284–85, 314, 315–16, 317
  Christian defined through, 97–103
  Church of England and, 79
  clarity of, 58–59, 92, 93
  continuity of the Church and, 97–103
  debate over, 76–85
  definition of, 76–78
  as directly from Messiah, 9, 58, 75–76, 80, 82–83, 97–103
  doctrinal minimalism about, 9, 73–76, 92–94, 96, 98–99, 102–3, 113n.7
  epistemological principle of, 85–90
  faith defined through, 85–90
  God exists article, 21–22, 46–47, 51–52, 57, 79–80, 128–29, 167, 284–85, 315–16
  heresy and, 35
  historical context of, 76–85
  Jesus is Messiah article, 21–22, 46–47, 57, 58–59, 60, 79–80, 82–83, 93–94, 98–99, 128–29, 167, 284–85, 315–16
  Latitudinarianism and, 76–77, 83
  Letter and, 30, 35–36, 44, 100–2, 103
  other doctrinal minimalist fundamentals, 82–85, 95–97
  overview of, 76–82
  poor and uneducated and, 92–97
  Protestant Reformation and, 76–77, 79, 85–86
  reason and, 97–103
  revelation and, 95
  ROC and, 1, 9, 22–23, 44, 46–47, 53–54, 57–59, 64, 69–70, 73–75, 77–78, 79–80, 87, 97–98, 101–2, 103, 285
  Roman Catholicism and, 76–77, 85–88
  scholarship on, 73–75, 90–91, 102–3
  Scripture and, 79–81, 87, 97–98, 102–3
  Socinianism and, 76–77
  STCE and, 44
  sufficiency of Scripture and, 102–3
  toleration and, 9, 53–54, 75–76, 103–8
  violence resulting from debates on, 53–54

God. *See also* Christology; Holy Spirit; Trinitarian debates
  free will and, 184, 198–200, 213, 306–9
  fundamental articles and, 21–22, 46–47, 51–52, 57, 79–80, 128–29, 167, 284–85, 315–16
  incomprehensibility and, 306–9
  miracles proving existence of, 37, 154, 155–57
  sovereignty of, 26, 27–28, 44, 184, 198–99, 212, 213, 309, 311
the Gospels. *See* Scripture
grace
  avoidance of Locke in taking sides on, 316
  faith and, 60, 145–46
  free will and, 183, 212–13
  Holy Spirit and, 145–46, 212
  obedience and, 60
  Scripture and, 147–48
  soteriology and, 60, 191–92
Grant, Ruth, 16
Green, Michael, 135
Griffin, Martin, Jr., 6–7, 75–76n.4, 83, 85–86

Hall, Joseph, 102, 277–78
Hallywell, Henry, 219–22, 223–24, 249–50
Hampton, Stephen, 51–52, 64–65, 75–76n.4, 194–95
Harris, James, 10–11, 41, 179–81, 182, 183, 195–97, 214
Harrison, Peter, 141n.10
Helm, Paul, 139–41, 143–44
heresy
  definition of, 100–1
  fundamental articles and, 35
  Letter and, 34–35, 100–1, 106
  Locke as paving way for, 250, 268, 291
  ROC and, 69–72
  schism distinguished from, 35–36, 100–1
  toleration and, 34–35, 106
  types of, 35
Hertzberg, Benjamin, 16
Higgins-Biddle, John C., 47–49, 51, 64, 265

Hobbes, Thomas
   Bramhall's debate with, 183, 185–90
   definition of free will for, 187–88
   free will and, 179–81, 183, 184–90, 195–96
   ideas and, 310
   necessitarianism and, 179–81, 188, 195–96
Holy Spirit
   Arminianism and, 71–72
   assistance given by, 71–72, 129, 154–55, 159–60, 161, 174, 226
   authority of Scripture and, 143–44, 145–46, 147–48
   Christ and, 317
   divinity of Scripture and, 147–48
   ecumenism and, 174
   grace and, 145–46, 212
   historical context of, 50–51
   justification and, 59, 67–68
   miracles and, 154–55, 174
   personhood and, 67–68
   Pneumatology of, 9, 49–51, 59–69
   Protestant Reformation and, 143–44
   reason and, 159–60
   revelation and, 226
   ROC and, 59–69, 71–72
   Roman Catholicism and, 145–46
   soteriology and, 67–68
   Trinitarian debates and, 263–64, 265
Houston, Joseph, 139–41
Hudde, Johannes, 21, 69–70
Hume, David, 139–41, 141n.10, 146–47

ideas. *See also* innate ideas
   abstraction and, 261n.9, 270–71, 301–2, 310
   adequate and inadequate distinction in, 310
   Aristotelianism and, 269–70
   assent and, 272–73, 276–77, 294–96
   clear and distinct ideas, 224, 245, 248, 254, 268, 270–71, 272–73, 274, 276–78, 287–88, 290–91
   definition of, 269–71, 301–2
   deism and, 276
   epistemological limitations and, 274–77
   Essay and, 269–71, 279–80, 286–87, 307, 310–11
   images and, 269–70, 271–72, 310–12
   incomprehensibility and, 271–74, 277–78, 310–12
   knowledge and, 279–82
   pure intellect and, 272, 278, 286, 305–6, 310
   scholarship on, 259n.4, 272, 281–82, 310
   scholasticism and, 269–70
   Trinitarian debates and, 269–79
   pure understanding/pure intellect distinguished from imagination and, 271–72
   way of ideas, 11, 269–75, 306
illumination, 67–68, 143–44, 153–55, 159–60
images, 269–70, 271–72, 310–12
Imbrosciano, Anthony, 139–41
implicit faith, 9, 36, 75–76, 85–90, 119, 169, 219–20, 221–24, 249–50
incomprehensibility
   above reason propositions and, 11, 218–19, 233, 235–38, 244–45, 247–48, 249–50, 253, 255–56, 264–65, 274–75, 287–88, 299, 300, 307–8
   Arianism and, 302–3
   assent and, 249–50, 252–53, 261–63, 271, 273–76, 278–79, 286, 288–89, 298, 301, 306
   contradiction and, 226–27, 230–31, 238, 243, 255, 264–65, 276–77, 290–91, 293–94, 296, 300, 307
   deism and, 276
   Essay and, 286–87, 307, 309
   free will and, 306–9
   God's sovereignty and, 306–9
   ideas and, 271–74, 277–78, 310–12
   images and, 310–12
   incompossible distinguished from, 229–30
   Locke's acceptance of, 11, 215, 218, 244–45, 247–50, 261–63, 278–88, 300, 305–12
   poor and uneducated and, 249–50, 285–86, 309
   problems with rejecting, 306–11
   ROC and, 284–85
   scholarship on, 244–45, 262–63n.10, 309

incomprehensibility (*cont.*)
　Socinianism and, 235–36
　Trinitarian debates and, 264–65, 269–79, 302–3
　undiscoverability and, 232, 233–36, 239, 248, 255–56, 300
　unsociability and, 306
innate ideas
　ancient philosophers and, 129–30
　arguments against, 9–10, 117–19, 123–28, 131–32, 133, 281–82
　assent and, 116–17, 119, 125–26, 131–32
　authority of Scripture and, 134
　Calvinism and, 117
　Cambridge Platonists and, 117–19
　common religious notions and, 124–25, 127–30
　controversy surrounding, 115–19
　cultural evidence against, 129–32
　deism and, 9–10, 119–24, 127–28
　enthusiasm and, 119
　Essay and, 9–10, 17–19, 24–25, 111–14, 117–19, 128–29, 130–31
　faith and, 119
　historical context of, 115–19
　justification and, 130
　knowledge and, 281–82, 286
　morality and, 9–10, 111–12, 114–15, 117, 126–27, 130–32
　necessity of Scripture and, 9–10
　poor and uneducated and, 126
　Protestant Reformation and, 117
　revelation and, 120, 125, 128–34
　ROC and, 17–19, 128–29
　Roman Catholicism and, 119
　scholarship on, 9–10, 115n.12, 116–19, 118n.23, 261n.9
　tabula rasa alternative to, 115–16, 123
In Pursuit of Purity, Unity, and Liberty (Lim), 102
Institutes of Elenctic Theology (Turretin), 60, 76–77
irenicism
　Church of England and, 52
　Essay and, 10–11
　justification and, 49–50
　preliminary evidence of, 53–56
　ROC and, 3–6, 9, 19–21, 46–47, 49–50, 53–56, 69–71, 258–59
　scholarship on, 5–6, 61–62, 69, 71
　Trinitarian debates and, 258–60, 285

Jesus is Messiah fundamental article, 21–22, 46–47, 57, 58–59, 60, 79–80, 82–83, 93–94, 98–99, 128–29, 167, 284–85, 315–16. *See also* Christology
Joldersma, Clarence, 16n.2
Jolley, Nicholas, 4–5, 16–17, 17n.4, 139n.3, 217–18n.6
Judgment and Advice (Baxter), 102–3
justification. *See also* fundamental articles; soteriology
　antinomianism and, 9, 49–50, 51–53, 68–69
　Church of England and, 51–52
　debates over, 22–23, 51–53, 108
　deism and, 22–23, 68–69, 130
　ecumenism and, 49–50, 65–66
　faith and, 47–49, 64
　freedom of religion and, 314
　Holy Spirit and, 59, 67–68
　innate ideas and, 130
　irenicism and, 49–50
　language use and, 61–63
　obedience and, 51–53, 64–65, 66–67
　Protestant Reformation and, 47–49, 51–52, 61–62, 64–66, 67–68
　requirements for, 51–52, 57–59, 62–63, 64, 84–85, 94, 97, 314, 315–16
　Roman Catholicism and, 64–65, 67–68
　scholarship on, 47–49, 51–52, 61–62, 64–66, 64n.72
　Scripture and, 58, 61–62, 66–67, 97
　Socinianism and, 65–66
　works and, 49, 51–52, 61–62, 64–68

knowledge
　above reason propositions and, 226–30, 247
　assent and, 284–88
　definitions of, 280–81, 292
　Essay and, 280–82, 284
　faith and, 292
　foreknowledge, 184

free will and, 184–86
ideas and, 279–82
innate ideas and, 281–82, 286
middle knowledge, 184–86, 213n.95
religious epistemology, 16–17, 139–42, 146–47, 174, 215, 260–63, 276–77, 291
scholarship on, 281–82
Trinitarian debates and, 284, 292
Kurun, İsmail, 17–19, 29–30, 75–76n.4

Latitudinarianism, 6–7, 24, 52, 73–75, 76–77, 83, 214
Letter Concerning Toleration, A (Locke)
aim of, 36
autonomy in, 31
Christology in, 17–19
church and state relationship in, 24, 30–33, 36, 136–37
definition of religion in, 100
doctrines in, 33–34
faith in, 17–19, 30–33
fallibility in religion in, 88–89
free will in, 41
fundamental articles in, 30, 35–36, 44, 100–2, 103
heresy in, 34–35, 100–1, 106
Latitudinarianism compared to, 24
ROC's relation to, 17–19, 36, 101–2
schism in, 35–36
scholarship on, 4, 16–19
Scripture in, 44–45, 88–89
soteriology in, 30–31, 34, 36, 44, 136–37
theological aspects of, 4, 17–19, 24, 30–36
Treatises' relation to, 36
Letter in Answer to a Book Entitled Christianity Not Mysterious, A (Browne), 301–2, 303–4
Lewis, C. S., 175, 221n.22
libertarianism, 179–81, 183, 195–97, 198–99, 200, 206, 212–13
liberty. *See* free will
Lim, Paul, 61–62, 75–76n.4, 102–3, 301
Limborch, Philip Van
authority of Scripture and, 145–46, 147–48
divinity of Scripture and, 145–46

fallibility in religion and, 89
fundamental articles and, 83–84
Locke defended by, 19–20, 21, 83–84
miracles and, 154
morality in, 147–48
Roman Catholicism and, 104
soteriology and, 65–66
toleration and, 104–5
Trinitarian debates and, 259–60
Livingston, James C., 48n.7, 215–16n.2
Locke, John. *See also* scholarship on Locke
approach of present volume to, 8–11
exile of, 23–24
major works overview of, 19–44
overall argument on theology of, 3–4, 313–18
overview of, 1–11, 15–45, 313–18
personal views distinct from writings of, 3–6, 9, 49–50, 69–70, 313, 315–17
LoLordo, Antonia, 181n.3, 217–18n.6
Lowde, James, 116
Lucci, Diego, 5–6n.4, 48–49n.8, 112n.5, 217n.5
Lutheranism, 4, 34–35, 56, 65–66, 76–78, 100, 212, 231, 291

MacIntosh, J. J., 141–42, 153–54
Malebranche, Nicolas, 183, 191–94
Mander, W. J., 300, 300n.134
Marshall, John, 4–5, 6–7, 48–49n.8, 90–91, 258–59n.3–4
McLachlan, Herbert, 6–7, 258–59nn.3–4
Measuring the Distance (Marko), 242, 291
Meditations on First Philosophy (Descartes), 270, 271
methodology. *See* scholarship on Locke
middle knowledge, 184–86, 213n.95
Milner, John, 117n.22
minimalism about doctrines, 9, 73–75, 92–94, 96, 98–99, 102–3, 113n.7
miracles
advantages of, 161–63, 170–71
assent and, 142–43, 156, 157–58, 159–60, 167–70
context principle for judging, 141–42, 153–54, 166
definitions of, 140n.7, 150–51, 152, 164–66

miracles (*cont.*)
  deism and, 10, 142–43, 174
  divinity of Scripture and, 10, 37, 139–45, 146–47, 149–53, 154–57, 163, 166–67, 169, 173–75
  empiricist use of, 146–48
  enthusiasm and, 139–41
  Essay and, 37, 155–60
  God's existence proved by, 37, 154, 155–57
  historical context of, 143–55, 175
  Holy Spirit and, 154–55, 174
  Lockean-era theologians on, 148–55
  monotheism and, 164–65
  morality and, 132–33, 161–63, 170–74
  moral probability arguments and, 146–48
  overview of, 155–67
  polytheism and, 164–65, 170–71
  poor and uneducated and, 10, 142–43, 167–70, 174
  Protestant Reformation and, 143–48, 151
  rarity of, 161
  reason and, 157–58, 161–62, 164–67, 169–70, 174
  religious epistemology and, 139–42, 146–47, 174
  requirements for genuine, 164–66
  revelation and, 10, 37, 138–43, 146–47, 153–54, 155–59, 161–63, 166
  ROC and, 4–5, 37, 160–63, 174–75
  Roman Catholicism and, 150–51
  scholarship on, 7, 10, 138–42, 146–50, 175
  use of miracles in theological arguments, 146–48
Mitchell, Joshua, 17–19
Molinism, 184–86
Molyneux, William, 37–38, 39–41, 179–82, 191, 192–93, 197–201, 208–9, 214
Mooney, Brian, 139–41
Moore, J. T., 112n.5, 134n.84
morality
  antinomianism and, 61–62
  authority and, 132–33
  certainty and, 126–27, 132–33
  deism and, 68–69, 121–23, 170–71, 173
  demonstrability of, 111–12, 126–27, 161–62
  divinity of Scripture and, 173
  Essay and, 9–10, 44–45, 133–34
  free will and, 211
  improvement of society and, 9–10, 134–37, 170–73
  innate ideas and, 9–10, 111–12, 114–15, 117, 126–27, 130–32
  miracles and, 132–33, 161–63, 170–74
  moral probability arguments, 145–48
  obedience and, 44, 49–50
  pagan morality, 95, 129–33, 134, 171–74
  reason and, 131, 161–62
  revelation and, 68–69, 95, 129–35, 161–62
  ROC and, 22–23, 111–14, 133–34, 161–62, 170–71
  scholarship on, 9–10, 135
  Scripture and, 9–10, 22–23, 44–45, 95, 114, 131–33, 134–35, 136–37
  Socinianism and, 131–32n.74
  soteriology and, 41–42, 134–37
  STCE and, 41–42, 44–45
  unnatural progress of, 170–73
Müller, Patrick, 6–7
Muller, Richard A., 79, 85–86, 143–44, 162, 173, 189–90, 212n.92, 230–31, 259n.4, 266
Myers, Peter, 17–19

Naked Gospel, The (Bury), 266–67
natural religion. *See* deism
Nature and Grace (Malebranche), 191–93, 194
necessitarianism, 179–81, 183, 187–91, 195–96, 197, 198–99, 206, 212–13, 308
necessity of Scripture, 3, 7–8, 9–10, 17–19, 318
New Testament. *See* Scripture
Norris, John
  above reason propositions and, 216–18, 219–20, 235–39, 244, 248, 264–65, 274–75, 298–300, 300n.134
  clear and distinct ideas and, 272–73
  contradictions and, 238, 300

contrary to reason propositions and, 235–37, 238–39, 298–300
  ideas and, 272–73, 274–75
  impossibility and, 299
  incomprehensibility and, 235–38, 244, 273–75, 298–300
  innate ideas and, 116
  response to Boyle of, 235–39
  Socinianism and, 235–36
  Trinitarian debates and, 264–65, 298–300
Nuovo, Victor, 4–5, 48–49nn.7–8, 112n.5, 141–42, 153–54
Nye, Stephen, 51, 265, 266–68, 274, 276–77, 279, 296

obedience
  antinomianism and, 49–50, 68–69
  deism and, 121–22
  faith and, 66–67, 249–50
  grace and, 60
  justification and, 51–53, 64–65, 66–67
  morality and, 44, 49–50
  repentance and, 60
  Socinianism and, 76–77
  soteriology and, 64
Of Libertie and Necessitie (Hobbes), 183, 187–88
Of Liberty and Necessity (Harris), 10–11, 187, 195–97
"Of Power" *(Essay)* (Locke), 10–11, 37–41, 179–81, 182, 191–92, 195–96, 198–99, 201–14, 306–7
O'Higgins, James, 215–16n.2, 260n.6
Old Testament. *See* Scripture
Organum Vetus (Burthogge), 288–89
original sin, 21, 29–30, 69–71
Owen, John, 48n.7, 52–53, 64, 149–50

pagan morality, 95, 129–33, 134, 171–74
Paraphrase and Notes on the Epistles of Paul, A (Locke), 91, 258–59
Patriarcha (Filmer), 23–24, 26
Patrick, Simon, 82–83, 90
Platonists, Cambridge. *See* Cambridge Platonists
Pneumatology, 9, 49–51, 59–69. *See also* Holy Spirit

poor and uneducated
  assent and, 142–43, 167–70
  faith and, 36
  fundamental articles and, 92–97
  incomprehensibility and, 249–50, 285–86, 309
  innate ideas and, 126
  miracles and, 10, 142–43, 167–70, 174
  ROC and, 3–4, 22, 56, 167–69
  soteriology and, 22, 284–85
Proast, Jonas, 24
probability arguments, 145–48
Procedure, Extent, and Limits of Human Understanding (Browne), 301–2, 303–4
proposition categorization, 7, 37, 215–19, 245–46, 256, 259–60, 268, 287–88, 290–91, 294–95, 297–98, 300. *See also* above reason propositions; according to reason propositions; contrary to reason propositions; unsociable propositions
Protestant Reformation
  above reason propositions and, 219–20, 224–31
  authority of Scripture and, 143–48
  deism and, 122–23
  divinity of Scripture and, 143–46
  free will and, 184–86, 189–90, 200
  fundamental articles and, 76–77, 79, 85–86
  Holy Spirit and, 143–44
  innate ideas and, 117
  justification and, 47–49, 51–52, 61–62, 64–66, 67–68
  miracles and, 143–48, 151
  ROC and, 3–4, 47–49
  soteriology and, 47–49, 59–60
providence, 148–49, 184, 199–200, 248
pure understanding/pure intellect, 271–72, 278, 286, 305–6, 310
Pyrrhonism, 146–47

Rabieh, Michael S., 4–5, 16–17
reason. *See also* above reason propositions; according to reason propositions; contrary to reason propositions
  assent and, 219–22, 226, 239–42, 271

reason (cont.)
  authority of Scripture and, 136
  definitions of, 216–18, 225–26, 239, 242–43, 244–46, 250–51
  enthusiasm and, 240, 244
  Essay and, 40–41, 107, 157–59, 216–18, 239
  faculties and, 239–41
  faith and, 103–4, 157, 220–21, 224–25, 228–29, 240–46, 247–48
  free will and, 39–41, 207–12
  fundamental articles and, 97–103
  Holy Spirit and, 159–60
  miracles and, 157–58, 161–62, 164–67, 169–70, 174
  morality and, 131, 161–62
  overview of, 239–44
  revelation and, 7, 157–59, 241–44, 252–53, 316
  right reason, 219–21, 225–26, 227–29, 231, 232–33, 234–35, 238, 240, 243, 244
  Roman Catholicism and, 231
  scholarship on, 7, 216–18
Reasonableness of Christianity, The (ROC) (Locke)
  above reason propositions in, 37, 112n.5, 134n.84
  according to reason propositions in, 37, 112n.5, 134n.84
  antinomianism excluded in, 9, 49–50, 68–69, 72
  Arminianism charge against, 4–5, 47–49, 71–72
  authority of Scripture in, 4–6, 135–36, 139–41
  Calvinism and, 47–49, 71–72
  Christology in, 9, 21–23, 44–45, 49–50, 57–59
  contrary to reason propositions in, 37
  deism as target of, 22–23, 46–49, 53–54, 68–69, 72, 112–13, 129, 131–32, 170–71
  divinity of Scripture in, 10, 163, 174
  doctrinal minimalism of, 73–75, 92
  ecumenical intent of, 3–6, 9, 21, 46–50, 53–56, 65–66, 69–72, 103, 111–12, 258–59
  Essay's relation to, 4–5, 9–10, 17–19, 41, 55–56, 111–14, 112n.5, 128–29, 133–34, 134n.84
  evangelical intent of, 46–49, 53–54
  faith in, 41, 62–63, 249–50
  fundamental articles in, 1, 9, 22–23, 44, 46–47, 53–54, 57–59, 64, 69–70, 73–75, 77–78, 79–80, 87, 97–98, 101–2, 103, 285
  heretical red herrings in, 69–72
  Holy Spirit in, 59–69, 71–72
  incomprehensibility in, 284–85
  innate ideas in, 17–19, 128–29
  irenic intent of, 3–6, 9, 19–21, 46–47, 49–50, 53–56, 69–71, 258–59
  justification in, 9, 22–23, 46–50, 52–54, 55, 61–68, 72, 97, 314
  language use in, 61–63
  Letter's relation to, 17–19, 36, 101–2
  Locke's personal views distinct from, 3–6, 9, 49–50, 69–70, 313
  miracles in, 4–5, 37, 160–63, 174–75
  morality in, 22–23, 111–14, 133–34, 161–62, 170–71
  necessity of Scripture in, 3, 9–10, 17–19
  original sin in, 20, 29–30, 69–70
  overview of, 1–11, 19–24
  poor and uneducated in, 3–4, 22, 56, 167–69
  Protestant Reformation context of, 3–4, 47–49
  publication of, 1, 19–20, 257n.1
  redemption in, 53–54
  revelation in, 3, 9–10, 37, 53–54, 68, 112–13, 120–21, 133, 163
  scholarship on, 2–7, 19–20, 46–49, 48n.7, 69, 71–72, 73–75, 111–13, 112n.5, 133
  Scripture in, 3, 4–6, 9–10, 17–19, 21, 44–45, 46–47, 53–54, 55–56, 61–62, 87, 97–98, 135–36, 139–41, 145, 163, 317
  Second Vindication of, 1, 3–4, 19–20, 46–47, 54, 55, 61–62, 81, 82, 94, 98, 249–50, 285, 286, 297–98
  Socinian charge against, 1–3, 4–5, 19–20, 46–49, 65–66, 71–72, 257–58

INDEX   351

soteriology in, 5–6n.4, 8–10, 19, 21–22, 44, 46–50, 53–54, 59–69, 71–72, 167–69, 284–85, 313
theological context of, 3–6, 9, 19–20, 46–47, 50–53, 313
toleration in, 46–47, 108, 136–37
Vindication of, 1, 3–4, 19–20, 46–47, 81, 93, 285
Reflections upon a Theological Distinction (Boyle), 231–32, 233, 235
Reformation. *See* Protestant Reformation
religious epistemology, 16–17, 139–42, 146–47, 174, 215, 260–63, 276–77, 291
religious freedom, 24, 30–33, 36, 136–37, 314–15
revelation. *See also* Scripture
  above reason propositions and, 221–29, 274–75, 287–88
  according to reason propositions and, 239
  assent and, 244, 245–46, 247
  deism and, 53–54, 111–12, 119–20
  Essay and, 37, 132–34, 155–60, 163
  fundamental articles and, 95
  Holy Spirit and, 226
  innate ideas and, 120, 125, 128–34
  miracles and, 10, 37, 138–43, 146–47, 153–54, 155–59, 161–63, 166
  morality and, 68–69, 95, 129–35, 161–62
  reason and, 7, 9–10, 157–59, 241–44, 252–53, 316
  ROC and, 3, 9–10, 37, 53–54, 68, 112–13, 120–21, 133, 163
  scholarship on, 7, 217n.5, 260n.6
Rickless, Samuel, 118n.23, 124–25, 187–88n.24
River, Isabel, 75–76n.4
ROC. See Reasonableness of Christianity, The (Locke)
Rogers, G. A. J., 6–7, 258–59n.3
Roman Catholicism
  above reason propositions and, 231
  authority of Scripture and, 143–44
  deism and, 122–23
  faith and, 87, 88, 119
  free will and, 184–86
  fundamental articles and, 76–77, 85–88
  Holy Spirit and, 145–46
  innate ideas and, 119
  justification and, 64–65, 67–68
  miracles and, 150–51
  reason and, 231
  sacraments and, 67–68
  Scripture and, 34–35, 56
  toleration and, 104
  transubstantiation in, 56n.34, 184–85, 226–27
Rowe, William, 186–87
Rust, George, 219–25, 234n.77, 243, 249–50, 292

salvation. *See* soteriology
schisms, 34–36, 105
scholarship on Locke
  above reason propositions and, 7, 215–19, 215–16n.2, 244–45, 256, 259–60
  Arminianism and, 4–5, 48–49nn.8–9, 71n.100, 73–75, 259n.5
  authority of Scripture and, 4–5, 139–41
  Calvinism and, 4, 49n.9, 64, 259n.5
  Cambridge Platonists and, 6–7
  Christology and, 17–19
  Church of England and, 75–76n.4
  coherence of major works in, 15–19, 313–18
  compartmentalized approaches in, 4
  deism and, 6–7, 112–13, 123
  divinity of Scripture and, 141–42, 143–44, 173
  ecumenism and, 4–6, 17n.4, 61–62, 112–13
  Essay and, 4–5, 16–19, 36–37, 111–13, 179–81, 181–82n.6
  faith and, 17–19, 217n.5
  free will and, 41, 179–81, 183, 186–87, 191–92, 195–97, 206
  fundamental articles and, 73–75, 90–91, 102–3
  groupings of scholars in, 4–6, 15
  heterodox views in Locke's theology and, 1–3, 5n.3, 20–21, 29, 41, 47–49, 71, 82–83, 113n.7, 318
  ideas and, 259n.4, 272, 281–82, 310

scholarship on Locke (*cont.*)
  incomprehensibility and, 244–45, 262–63n.10, 309
  innate ideas and, 9–10, 115n.12, 116–19, 118n.23, 261n.9
  irenicism and, 5–6, 61–62, 69, 71
  issues not sufficiently addressed by Locke and, 317
  justification and, 47–49, 51–52, 61–62, 64–66, 64n.72
  knowledge and, 281–82
  Letter and, 4, 16–19
  miracles and, 7, 10, 138–42, 140nn.6–7, 146–50, 175
  morality and, 9–10, 135
  narratives in, 6–7
  orthodox views in Locke's theology and, 2–3, 11, 21, 88, 103, 123, 215, 218, 244–45, 256, 259–60, 261, 317, 318
  overall argument on theology in, 3–4, 313–18
  overview of, 2–7, 15–19
  personal views distinct from writings and, 3–6, 9, 49–50, 69–70, 313, 315–17
  reason and, 7, 216–18
  revelation and, 7, 217n.5, 260n.6
  ROC and, 2–7, 19–20, 46–49, 48n.7, 69, 71–72, 73–75, 111–13, 112n.5, 133
  sectarian interpretation in, 4–5, 15, 17–20, 46–49, 55, 65–66, 68–70, 73–75, 112–13, 315
  sincere interpretation in, 5–6, 10, 15–19, 47–49, 73–75, 112–13, 139n.3
  Socinianism and, 6–7, 48–49n.8, 71, 71n.100, 259n.5
  soteriology and, 8, 19, 37–38, 71, 313–16
  STCE and, 16, 26
  surreptitious interpretation in, 4–5, 15–17, 47–49, 73–75, 112–13, 134, 139n.3
  theological program of Locke and, 1, 3–4, 5–6, 7–8, 16, 29–30, 47–49, 316–17
  toleration and, 17–19
  Treatises and, 16–17, 29–30
  Trinitarian debates and, 11, 36–37, 257–61, 258–59n.3, 259n.4, 260nn.7–8, 266, 268–69, 285, 301
Unitarianism and, 258–59n.3

scholasticism, 154–55, 187–89, 194–95, 269–70
Schuurman, Paul, 191–92, 261n.9, 272n.39
scriptural references
  1 Peter
    3:15, 220–21
  Galatians
    5:6, 66–67
  James
    2:24, 51–52, 66–67
  John
    1:49, 82–83
    15:15, 80
  Romans
    1:18–21, 117
    2:14–15, 117
    4:3–8, 61–62
Scripture. *See also* authority of Scripture; clarity of Scripture; divinity of Scripture; necessity of Scripture; sufficiency of Scripture
  above reason propositions and, 11, 222–28, 233–34, 239
  according to reason propositions and, 239
  antinomianism and, 68–69, 316
  assent and, 167, 252–53, 284–85
  contrary to reason propositions and, 223
  Essay and, 44–45
  fundamental articles and, 79–81, 87, 97–98, 102–3
  grace and, 147–48
  Holy Spirit and, 143–44
  justification and, 58, 61–62, 66–67, 97
  Letter and, 44–45, 88–89
  morality and, 9–10, 22–23, 44–45, 95, 114, 131–33, 134–35, 136–37
  ROC and, 3, 4–6, 9–10, 17–19, 21, 44–45, 46–47, 53–54, 55–56, 61–62, 87, 97–98, 135–36, 139–41, 145, 163, 317
  Roman Catholicism and, 34–35, 56
  STCE and, 41–45
  Treatises and, 26, 27–28
Second Vindication, A (Locke), 1, 3–4, 19–20, 46–47, 54, 55, 61–62, 81, 82, 94, 98, 249–50, 285, 286, 297–98

Sell, Alan P. F., 5–6, 119, 217n.5, 261n.9
Sheerin, F. L., 184–85
Sherlock, William, 266–68
Short Discourse of the True Knowledge of Jesus Christ, A (Bold), 55, 84
Smith, Donald, 49n.9
Snobelen, Stephen D., 4–5, 47–49, 69, 71–72
Socinianism
   above reason propositions and, 231, 235–36, 300
   Arianism associated with, 51, 265
   assent and, 273
   contrary to reason propositions and, 235–36, 265, 266–67
   definition of, 50–51
   fundamental articles and, 76–77
   incomprehensibility and, 235–36
   justification and, 65–66
   morality and, 131–32n.74
   obedience and, 76–77
   ROC charged with, 1–3, 4–5, 19–20, 46–49, 65–66, 71–72, 257–58
   scholarship on, 6–7, 48–49n.8, 71, 71n.100, 259n.5
   soteriology and, 71
   theological context of, 50–51, 52–53
   Trinitarian debates and, 265, 266–67
   Unitarians associated with, 51
Socinianism Unmask'd (Edwards), 81, 98–99
Some Thoughts Concerning Education (STCE) (Locke)
   dearth of scholarship on, 16, 26
   deism in, 43–44
   fundamental articles missing from, 44
   God's sovereignty in, 41–42, 44
   morality in, 41–42, 44–45
   overview of, 26, 41–44
   relation to other works, 16
   Scripture in, 41–45
   soteriology in, 41–42, 44
   theological aspects of, 16
Some Thoughts Concerning the Several Causes and Occasions of Atheism (Edwards), 81–82
soteriology. *See also* fundamental articles; justification

annihilation and, 40, 41, 211, 313–14
antinomianism and, 9, 60–61, 68
Arminianism and, 59–60, 71–72, 212
authority of Scripture and, 134–37
Calvinism and, 64
Cambridge Platonists and, 219–20
Church of England and, 52, 75–76n.4
conscience and, 105
deism and, 119–20, 297–98
ecumenism and, 9, 49–50, 71–72
Essay and, 37–41, 44
faith and, 59–60, 64, 223–24
freedom of religion and, 314–15
free will and, 37–40, 184, 194–95, 206, 208–13, 214
grace and, 60, 191–92
historical context of, 51–53
Holy Spirit and, 67–68
Letter and, 30–31, 34, 36, 44, 136–37
morality and, 41–42, 134–37
obedience and, 64
poor and uneducated and, 22, 284–85
Protestant Reformation and, 47–49, 59–60
reason and, 9–10, 167–69
ROC and, 5–6n.4, 8–10, 19, 21–22, 44, 46–50, 53–54, 59–69, 71–72, 167–69, 284–85, 313
scholarship on, 8, 19, 37–38, 71, 313–16
simplicity in, 167–69, 284–85, 315–16
Socinianism and, 71
STCE and, 41–42, 44
toleration and, 34, 46–47, 297–98
Treatises and, 29–30, 44
Trinitarian debates and, 263
South, Robert, 266–68
sovereignty of God, 26, 27–28, 44, 184, 198–99, 212, 213, 309, 311
Spinoza, Benedict de, 122, 148–49, 154, 164, 279
Stanton, Timothy, 15–16n.1, 17–19
state and church relationship, 24, 30–33, 36, 136–37, 314–15
STCE. See Some Thoughts Concerning Education (STCE) (Locke)
Stephens, William, 122, 295–96
Stewart, M. A., 141n.10

Stillingfleet, Edward
  above reason propositions and, 250
  innate ideas and, 116–19
  Locke critiqued by, 2, 25, 36–37, 250, 257–58, 260–61, 268, 269–70, 291
  Locke's responses to critiques by, 2, 25, 309
  Trinitarian debates and, 36–37, 260–61, 268–69, 307, 309
  way of ideas and, 269–70
Strauss, Leo, 4–5, 16–19, 138–39
sufficiency of Scripture, 7–8, 102–3
Summary Account of the Deists' Religion, A (Blount), 121–22
suspension of the will, 180n.2, 181n.4, 191–94, 196, 205–12
Svensson, Manfred, 48n.7, 113n.7
Synod of Dordrecht (1618–1619), 185–86

tabula rasa, 115–16, 123
Theologia Christiana (Limborch), 83–84
theological program of Locke, 1, 3–4, 5–6, 7–8, 16, 29–30, 47–49, 316–17
Thiel, Udo, 260n.8
Thomas Aquinas, 184–86, 190–91
Tillotson, John
  divinity of Scripture and, 150–54
  free will and, 307–8
  incomprehensibility and, 307–8, 309
  justification and, 64–65
  miracles and, 142–43n.16, 150–54
  religious epistemology and, 276–77
  Scripture and, 151–52
  Trinitarian debates and, 276–77, 307–8
Tindal, Matthew, 120–21, 123
Toland, John. *See also Christianity Not Mysterious* (Toland)
  above reason propositions and, 7, 11, 215–18, 215–16n.2, 250, 253–56
  according to reason propositions and, 255–56
  assent and, 250–53, 255
  contradictions and, 255
  contrary to reason propositions and, 254, 255–56, 293
  definition of reason and, 250–51
  deism and, 2, 250
  divinity of Scripture and, 152–53

  faith and, 251–52, 292–94
  incomprehensibility and, 255, 293–94
  knowledge and, 292, 294–95
  Locke's influence on, 2, 6–7, 142–43n.16, 250, 268, 291–92, 294–95
  miracles and, 152–54, 254, 294
  propositions and, 6–7, 11
  reason and, 250–53
  revelation and, 11, 252–53, 316
  scholarship on, 6–7, 215–16n.2, 250
  Socinianism and, 2
  Trinitarian debates and, 268, 291–95
toleration. *See also Letter Concerning Toleration, A* (Locke)
  assent and, 107
  Christology and, 17–19, 32
  Church of England and, 24, 83, 103–4, 194–95
  conscience and, 105, 106–7
  definition of, 32
  doctrines and, 33–34
  Essay and, 86–87, 107–8, 136–37
  freedom of religion and, 24, 30–33, 36, 136–37, 314–15
  free will and, 194–95
  fundamental articles and, 9, 53–54, 75–76, 103–8
  heresy and, 34–35, 106
  historical context of, 103–5
  Letter and, 24, 32, 136–37
  limits of, 32
  overview of, 106–8
  reason and, 107
  ROC and, 46–47, 108, 136–37
  Roman Catholicism and, 104
  schisms and, 34–35, 106
  scholarship on, 17–19
  soteriology and, 34, 46–47, 297–98
transubstantiation, 56n.34, 184–85, 226–27
Treatises. See Two Treatises on Civil Government (Locke)
Trinitarian debates
  above reason propositions and, 218–19, 224, 226–27, 233n.74, 259–60, 261–63, 264–65, 268–69
  analogy and, 303–6
  Arianism and, 50, 266–67

Aristotelianism and, 258–59, 266–68, 269–70
assent and, 261–63, 303
avoidance of Locke in taking sides in, 8, 11, 36–37, 257–61, 285, 316
contrary to reason propositions and, 265, 266–67
deism and, 295–96
ecumenism and, 258–59, 263, 266, 311–12
English Trinitarian debates, 263–69
Essay and, 36–37, 268–69, 309, 311–12
faith and, 249–50
historical context of, 263–79
Holy Spirit and, 263–64, 265
ideas and, 269–79
incomprehensibility and, 264–65, 269–79, 302–3
irenicism and, 258–60, 285
knowledge and, 284, 292
Locke as antitrinitarian, 288–98
Locke as not antitrinitarian, 298–306
Locke-Stillingfleet debate and, 268–69, 307
mature doctrine on, 263–64
overview of, 257–63
propositions and, 283–84
scholarship on, 11, 36–37, 257–61, 258–59n.3, 259n.4, 260nn.7–8, 266, 268–69, 285, 301
Socinianism and, 265, 266–67
soteriology and, 263
Tuckness, Alex, 17–19
Turretin, Francis
above reason propositions and, 216–18, 224–31
according to reason propositions and, 226–28
Arminianism and, 76–77
authority of Scripture and, 143–44, 147–48
contradictions and, 224–27, 229–31
contrary to reason propositions and, 228–29, 230–31
faith and, 77–78, 224–25
free will and, 199–200
fundamental articles and, 76–79, 82
God's sovereignty and, 199–200

innate ideas and, 115–16, 116n.13
knowledge and, 226–28
Locke influenced by, 224–25
Protestant Scholasticism of, 224–31
reason and, 224–26
revelation and, 229–30
Socinianism and, 76–77, 116n.13, 231
Two Treatises on Civil Government (Locke)
aim of, 23–24
children's relation to parents in, 27–28
divine right of kings as catalyst for, 23–24
equality in, 23–24, 26–28
freedom in, 23–24, 26–28
free will in, 29, 41
God's sovereignty in, 26–30, 44–45
government as restraining violence in, 27
influences on, 23–24
law of nature in, 27–29
legislative power in, 27–28
original sin in, 29–30
overview of, 23–24
Patriarcha as target of, 23–24, 26
rebellion in, 27
retribution in, 27
scholarship on, 16–17, 29–30
Scripture in, 26, 27–28
slavery in, 27–28
soteriology in, 29–30, 44
state of nature in, 23–24, 26–27
theological aspects of, 16–17, 23–24, 26–30
war in, 27

undiscoverability, 232, 233–36, 239, 248, 255–56, 300
the uneducated. *See* poor and uneducated
Unitarianism, 6–7, 51, 103–4, 258–59n.3, 265
unsociable propositions, 233, 248, 254, 264, 274–75, 283–84, 306, 307–8
Uzgalis, William, 260n.6

Vickers, Jason, 259–60, 259nn.4–5
Vindication of The Reasonableness of Christianity, A (Locke), 1, 3–4, 19–20, 46–47, 81, 93, 285

virtue. *See* morality
voluntarism, 190–91

Wallace, Dewey, 61–62, 64n.72
Wallis, John, 266–68
Walmsley, Jonathan, 261n.9, 310
"Way of Ideas," 11, 269–75, 306
weakness of will, 191, 193–94
Welch, Claude, 215–16n.2

Westminster Confession, 59–60, 183–84n.7
Winkler, Kenneth, 272
Wolterstorff, Nicholas, 5–6, 15–16n.1, 138–41
works, 49, 51–52, 61–62, 64–68

Yaffe, Gideon, 181–82n.6
Yolton, John, 16, 17–19, 115n.12, 116, 117–19, 118n.23, 260n.7, 261n.9, 288